MANAGEMENT SCIENCE

MANAGEMENT SCIENCE:
An Introduction to Modern Quantitative Analysis and Decision Making

Gerald E. Thompson, Ph.D.

Professor of Economics and Management
University of Nebraska-Lincoln

McGraw-Hill Book Company

New York
St. Louis
San Francisco
Auckland
Düsseldorf
Johannesburg
Kuala Lumpur
London
Mexico
Montreal
New Delhi
Panama
Paris
São Paulo
Singapore
Sydney
Tokyo
Toronto

MANAGEMENT SCIENCE:
An Introduction
to Modern
Quantitative
Analysis and
Decision Making

1234567890KPKP79876

This book was set in Times Roman by University Graphics, Inc. The editors were William J. Kane and Claudia A. Hepburn; the cover was designed by Joseph Gillians; the production supervisor was Dennis J. Conroy. The drawings were done by Danmark & Michaels, Inc.
Kingsport Press, Inc., was printer and binder.

Library of Congress Cataloging in Publication Data

Thompson, Gerald E
    Management science.

    1. Decision-making—Mathematical models.
I. Title.
HD69.D4T5   658.4'033   75-17666
ISBN 0-07-064360-1

Contents

PREFACE   **vii**

PART ONE   BACKGROUND AND INTRODUCTION

  1   Introduction to Quantitative Analysis for
Decision Making   3

**PART TWO   AN APPROACH TO DECISION MAKING
UNDER UNCERTAINTY: DECISION
ANALYSIS**

  2   Making Decisions under Uncertainty   13
  3   Interpretations of Probability: Relative
Frequency and Subjective   26
  4   Prior Knowledge and Bayesian Posterior
Probabilities   54
  5   Making the Decision after Obtaining
Additional Information and Revising the Prior
Probabilities   77
  6   Using Additional Information from a Sample:
What Is It Worth?   97
  7   Opportunity Losses and Utilities in Decision
Making under Uncertainty   118

**PART THREE   AN APPROACH TO DECISION MAKING
UNDER CERTAINTY: LINEAR-
PROGRAMMING ANALYSIS**

  8   Linear Programming and Decisions   143
  9   Analysis for the Planning of Facilities,
Equipment, and Other Resources: A Graphic
Introduction to Sensitivity Analysis and
Parametric Programming   168

v

10   Solving Larger Problems: An Elementary
     Discussion of the Simplex Method   191
11   More on the Simplex Method   210
12   Sensitivity Analysis and the Dual Linear-
     Programming Problem   229
13   Decision Making When More than
     One Technique of Production
     Is Available   244
14   More than One Objective and Other Decision
     Problems   270
15   Transportation-related Decision Problems
     and the Location of New Facilities   286

**PART FOUR   OTHER APPROACHES TO DECISION
              PROBLEMS**

16   Approaches to Inventory Decisions   319
17   Markov Processes and Decisions   345
18   Project Analysis: PERT and CPM   367
19   Simulation: A Supplementary Method for
     Making Predictions and Decisions   381
20   Waiting-Line Problems   403
21   Interdependent Decision Making and the
     Game-Model Approach   423

Suggestions for Further Reading   **443**

INDEX   **447**

Preface

The purpose of this book is to introduce as simply as possible the main modern quantitative approaches to decision making. Only a high school mathematics background is assumed.

The book includes a discussion of the main approaches to decision making under conditions of *uncertainty* as well as conditions of *certainty*. These approaches compose the main segment of the growing field of *management science,* a field of study that is also known as *operations research* and sometimes is referred to as *systems analysis*.

Because of their central importance, two topics receive special attention. The first is *decision analysis,* the widely applicable procedure for decision making under uncertainty. The other is *linear programming,* the main quantitative approach to decision making under conditions of certainty. Other topics include approaches to inventory decisions, Markov processes and decisions, project analysis through PERT and CPM, simulation as a supplementary approach to prediction and decision making, waiting-line problems, and interdependent decision making and the game-model approach.

To be sure, when we proceed at a high school mathematical level it turns out that the discussion of some of the topics cannot be pursued fully. However, in teaching these topics to students with a very modest mathematical background, we have discovered that the essential ideas of the main modern quantitative approaches to decision making can be understood. In one way, this relaxation on the mathematical side permits us to focus more fully on some of the important applications and real-world interpretations of modern quantitative methods, both of which are crucially important when we come to the making of decisions of consequence in complex real-world situations.

The approach throughout the book emphasizes the use of small, simple, and clear-cut examples to illustrate the procedures of decision analysis, linear programming, and other quantitative topics, each of which extends to the study of the large, practical, real-world problems. If students' first brush with these topics is in terms of a complicated application, their conception of the approach usually is not clear, and all too often they are simply overwhelmed. Therefore, the primary aim of this book is to help prepare students conceptually and computationally for the more complicated applications to be encountered in their work as well as in later courses in their academic program.

Although the mathematics used throughout the book is kept simple, it must be said also that the ideas discussed are quite sophisticated and appeal to students at all levels. Thus, the book can be used effectively in a variety of courses.

For freshmen and sophomores, a selection of the more introductory chapters provides a very useful survey course. We have actually done this using Chapters 1, 2, 3, 4, and 5 on decision analysis; Chapters 8, 9, 10, and 15 on linear programming; and Chapters 16, 18, 19, and 20 on inventory analysis, project analysis (PERT and CPM), simulation, and waiting-line problems.

Numerous problems to be worked by the student appear at the end of each chapter, and there is a close tie-in between the problems and the discussion (and worked-out examples) in the text. The instructive approach of the problems permits virtually all students to acquire the necessary skills to use and understand the procedures.

An unusually complete instructor's manual accompanies the text and provides detailed solutions to the many end-of-chapter problems. Thus, the instructor's burden of showing a student just where he or she went wrong can be somewhat lightened.

A very practical aspect of the manual then is that a busy instructor with many preparations can assign problems in advance of having worked them out. As a matter of fact, in the freshman-sophomore course in which the text was used, it was found that one of the most effective ways to proceed was to assign problems in advance and then spend part of each class period going through the solutions, usually discussing at some length those points that were found to need more attention. The instructor's manual also helps out by providing numerous easy-to-use examination questions and problems.

For juniors and seniors (and beginning MBA students), the book has also been found to be very effective. At these levels, most all the chapters of the book were used. Thus, by including the more advanced discussions and the more challenging end-of-chapter problems, it is possible to provide for the more mature student, too, a sound and balanced introduction to the main modern quantitative methods for decision making.

Although the contributors to modern quantitative analysis are numerous, many of the basic ideas in this book are principally due to George B. Dantzig, Tjalling C. Koopmans, Howard Raiffa, and Robert Schlaifer.

Reviews of the manuscript and comments of much value were provided by Jerry G. Hunt of New Mexico State University, Paul Merry of the University of Denver, Marvin Rothstein of the University of Connecticut, and Paul Schmidbauer of California State University in San Francisco. Kenneth Bond of Creighton University also made useful suggestions.

The Ford Foundation and the University of Nebraska have given generous support. Other institutions that have given much in many ways are the University of Iowa, Harvard University, and the University of Michigan.

Gerald E. Thompson

MANAGEMENT SCIENCE

Part One

Background and Introduction

Introduction to Quantitative Analysis for Decision Making

In recent years important advances in quantitative analysis for decision making have taken place. These developments have created a field of study that we call *management science,* a field that is also referred to as *operations research* and *systems analysis.* Knowledge of these procedures and an ability to use them can contribute greatly to our skills in making good decisions. The aim of this book is to provide an elementary introduction to these main developments.

All persons and all organizations must make decisions. How well we make these decisions can affect our level of well-being and even our very survival. Important decisions must be made on what to do in the circumstances in which we find ourselves. Typically, they are made with limited knowledge and with many physical, financial, and moral-legal restrictions facing us.

In this book we shall see that quantitative analysis in two general ways can help in making good decisions. The direct application of a formal procedure to a decision problem is no doubt the obvious way, but its indirect effect upon our intuitions is perhaps of even greater significance.

Most real-world decision making is essentially of an intuitive type; that is, no formal methods are used. But one of the great benefits of studying the formal decision-making procedures is the favorable effect that it has upon our intuitive decision-making skills.

This effect appears to involve developing and channeling our intuitive processes so that we are alerted to the more important factors and uncertainties present in particular real-world decision problems. It can be a means of gaining at an earlier age than would otherwise be possible a desirable maturity and sophistication in dealing with complex decision problems of consequence.

Generally speaking, quantitative analysis is involved in the interpretation of data and using it in making predictions and decisions. From a broad view, the data can involve all of our experience and that of others. From a more limited view, the data may include only the results from a particular test, survey, or sample.

Although this book focuses on some of the main quantitative procedures that assist prediction and decision making, concepts and procedures are discussed in terms of very simple examples so as to facilitate understanding. The main motive is to use the small examples to illustrate procedures that extend to large problems.

Often, the best decision (or solution) in an example that we use may be apparent even before applying any formal procedure. But the larger real-world problem is what we have in mind. In the larger problem the intuitive procedures sometimes break down due to our limited capacity to take many factors and their interrelationships into account simultaneously. It is then that the more formal procedure is of special value.

However, we do not mean to imply that intuitive judgments are unimportant in large practical problems where formal quantitative analysis is used. It is quite the opposite. The scarce, highly developed human powers should be applied where there is really no substitute for them. Typically, some important elements in reality cannot be satisfactorily quantified and represented in the analysis Usually, this deficiency in the analysis has to be taken into account through the use of human judgment. Also, the selection of the particular quantitative model to use in a given situation and the interpretation of its results require a high order of human judgment. Before examining any specific procedure, however, let us look at some characteristics that all models (and even all thinking) have in common.

MODELS AND REALITY

In order to make good predictions and good decisions in reality, we must first closely observe the reality in which we are interested with a view to selecting those elements (or factors) that appear to be the most influential in shaping the unfolding events in that reality. Then, we must in some way represent these elements and their interrelationships in our thinking.

In informal intuitive thought, we are usually not very conscious of the way in which elements in reality are represented in our thinking. However, in explicit formal thinking (such as in quantitative analysis), where ultimately one of the goals is to represent many more elements of the reality and their interrelationships than is possible by intuitive methods, much attention needs to be given to the selection of these elements and to the form of their representation.

Thus, as depicted in the upper section of Figure 1-1, we try to distinguish clearly between a segment of reality and a *representation* of selected elements of that reality. Usually, our representation of selected elements and their interrelationships is called a *model* or *theory* of that segment of reality. Such models or theories can be either verbal or quantitative in form, and many different models or theories can be constructed to represent the very same reality. It is no easy task to choose or to construct some "best" one.

It should be made clear that many elements in the reality, even in large models, are not represented in a given model. All models in some sense are incomplete. This is true whether they are in the form of a quantitative model or a verbal model. In both types of models we take the important step of selecting elements of the reality and then representing them by words and phrases or by quantitative terms. This step is sometimes referred to as the *abstraction* step. We say that selected elements are "abstracted out" of reality.

Before examining particular models, it may be well to note that models usually are constructed with a view toward using them to help predict events in a future reality or to designate a future course of action that is in some sense best. The full diagram in Figure 1-1 indicates this use.

On the left side of Figure 1-1 the movement in time from the present reality to some future reality is given. Usually this is the section of most interest to us in real situations. But often we wish to make some prediction or decision with respect to some particular segment of the reality.

On the right side of the diagram the representation of reality in the form of models or theories is shown, together with their typical use, that is, obtaining predictions or theoretical conclusions about a yet-to-unfold reality.

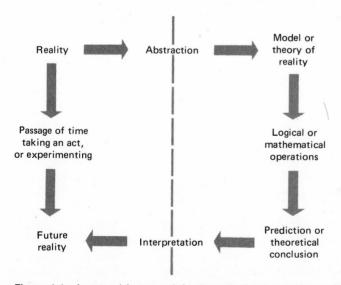

Figure 1-1 A general framework for the construction and use of models and theories.

We shall illustrate the preceding points soon, but right here we should note that a thorny problem usually accompanies any prediction or conclusion obtained from a model. The problem is this: How sure are we that the predicted event will occur or that the indicated "best" course of action will in fact be the best act? This is a difficult but very important question on which to get some answer. Putting it most directly, there must be some sort of evaluation or interpretation of the prediction (or conclusion). We say that a "gap" of some sort exists between a prediction and the future reality. The bridging of this gap involves what we call in Figure 1-1 the *interpretation* of a prediction or conclusion.

Generally, the most satisfactory way to interpret the conclusions of any thinking or reasoning is to go back to the beginning of that thinking; that is, we must examine the assumptions made at the start. Do they fit the reality well? Is the correspondence close? Are there possibly important elements in reality that are left out of the model? If they are left out, then it is assumed implicitly that they have little or no influence on the reality of interest. Is this deletion justified?

These are some of the questions to be asked; and in considering them, we come to see that different assumptions can lead to different predictions and decisions. Thus, in interpreting a prediction we must go back to the abstraction step and examine the fit (the correspondence) of the model to the segment of reality. If the fit is a poor one, consideration of a new or modified model should be undertaken.

Perhaps we should discuss further what is meant by the "fit" of a model or theory. For example, the word "redhead" clearly fits some persons (some reality) and does not fit others (some other reality). In some cases the fit is not very clear.

Let us take another example. The phrase "out of order" printed on a sheet of paper and placed on a copying machine may fit or it may not (the machine actually may function normally). Also, it is possible that the phrase may be only an approximate fit.

This is true of sentences, paragraphs, and their counterparts in quantitative models that we discuss in this book. The fit to reality may be good, poor, or approximate. Thus, the conclusions from our thinking (or reasoning) must be interpreted with the fit in mind.

In summary, a sound interpretation of the prediction or conclusion of a model requires not only full knowledge of the model and its premises but also a deep knowledge of the complex reality it represents. Thus, assessing the fit of a model to a segment of reality requires both theoretical knowledge and real-world experience. Therefore, at some point in the use of a model the ever-present gap between the predictions of a model and the actual events in the future reality requires sound human judgment.

A QUANTITATIVE MODEL

A distinguishing characteristic of quantitative models is that elements in reality and their interrelationships are usually represented by variables, constants, equations, and inequalities. We shall discuss this more fully later, but let us say at this point that in verbal models or theories the rough counterparts of variables and constants are words and phrases. Sentences are analogous to equations (also, to inequalities), and paragraphs are analogous to sets of equations (or to sets of inequalities). Good illustrations of this will appear in Part Three of this book.

With representations of reality in the form of quantitative models, it becomes possible to apply particular chains of reasoning (logic) which are known as mathematical operations. Simple examples of these operations are addition and multiplication, which permit conclusions or predictions (solutions) to be obtained that may be impossible to obtain through the sole use of verbal models or intuitive thinking. A verbal model can be very rich in terms of the number of elements in reality that it can represent, but it suffers greatly with respect to the yield of useful conclusions from any reasoning. This is largely because we cannot perform the logical-mathematical operations (such as addition, multiplication, and so forth) on words and sentences that we can on constants, variables, and equations.

In the development and construction of all types of models, we seek to identify the most important elements in the reality of interest. The aim in quantitative models is to represent these elements and their interrelationships by variables, constants, equations, and inequalities. Thus, in a given problem we look for those elements (factors) which normally vary or can be varied by choice. These elements are then represented by letters such as x and y and are referred to as *variables*. For example, the number of hours that a particular machine is operated may be variable, and the number of hours of operation can be represented by the letter x. Thus, the letter x refers to any one number (hours of operation) from a set of possible numbers (possible hours of operation).

Elements (factors) in reality that remain more or less fixed for the period under consideration are each represented by a constant value and are called *constants*. For example, the amount of product output from each hour of operation of the machine referred to above may be approximately constant and may be so treated in a model of that operation. Suppose that over a period of time the average output for an hour of machine operation is 10 units. This may be assumed to be one of the constants in a model of this operation which is designed to predict the total output from operating the machine for various lengths of time.

Although a model of this operation can be quite informal and verbal, let us use this simple example to illustrate a more formal expression of the relationship between the hours of machine operation and product output as follows:

$10x = $ total output

The letter x refers to the number of hours of machine operation. The constant 10 represents the hourly rate of output of the machine and is assumed to remain unchanged for the period under consideration. As shown in Figure 1-2, we use this example to illustrate the general framework for the construction and use of a model.

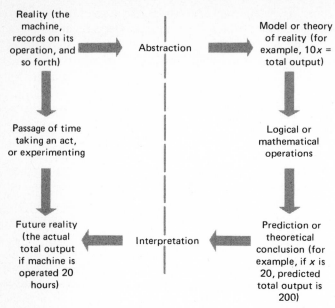

Figure 1-2 A simplified illustration of the use of the general framework for the construction and use of a model.

Thus in Figure 1-2 we have a specific (though simple) model to represent selected elements in reality (the machine, the records on its operation, and so forth). But what is desired is a prediction of total output if the machine is operated for a given number of hours.

We can obtain such a prediction of total output by simply substituting a specific value for x and multiplying it by 10. For example, an x-value of 20 hours gives a predicted total output of 200: $10x = 10(20) = 200$. This can be obtained before the actual operation of the machine for the 20 hours with its actual total output.

As shown in Figure 1-2, an interpretation of any prediction is necessary. Once again, the need to examine the initial assumptions is clear. For example, is the assumed constant value of 10 valid? If the output per hour has not stayed at 10 in the past, there is good reason to expect a variation in total output from one 20-hour period of operation to the next; and thus a prediction of 200 units for a given 20-hour period becomes far from a certainty.

Aside from this possible error, some other elements in reality affecting total output may be completely left out of the model. For example, the quality of raw materials (or the quality of labor) may not be constant and thereby may affect total output. Thus, consideration of the accuracy of the assumptions made (such as the output per hour of 10 units and no raw-material or labor-quality changes) will be important in deciding how much confidence to place in a particular prediction.

The little model we have been examining might also be described as a *certainty* (or deterministic) model. Essentially, the basis for this description is that the constants are known and remain fixed or certain. Remember that the constants are assumed to remain unchanged even though other elements in reality vary (that is, the factors represented by variables).

However, even though we may know that these elements in the reality that are assumed to be constant do not remain that way, we may still make use of the certainty model to obtain predictions. However, appropriate adjustments will be planned in the interpretation of the predictions or conclusions. A partial alternative to this procedure is to represent explicitly in the model the degree of uncertainty (using probabilities) regarding particular elements in models. An elementary introduction to this procedure appears in Part Two, where procedures for decision making under conditions of uncertainty are examined. In these chapters the possibility of gaining further information before making a particular decision is also explored.

In Part Three we examine one of the most commonly used quantitative procedures for making decisions under certainty. *Linear programming* is the name of this procedure. As we shall see, it need have no connection at all to computer programming, but in actual practice computers are used to solve linear-programming problems. Linear programming by itself is a procedure for choosing one course of action from many possible courses of action. The methods of linear programming are especially useful where the courses of action are very numerous and the restrictions upon activities are many. Typically, the restrictions are imposed by such factors as scarce resources, limited budgets, and regulatory laws. In Part Four of the book, other relevant topics in quantitative analysis are examined. These topics include inventory analysis, Markov processes and decisions, project analysis through PERT and CPM, simulation as a supplementary method for making predictions and decisions, waiting-line problems, and the game-model approach to interdependent decision making.

SUMMARY

1 Our everyday informal thinking as well as our more formal analysis (as in quantitative analysis) is usually incomplete. It is incomplete in the sense that elements in reality are left out (either by design or oversight). This is one of the main reasons for decision errors.

2 Another reason for decision errors is that in our thinking (and in our more formal analysis, too) assumptions are made that are simply not true or are not quite true.

3 To properly interpret the predictions and decisions indicated by the analysis requires knowledge of two types: (*a*) knowledge of the thinking or the analysis that was done in arriving at the prediction or decision (that is, the assumptions made and the logical-mathematical operations used) and (*b*) a deep perceptive knowledge of the relevant segment of the real world.

4 When a segment of reality is represented in the form of a quantitative model, the use of mathematical operations can yield results not obtainable through the sole use of verbal models or intuitive thinking.

PROBLEMS

1-1 Describe possible relationships of words, phrases, and sentences to a segment of reality. What is the nature of the relationship that is necessary in clear thinking and reasoning? Explain.

1-2 What is the desired relationship of a model or theory to a segment of reality? Is the relationship altered as the model or theory takes a more quantitative form?

1-3 Discuss the nature of the possible gain in the use of quantitative analysis over verbal analysis and intuitive thinking in the study of real-world problems. What may interfere with achieving this gain?

1-4 In assembling steel chairs, some of the parts must be welded together. It is found that each chair requires the welding equipment for about 3 minutes. Suppose that we can choose (vary) the number of chairs we produce. Form a quantitative model (an equation) of this operation which will predict (for various outputs of chairs) the total amount of welding-equipment time that would be needed.

1-5 Using the quantitative model that you created in Problem 1-4, indicate the total amount of welding-equipment time that would be needed to assemble 100 chairs.

1-6 Discuss the difficulties usually encountered (especially in larger problems) in interpreting predictions, such as the one obtained in Problem 1-5. In your answer refer to the abstraction step and the implicit as well as the explicit assumptions made in the model.

Part Two

An Approach to Decision Making under Uncertainty: Decision Analysis

Chapter 2

Making Decisions
under Uncertainty

Choosing and deciding are some of our most familiar experiences. But these experiences are also some of the most perplexing to us because we often cannot know for sure what the consequences of various acts will be. Sometimes the chosen acts in retrospect appear to have been wise. At other times there is cause for regret. It is common to reflect on errors made in earlier decisions and to attempt to reduce such errors in the future.

In a general way these thoughts provide some relevant background for Part Two of this book in which we study the making of decisions under uncertainty. Our focus shall be on decisions in our professional work, but much of what we discuss can shed light on decision making in our private lives as well.

We start from the situation in which a choice of a single course of action from many courses of action is to be made and in which there is the desire to consider the consequences of the acts so that the act selected has the most desirable consequence.

Now if the consequence of each act can be known in advance (with certainty), the problem of decision is essentially one of identifying the act with the best consequence. In some cases this is a simple task, whereas in others it is a very complicated one. Thus, when the consequences can be known in advance (and when the thought or the model encompasses all of the relevant aspects of the reality), errors in decision are essentially avoided.

However, our principal concern in this part of the book is to examine decision making under conditions of *uncertainty*, that is, where the consequence of each course of action is not definitely known. Thus, we recognize uncertainty explicitly and examine ways of making good decisions under such conditions.

We shall see that procedures exist by which some best course of action can be selected in light of our present limited knowledge. Also, in later chapters we shall study ways of revising our state of knowledge as additional information is obtained and of making decisions after such revision.

Even beyond this, we shall examine procedures that enable us to determine the value (the expected value) of additional information which we may be in a position to obtain by such means as testing or sampling. In simple terms, we can estimate how much better off we would be by possessing the additional information.

By knowing the expected value of additional information and its cost, we can then determine in advance whether it is worthwhile to obtain this information before making the decision of interest. It should become quite clear that the expected value of additional information depends mainly upon three factors: our present knowledge, the record of the proposed predictor, and the consequences of decision error if they occur.

In the remaining portion of this chapter let us discuss some of the main elements of the procedures for good decision making under conditions of uncertainty.

DECISION MODELS INCORPORATING UNCERTAINTY

How do we define decision making? Essentially, we define it as we do in everyday usage: The choosing of one course of action from various possible courses of action.

An important aspect of modern quantitative decision analysis is that it builds on good, everyday, intuitive decision procedures. It develops, refines, and extends them so that better decisions can be made in complex situations where decisions are quite difficult. Intuitive knowledge is not discarded but is incorporated explicitly into the analysis.

Before proceeding further, let us focus on some of the main elements generally found in models of decision under uncertainty. These elements are:

1 A set of *alternative courses of action* from which the choice is to be made.

2 A set of *different possible consequences of each course of action*. First, this requires a set of *events* that can occur and then the *consequence* of each act-event combination. Each consequence refers to the effect of an act-event combination upon an objective (such as profit).

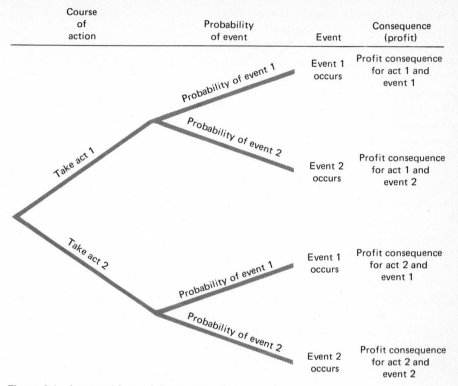

Figure 2-1 A general form of the decision tree.

3 The *degree of uncertainty associated with each possible consequence.* Here, the chances of each profit outcome for each act are represented.

4 The *criterion* to be used in choosing a single course of action. Very roughly, the use of a decision criterion involves obtaining a measure of the effect of each course of action upon an objective and then selecting the act with the most desirable effect upon the objective.

DECISION TREES

A diagram that provides a very useful way of representing the elements of a decision model is the *decision tree.* It is a diagram that represents the sequence (or flow) of decisions, events, and consequences.

A general form of the decision tree for two acts and two events is shown in Figure 2-1. By convention, the decision tree "grows" from left to right in a quite unconventional horizontal fashion. The possible courses of action are represented first, then the possible events with their probabilities, and finally, the consequences (such as profits).

Taking a particular course of action can be thought of as "going down" a particular branch of the decision tree. The actual event that will occur is subject to chance (it is often referred to as a "chance event," and going down a branch that involves a chance event is thought of as a "chance process").

A profit consequence for each act-event combination usually can be estimated even though we are uncertain about which event will occur. Of course our uncertainty regarding the occurrence of the event makes the profit consequence of a particular act uncertain, too.

Represented in the form of a decision tree, the flow of decisions, events, and consequences in a problem can easily be studied before the actual decision is made (and, also, after it has been made). The value of using it for analysis before the decision is made is that it can facilitate the identification of the best course of action under the present limited knowledge and also (as we shall see later) under possible future states of knowledge when additional information from tests, surveys, or samples has been obtained.

PROBABILITY AND UNCERTAINTY

As we try to describe in everyday words the degree of uncertainty that we attach to the occurrence of a particular event, there remains a general vagueness in our statements. Fortunately, the concern for a more quantitative expression of ideas and relationships has led to ways of describing the uncertainty of events more precisely. *Probability* is the name given to the common quantitative measure of uncertainty. We shall discuss it in some detail in Chapter 3, noting here only some of its main properties.

Probability is a quantitative measure of the uncertainty associated with the occurrence of a particular event. If an event is considered certain to occur, it is associated with a probability of 1.00. If its occurrence is considered impossible, the associated probability is 0.00. Those events whose occurrence is considered possible but uncertain are associated with the probabilities between 0.00 and 1.00: those considered more likely, having a probability closer to 1.00; those events considered less likely, having a probability further from 1.00.

Although the use of probabilities to represent the degree of uncertainty makes possible a more precise description of the uncertainty, it also permits the identification of a best course of action by allowing the computation of an *expected profit* (to be defined later) for each course of action. A common criterion for decision making is to select the course of action with the highest expected profit. Let us illustrate this in the following paragraphs with a small example. Some aspects of this procedure will be discussed in more detail in later chapters.

AN EXAMPLE OF DECISION MAKING UNDER UNCERTAINTY

To illustrate the main quantitative procedure for decision making under conditions of uncertainty, let us examine a problem that is related to the machine example discussed in Chapter 1. In that earlier discussion there was no uncertainty and no possibility for choice. Now we have both.

EXAMPLE

We have two packaging machines (an old one and a new one) that can be used to wrap and seal products for distribution.

We must select just one of the two machines to run for a period of time. There would be no problem if the quality of the raw materials used by the machines could be known beforehand. The new machine is the more efficient of the two if the materials are of good quality. But if the materials are of poor quality, the old machine performs better because it does not become jammed like the new one.

The main problem is that the decision as to which machine to use has to be made before the quality of the materials is known.

For each machine the output per hour of operation (and thus the profit) is affected by the quality of the materials. The materials can be either good or poor, but their quality cannot be known before the decision has to be made. We have the following information:

Of the past shipments of the materials 80 percent have been of good quality and 20 percent of poor quality.

Using the old machine, profit for the period would be $200 if the materials turn out to be of good quality but only $160 if they are of poor quality.

Using the new machine, profit for the period would be $240 if the materials turn out to be of good quality but only $80 if they are of poor quality.

Given the above information, should we use the old or new machine to maximize expected profit?

Suppose that we look at this decision problem in terms of the four elements of decision models discussed earlier: (1) the alternative courses of action, (2) the possible consequences of each course of action, (3) the degree of uncertainty, and (4) the criterion to be used.

The Alternative Courses of Action

There are only two courses of action from which to choose: "use old machine" or "use new machine." We can represent each course of action in a decision tree by a separate branch as is done for this problem in Figure 2-2. The flow of decisions, events, and consequences is from left to right.

The Possible Consequences of Each Course of Action

First, the possible *events* that can occur with each course of action must be listed. This is most easily done by representing each event by a separate branch on the tree following each course of action. We list the basic events for this problem, "good-quality materials in the shipment" and "poor-quality materials in the shipment," at the tips of the second set of branches as shown in Figure 2-2.

Then for each *act-event combination* we must estimate the profit that could be realized and place these profit consequences at the appropriate positions in Figure 2-2. For example, given the occurrence of the event "good-quality materials in the shipment," the profit consequence is $200 provided the act "use old machine" is taken. This same event "good-quality materials in the shipment" when combined with the act "use new machine" results in a profit of $240.

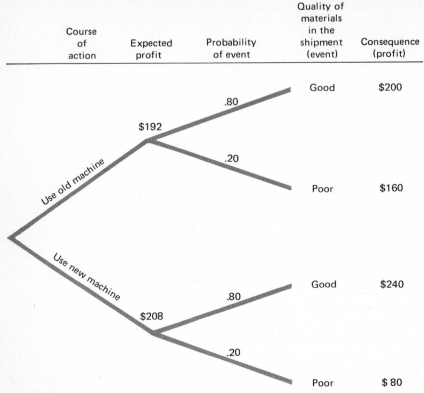

Course of action	Expected profit	Probability of event	Quality of materials in the shipment (event)	Consequence (profit)

Figure 2-2 An example of a decision problem in tree form.

The Degree of Uncertainty Associated with Each of the Events and Each of the Profit Consequences

We indicated above that the use of probabilities permits a more precise description of the amount of uncertainty to be attached to each event. From the data given, we have the relative frequency (percentage of the time) the shipments were of good and poor quality. Provided that all other conditions remain essentially the same, we can use these relative frequencies as the basis for probability assignments to the future events "good-quality materials in the shipment" and "poor-quality materials in the shipment."

Since 80 percent of the shipments have been of good quality and 20 percent of poor quality, we assign a probability of .80 to the possible future event "good-quality materials in the shipment" and a probability of .20 to the event "poor-quality materials in the shipment."

The probabilities assigned to each event in Figure 2-2 also are the appropriate probabilities to be attached to the associated profit consequences of particular act-event combinations. For example, let us examine the uppermost branches of the tree in Figure 2-2 representing the act-event combination "use old machine" and "good-quality materials in the shipment." The probability of the event "good-quality materials in the shipment" is .80, and this also is the probability of realizing the profit of $200 associated with this particular act-event combination.

Looking at the lower section of the tree, we see that this same event "good-quality materials in the shipment" can be combined with the act "use new machine." The probability of this event is, of course, .80; but now the profit consequence is $240. Thus, the probability of this profit consequence is .80 (given the act "use new machine").

The Criterion to Be Used in Choosing a Course of Action

As noted earlier, a common criterion for choosing a course of action is to select that course of action for which the expected profit is the largest. However, the term "expected profit" used here has a specific technical meaning and often is not identical with the meaning of the term as it is used in common speech.

The *expected profit for each act* is defined as the *average* profit that would tend to be realized for each act if it were taken time after time with the probabilities and profit consequences holding at their assigned amounts.

Thus, the computation of the expected profit for each act involves multiplying the probability of each profit consequence by the associated profit consequence and then adding all these products of the appropriate multiplications.[1] We can express it in a general form as follows:

[1]*Background note:* Most persons are familiar with the computation of an average value from a set of values by adding all the values (repeating a value each time it occurs) and dividing the sum by the number of possible values. For example, if the values are 1, 1, 1, 3, and 4, the average value is 2:

$$\frac{1 + 1 + 1 + 3 + 4}{5} = \frac{10}{5} = 2$$

An alternative procedure (especially useful when probabilities are involved) is to associate a relative frequency (or probability) with each possible value and then multiply each possible value by its relative frequency (or probability). Adding the resulting products of the multiplications gives us the same average value (or expected value). This alternative procedure is used as follows to obtain the same average value of 2 in the example above:

Possible value	Absolute frequency	Relative frequency	Possible value times its relative frequency
1	3	⅗ (or .60)	1 × .60 = .60
3	1	⅕ (or .20)	3 × .20 = .60
4	1	⅕ (or .20)	4 × .20 = .80
	5		Average (or expected value) = 2.00

A probability is essentially to be thought of as an estimated (usually future) relative frequency of a value. Thus, when probabilities of values (such as profit values) are given in a particular situation, this procedure enables us to compute the expected profit value.

$$
\begin{pmatrix}
\text{Expected} \\
\text{profit for} \\
\text{a course} \\
\text{of action}
\end{pmatrix}
=
\begin{pmatrix}
\text{probability} \\
\text{of one} \\
\text{particular} \\
\text{profit} \\
\text{consequence}
\end{pmatrix}
\begin{pmatrix}
\text{the} \\
\text{associated} \\
\text{profit} \\
\text{consequence}
\end{pmatrix}
+
\begin{pmatrix}
\text{probability} \\
\text{of} \\
\text{another} \\
\text{particular} \\
\text{profit} \\
\text{consequence}
\end{pmatrix}
\begin{pmatrix}
\text{the} \\
\text{other} \\
\text{particular} \\
\text{profit} \\
\text{consequence}
\end{pmatrix}
$$

To obtain the expected profit for the act "use old machine," first we multiply the probability of the $200 profit consequence which is .80 by the $200 profit. To this product we add that obtained by multiplying the .20 probability of the $160 profit consequence by the $160 profit. The sum of these products is $192, the expected profit of the act "use old machine." We summarize our computations as follows:

$$
\begin{pmatrix}
\text{Expected} \\
\text{profit} \\
\text{for the} \\
\text{act} \\
\text{"use old} \\
\text{machine"}
\end{pmatrix}
=
\begin{pmatrix}
\text{probability} \\
\text{of the} \\
\$200 \\
\text{profit} \\
\text{consequence}
\end{pmatrix}
\begin{pmatrix}
\text{the} \\
\$200 \\
\text{profit} \\
\text{consequence}
\end{pmatrix}
+
\begin{pmatrix}
\text{probability} \\
\text{of the} \\
\$160 \\
\text{profit} \\
\text{consequence}
\end{pmatrix}
\begin{pmatrix}
\text{the} \\
\$160 \\
\text{profit} \\
\text{consequence}
\end{pmatrix}
$$

$$= (.80)(\$200) + (.20)(\$160)$$
$$= \$160 + \$32$$
$$= \$192$$

For the act "use new machine" we obtain an expected profit of $208 as follows:

$$
\begin{pmatrix}
\text{Expected} \\
\text{profit} \\
\text{for the} \\
\text{act} \\
\text{"use new} \\
\text{machine"}
\end{pmatrix}
=
\begin{pmatrix}
\text{probability} \\
\text{of the} \\
\$240 \\
\text{profit} \\
\text{consequence}
\end{pmatrix}
\begin{pmatrix}
\text{the} \\
\$240 \\
\text{profit} \\
\text{consequence}
\end{pmatrix}
+
\begin{pmatrix}
\text{probability} \\
\text{of the} \\
\$80 \\
\text{profit} \\
\text{consequence}
\end{pmatrix}
\begin{pmatrix}
\text{the} \\
\$80 \\
\text{profit} \\
\text{consequence}
\end{pmatrix}
$$

$$= (.80)(\$240) + (.20)(\$80)$$
$$= \$192 + \$16$$
$$= \$208$$

The highest of the expected profit amounts is $208. Because it is associated with the act "use new machine," this is the best act by this criterion. Generally, as we work our way back through a tree that we have laid out, we follow the practice (as shown in Figure 2-2) of placing the computed expected profit amounts just above the point where the branches emerge representing the various possible chance events.

A NOTE ON ANOTHER CRITERION

It is possible in decision making under uncertainty to assume that the worst (or best) consequence for each act will occur and then make a decision on either of these assumptions. If the worst consequence for each act is assumed in our problem above, the preferred act is "use old machine." The worst consequence for "use old machine" ($160) is higher than the worst consequence for "use new machine" ($80). (This "pessimist" criterion is also known as the "maximin" or "minimax" criterion.)

At the other extreme, if the occurrence of the best consequence for each act is assumed, the preferred act is "use new machine." The best consequence for "use old machine" is only $200, whereas for "use new machine" it is $240.

We can see that for a large problem with many possible consequences for each act this procedure may make it a lot simpler to select an act, and sometimes this criterion may be justified. But, generally, the assumption that a particular consequence *will* occur is not warranted. Usually, it is more desirable to take into account all the various consequences that can occur and the chances (probabilities) of their occurrence. The computation of an expected profit for each of the acts does this, as we have demonstrated above. In Chapter 7 we also take into account cases where some undesirable outcomes cannot be tolerated and also where identical additional amounts of profit are not valued equally.

SUMMARY

Through the use of more explicit quantitative decision procedures it becomes possible to introduce more reason and rationality into the analysis of large and complex decision problems. Some of the more important ways this comes about are as follows:

1 The number of courses of action that can be considered is enlarged. Intuitive procedures are extremely limited in this regard.
2 An explicit representation can be provided of the degree of uncertainty regarding the occurrence of particular events and consequences.
3 An estimate is provided of the consequences of each of the various courses of action in complex situations.
4 A procedure can be used in large decision problems to select a course of action that is based on reason and consistency. — most desirable consequence
5 A more explicit representation of a problem, especially in the form of a decision tree, lends the problem to fairly easy programming on a computer. In this way quite complex problems can be studied.

PROBLEMS

2-1 A timber-products firm produces two products from logs that it acquires periodically. One of the products is plywood. The other product is regular lumber.

The quality of the logs sometimes is good, and at other times it is poor. Usually, it can be classified into one of these two states (good or poor), but the state cannot be known in advance.

The problem is this: A decision has to be made on which product to make from the logs before the quality of the logs is known.

Construct a decision tree that represents the act-event combinations of the problem.

2-2 Suppose that the timber-products firm in Problem 2-1 has records that show that one-half of the past batches of logs have been of good quality and one-half have been of poor quality. Thus, it is judged reasonable to assign a probability of .50 to the next batch being of good quality and a probability of .50 to it being of poor quality.

Further information reveals that if plywood is made and if the quality of logs is good, the profit for the period will be $50,000; if the quality is poor, the profit will be $20,000 in producing this product. If regular lumber is made from the logs, the profit is $42,000 providing the logs are of good quality; but it is $30,000 if the quality is poor.

a Insert the probabilities on the appropriate branches of the tree that you constructed in Problem 2-1.

b Place the profit consequences of each act-event combination at the tips of the branches.

c Compute an expected profit for each act, and indicate the act with the highest expected profit.

2-3 A firm that manufactures bicycles needs to expand its production facilities but is undecided as to whether a large plant or a small plant should be constructed.

An important relevant event is the state of the market for the product to be made in the new facilities. Suppose the state of the market is either good or fair but is uncertain at the time of the decision.

To facilitate the analysis of the decision problem, construct a decision tree showing the acts and the possible events associated with each act.

2-4 The bicycle maker in Problem 2-3 is concerned with the state of the market for the units to be produced in the proposed new facilities. A plant that is too large will incur quite high average costs of production when it is only partly utilized. Suppose the existing information about the market provides a probability assignment of .50 to the market being good and .50 to it being fair.

Further, the estimated profit is $500,000 if the small plant is built and the market is good; it is $100,000 if this act is taken and the market is fair. If the large plant is built and the market is good, the profit is estimated to be $700,000; but a negative profit (a loss) of $200,000 is incurred if the market is fair and the same act is taken.

a Using the decision tree, compute the expected profit of each act.

b What is the best-size plant to construct in terms of expected profit?

2-5 An investment decision must be made on the use of a given amount of funds. Suppose that consideration is given to investing the entire amount in only one of three securities: security 1, security 2, or security 3.

The state of the securities market at the end of a particular period is of great relevance for this decision. However, this cannot be known in advance and is uncertain at the time the investment decision is to be made. It is judged that we can satisfactorily classify the status of the securities market as either depressed or rising.

a   Construct a decision tree for this investment decision problem.

b   How many act-event combinations would we have if consideration was given to the purchase of a fourth security?

2-6   In Problem 2-5 suppose the probability of a depressed securities market at the end of the period is judged to be .40 and the probability of a rising market is judged to be .60.

Also, assume the following profit estimates for the act-event combinations involving the purchase of one of the following three securities with all the funds. (Profit here refers to dividends during the period plus the amount of appreciation or depreciation in the price of the security.)

Course of action	Profit (in thousands of dollars) given the state of the securities market	
	Depressed market	Rising market
Buy security 1	$ 90	$120
Buy security 2	80	140
Buy security 3	100	110

a   Compute an expected profit for the purchase of each security.

b   Which security purchase will maximize expected profit?

2-7   In agriculture, a factor that can have a significant effect upon product output is the presence or absence of harmful insects. Usually, the level of infestation that would occur in a future production period cannot be known before a decision has to be made on the application of an insecticide.

Suppose that the level of infestation can be classified as heavy, moderate, or slight. From historical data the probabilities assigned to the levels of infestation in the future production period are .10, .50, and .40, respectively.

a   Construct a decision tree for the problem showing the act-event combinations for applying an insecticide and for not applying one.

b   Insert the probabilities on the appropriate branches leading to the events.

2-8   In Problem 2-7 it is estimated that if no insecticide is applied the possible outputs (in bushels per acre) are 15 if the infestation is heavy, 28 if it is moderate, and 31 if it is slight. If an insecticide is applied, the output is estimated to be 32 regardless of the level of infestation that would have occurred without the application.

Suppose further that the revenue (price) per bushel is $3 and the cost of the insecticide (including its application) is $11 per acre.

a   Compute an expected net revenue for applying the insecticide and also for not doing so. Obtain a net revenue consequence for each act-event combination. (Interpret net revenue as total revenue from a particular output less any insecticide cost.)

b   Which is the best act in terms of expected net revenue?

2-9   A new camera has been developed by a firm, and it is being considered for introduction to a large national market. Experience with the introduction of similar products indicates some uncertainty with respect to the state of the market for such new products.

Suppose it is reasonable to think of the market for the new product being in one of three possible states: good, fair, or poor. Respective probability assessments of .10, .80, and .10 were obtained through the examination of previous studies of the market for this product and through the use of the judgments of the market by experienced persons.

If the new camera is introduced, the profit consequences (in millions of dollars) with a good, fair, or poor market for the new camera are estimated to be $90, $50, or − $10, respectively. The firm also produces products that have been on the market for some time. Thus, if it does not introduce the new camera, the profit consequences (in millions of dollars) of the act "do not introduce the new product" are $70 if the market for the new camera is good, $60 if the market for it is fair, and $10 if the market is poor.

a   Construct a decision tree of the problem and insert the probabilities of the events and the consequences of the act-event combinations.

b   Compute an expected profit for each act and indicate whether or not the new camera should be introduced in terms of expected profit.

2-10 In the oil industry there are some firms that begin drilling operations with little knowledge on which to base their drilling decisions. Such "wildcatters" will usually know what others have found when they drilled in particular areas, but they may know little else about the existence of oil.

Suppose that one of these firms is considering drilling in a region where only 10 percent of past drillings have encountered oil. From this knowledge the firm assigns a probability of .10 on encountering oil in its drilling operations under consideration. Also, a probability of .90 is assigned to the event "no oil."

The cost of drilling is estimated to be $50,000. If oil is found, the estimated (net) revenue (not taking into account the drilling costs) that would be forthcoming over the expected productive life of the well is $650,000.

a   Construct a tree of the problem to help in the decision as to whether or not to drill. Represent in the tree the profit consequences of the act-event combinations. Incorporate the drilling costs and treat any losses as negative profits.

b   Should drilling be undertaken in this area in terms of expected profits?

2-11 A government agency is considering entering into a contract for 1 year with one of two firms that will supply the agency with time-sharing computer services. The firms' bids are such that the direct cost to the agency is approximately the same for each of the firms. However, taking all data processing costs into account, one firm appears to be preferred although the chances of an early successful installation of the services by that firm is somewhat uncertain.

More specifically, it is believed that firm 1 has the potential to provide services that can result in lower costs. If the firm's system is satisfactory in a short period of time, the overall cost estimate is $30,000. However, it is also estimated that the probability is only .60 that this cost can be realized.

The probability is .40 that firm 1's system will be unsatisfactory, with an overall cost consequence of $60,000.

Firm 2 cannot provide as efficient a system, but the probability of its being satisfactory is judged to be .70. The cost consequence is $40,000 if this is the state of the system. The probability is .30 that firm 2's system would be unsatisfactory, with a cost of $60,000 to the agency.

a   Construct a decision tree of the problem and insert where appropriate the probabilities of the events and the cost consequences of the act-event combinations.

b   With which firm should the agency sign the contract if it wants to minimize expected cost?

c   What would be the choice using the pessimist criterion? Explain.

2-12   Suppose that a firm summarizes its profit outcomes for the possible act-event combinations as follows:

	Event 1	Event 2	Event 3
Act 1	$46	$20	$ -5
Act 2	$20	$60	$ -5
Act 3	$ 0	$20	$100
Act 4	$10	$20	$ 70

a   Construct a tree of the decision problem.

b   Under the pessimist criterion, which is the best act?

c   Compute an expected profit for each act if the probabilities of events 1, 2, and 3 are .50, .30, and .20, respectively.

d   Give an intuitive interpretation to the expected profit for each act obtained in c.

e   Identify the optimal act under the maximization-of-expected-profit criterion.

Chapter 3

Interpretations of Probability: Relative Frequency and Subjective

In this chapter we shall give more careful examination to the concept of probability and to some of the main rules regarding the use of probabilities. In Chapter 2 we referred to probability as a measure of the degree of uncertainty with regard to the occurrence of a particular event. Recall that a probability can be as high as 1.00 (certainty) or as low as 0.00 (impossibility). For more likely events we assign a value closer to 1.00, for less likely events, a value further from 1.00.

Moreover, if our list of the possible events of a chance process is *exhaustive* (that is, all possible events are listed) and *mutually exclusive* (only one of them can occur), the sum of the probabilities assigned to each of the events must be equal to 1.00. The requirement that these probabilities sum to 1.00 is simply equivalent to the verbal statement that only one of the events *can* occur, but one of them *must* occur. In this chapter we shall illustrate events that are mutually exclusive and a set of events of a chance process that is exhaustive.

INTERPRETATIONS OF PROBABILITY

Currently, there are two main interpretations or definitions of probability that are held by those working in probability and statistics. One interpretation is often called the *relative-frequency* interpretation; the other, the *subjective* (or *personalistic*) interpretation.

Relative-Frequency Interpretation of Probability

Loosely stated, the relative-frequency interpretation of probability limits the use of probabilities to those situations where a particular type of historical data is available on the occurrence of the relevant events. Thus, in some contexts the relative frequency of an event can be thought of as the percentage of the time the particular event occurs. The relative frequency that an event has occurred is then used as the basis for a probability assignment to the occurrence of this particular event in some future period.

In a more technical sense the probability of an event is defined as being equal to its long-run relative frequency. However, in practical applications such long-run relative frequencies are not obtainable, and thus an estimate of the long-run relative frequency must be obtained by using the relative frequency computed from the available data.

To provide an illustration of a relative-frequency-based probability assignment, let us take a familiar object, such as a soda bottle cap. Suppose that we are interested in the probability that the flat side of the bottle cap would face upward after tossing it into the air several feet.

We toss the bottle cap 100 times, record the absolute frequency of the flat side facing upward, and find it to be 30. The absolute frequency of the open side facing upward was 70. Thus, the *relative* frequency that the flat side faced upward was 30/100 or .30; and that the open side faced upward, 70/100 or .70.

Following the relative-frequency interpretation, we would for a future toss (toss 101) assign a probability of .30 to the event "flat side up" and a probability of .70 to the event "open side up."

In this example the conditions (the reality) under which toss 101 is to be made could be very close to the conditions under which the past 100 tosses were made. From a practical standpoint we could perhaps consider the conditions to be the same even though some changes have occurred in the relevant reality (for example, the conditions in the air, the surface on which the object is to fall, and so forth).

Of course if the changes are great enough for us to detect them and consider their effect on the chances of the outcomes, we may begin to question the use of the relative frequencies as the sole basis for the probability assignments.

Subjective (or Personalistic) Interpretation of Probability

The point of view usually taken in a subjective (or personalistic) interpretation of probability is that the probabilities assigned to the events cannot be disassociated from some specific person or persons. This is held to be true even in the use of the relative-frequency interpretation just discussed.

At some point in the use of probabilities a choice has to be made with regard to the particular probability assignments to be used. Even if the final probability assignments are identical to the historical relative frequencies of the occurrence of the events, some personal judgment has to be made on the adequacy of the probability assignments.

Because reality in a large sense never repeats itself, the future events being considered will emerge (if they occur) out of a different reality from that which the past events emerged. Therefore, it is inescapable that some personal judgment be made (perhaps implicitly) on the closeness of the analogy between the past reality (in which the relative-frequency data were obtained) and the reality in the future when the particular events may occur.

Since the analogy between past reality and future reality is never perfect, and often diverges considerably, the role of personal judgment (perhaps supplemented by various tests) is an important element in the intelligent use of probabilities and, also, of statistical procedures generally.

Thus, even when relative-frequency data are available, important judgments must be made by someone on the validity of these data for the reality on which we are focusing. But what should be done in a situation where the past relative frequencies of events are simply not available? What probability assignments can then be made to the events? Let us look at these questions with reference to the bottle-cap example.

Suppose that we could *not* have tossed the bottle cap 100 times—not even a single toss. What probability would we want to assign to the events "flat side up" and "open side up"? A strict follower of the relative-frequency interpretation would say that probability assignments simply should not be made to these events under these circumstances. This person would say: "Let us wait until we have some adequate relative-frequency data."

But looking at our professional work (and private lives, too), we see a continuing procession of choices and decisions to be made under conditions of uncertainty where there are no adequate relative-frequency data available on which to base probability assignments to the events (events that are often of considerable importance to us).

Thus, even though relative-frequency data on the occurrence of the particular events are highly desirable, in many situations the only data available may be of a non-relative-frequency type. By this we mean the accumulated experience and general knowledge possessed by persons.

Thus, suppose that in the bottle-cap example we were forced to make a probability assignment to the events "flat side up" and "open side up" without first being able to make repeated tosses to obtain some relative frequencies. What could we do? We could draw upon our general knowledge of similar objects and our experience with them. For example, we might observe that the flat side is heavier (the center of gravity may appear to be closer to that side) but that the open side has a larger surface.

We can see that even without being able to toss the bottle cap (to get some relative frequencies) we may make useful probability assignments based upon our best personal judgment. If we cannot delay in the assignment of probabilities (and the events are of considerable consequence), we would want to make the best probability assignments to the events in light of our present knowledge and experience.

We should emphasize that what we desire in a subjective probability assignment is a representation of our best personal judgment of the chance of a particular event occurring. Most assuredly, it does not refer to a casual or whimsical assessment but to a careful and honest assessment of the chance of an event occurring (in light of our present knowledge).

Also, we could refer to this probability assessment as our subjective judgment of the chance that a particular "fact" will emerge (usually a future "fact"). This is to be contrasted with the subjective judgments of "value" or "preference" that may be involved in determining the relative attractiveness of the consequence of a particular event associated with a particular act. (This aspect of decision making under uncertainty is explored in Chapter 7.)

Furthermore, it is important in making subjective probability judgments regarding the occurrence of events that we not be influenced by our desire for particular events to occur. There appears to be a persistent human tendency implicitly to place higher-than-justified probabilities on strongly preferred consequences.

Different persons will, of course, possess different knowledge and experience. Thus, it is to be expected that different persons will perhaps assign different probabilities to the events. In our bottle-cap example, someone might assign a probability of .50 to "flat side up," whereas someone else might assign a probability of .40 to this same event.

This variation in subjective or personalistic probability assignments from person to person leads some to refer to the relative-frequency-based probabilities as being "objective" probabilities. In some sense there is a greater objectivity to these probabilities since each person using the relative-frequency procedure would, upon examining the relative-frequency data, make the same probability assignments to the events.

However, as we noted above, subjective judgments must subsequently be made with regard to the appropriateness of the relative-frequency-based probabilities in any particular application. Thus, although there is this desirable element of objectivity in this procedure (the assignment of probabilities from relative frequencies) that is absent in the purely subjective or personalistic procedure, it is well to note that its use is not free from subjective judgments either.

The main point of this section is that it is useful to assess carefully the chances of particular events occurring by using all the data that are available. Some of the data at times may be of the relative-frequency type and some may not. A general interpretation of probability permits all data to be used in making the probability assignments to events of interest to us.

Again, we should say that relative-frequency data are highly desirable. But if they are not available (or if the relative-frequency data that are available are to be considered with reference to a set of real conditions different from those under which they were obtained), the use of probability assignments based upon the general knowledge and experience of perceptive persons is very desirable.

EVENTS AND SETS

An accurate assignment of probabilities to events is aided if we think of the possible events that can occur as elements of a set. Some events are referred to as *simple* events, whereas others are called *compound* events.

Simple Events

If the possible events of a chance process are broken down as finely as possible we have the set of simple events of that chance process.

For example, suppose that a copying machine is to be used to make two copies of an important document. However, it is common for some of the copies from this machine to be defective in some way. Thus, for each copy produced, the possible outcomes are "good copy" (let us refer to this event by the letter *g*) or "defective copy" (let us refer to this outcome by the letter *d*). Therefore, the possible simple events *in producing two copies* are four in number:

    1 "Good copy" on the first one made and "good copy" on the second one made (*gg*).
    2 "Good copy" on the first and "defective copy" on the second (*gd*).
    3 "Defective copy" on the first and "good copy" on the second (*dg*).
    4 "Defective copy" on the first and "defective copy" on the second (*dd*).

These four simple events comprise a set of events that is "exhaustive." This means that we have listed all the possible events that can occur in this chance process of making two copies of the document. Therefore, we say that one of the events *must* occur (that is, it is a certainty with a probability of 1.00), and therefore the sum of the probabilities assigned to each of the simple events must be 1.00.

The possible occurrence of any one of these four simple events can be represented in different ways. In Figure 3-1 we show the possible simple events through the use of a tree diagram. From left to right, the first copy made has two possible outcomes, and the second copy made also has two possible outcomes. Thus, the simple events represented in Figure 3-1 are referred to as: *gg, gd, dg,* and *dd*.

As we think of the simple events as elements of a set, a Venn diagram, as in Figure 3-2, is a quite appropriate form of representation. Such diagrams (named after the nineteenth-century English philosopher John Venn) help us visualize the elements of a set.

In Figure 3-2 the same simple events *gg, gd, dg,* and *dd* are represented by points enclosed by a solid line. All the simple events taken together are referred to as the *sample space* of the chance process. (In more advanced discussions

First copy	Second copy	Simple event

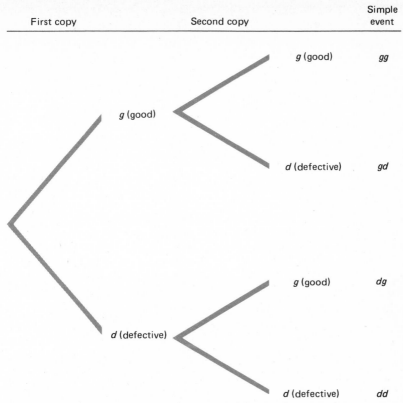

Figure 3-1   The simple events in making two copies of the document.

each simple event is referred to as a *sample point*.) Of course each simple event can be thought of as an element of the set of all simple events, the sample space. Recall that in our problem any one of the simple events *can* occur, but one of them *must* occur.

Compound Events

In practical problems, the events in which we are usually interested are *compound events*. In set terms, a compound event is comprised of a set of more than one of the simple events. Further, we could describe a compound event as a subset of the sample space, the subset being comprised of more than one element (more than one simple event).

Thus, a compound event is said to occur if any *one* of a set of simple events occurs. Let us illustrate this with the example of the copying machine making two copies of the document.

Suppose that we are interested in the possibility of obtaining *at least one good copy* when two are made. Let us refer to this compound event (at least one good copy) by the letter *L*.

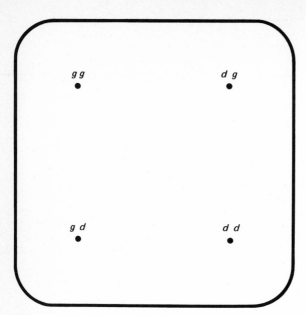

Figure 3-2 A Venn diagram showing the simple events in making two copies of the document.

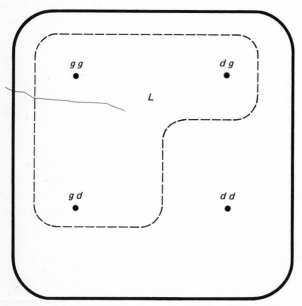

Figure 3-3 The simple events associated with the compound event *L* ("at least one good copy").

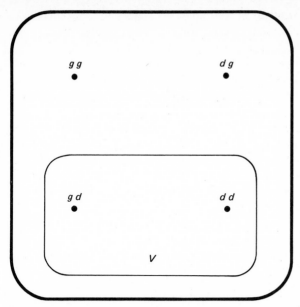

Figure 3-4   The simple events associated with the compound event V ("last copy defective").

A look at Figure 3-3 reveals that there are three possible simple events (*gg, gd,* or *dg*) any one of whose occurrence would cause the compound event *L* to occur (that is, at least one good copy is made). Also, we might describe this compound event by listing these simple events as follows:

$$L = \{gg, gd, dg\}$$

In Figure 3-3 we enclose the points *gg, gd,* and *dg* with a dashed line to indicate that they are elements of the set associated with the compound event *L*, "at least one good copy." Only the simple event *dd* is excluded from this set.

Another compound event could be of interest in this same chance process of making two copies. Suppose it is the event "last copy defective" as two are made. Let us refer to this compound event by the letter *V*. In Figure 3-4 we identify the simple events *gd* and *dd* (which would cause *V* to occur) and enclose them with a solid line. Another way to describe this compound event is as follows:

$$V = \{gd, dd\}$$

We have referred to two different compound events with regard to the same chance process of making two copies and observing the occurrence of a single simple event. An obvious point of interest in many such problems is whether or not *both* compound events can occur in one run of the chance process (that is, in making two copies). If we identify the compound events *L* and *V* on a Venn diagram (as we do in Figure 3-5), we see that *both* of these compound events can occur. Of course, intuitively, too, we know that in making two copies we can get at least one good copy and also have the last copy turn out defective. In large problems, however, our intuition typically fails in providing answers to such questions.

In set terms, there is an element (*gd*) that is a member of both of the sets associated with the compound events *L* and *V*. In terms of events, this means that if the simple event *gd* occurs, *both* the events *L* and *V* occur. Therefore, the compound events *L* and *V* are *not* "mutually exclusive." All the simple events are not exclusively members of just one of the subsets corresponding to the compound events.

More on Set Terms

Elements that have membership in two different subsets of the sample space (such as *gd* with regard to the compound events *L* and *V*) are described as being elements of another set referred to by $L \cap V$. This is read *L* intersect *V*. In our example, the sole member of this set is the simple event *gd*. More formally, we have:

$$L \cap V = \{gd\}$$

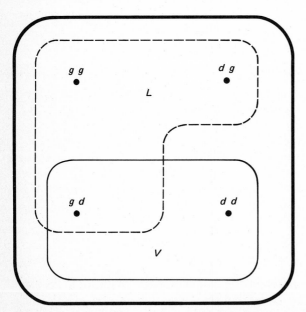

Figure 3-5 The possibility of the occurrence of both of the compound events *L* and *V*.

The set $L \cap V$ is important because it is comprised of those simple events which, if any of them occur, cause *both* of the compound events L and V to occur. This has important implications for predicting some events given the occurrence of other events (as we shall see in Chapter 4).

At other times we may be interested in the occurrence of one compound event *or* the other. Suppose that in our example we are interested in the occurrence of either L (at least one good copy) or V (last copy defective). In set terms the appropriate concept is that of the union of the two sets L and V. Thus, the occurrence of *either* L or V is represented by $L \cup V$ which is read L union V. More formally, we list the simple events that have membership in at least one of the sets L or V.

$$L \cup V = \{gg, gd, dg, dd\}$$

It turns out in the illustration that all the simple events are members of one of the sets or the other.

ASSIGNING PROBABILITIES TO SIMPLE AND COMPOUND EVENTS

What probabilities should be assigned to the simple events in our copying-machine example? First, we must assign probabilities to the outcomes at each step in the chance process. In our example this means that we must assign a probability to "good copy" (g) and "defective copy" (d) at each step (that is, for each copy made).

Suppose that in the past about one-half of the copies have been defective. Thus a probability of .50 is assigned to the occurrence of d and a probability of .50 to g for each copy made. We shall see that this example is an illustration of the special case of each outcome having an equal probability. In all such cases it turns out that each of the simple events will have an equal probability of occurrence. Thus, in making two copies, the simple events are four in number: *gg, gd, dg,* and *dd*. With four simple events, the probability of any one of them occurring is equal to the reciprocal of the total number of simple events. Thus, for our copying-machine example, the probability of each simple event is ¼ or .25.

$$\frac{\text{Probability of}}{\text{each simple event}} = \frac{1}{\begin{array}{c}\text{number of}\\\text{simple events}\end{array}}$$

$$= \text{¼ or .25}$$

In Figure 3-6 we have attached a marker to each point representing a simple event and have placed on each marker the appropriate probability.

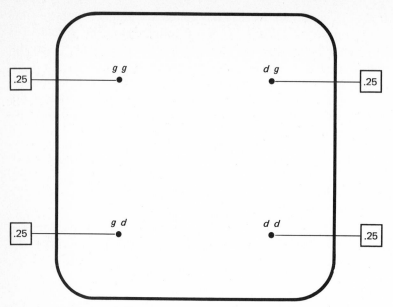

Figure 3-6   The probabilities of the simple events in the copying-machine example.

The Multiplication Rule

In Figure 3-7 we have once again laid out the tree diagram pertaining to the chance process of making two copies of the document. Now, however, we have placed the appropriate probabilities of .50 for g and .50 for d at each step in the chance process.

As indicated above, the case of equal probabilities of each outcome at each step in the chance process leads one to an equal probability of occurrence of the simple events, each being .25 in the above case. However, we can also obtain these probabilities of the simple events by multiplying the probabilities on the branches in Figure 3-7 leading to each of the simple events. For example, the probability of the simple event gg is .25: (.50)(.50) = .25.

Should a chance process *not* be characterized by such equally probable outcomes at each step, the calculation of the probabilities of the simple events *must* use this multiplication procedure. Sometimes this multiplication procedure is referred to as the "multiplication rule." Also, since one of the simple events in a chance process must occur, and since no more than one of them can occur, the sum of the probabilities of the simple events must be equal to 1.00.

The Probabilities of Compound Events

Earlier we considered the occurrence of two compound events, L and V. (L pertained to the occurrence of "at least one good copy" and V to "last copy defective.") We described these compound events by listing the simple events that comprise them. Now we have a probability of .25 to assign to each of the simple events. But what probability should we assign to L or to V?

It turns out that the probability of a compound event is simply the sum of the probabilities of the simple events that comprise it. Thus, since the compound event L is comprised of the simple events gg, gd, and dg, we can obtain the probability of L as follows (*Note:* We use the upper case letter P to refer to the probability of the event enclosed in the parentheses immediately following the letter P):

$$P(L) = P(gg) + P(gd) + P(dg)$$
$$= .25 + .25 + .25$$
$$= .75$$

In terms of the Venn diagram in Figure 3-8, this corresponds to the summing of the probabilities on each of the markers attached to the points representing the simple events gg, gd, and dg associated with the compound event L.

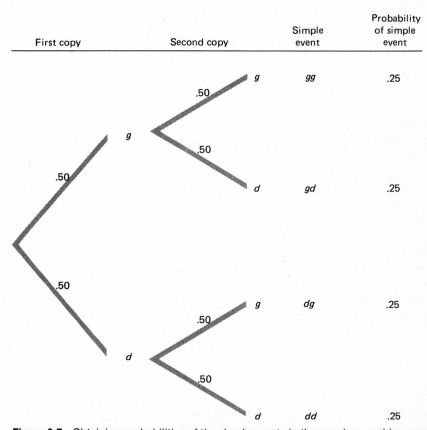

Figure 3-7 Obtaining probabilities of the simple events in the copying-machine example.

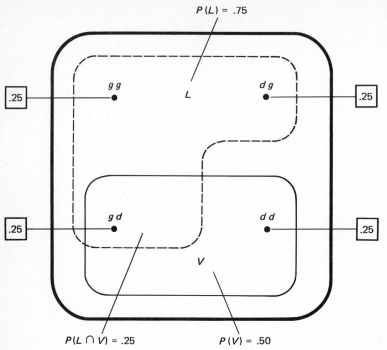

Figure 3-8   The probability of the occurrence of both of the compound events *L* and *V*.

In similar fashion, the probability of the compound event *V* is obtained. The associated simple events are *gd* and *dd*. Thus, the probability of *V* is obtained as follows:

$$P(V) = P(gd) + P(dd)$$
$$= .25 + .25$$
$$= .50$$

But what about the probability of the occurrence of *both* the compound events *L* and *V*? Most simply, we can, from Figure 3-8, observe whether or not there are simple events that have common membership in the two sets corresponding to the compound events *L* and *V*. There is one such simple event, *gd*. It has a probability of .25. Thus, the probability of *both L* and *V* occurring is .25. More formally, the probability of *L* and *V* is as follows:

$$P(L \cap V) = P(gd)$$
$$= .25$$

Also, we can obtain the probability of the occurrence of one compound event *or* another by summing the probabilities of the appropriate simple events.

Recall that

$$L \cup V = \{gg, gd, dg, dd\}$$

Therefore,

$$
\begin{aligned}
P(L \cup V) &= P(gg) + P(gd) + P(dg) + P(dd) \\
&= .25 + .25 + .25 + .25 \\
&= 1.00
\end{aligned}
$$

As noted before, every simple event in the sample space is a member of the set corresponding to the event L or the set corresponding to the event V. Thus, either the compound event L or the compound event V must occur.

ASSOCIATING QUANTITATIVE OUTCOMES (CONSEQUENCES) WITH THE EVENTS

So far in this chapter we have examined illustrations of events (both simple and compound) and have seen how probabilities can be associated with such events. In our copying-machine example we associated the probabilities with the simple events as shown in the first two columns of Table 3-1.

Random Variables

The mere assignment of the probabilities to the events may indeed be a useful step, but often in various real-world problems the occurrence of each of the events can in part be described by a quantity (or a number), such as profit, cost, or output. This second step is referred to as "defining a *random variable* on the events of a chance process." Thus, we have the following definition:

Random variable   The set of numerical outcomes of a chance process (one outcome being associated with each of the possible events); hence, a variable in which the value that occurs is subject to chance.

Table 3-1   Simple Events, Probabilities, and a Random Variable in the Copying-Machine Example

Simple event	Probability of simple event	Random variable (number of good copies)
gg	.25	2
gd	.25	1
dg	.25	1
dd	.25	0

In the copying-machine example we might be interested in all the different numbers of good copies that we could obtain. Thus, in Table 3-1 we show in the third column the different numbers of good copies associated with each of the simple events. We say that this set of numerical values is a random variable defined on this set of simple events. (*Note:* In more mathematical discussions a random variable is referred to as a "rule" or a "function" that assigns numerical values to chance events.)

But what *probabilities* can we assign to these numerical outcomes? It turns out that the probabilities that we already associated with the possible events can, in turn, be associated with the values of the random variable defined on those events.

Thus, we show in Table 3-2 the probability associated with each of the values of the random variable. The probability of two good copies is the same probability as that assigned to the event *gg*. It is .25. One good copy can be obtained through the occurrence of either of the simple events *gd* or *dg*; thus, the probability of one good copy equals the probability of *gd or dg*. This probability is .50, the sum of their individual probabilities: .25 + .25 = .50. The probability of not obtaining a single good copy is the probability of *dd,* which is .25.

Probability Trees and Probability Graphs

In Figure 3-9 we show two other ways to represent the same copying-machine example—the possible values of the random variable along with their probabilities. The probability tree in Figure 3-9*a* lends itself to the analysis of complex decision problems involving uncertainty, whereas the probability graph in Figure 3-9*b* shows well the "scatter" of the possible values of the random variable and the magnitude of their probabilities. In some situations we may find that the probability tree is the more effective form of representation; in other instances, the probability graph may be more useful.

Expected Value

It becomes quite apparent now that defining a random variable on a set of events whose probabilities are available permits us to compute the *expected value* of the random variable. (Also, it permits us to compute some other useful measures that we shall discuss later.)

Table 3-2 A Random Variable and Associated Probabilities for the Copying-Machine Example

Random variable (number of good copies)	Probability of this number of good copies
0	.25
1	.50
2	.25

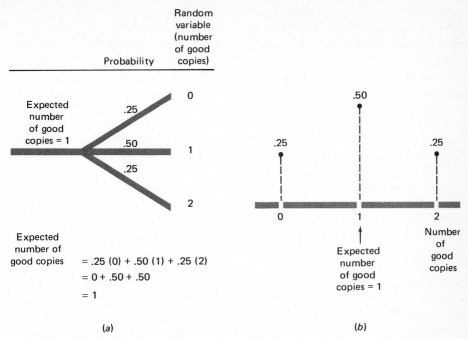

Figure 3-9 A probability tree and a probability graph for the copying-machine example.

Recall from Chapter 2 that we noted the similarity of an expected value to an ordinary average. The meaning we give to the term "expected value" is not identical to what most persons have in mind when in ordinary speech they use the word "expect." We define expected value as follows:

Expected value The long-run average value of a random variable, thus, the number obtained by multiplying each value of the random variable by its probability of occurrence and then summing the products of the multiplications.

Inasmuch as random variables represent such quantities as profit, cost, or numbers of product output, the expected value of each random variable will usually be referred to simply as expected profit, expected cost, or expected output.

In our copying-machine example the expected value (here, the expected number of good copies) is 1.

$$\text{Expected number of good copies} = .25(0) + .50(1) + .25(2)$$
$$= 0 + .50 + .50$$
$$= 1$$

Another Example: Two Random Variables
Defined on the Same Set of Events

Suppose that we are engaged in the manufacture of steel roller bearings. We have found that most of the time they are machined to an acceptable size, but some of the time they are too large, and occasionally they are too small.

Let us refer to the possible states (events) as good, oversize, and undersize. Furthermore, we have records that show that 70 percent of the time the state has been good, 20 percent of the time oversize, and 10 percent of the time undersize. Thus, using these relative frequencies as the basis for the probabilities assigned to the occurrence of these states in future production, we can represent this chance process by the tree shown in Figure 3-10a.

If one of our roller bearings is oversized, it can be machined again to attain an acceptable size; but this would incur additional cost. If a bearing is undersized, there is nothing that can be done to make it acceptable. We must begin again with a new piece of material. This would involve even greater additional cost.

Thus, different additional costs would accompany the occurrence of different states. In Figure 3-10a we show additional costs of 10 cents per unit if the bearing is oversized and 40 cents if it is undersized. No additional costs are incurred if it is of acceptable size.

In technical terms, we would say that we have defined a random variable on the set of basic events. It is a cost random variable that also permits us to compute the expected (additional) cost of each roller bearing that we may produce.

As before, we obtain the expected value (here, the expected cost) by multiplying the various cost amounts each by its probability of occurrence and then summing the products of the multiplications. The expected (additional) cost in this example is 6 cents per unit.

$$
\begin{aligned}
\text{Expected cost} &= .70(0) + .20(10) + .10(40) \\
&= 0 + 2 + 4 \\
&= 6 \text{ cents}
\end{aligned}
$$

We insert this expected cost at the appropriate points in the tree in Figure 3-10a and in the graph in Figure 3-10b.

This example also shows that another random variable in the same problem may be of interest. Suppose that we need to make plans to have raw materials available for use in this production. One thing we may need to know is how much additional raw material would be needed to produce replacements for the undersized units.

Of course when the basic events (states) are uncertain, we can only hope to obtain an *expected* amount of additional materials needed. But this is not much trouble for us in this case because we already have a probability for each of the basic events. All that we need to do is associate an amount of additional raw materials needed for each of the possible states.

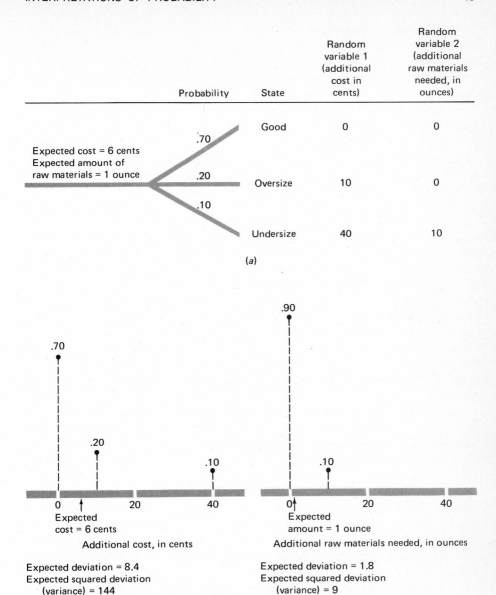

	Probability	State	Random variable 1 (additional cost in cents)	Random variable 2 (additional raw materials needed, in ounces)
	.70	Good	0	0
	.20	Oversize	10	0
	.10	Undersize	40	10

Expected cost = 6 cents
Expected amount of
raw materials = 1 ounce

(a)

.70

.20

.10

| 0 | 20 | 40 |

Expected
cost = 6 cents

Additional cost, in cents

Expected deviation = 8.4
Expected squared deviation
 (variance) = 144
Standard deviation = 12

(b)

.90

.10

| 0 | 20 | 40 |

Expected
amount = 1 ounce

Additional raw materials needed, in ounces

Expected deviation = 1.8
Expected squared deviation
 (variance) = 9
Standard deviation = 3

(c)

Figure 3-10 Probability tree and probability graphs for the roller-bearing example.

No additional materials are needed if the bearing is either of acceptable size or is oversized. However, some material is needed if the unit is undersized. If it is undersized, the amount of additional materials needed per unit is 10 ounces. Thus, we show this second random variable (defined on the same set of events) in the right-hand column of Figure 3-10a.

The original probabilities of the basic events provide us with the probabilities for the values of this second random variable, too. The expected value (here, the expected amount of additional materials needed) is obtained in the usual fashion as follows:

$$\text{Expected amount of materials} = .70(0) + .20(0) + .10(10)$$
$$= 0 + 0 + 1$$
$$= 1 \text{ ounce}$$

In order to illustrate different forms of representation, we insert this expected value in the tree in Figure 3-10a and also in the appropriate graph for this random variable in Figure 3-10c.

Measures of the Scatter of the Possible Outcomes

Through the use of probability graphs, such as in Figure 3-10b and c, we get a visual awareness of the scatter of the possible values of a random variable.

We can see in Figure 3-10b that the possible values of the cost random variable range from 0 to 40, whereas in Figure 3-10c the extreme values of the raw-materials random variable are 0 and 10. Thus, one rough measure of the scatter is obtained by computing the difference between the highest and lowest values of the random variable. This measure is appropriately called the *range*. For the cost random variable in Figure 3-10b the range is 40: 40 − 0 = 40. The raw-materials random variable in Figure 3-10c has a range of only 10: 10 − 0 = 10.

Although the range usually is an easy-to-obtain measure of the scatter, it does not take into account the outcomes between the extremes nor the *probabilities* of their occurrence. The more commonly used measures (to be discussed later) incorporate these probabilities in the computation of the measure.

Also, these common measures focus on the *possible deviations from the expected value and their probabilities of occurrence*. In other words, when any one of the possible values of a random variable occurs, it also represents a deviation of some amount from its expected value. (Of course the "deviation" is 0 if the value that occurs was also the expected value.) The elementary idea here is to represent *the deviation that one can expect* each time before a single value of the random variable occurs. Such a measure would provide an indication of our uncertainty regarding the random variable of interest.

In the case of certainty, there would be no deviations at all. Only one value can occur, and the probability of its occurrence is 1.00. On the other hand, under extreme uncertainty the possible values of the random variable generally would extend over a very wide range, and thus very large deviations could occur.

In our roller-bearing example shown in Figure 3-10*b* the expected cost of each unit is seen to be 6 cents. However, if the bearing turns out to be undersized, the cost is 40 cents. The 40-cent cost outcome represents a deviation of 34 cents from the expected cost of 6 cents: $40 - 6 = 34$ cents. In similar fashion we can consider each possible cost outcome (that is, each value of the random variable) and obtain its deviation from the expected cost (the expected value). This is done for the cost random variable in the fourth column of Table 3-3.

Furthermore, we can assign the same probability to each of these deviations that we had originally assigned to the associated possible cost outcomes. In the roller-bearing example, this means that the probability of the 34-cent deviation is .10, the same probability that was assigned to the 40-cent cost possibility.

The simplest measure of the overall scatter (around the expected value) is the *expected deviation*. Essentially, it is the deviation one can expect each time a single value of the random variable occurs. The expected deviation takes into account both the absolute deviation of each outcome (here, each cost outcome) from its expected value (here, expected cost) and its associated probability of occurrence. We define it as follows:

Expected deviation A measure of the scatter of the possible values of a random variable around its expected value in which (1) the deviation (absolute) of each possible value of the random variable from its expected value is multiplied by its associated probability and (2) the products of the multiplications are summed.

As seen in Figure 3-10*b* the possible cost outcomes of 0, 10, and 40 represent absolute deviations (from the expected value of 6) of 6, 4, and 34. We take the probabilities of .70, .20, and .10 associated with the cost outcomes of 0, 10, and 40, respectively, and assign them to the deviations of 6, 4, and 34. Thus, the expected deviation of the cost random variable is 8.4 cents as follows:

$$
\begin{aligned}
\text{Expected deviation of the cost outcomes} &= .70(6) + .20(4) + .10(34) \\
&= 4.2 + .8 + 3.4 \\
&= 8.4 \text{ cents}
\end{aligned}
$$

We would say that the expected cost per unit is 6 cents and that the expected deviation is 8.4 cents. If this production is to be repeated for a very long time, the cost per unit would tend to average 6 cents and the cost outcomes would on the average deviate by 8.4 cents from the 6 cents expected cost.

In Figure 3-10*c* the materials random variable is represented with its associated probabilities. A glance at the probability graph suggests much less scatter for this random variable than for the cost random variable in Figure 3-10*b*. The expected deviation of the materials random variable is only 1.8 ounces, whereas the expected deviation of the cost random variable is 8.4 cents. The possible amounts of raw materials needed are 0 and 10 ounces, which represent absolute deviations of 1 and 9 from the expected amount of materials needed of 1 ounce.

The probability is .90 for the deviation of 1 and is .10 for the deviation of 9. Thus, we have the following:

$$\text{Expected deviation of materials needed} = .90(1) + .10(9)$$
$$= .9 + .9$$
$$= 1.8 \text{ ounces}$$

A summary of the computations of the expected value and expected deviation for the cost random variable is shown in the first two sections of Table 3-3. It is a form in which the computation of these measures and other measures of scatter is easily organized. A comparable summary for the materials random variable is found in the first two sections of Table 3-4.

It is unfortunate that the expected deviation, the most direct and intuitive measure of scatter that incorporates all of the deviations and their probabilities, has some drawbacks for use in more advanced work. One of the difficulties is that the computation of the expected deviation involves absolute values that create problems later on.

Thus, if we are to avoid the use of absolute values when we compute the deviations, we are left with some negative deviations as shown in the middle section of Table 3-3. In this case, when the cost outcome is 0, the algebraic deviation is −6. But if we leave the deviations in this form (some of them negative) and multiply the deviations by their associated probabilities and sum the products, we will always get an expected deviation of 0. This, of course, provides us with no measure of scatter at all.

The simplest measure of scatter that does not require the use of absolute values (but uses the deviations and their probabilities) is the *expected squared deviation* (or *variance*). In this measure every deviation (positive or negative) is multiplied by itself; that is, each deviation is squared.

Of course this squaring of the deviations removes the negative signs but greatly exaggerates the deviations. Each of the squared deviations is in turn multiplied by its associated probability, and the sum of the products of these multiplications gives us the expected squared deviation (or variance) of the random variable.

Expected squared deviation (variance)   A measure of the scatter of a random variable around its expected value, in which: (1) each deviation is squared, (2) the resulting squared deviations are each multiplied by their associated probabilities, and (3) the products of the multiplications of the probabilities times the squared deviations are summed.

For the cost random variable in the roller-bearing example, the computation of the expected squared deviation (variance) is summarized in the right-hand section of Table 3-3. It is found to be 144.

$$\text{Expected squared deviation (variance)} = .70(36) + .20(16) + .10(1,156)$$
$$= 144$$

Table 3-3 Computation of Measures of Scatter of the Cost Random Variable

Random variable 1 (possible additional cost, in cents)	Probability of this cost	Possible cost times its probability	Deviation of this cost from the expected cost of 6 cents	Deviation (absolute) times its probability	Deviation squared	Deviation squared times its probability
0	.70	.70(0) = 0	0 − 6 = −6	.70(6) = 4.2	36	.70(36) = 25.2
10	.20	.20(10) = 2	10 − 6 = 4	.20(4) = .8	16	.20(16) = 3.2
40	.10	.10(40) = 4	40 − 6 = 34	.10(34) = 3.4	1,156	.10(1,156) = 115.6
		Expected cost = 6		Expected deviation = 8.4		Expected squared deviation = 144
						Standard deviation = 12

Expected cost = .70(0) + .20(10) + .10(40) = 6
Expected deviation = .70(6) + .20(4) + .10(34) = 8.4
Expected squared deviation (variance) = .70(36) + .20(16) + .10(1,156) = 144
Standard deviation = square root of variance = 12

Table 3-4 Computation of Measures of Scatter of the Raw-Materials Random Variable

Random variable 2 (possible additional raw materials needed, in ounces)	Probability of this amount	Possible amount times its probability	Deviation of this amount from the expected amount of 1 ounce	Deviation (absolute) times its probability	Deviation squared	Deviation squared times its probability
0	.90	$.90(0) = 0$	$0 - 1 = -1$	$.90(1) = .9$	1	$.90(1) = .9$
10	.10	$.10(10) = \underline{1}$	$10 - 1 = 9$	$.10(9) = \underline{.9}$	81	$.10(81) = \underline{8.1}$
		Expected amount = 1		Expected deviation = 1.8		Expected squared deviation = 9.0 Standard deviation = 3

Even though the expected squared deviation (variance) is often used as a measure of scatter, it has some disadvantages, too. The squaring of the deviations overstates the extent of the deviations and also provides a measure in which the units are confusing. In our roller-bearing example the cost deviations are in cents. The squaring of the deviations gives us "cents squared," and thus the final measure is in "cents squared," too.

We can think of this measure of scatter (expected squared deviations) in a long-run sense, also. If production were to continue over a very long period of time, the average cost per unit would tend toward 6 cents and the deviations of the cost outcomes squared would average about 144.

You may recall that the expected (absolute) deviation for this cost random variable is 8.4 cents. Thus, we can see in this example how the squaring of the deviations exaggerates the extent of the deviations and additionally gives us a measure of scatter in "cents squared." But it has some good characteristics, especially for mathematical operations, and this helps account for its widespread use.

Perhaps you are thinking that it would be nice to have a measure of scatter in the original units (cents) and also without the great exaggeration of the scatter. Maybe you have already guessed that there is such a measure. It is called the *standard deviation.*

Let us go back to the expected squared deviation (variance) and take its square root (the reverse of squaring). When we take its square root we are in a sense "undoing" the squaring of the deviations that was done in its computation. But by taking the square root we get something we want: A measure of scatter back in the original units (cents). Also, we get a measure of the scatter somewhat near in magnitude to the simple expected (absolute) deviation. For the cost random variable in our roller-bearing example, the square root of 144 (the expected squared deviation) gives us a standard deviation of 12 cents. We summarize this with the following definition:

Standard deviation A measure of the scatter of a random variable which is obtained by taking the square root of the expected squared deviation (variance).

It is important to note, however, that while the standard deviation as a measure of the scatter cuts back on the overstatement of the scatter, it does not bring us back to a measure of the scatter that is equal to the expected (absolute) deviation. In the cost random variable of Table 3-3 the standard deviation is 12 compared with an expected (absolute) deviation of 8.4. In the materials random variable of Table 3-4 the standard deviation is 3, whereas the expected (absolute) deviation is 1.8.

Thus, it is apparent that the standard deviation does not have the easy and direct intuitive interpretation of the expected (absolute) deviation. However, the standard deviation has very desirable mathematical properties and is widely used in probability and statistics.

SUMMARY

1 *Probability* is a quantitative measure of the degree of uncertainty regarding the occurrence of an event. A probability of 1.00 represents certainty, and a probability of 0.00 represents impossibility. Events that are more likely to occur are assigned probabilities closer to 1.00; those less likely to occur are assigned values further from 1.00.

2 A set of events is *exhaustive* if all possible events are listed in the set. A set of events is *mutually exclusive* if only one of the events in the set can occur.

3 The *relative-frequency* interpretation of probability essentially restricts the use of probabilities to those situations in which the probability assignments to events can be based directly on the relative frequency of these events in the past.

4 The *subjective* or *personalistic* interpretation of probability is very broad. It does not limit the use of probabilities to those based directly on the relative frequency of events. It allows probabilities to be based wholly or in part on data or experience that is obtained through subjective judgments or assessments by persons of the chances of the particular events occurring.

5 The use of relative-frequency-based probabilities is not free of subjective judgments either. Judgments have to be made regarding the fit of the probabilities (based on relative frequencies) to the reality of interest which often lies in the future and invariably is different from the reality in which the relative frequencies were collected.

6 The making of good predictions and good decisions requires the careful use of all data and experience whether they are of a relative-frequency or subjective type.

7 *Compound events* occur when any one event from a set of more than one *simple event* occurs.

8 A *random variable* is defined on a set of events when a numerical value is associated with the occurrence of each of the events. More than one random variable can be defined on the same set of events.

9 A *probability distribution* for a random variable is obtained when a probability is assigned to each value of the random variable.

10 The *expected value* of a random variable can be thought of as the future long-run average value of the random variable.

11 Measures of the scatter of the values of a random variable are: the *range,* the *expected (absolute) deviation,* the *expected squared deviation* (the variance), and the *standard deviation* (the square root of the variance). Each measure has some advantages and disadvantages.

PROBLEMS

3-1 A school follows a grading system based on possible reports for each student of A, B, C, D, F, or I (incomplete) for each course. Indicate whether the following sets of events for a student in a course are exhaustive, mutually exclusive, or both.

a "Passing grade" and "nonpassing grade"

b "Passing grade" and "grade of I"

c "Grade of F or above" and "passing grade"

3-2 a Discuss the main points of difference in the relative-frequency and subjective interpretations of probability.

b Is your uncertainty with respect to particular real-world events any less if you adhere to a strict relative-frequency interpretation of probability?

3-3 a Comment on the role of subjectivity in making probability assignments to future events.

b What are some of the advantages and some of the dangers of using subjective probabilities?

3-4 Consider the copying-machine example discussed in this chapter. Instead of making two copies of the document, suppose that we make *three* copies. Each copy can be either good or defective.

a Construct a tree (as in Figure 3-1) that shows a way to obtain the simple events of the "chance process" in producing three copies of the document.

b Construct a Venn diagram of the chance process involved in making three copies. Label each of the simple events.

3-5 a Suppose in Problem 3-4 we need at least two good copies of the document. Let us refer to this event "at least two good copies" by the letter *A*. Represent this event in the Venn diagram constructed in Problem 3-4.

b Also, let us consider another event *D* (last copy defective). Represent this event in the Venn diagram of Problem 3-4, also.

c Are the events *A* and *D* exhaustive?

d Are the events *A* and *D* mutually exclusive?

3-6 Continue with Problem 3-5.

a Consider still two other events, *B* (at least two defective copies) and *C* (last copy good). Represent these events, too, in a Venn diagram.

b Indicate whether each of the following pairs of events is exhaustive and whether it is mutually exclusive: *A* and *B*, *A* and *C*, *B* and *C*, *B* and *D*, and *C* and *D*. A new Venn diagram for each pair of events will show these characteristics most clearly.

3-7 a If in Problem 3-4 each copy has a probability of .50 of being defective, what is the probability of each simple event?

b What is the probability of *A* (at least two good copies)?

c What is the probability of *D* (last copy defective)?

d What is the probability of *A and D* occurring?

e What is the probability of *A or D* occurring?

3-8 Suppose the copying machine in Problem 3-4 now has been carefully adjusted so that only 20 percent of the copies are defective. *Three* copies of the document are made.

a After the adjustment, what is the probability of each of the simple events? In a Venn diagram place the probability of each simple event on a marker attached to the point representing that simple event.

b Now, what is the probability of getting at least two good copies out of three (event *A*)?

c What is the probability of *D* (last copy defective)?

d What is the probability of *A and D*?

e What is the probability of *A or D*?

3-9 Let us consider a variation of the copying-machine example discussed in this chapter. We want to make *two* copies of a document *after the machine has been adjusted*. After adjustment the probability of each copy being defective is .20.

    a What is the probability of each of the simple events?

    b What are the possible values of the random variable obtained by counting the number of good copies when two are made?

    c What are the probabilities associated with each of the values of the random variable in *b*? Represent them in a tree diagram and also by a probability graph.

    d What is the expected number of good copies when two copies are made?

3-10 Continue with Problem 3-9. Consider the random variable obtained by counting the number of *defective* copies in making two copies.

    a Represent the probabilities in a tree and also in a probability graph.

    b What is the expected number of defective copies?

3-11 A cost random variable can take one of two possible values, $0 or $10. The probabilities are .2 and .8, respectively.

    a Construct a tree diagram of this chance process and insert the probabilities and values of the random variable.

    b Represent the probabilities in the form of a probability graph.

    c What is the expected cost?

    d What is the range of possible costs?

    e Compute the expected (absolute) deviation. Interpret your answer.

    f Compute the expected squared deviation (the variance). Interpret your answer.

    g Obtain the standard deviation. Interpret your answer and compare it with the measure of scatter obtained in *e*.

3-12 The possible values of a profit random variable are $2 and $8 with associated probabilities of .4 and .6, respectively. Compute the following:

    a Expected profit

    b Range

    c Expected (absolute) deviation

    d Expected squared deviation (the variance)

    e Standard deviation

3-13 Consider again the packaging-machine example in Chapter 2 (represented in Figure 2-2). In Chapter 2 we did not obtain any measures of scatter of the profit outcomes.

    a What is the profit range *for each act?*

    b Compute, compare, and interpret the expected (absolute) deviation for each act.

    c Compute the expected squared deviation (variance) for each act.

    d Obtain the approximate standard deviation for each of the acts.

3-14 There are two measures other than the expected value (or average) that provide a quick, single-number summary of the information in a probability distribution (or a frequency distribution).

    One of these measures is the *mode;* the other is the *median*. The mode refers to the most probable (or most frequent) value. The median refers to the value below which one-half of the values lie.

    To obtain the median value we place the values in an array in order of magnitude from the lowest to the highest value, repeating a value if it occurs more than once. Beginning with the lowest value in the array, we count off one-half of the total number of items in the array. The item at the half-way point is the median value.

    Suppose we have the following outputs per hour from a machine: 2, 2, 6, 10, and 15. Compute the following:

    a The average

    b The mode

    c The median

    d The median when a sixth output of 16 is included. (*Note:* When the number of items in an array is even, the median will fall between two numbers. In this case, the median is usually defined as the midpoint between the two numbers, even if it is a fractional amount.)

3-15 From the output data in Problem 3-14 obtain the following measures of scatter. (*Note:* When the data are in an array as in Problem 3-14, where each value is repeated if it occurs again, simply multiply each deviation or squared deviation by its relative frequency $1/n$, where n refers to the number of items in the array. A shortcut is to sum the deviations or squared deviations and then multiply the sum by $1/n$; or, simply divide the sum by n.)

    a The average absolute deviation

    b The variance

    c The standard deviation

Chapter 4

Prior Knowledge and Bayesian Posterior Probabilities

Each of us every day usually makes conditional statements of one sort or another. That is, we say that *if* a particular event occurs (for example, if the skies become overcast) then some other event (such as rain) is likely to occur. Such statements are elementary versions of *conditional probability* statements.

CONDITIONAL PROBABILITIES

The key idea of conditional probability is that the probability assigned to one particular event (rain) is affected by the occurrence of some other event (clear or cloudy skies). This is a simple idea and one that is very much a part of our ordinary thinking. But by representing the procedure in a more explicit (and quantitative) fashion, much improvement can be made in our decision making and in our general level of knowledge. We shall see that through the use of more explicit and quantitative methods we can effectively consider more alternative courses of action and take into account the occurrence of many more events.

Prior Probabilities

Conditional probabilities give a quantitative form for the *change* of our opinion (change in our state of knowledge) with respect to the occurrence of particular events. For example, as we awaken in the morning with the shades drawn we may believe that the chances are quite low that the day will bring rain. But as we raise the shades and observe cloudy skies we revise our belief and then say that the chance of rain is quite high.

We shall refer to the belief (rain) *before* the shades are raised as the *prior* belief or the *prior state of knowledge*. Should a probability (say, .20) be assigned to the event (rain) before the shades are raised, we would refer to it as the *prior probability* of rain. The word "prior" here indicates that we are referring to the state of knowledge *before* making any observations of relevant events (such as clear or cloudy skies).

Posterior (Conditional) Probabilities

However, after observing a relevant event (such as clear or cloudy skies), we typically *revise* our belief regarding the event of interest (rain). Thus, if a probability is assigned to the event "rain" (say, .80) *after* observing cloudy skies, we would refer to it as *a posterior probability* of rain.

The word "posterior" as we use it here indicates that we are referring to a state of knowledge *after* making a particular observation of a relevant event. We say *a* state of knowledge because the belief that it will rain may be quite different if the skies are clear from if they are cloudy. The posterior probability of rain may be .80 after observing cloudy skies, whereas it may be only .10 after observing clear skies.

To summarize: The prior probability of rain is .20. It is revised upward to .80 if cloudy skies are observed. But the .20 prior probability of rain is revised downward to .10 if clear skies are observed. Thus, each of the posterior probabilities is also a *conditional probability*. When the probability of an event is affected by the occurrence of another event, we refer to it as a conditional probability. (*Note:* We are not asserting that one event causes another; we are only saying that the probability assigned to one event is affected by the occurrence of another.)

More compactly we represent conditional probabilities by some special notation. For example, the conditional (and posterior) probability of rain given that we have observed cloudy skies can be represented as follows: (*Note:* The vertical line below is equivalent to the word "given." Thus, the following statement is read: "The probability of rain *given* overcast skies is .80.")

$$P(\text{rain} \mid \text{overcast skies}) = .80$$

And the other conditional posterior probability of rain is the following:

$$P(\text{rain} \mid \text{clear skies}) = .10$$

Of course there are still other conditional probabilities that may be of interest in this problem, but the two that we selected provide good illustrations.

Unconditional Probabilities

We should note at this point, too, that prior probabilities usually are *unconditional* probabilities. That is, in the prior probabilities we are not assigning probabilities to events (such as rain) on the assumption that we observe some other event (such as cloudy skies). We simply assign a probability to the event rain *in light of what we know at the present time*. It is in that sense that the probability is unconditional. Of course, too, unconditional probabilities are not necessarily prior probabilities. We shall see an illustration of this later in this chapter.

In the rain example the prior-probability assignment would typically be based on the past relative frequency of rain. If over a number of years 20 percent of the days have included rain, a reasonable prior probability of rain would be .20. Such unconditional probabilities are more compactly stated as follows (without any conditional event appearing in the statement):

$$P(\text{rain}) = .20$$

The Importance of Prior Probabilities

Before going on to another example to illustrate how we revise the prior probabilities, another point should be made. It is this: Most thoughtful persons take the position that we always have some prior knowledge about events of interest to us even though this knowledge may be slight and we feel quite ignorant. Many hold that we can always assign prior probabilities to these events. Of course, most of the prior probabilities in this general sense would be based on subjective judgments. The importance of this step, however, is that taking it allows the concepts and procedures discussed in these chapters to be applied (perhaps sometimes in subtle ways) to virtually every decision that we face in our professional work and in our private lives.

The rain example gave us a good illustration of prior and posterior probabilities. But in that example we really paid no attention to any procedure for revising the prior probabilities. There is a valid procedure by which the revision can be made. It is known as the *bayesian procedure*. The copying-machine example will serve as a good illustration of how this bayesian procedure accomplishes the revision.

REVISING THE PRIOR PROBABILITIES BY THE BAYESIAN PROCEDURE

The main objective of this chapter is to discuss and illustrate the general procedure for revising our prior probabilities as we observe the occurrence of particular relevant events. This procedure is called the bayesian procedure because it was first associated with the eighteenth-century English philosopher Thomas R. Bayes. Although the basic elements of the procedure have long been known, it is only within the past 20 years that its general usefulness has been widely recognized.

The Copying-Machine Example Again

Let us try to illustrate the bayesian procedure in the simplest possible way with the already-familiar copying-machine example. In larger and more realistic problems the procedure is the same, but it is less clear to our intuition.

You will recall that in the copying-machine example we made two copies of a document without learning the results. The first copy could be good or defective, and the second copy could be good or defective. But since we know the machine makes defective copies 50 percent of the time, the probability is .50 of a copy being defective each time one is made. Thus, in making two copies the probability of each of the four simple events is .25 as shown in Figure 4-1. (Review the previous chapter on this point if necessary.)

In Figure 4-1 we also have represented the two compound events we discussed in the last chapter. The compound event L refers to the occurrence of "at least one good copy."

The event L would occur if any one of the simple events enclosed by the dashed line would occur: gg, gd, or dg. The (unconditional) probability of L is .75, the sum of the probabilities of the three simple events comprising the compound event L: $.25 + .25 + .25 = .75$.

The compound event V refers to the occurrence of "last copy defective." The event V would occur if either of the simple events gd or dd would occur.

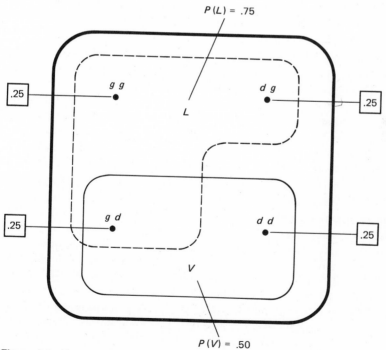

Figure 4-1   Two events in the copying-machine example.

The (unconditional) probability of V is .50, the sum of the probabilities of *gd* and *dd:* .25 + .25 = .50.

Prior Probabilities   We have said that the unconditional probability of L (at least one good copy) is .75. Thus, we might refer to this probability as our *prior* probability of L if there is some other relevant event that could occur and lead to a revision of this probability assignment.

Bayesian Posterior Probabilities   Suppose it is known that event V (last copy defective) has actually occurred. We can think of our being able to look directly at the last copy made and see that it is a defective copy.

What does the observation of this event mean to us? Of course most obviously it means that we cannot have two good copies (we are making only two). Under our prior (original) information we would have said that the probability of two good copies out of two is .25. Now, having observed that the last one is defective, we would say that the occurrence of two good copies out of two is impossible. Thus, the prior probability of two good copies was .25. Given that we have observed that the last unit is defective, we say that the probability of two good copies is revised downward to 0.00. This 0.00 probability is a posterior (and conditional) probability.

But suppose we are more interested in event L (at least one good copy). Again, if we have observed that event V (last copy defective) has occurred, intuitively we would also want to revise downward the probability of L (at least one good copy).

Yes, we would want quickly to revise downward our prior probability of .75 on event L. But how much should we lower it? To 0.00? No, it is still possible to have one good copy even if the last copy is known to be defective. Then what is the correct posterior probability?

The full bayesian procedure answers this question, but it is still a bit involved for the intuition. Thus, before getting into the formal procedure, let us take a look at Figure 4-1 where we can see directly the key ideas in the bayesian procedure for revising the prior probabilities to obtain the various posterior (conditional) probabilities.

The main point is this: *If event* V (last copy defective) *has occurred, to us the only simple events that can now occur are* gd *or* dd (that is, the simple events comprising the compound event V). Since each of these simple events is equally likely, the probability of each of the simple events (*gd* and *dd*) must be .50.

Let us go back to event L (at least one good copy). Event L can now occur *only* if *gd* occurs. Since *gd* has a probability of .50 we say now that the probability of L is .50. Thus, the correct revision of the prior probability of L, .75, is to .50 (given that event V has occurred).

In summary, we would say that the prior (unconditional) probability of "at least one good copy" was .75. More compactly, we would put it as follows:

P(at least one good copy) = .75

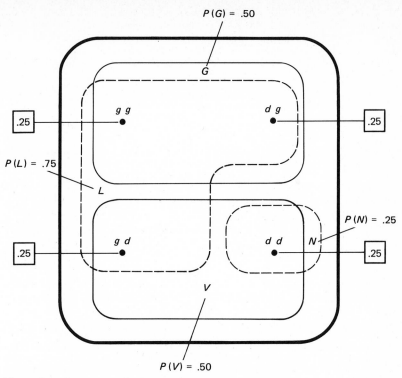

Figure 4-2 Four events in the copying-machine example.

However, if we observe the event "last copy defective," the posterior (and conditional) probability of "at least one good copy" is revised downward to .50. This is a bayesian posterior probability and can be stated as follows.

P(at least one good copy | last copy defective) = .50

The More Formal Bayesian Procedures By now we should have a grasp of the concept of prior probabilities and roughly how they may be revised in light of the occurrence of some other relevant event.

What we want now is a general procedure that is widely applicable and would allow us to obtain such posterior probabilities for larger and more realistic problems. The bayesian procedure does this, and we can illustrate it with the familiar and simple copying-machine example.

For the copying-machine example we already know that one of the bayesian posterior probabilities is .50: P(at least one good copy| last copy defective) = .50. But let us see how we arrive at this very same posterior probability (and others) by the formal bayesian procedure. To illustrate the procedure more fully we define more events and represent them in the diagram in Figure 4-2.

There are three main steps in the procedure:

1 Construction of an initial probability tree
2 Formation of a joint and marginal probability table
3 Construction of a reverse probability tree

Step 1: Construction of an Initial Probability Tree   In this tree we lay out (from left to right) first the events of primary interest (we call these events the "states") and then the events that reveal additional information. *Illustration:* In our copying-machine example an event of primary interest is event *L* (at least one good copy). In Figure 4-3 we have constructed an initial probability tree for this example. The first two events (states) are *L* (at least one good copy) and *N* (not a single good copy).

The events that can give us additional information in this example are event *V* (last copy defective) and event *G* (last copy good). Thus, at the tips of the second set of branches in Figure 4-3 we have these events represented. We represent them twice, once after each of the possible states.

The *probabilities* of the events in our initial probability tree are next. The

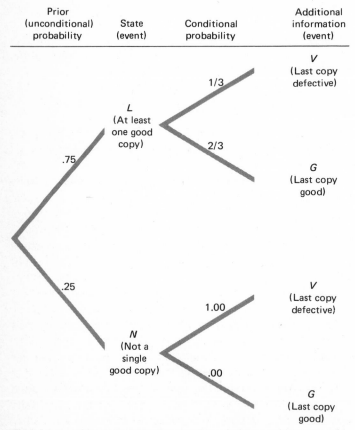

Figure 4-3   Initial probability tree for the copying-machine example.

first branches from the left require the prior (unconditional) probabilities of the states. We can obtain these directly from Figure 4-2 in this example. The prior probability of L is .75, and the prior probability of N is .25. Remember, too, that whatever the number of states, the prior probabilities must sum to 1.00.

The second set of branches requires conditional probabilities. After all, the upper branches emanate from event L, and at that point it is assumed that event L has occurred. Let us go to Figure 4-2 and see what the probability of V is given that L has occurred. Given that event L has occurred, the only possible simple events are gg, gd, or dg. Each of these is equally likely. Since there are three of them, each must have a probability of $\frac{1}{3}$.

However, V can occur only if gd occurs. Thus, since gd has a probability of $\frac{1}{3}$, the probability of V is $\frac{1}{3}$ (given that L has occurred). This probability (a conditional probability) is inserted on the branch leading to event V in Figure 4-3. From Figure 4-2 we see that event G has a probability of $\frac{2}{3}$ given that L has occurred. Either gg or dg would cause G to occur; thus the probability of G is $\frac{2}{3}$, the sum of their individual probabilities: $\frac{1}{3} + \frac{1}{3} = \frac{2}{3}$.

Going to the lower-right section of Figure 4-3, we see branches leading to V and to G, too; but now it is assumed that event N (not a single good copy) has occurred.

If event N has occurred, we see from Figure 4-2 that the simple event dd has occurred. Thus we know for certain that V (last copy defective) has occurred. Therefore, we place a probability of 1.00 on the branch leading to V.

Similarly, if we know that dd occurred, we see in Figure 4-2 that event G (last copy good) could not have occurred. Therefore, we place a probability of 0.00 on the branch leading to the event G.

Step 2: Formation of a Joint and Marginal Probability Table   Our aim in this step is to obtain the joint and marginal probabilities that are necessary to compute the desired posterior probabilities of the states.

A *joint probability* refers to the probability of the joint (or simultaneous) occurrence of two events. It turns out that if we have the appropriate events and their probabilities in an initial probability tree, we can get their joint probabilities by systematically multiplying through the entire tree so that all branches are so treated. We do this in Figure 4-4 and record the results at the extreme right-hand side.

Starting from the top of the right-hand column in Figure 4-4 we see that the first joint probability is .25. It is the probability of *both* L and V occurring. (We could also say it is the probability of L intersect V.) This joint probability of .25 is obtained simply by multiplying through the uppermost branches of the tree: $P(L)$ · $P(V \mid L) = (.75)(\frac{1}{3}) = .25$. In similar fashion the remaining joint probabilities are obtained. Next, the joint probabilities are represented in table form for convenient computation of the marginal probabilities. Notice how in Table 4-1 we list the states across the top and the events providing additional information down the left-hand side. A joint probability is inserted in each cell of the table representing the joint occurrence of the appropriate events. For example, in the upper-left corner of Table 4-1 the probability of the joint occurrence of the events

L and V is listed. It is .25: $(.75)(\frac{1}{3}) = .25$. We complete the table in similar fashion inserting the joint probabilities obtained in the right-hand column of Figure 4-4.

Now it turns out that if we add the joint probabilities in a particular row of our table it will provide us with the probability of that particular event providing additional information. Thus in Table 4-1 we see that the probability of V (last copy defective) is .50, the sum of the joint probabilities in the first row: $.25 + .25 = .50$. The probability of G (last copy good) is .50, too: $.50 + .00 = .50$.

Each of these probabilities of events providing additional information is called a *marginal* probability. The word "marginal" is used simply because the computation of these probabilities appears at the margin of the table. They are also referred to as "unconditional probabilities of the particular events providing additional information." (*Note:* In this example it happens that the marginal probabilities are both .50, but in most problems they would not be equal.)

Step 3: Construction of the Reverse Probability Tree It is in this step that we obtain the posterior probabilities of the states (the events of primary interest). The reverse tree implies that something is reversed, and indeed this is so. It is the initial tree that is reversed, that is, the sequence of the events from left to right.

In the initial tree we listed the states first and then the events providing

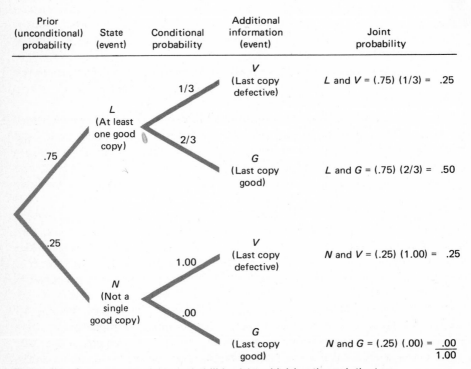

Figure 4-4 Computing the joint probabilities by multiplying through the tree.

Table 4-1   Joint and Marginal Probabilities for the Copying-Machine Example

Event providing additional information	State		Marginal probability
	L (at least one good copy)	*N* (not a single good copy)	
V (last copy defective)	$(.75)(\frac{1}{3}) = .25$	$(.25)(1.00) = .25$	$.25 + .25 = .50$
G (last copy good)	$(.75)(\frac{2}{3}) = .50$	$(.25)(.00) = .00$	$.50 + .00 = .50$
			1.00

additional information. In the reverse tree the events providing additional information appear first, followed by the states.

The order in the reverse tree is the desired order for our posterior probabilities. Recall that the posterior probabilities are computed on the assumption of the occurrence of some particular event that provides additional information. In Figure 4-5 we lay out the reverse tree for our copying-machine example. Notice how events *V* and *G,* which provide additional information, appear first. Next, we have the events *L* and *N* of primary interest (the states). We repeat the events *L* and *N* after each of the events (*V* and *G*) that provide additional information. They are repeated because their probabilities are usually different after the occurrence of each event providing additional information. These probabilities of the states are, of course, posterior probabilities.

Now let us see how we obtain the probabilities to insert on the branches of the reverse tree. The first probabilities needed are the (unconditional) probabilities of the events *V* and *G* providing additional information. But these are the marginal probabilities we already computed in Table 4-1. Therefore, we simply transfer the marginal probabilities from the right-hand margin of the table to the first set of branches of the reverse tree in Figure 4-5.

The important posterior probabilities of the states come next, and it is right here where most of the computation lies (and potential difficulties, too). Let us put it as simply as possible: We need first a probability of *L* to place on the uppermost branch (of the second set of branches) in Figure 4-5. At that point it is assumed that *V* has occurred. Thus, we focus on the first row of Table 4-1 (the joint and marginal probability table).

It turns out that the posterior probability of *L* is obtained by dividing the marginal probability for that row, .50, into the appropriate joint probability, .25. More specifically, the posterior probability of *L* is obtained simply by dividing the marginal probability of *V*, .50, into the joint probability of *V* and *L*, .25. This gives us a .50 posterior probability of *L* as follows:

Marginal (unconditional) probability	Additional information (event)	Bayesian posterior (conditional) probability	State (event)

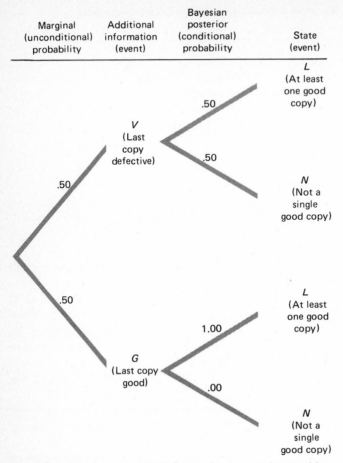

Figure 4-5 The reverse probability tree for the copying-machine example.

$$\text{Posterior probability of } L \text{ given that } V \text{ has occurred} = \frac{\text{joint probability of } V \text{ and } L}{\text{marginal probability of } V}$$

$$= \frac{.25}{.50}$$

$$= .50$$

This is the very same .50 posterior probability of L that we obtained by the more direct and intuitive method earlier. This posterior probability of L (given V) is the posterior probability that goes on the uppermost branch of the second set of branches in Figure 4-5.

Thus, we have one of the posterior probabilities for our reverse tree. The others are obtained in similar fashion. For the remaining posterior probabilities on the branches emanating from V (there is just one more in this example), we continue to divide by the same marginal probability of V, .50, but the joint probability changes. Since we now want the posterior probability of N, we divide the .50 marginal probability of V into the joint probability of V and N. In this simple example this joint probability turns out to be .25, too, the same as the earlier joint probability. Thus, the second posterior probability (also .50) is obtained by the following:

$$\begin{array}{l} \text{Posterior} \\ \text{probability} \\ \text{of } N \text{ given} \\ \text{that } V \text{ has} \\ \text{occurred} \end{array} = \frac{\text{joint probability of}}{\text{marginal probability}} \\ \qquad\qquad\qquad\; V \text{ and } N \\ \qquad\qquad\qquad\;\; \text{of } V$$

$$= \frac{.25}{.50}$$

$$= .50$$

Given that event G has occurred, we move to the second row of Table 4-1. The posterior probability of L now is 1.00 as shown by the following:

$$\begin{array}{l} \text{Posterior} \\ \text{probability} \\ \text{of } L \text{ given} \\ \text{that } G \text{ has} \\ \text{occurred} \end{array} = \frac{\text{joint probability of } G \text{ and } L}{\text{marginal probability of } G}$$

$$= \frac{.50}{.50}$$

$$= 1.00$$

Given the same event (G has occurred), the posterior probability of N is 0.00 as follows:

$$\begin{array}{l} \text{Posterior} \\ \text{probability} \\ \text{of } N \text{ given} \\ \text{that } G \text{ has} \\ \text{occurred} \end{array} = \frac{\text{joint probability of } G \text{ and } N}{\text{marginal probability of } G}$$

$$= \frac{0.00}{.50}$$

$$= 0.00$$

These last two posterior probabilities are placed in the lower-right section of the reverse tree in Figure 4-5. With the reverse tree now completed, we have all of the posterior probabilities of interest as well as the marginal probabilities. The marginal probabilities will be seen to be of special value in the next chapter.

Another Illustration of the Bayesian Procedure

Let us look at another example to be sure that the essential steps in obtaining the posterior probabilities are understood.

Suppose in this example the event we are interested in is whether or not we have the lung disease known as tuberculosis (TB). We are interested in whether the event (the state) is "TB" or "no TB." We have some prior knowledge regarding these states, but the possibility also exists of gaining additional information through a test, specifically, a chest x-ray.

We have the prior knowledge that 2 percent of the persons in groups such as ours actually have TB. Thus, before getting any further information at all we can say that a person in the group picked at random has a 2 percent chance of having TB. This being information we already possess, we would at this point assign a probability of .02 to anyone having TB whom we selected. This also implies a prior probability of .98 for the state "no TB."

Suppose we can gain additional information by taking a chest x-ray that detects fairly well the presence of TB. However, it is not a *perfect predictor*. If it were, it would always detect TB if it is present and never indicate that it is present when it is not. We call it an *imperfect predictor* because of its inability to detect TB perfectly and other incorrect indications.

A chest x-ray result that indicates (predicts) the presence of TB is described as a "positive x-ray." One that indicates (predicts) the person has no TB is termed a "negative x-ray."

What is usually desired in practical problems like this is an answer to questions such as the following: What is the probability that a person selected has TB if his or her chest x-ray is positive (that is, the chest x-ray indicates the presence of TB)? The bayesian procedure will provide an answer to this question and to others. Let us apply it to this problem and find out the probabilities.

In applying the bayesian procedures, as before, we first lay out the initial probability tree. This we do in Figure 4-6a. From left to right, we list the states (TB and no TB). Then we list the events that provide additional information (the predictions), that is, the test outcomes "positive x-ray" and "negative x-ray." We can get either of these test outcomes when a person has TB and also when a person does not have the disease.

Next, we need the probabilities on the branches of the initial tree. On the first set of branches we insert the prior probabilities of the states. As seen in Figure 4-6a they are .02 for the state "TB" and .98 for the state "no TB."

The probabilities on the second set of branches essentially constitute the record of the chest x-ray as a predictor of the state "TB." Thus, we first need the (conditional) probability of getting a positive x-ray result when a person is known to have TB. This, of course, would typically be based on a conditional relative

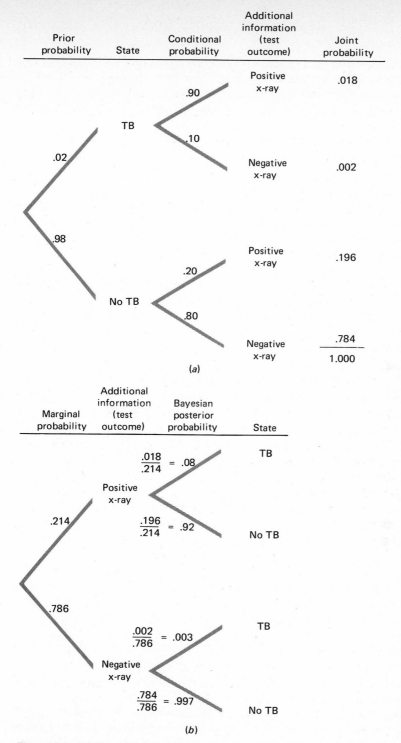

Prior probability	State	Conditional probability	Additional information (test outcome)	Joint probability
		.90	Positive x-ray	.018
	TB			
		.10	Negative x-ray	.002
.02				
.98				
		.20	Positive x-ray	.196
	No TB			
		.80	Negative x-ray	.784
				1.000

(a)

Marginal probability	Additional information (test outcome)	Bayesian posterior probability	State
		$\frac{.018}{.214} = .08$	TB
	Positive x-ray		
.214		$\frac{.196}{.214} = .92$	No TB
.786		$\frac{.002}{.786} = .003$	TB
	Negative x-ray		
		$\frac{.784}{.786} = .997$	No TB

(b)

Figure 4-6 *(a)* The initial probability tree and *(b)* the reverse probability tree for the TB example.

frequency of a positive x-ray when a person had TB. From records, such data can often be obtained (even though it may not have been known at the time of the x-ray that the person had TB). This conditional relative frequency would then ·serve as the basis for a conditional probability assignment to the test outcome "positive x-ray."

Thus, if 90 percent of the test outcomes were positive when TB was known to be present this would provide the conditional probability of getting that test outcome (in the case under consideration) given the presence of TB. Thus, a probability of .90 is placed on the first of the second set of branches in Figure 4-6*a*. Also on the same basis a conditional probability of .10 is assigned to the test outcome "negative x-ray" given the state "TB."

Similarly, if the relative frequency of the test outcome "positive x-ray" is 20 percent when no TB was present, we assign a conditional probability of .20 to "positive x-ray" given the state "no TB." Along with this, a conditional probability of .80 is assigned to the test outcome "negative x-ray" given the state "no TB."

The joint and marginal probabilities are next. Multiplying through the initial tree in Figure 4-6*a* provides us with the joint probabilities in Table 4-2. Summing the joint probabilities across each row gives us the marginal probabilities of the test outcomes.

The .214 marginal probability of getting a positive x-ray and the .786 marginal probability of getting a negative x-ray go on the first set of branches of the reverse tree in Figure 4-6*b*. The posterior probabilities come next. Let us illustrate the computation of one of them. For the posterior probability at the upper-right section of Figure 4-6*b* we have a probability of approximately .08. Let us set it down more explicitly as follows (*Note:* In this form it is referred to as Bayes' formula).

$$P(\text{TB}) \mid \text{positive x-ray} = \frac{P(\text{TB}) \cdot P(\text{positive x-ray} \mid \text{TB})}{P(\text{positive x-ray})}$$

$$= \frac{\text{a joint probability}}{\text{a marginal probability}}$$

$$= \frac{.018}{.214}$$

$$= .08$$

This first posterior probability provides the answer to the question we raised earlier: What is the probability that a person drawn from this group has TB given that his or her x-ray is positive (that is, it indicates the presence of TB)? The answer is .08.

Are you surprised that it is only .08? Most persons are. After all, the record of the chest x-ray as a predictor of TB looks pretty good from the initial tree in Figure 4-6*a*. We see in Figure 4-6*a* that when TB has been present, the x-ray predicted it correctly 90 percent of the time. When there was no TB, it predicted

Table 4-2 Joint and Marginal Probabilities for the TB Example

Additional information (test outcome)	State		Marginal probability
	TB	No TB	
Positive x-ray	.018	.196	.214
Negative x-ray	.002	.784	.786
			1.000

this state correctly 80 percent of the time. Then how is it that we come up with such a low probability of TB when it is predicted by the x-ray?

The explanation lies in the prior probabilities. For every 1,000 persons selected from this group, we would expect only 20 to have TB and 980 to have no TB: $(.02)(1,000) = 20$. From those 20 who have TB, we would expect to have 18 with positive x-rays: $(.90)(20) = 18$. From the 980 who have no TB, we would expect 196 positive x-rays: $(.20)(980) = 196$.

Thus, for the 1,000 persons, we would expect to obtain 214 positive x-rays (indicating the presence of TB). But most of these will come from persons with no TB! As indicated above, only 18 of the 214 will be from persons with TB. This is only 8 percent: $^{18}/_{214} = .08$. The other 92 percent will come from people with no TB.

The general inability of persons to take into account intuitively both the record of such predictors and the prior probabilities helps explain why the bayesian procedure is so valuable in modern thinking and decision making. Its benefits become even more obvious as the states and predictions become more numerous. Furthermore, it can be integrated with procedures for estimating how much a test or other predictor would be worth in a given situation. This is illustrated in the next two chapters.

SUMMARY

1   The probability of an event, given the occurrence of another event, is called a *conditional probability*. Although in a deep sense all probabilities are conditional probabilities, the term is typically used with reference to the occurrence of some particular related event that affects the probability of an event of primary interest.

2   The *prior probability* of an event is the probability assigned to an event *before* (prior to) receiving additional information regarding the occurrence of a related event. Thus, prior probabilities are *unconditional probabilities*.

3   A *posterior probability* of an event is the probability assigned to an event *after* the occurrence of another related event. Thus, posterior probabilities are conditional probabilities.

4   A general framework for viewing our changing knowledge with regard to the occurrence of an event is provided by the concepts of prior and posterior

probabilities. In our present knowledge, the probability assignments to the occurrence of an event of primary interest (a state) is termed a *prior* probability. Upon learning of the occurrence of another related event, we revise our prior probability of this event of primary interest to a *posterior* probability.

5   Although a revision of prior probabilities to posterior probabilities can be done in simple problems by using a Venn diagram, a more formal method known as the *bayesian procedure* is needed for larger problems.

6   The formal bayesian procedure for revising the prior probabilities in light of additional information is comprised of three steps: (*a*) construction of an initial probability tree, (*b*) formation of a joint and marginal probability table, and (*c*) construction of a reverse probability tree. It is in the construction of the reverse probability tree that the posterior probabilities are obtained.

7   The important practical point in connection with the bayesian procedure is that it provides a way of taking into account both the prior probability of an event and the record of a predictor in predicting the occurrence of that event. In a very loose sense, we can think of a posterior probability as representing the sum of (*a*) what we "knew" before receiving additional information (such as a prediction) plus (*b*) the knowledge obtained from the additional information. Our intuition is extremely limited in doing this effectively.

PROBLEMS

4-1 a   Distinguish between a state of prior information and a state of posterior information.

   b   Illustrate states of prior and posterior information from your own experiences, such as looking for a new apartment, bicycle, or car.

   c   Relate your discussions in *a* and *b* to prior and posterior *probabilities* of an event.

4-2   Differentiate between a conditional probability and an unconditional probability. What connections are there between these concepts and those of prior and posterior probabilities?

4-3   Consider again the copying-machine example discussed in this chapter. But now we are making *three* copies of the document instead of two. Recall that each copy we make has a .50 probability of being defective.

   a   Construct a Venn diagram showing the simple events in the chance process of making three copies of the document. Indicate on a small marker from each simple event its probability of occurrence.

   b   Suppose we need at least two good copies of the document. Let us refer to this compound event by the letter *A*. Represent this event in the Venn diagram constructed in *a*. What is the unconditional (prior) probability of *A*?

   c   Suppose that before knowing whether or not *A* (at least two good copies) has occurred, we can know whether or not another related event has occurred. This related event is event *D* (last copy defective). Still being interested in event *A*, we would like to know the probability of *A* given that *D* has occurred. Indicate event *D* on the Venn diagram constructed in *a*.

   d   Given that *D* has occurred, what are the simple events that could have occurred?

    e   Given that D has occurred, what are the simple events that could *not* have occurred?

    f   Knowing those simple events that could have occurred, what now is the probability that any one of them occurred?

    g   What simple events (in this set of simple events that could have occurred) would cause event A (at least two good copies) to occur?

    h   Thus, what is the (posterior) probability of A given that event D has occurred?

    i   What was the probability of A prior to knowing whether or not event D had occurred? Does your answer to h make sense? Explain.

4-4 In this problem let us obtain the posterior probability of A (at least two good copies) and other posterior probabilities using the initial and reverse trees in the bayesian procedure. To do so let us consider the following events in making three copies:

A = at least two good copies
B = less than two good copies
C = last copy good
D = last copy defective

    a   Represent the events A, B, C, and D in a Venn diagram.

    b   Suppose that the events of primary interest (the states) are A (at least two good copies) and B (less than two good copies). Additional information about events A and B can be obtained by knowing whether event C (last copy good) or D (last copy defective) occurred. Thus, construct an initial probability tree involving these four events.

    c   Place the appropriate unconditional probabilities and conditional probabilities on the branches of the initial probability tree in b. (Remember that the second set of branches requires conditional probabilities.)

    d   Form a joint and marginal probability table from the initial probability tree in c. (Remember to multiply through every branch from left to right in the initial tree to get the joint probabilities.)

    e   Construct the reverse probability tree of the problem. (Remember that the events are now in reverse order and that each posterior probability is a joint probability divided by a marginal probability.)

    f   Is the (posterior) probability of A (at least two good copies) given D (last copy defective) the same in e as you indicated in Problem 4-3h?

4-5 In connection with Problem 4-4, suppose we want to know the probability of at least *one* good copy given that the last copy is known to be defective. Let us refer to the event "at least one good copy" in making three copies by the letter E.

    a   Represent in a Venn diagram the simple events in making three copies. Then identify in the Venn diagram the event E (at least one good copy) and the event D (last copy defective).

    b   Obtain directly from the Venn diagram the (posterior) probability of E (at least one good copy) given event D (last copy defective).

4-6 Continue with the information given in Problem 4-5. Now we wish to obtain by using the initial and reverse trees in the bayesian procedure, the posterior probability of E (at least one good copy) and other posterior probabilities.

    a   Construct an initial probability tree. Our events of primary interest are E (at least one good copy) and F (not a single good copy) in making three copies of the document. The events providing aditional information are *D* (last copy defective) and *C* (last copy good). Use fractions to represent the probabilities of the events.

b   Form a joint and marginal probability table from the initial probability tree constructed in *a*.

c   Construct a reverse probability tree. Insert all the marginal and posterior probabilities on the branches of the reverse tree.

d   What is the (posterior) probability of *E* (at least one good copy) given the occurrence of event *D* (last copy defective)? Is it the same as you obtained in Problem 4-5*b* directly from the Venn diagram?

4-7   An important part of our copying machine has been replaced. Now it makes defective copies only 20 percent of the time instead of 50 percent. As in the discussion in this chapter, suppose we are going to make only *two* copies of the document and are interested in the same events, especially event *L* (at least one good copy) and event *V* (last copy defective).

a   Construct a tree (as in Figures 3-1 and 3-7) showing the simple events in making two copies. Insert the correct probabilities on the branches and obtain the probabilities of the simple events by multiplying through the tree.

b   Represent in a Venn diagram the simple events in making two copies.

c   Attach a marker to each point representing a simple event. On each marker, insert the probability of the simple event.

d   Represent event *L* (at least one good copy) and event *V* (last copy defective) in the Venn diagram formed in *b*.

e   Directly from the Venn diagram, obtain the prior (and unconditional) probability of *L* (at least one good copy).

f   Also directly from the Venn diagram, obtain the posterior (and conditional) probability of *L* (at least one good copy) given the occurrence of event *V* (last copy defective)?

4-8   Continue with the information in Problem 4-7 and that provided in the discussion of this chapter. Now we want to obtain by using the initial and reverse trees in the bayesian procedure the posterior probability of *L* (at least one good copy) and other posterior probabilities.

a   Construct an initial probability tree. Our primary interest is in the occurrence of event *L* (at least one good copy) and event *N* (not a single good copy) in making two copies. The events providing additional information are events *V* (last copy defective) and *G* (last copy good).

b   Form a joint and marginal probability table.

c   Construct a reverse probability tree. Insert the marginal and posterior probabilities.

d   What did you obtain for the (posterior) probability of *L* (at least one good copy) given the occurrence of *V* (last copy defective)? Is it the same as you obtained in Problem 4-7*f*?

4-9   In Problem 2-10 we examined the decision problem of an oil-drilling firm. The problem was whether or not to drill in a region where only 10 percent of the drillings encountered oil.

In this problem, however, we shall *not* focus directly upon whether or not to drill. Our focus now will be on the availability of additional information and how it permits the prior probabilities to be revised after receiving the additional information.

In this problem the events of primary interest (the states) are the presence of oil or its absence (that is, no oil). Now, in connection with these events suppose there are other events that are related to the presence or absence of oil, specifically the outcomes of seismological tests in the region under consideration. Furthermore, these other events (the seismic test outcomes) can occur before we know whether there is oil in a particular region. This, of course, is what makes these events potentially useful.

These seismic readings (test outcomes) are of two types. One type is an "oil reading" (that is, it predicts oil). The other type is a "no-oil reading" (a prediction of no oil). But this "seismic device," as we shall call it, is not a perfect predictor. In the past it has occasionally predicted oil when no oil was present. A summary of its record is given below:

Event of primary interest (state)	Relative frequency of this reading given each state	
	Oil reading (reading A)	No-oil reading (reading B)
Oil (state 1)	.60	.40
No oil (state 2)	.20	80

a Construct an initial probability tree that incorporates the prior probabilities of the events of primary interest and also the conditional probabilities of receiving the additional information. Let us use the conditional relative frequencies of the readings as the basis for the conditional probability assignments.

b Form a joint and marginal probability table from the initial tree constructed in *a*.

c Construct a reverse probability tree. Insert all the marginal and posterior probabilities on the branches of the reverse tree.

d Discuss the meaning of the marginal and posterior probabilities obtained in *c*. Do they appear to be reasonable? Explain.

4-10 In the oil-drilling example of Problem 4-9, suppose that now another, more promising region is considered for possible drilling. In the new region, oil has been encountered with a relative frequency of .20. Let us use this relative frequency as the basis for assigning a .20 prior probability to encountering oil if we drill in this region. Of course now the prior probability of oil not existing is .80.

The main purpose of this problem is to discover how changes in the prior probabilities affect the posterior probabilities even though the same additional information has been obtained.

a Construct an initial probability tree that incorporates the new prior probabilities. We are still considering the same additional information (the same seismic readings), and so the conditional relative frequencies of the seismic readings in

Problem 4-9 are used as the basis for the conditional probabilities of the seismic readings (as in Problem 4-9).

b Form a joint and marginal probability table from the initial probability tree constructed in *a*.

c Construct a reverse probability tree. Insert the new marginal and posterior probabilities computed from the table in *b*.

d Discuss the effect of the change in prior probabilities upon the marginal and posterior probabilities.

4-11 An agricultural decision under uncertainty was examined in Problems 2-7 and 2-8. In those problems we focused on whether or not to apply an insecticide given the existing (prior) information, specifically, the past relative frequencies of infestation.

In this problem we focus on the use of additional information that permits us to revise our prior probabilities after receiving additional information. The additional information in this case is in the form of an outcome of a test designed to detect the presence of larvae in the soil. The presence of larvae is often associated with subsequent infestation. However, the mere presence of larvae does not assure subsequent heavy infestation. Thus, the test for the presence of larvae is an imperfect predictor of the level of infestation. Its record as a predictor is indicated by the following relative frequencies of test outcomes given subsequent levels of infestation

Event of primary interest (state)	Event providing additional information (test outcome indicating the presence or absence of larvae given this state)	Relative frequency of this test outcome given this state
Heavy infestation	Larvae detected	.80
	No larvae detected	.20
		1.00
Moderate infestation	Larvae detected	.60
	No larvae detected	.40
		1.00
Slight infestation	Larvae detected	.10
	No larvae detected	.90
		1.00

a Construct an initial probability tree that incorporates both the prior probabilities of the states and the conditional probabilities of the test outcomes. Use the past relative frequencies of the states as the basis for the prior probabilities. They are .10 of heavy infestation, .50 of moderate infestation, and .40 of slight infestation. Use the conditional relative frequencies above as the basis for the conditional probabilities of the test outcomes.

b Form a joint and marginal probability table from the initial tree constructed in *a*.

    c   Construct a reverse probability tree including the marginal probabilities of the test outcomes and the posterior probabilities of the levels of infestation.

    d   Does the larvae information appear to be useful? Discuss the meaning of the posterior probabilities.

4-12 This problem is a forerunner of sampling problems that we shall encounter in the next chapter. Although it does not deal with a real-world-type problem, the following is a problem that helps us understand methods that are useful in interpreting additional information regarding such things as the quality of a shipment of products, the state of a market for a new product, and so forth.

    The problem is this: There are a large number of identical-looking earthen jars in a room. Each jar holds 10 balls, some of which are red and some of which are green. Some of the jars hold mostly red balls; the other jars hold mostly green balls.

    You are told that 80 percent of the jars hold mostly red balls, while the remaining 20 percent hold mostly green balls.

    a   If you were to select one of these jars at random what would be a reasonable probability of drawing a mostly red jar?

    b   Now you are told that each mostly red jar contains 6 red balls and 4 green balls. You are also informed that each mostly green jar contains 1 red and 9 green balls.

    Construct an initial probability tree that represents selecting one of the jars at random and then drawing one ball from the jar that you selected. You do not know which type of jar you selected. But the type of jar selected is the event of primary interest to you (in a real-world problem the predominantly red jar may be a predominantly defective shipment of products). The additional information comes in the form of drawing a red ball or a green ball. Of course a red ball or a green ball can come from either type of jar, but your initial probability tree should contain the conditional probabilities of drawing a red ball and also of drawing a green ball.

    c   Form a joint and marginal probability table from the initial probability tree constructed in *b*.

    d   Construct a reverse probability tree from the joint and marginal probability table obtained in *c*.

    e   Interpret the marginal and posterior probabilities obtained in *d* including a discussion of the revisions of prior probabilities. Do any of the posterior probabilities surprise you? Explain.

4-13 The bicycle maker in Problem 2-4 had to decide on whether a small plant or a large plant should be constructed in order to provide additional production facilities.

    In this problem we are not examining the final decision problem. Here, we shall only examine the effect that the results of a market survey have upon our prior probabilities.

    Recall that the event of primary interest is whether the state of the market for the product is good or fair. The prior probabilities on these states are .50 and .50.

    But there is a market survey procedure that is available and has been in use for some time so that a record of its predictions is available. The following shows the relative frequency of each prediction given each state of the market. The survey predictions in earlier uses were recorded along with the state of the market as it subsequently became known.

    a   Construct an initial probability tree.

    b   Form a joint and marginal probability table.

Event of primary interest (state of the market)	Event that provides additional information (prediction from the survey before the state of the market was known)	Relative frequency of this prediction given this state of the market
Good market	Good market predicted	.64
	Fair market predicted	.36
		1.00
Fair market	Good market predicted	.16
	Fair market predicted	.84
		1.00

c Construct a reverse probability tree.

d Discuss the revision of the prior probabilities of the states of the market to the posterior probabilities.

Making the Decision after Obtaining Additional Information and Revising the Prior Probabilities

We have examined in some detail the main properties of probability and random variables. It is time now to begin a more careful, in-depth analysis of decision making under conditions of uncertainty where the occurrence of particular events is represented by probabilities.

Because we are now familiar with the concept of conditional probability we can discuss two important factors: (1) a procedure for making a decision after receiving particular additional information and revising the prior probabilities and (2) a general procedure for estimating *the value of additional information* that may be obtained by tests, sampling, or other means.

Regarding the first point, we shall see that particular additional information will revise the prior probabilities such that the best act (by the maximization of expected-profit criterion) sometimes is *not* the one selected under prior information alone. On the second point it turns out that we can obtain the expected value of such additional information (what it would be worth to us) before actually being committed to obtaining it. Thus, by comparing the expected value of the information with its cost, we can determine whether or not we would (on the average) be ahead in obtaining it.

It is not uncommon in real situations for the cost of additional information to exceed the (expected) value of that information. In such cases, making the decision under existing (prior) information is the preferred alternative. However, there are many situations where the value of additional information exceeds its cost, and then the preferred alternative is to obtain the additional information before making the decision of interest.

SELECTING THE BEST ACT UNDER PRIOR
(EXISTING) INFORMATION ALONE

In Chapter 2 we discussed the use of expected profit in selecting an act from a set of alternative acts. The act associated with the maximum expected profit was identified as the best act under the maximization-of-expected-profit criterion.

In the machine example of Chapter 2 the two alternative acts were "use old machine" or "use new machine." The selection of one of these acts had to be made before the quality of the raw materials in a shipment was known. In Figure 5-1 we repeat the decision problem and observe that the best (optimal) act is "use new machine," with an expected profit of $208.

We now begin in Figure 5-1 the practice of enclosing within a square those points in the tree where a decision (a choice) is to be made. We enclose within a circle those points in the tree where chance factors determine the path taken. In large decision trees this practice permits an easy identification of the points of choice and the points of chance.

As we begin thinking about gaining additional information before making the decision on which machine to use, we realize that the tree in Figure 5-1 represents only the problem of decision under *existing* information or, as it is often called, *prior* information.

Prior information refers to the state of knowledge (the state of information) before (prior to) gaining any additional information. After we obtain additional information, the state of knowledge changes. In the next few paragraphs we shall examine decision making after we revise our prior information in light of additional information.

SELECTING THE BEST ACT AFTER OBTAINING ADDITIONAL
INFORMATION FROM A PERFECT PREDICTOR

As we examine the possibility of getting additional information before making the particular decision of interest, we must, in a sense, "back up" in our tree diagram to a decision point representing the choice to be made between making the decision under prior information or waiting until additional information has been obtained. We represent this decision point in the tree shown in Figure 5-2.

In the machine example we have already discovered the best expected profit that can be obtained under prior information. It is $208. But what we desire now is the *expected profit "using" additional information,* that is, delaying the decision on which machine to use until we have obtained additional information and revised the prior probabilities.

If we can obtain the expected profit using additional information (and we can), we are in a position to compare the "expected profit *using* it" with the

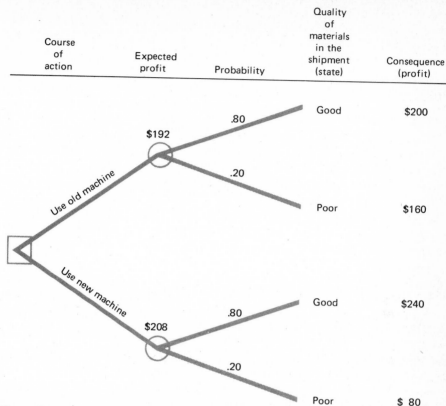

Course of action	Expected profit	Probability	Quality of materials in the shipment (state)	Consequence (profit)
		.80	Good	$200
Use old machine	$192			
		.20	Poor	$160
		.80	Good	$240
Use new machine	$208			
		.20	Poor	$ 80

Figure 5-1 The machine decision problem under prior information only.

"expected profit *not using* it" and observe the difference. The amount by which the expected profit using additional information exceeds the expected profit under prior information alone gives us the expected value of the additional information. Let us illustrate this with the machine example.

Expected Value of Additional Information in the Machine Example

In the machine example, suppose there is a test that can be run on the quality of the raw materials in a shipment before the decision is made on which machine to use. To make it as simple as possible also suppose that the test is a *perfect* testing device; that is, it is always correct.

The testing device gives two readings. One of the readings is a "good-quality reading," and the other is a "poor-quality reading." Whenever the shipment has been of good quality, the testing device has always given a "good-quality reading." When the shipments have been of poor quality, the outcome has always been a "poor-quality reading."

If we can use this perfect testing device to get a prediction of the quality of the materials before making the decision on which machine to use, what will the

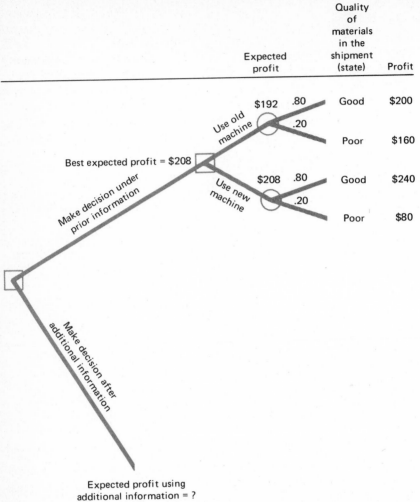

	Expected profit	Quality of materials in the shipment (state)	Profit
	$192 .80	Good	$200
	.20	Poor	$160
	$208 .80	Good	$240
	.20	Poor	$80

Use old machine

Best expected profit = $208

Make decision under prior information

Use new machine

Make decision after additional information

Expected profit using additional information = ?

Figure 5-2 Recognition of the choice point representing the making of the decision under prior information alone or after additional information has been obtained.

prediction (reading) be worth? To obtain its expected value we will have to further develop the lower section of the tree in Figure 5-2. We do this in Figure 5-3.

The Machine Example in Tree Form The lower section of the tree in Figure 5-3 represents the possible sequence of events, acts, events, and profit consequences that may be encountered if the path chosen is that of getting a reading from the testing device before making the decision on which machine to use.

If we proceed through the lower section of the tree in Figure 5-3, we encounter first either a "good-quality reading" or a "poor-quality reading" from the testing device. After we get a reading (a prediction), we make the decision on which machine to use. Once this decision is made, the quality of the raw materials becomes known and also the profit consequence.

But we want to obtain an overall expected profit of using this additional information in our decision making after we get a reading from the testing device. To get this expected profit, we first need to go through the tree and assign probabilities to the events (outcomes) at each of the chance points.

Going down the path of obtaining additional information (from left to right), we encounter a chance point with the possible outcomes (events) of the testing

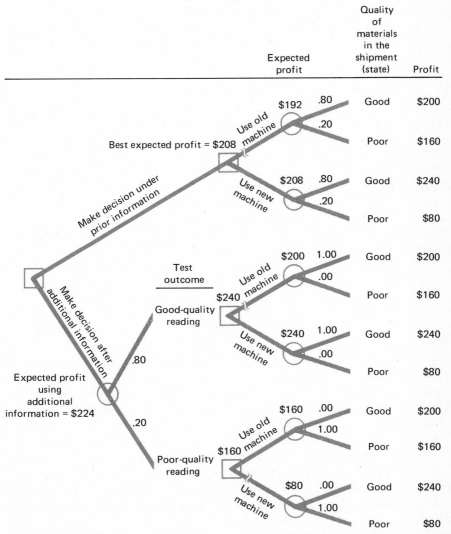

Figure 5-3 Obtaining the expected profit *using* additional information from a perfect predictor.

device, that is, "good-quality reading" or "poor-quality reading." But what probabilities should be assigned to the occurrence of each of these readings? At this point in our discussion let us provide only an intuitive basis for the probability assignments. (Later we shall see that the bayesian reverse-tree methods will provide these probabilities for us.)

If under our existing (prior) knowledge we assume a probability of .80 regarding the event "good-quality materials in the shipment," we should also assign a probability of .80 to receiving a "good-quality reading" from a testing device that is a perfect predictor. Similarly, we should assign a probability of .20 to the receipt of a "poor-quality reading" from a perfect predictor, since .20 is the current probability assigned to the occurrence of "poor-quality materials in the shipment."

Thus, we place a probability of .80 on the branch leading to the "good-quality reading" and a probability of .20 on the branch leading to the "poor-quality reading."

Proceeding further through the tree from left to right, we encounter a decision point. Actually, there is a decision point after each reading because the state of information is different after each reading. After a "good-quality reading," a perfect predictor (such as the perfect testing device) would cause the probability of "good-quality materials in the shipment" to be revised from .80 to 1.00, and the probability of "poor-quality materials in the shipment" to be revised from .20 to 0.00. In Figure 5-3, these revised (posterior) probabilities are assigned to the states *given* a "good-quality reading."

Similarly, after a "poor-quality reading" we would revise upward the prior probability of a poor-quality shipment from .20 to 1.00. The prior probability of "good-quality materials in the shipment" would be revised downward from .80 to 0.00. These revised (posterior) probabilities are recorded on the appropriate branches of the tree in Figure 5-3.

Now, after laying out sequentially in tree form the events, acts, events, and profit consequences, and then inserting the appropriate probabilities on the branches leading to chance events, we are in a position to start "moving back through the tree."

"Moving Back Through the Tree"   By the phrase "moving back through the tree," we mean that we start at the extreme right-hand side of the tree (at the very tips of the branches); and when a chance point is encountered, we compute an expected profit; when a choice point is encountered, we "turn around," look at the expected profits that were computed at each chance point, and then select the act that leads to the highest (optimal) expected profit. We place this best-expected-profit amount just above the relevant choice point. This procedure is continued until an expected profit is placed just above every choice point at that stage in the tree. Also, at this time it is useful to identify the optimal act so that if the path of getting additional information is actually taken, the act to be implemented after any of the predictions (readings) is readily known.

Let us illustrate what has just been said in terms of the example. In Figure 5-3, just after the receipt of a "good-quality reading," we place right above the chance point associated with the act "use old machine," the expected profit of $200: 1.00($200) + 0.00($160) = $200. Above the chance point associated with the act "use new machine," we place the expected profit of $240. Clearly, the best expected profit is $240, which we place above the *choice* point just posterior to "good-quality reading." Also, we choke off the act not to be taken (the nonoptimal act "use old machine").

Posterior to a "poor-quality reading," we have expected profits of $160 for "use old machine" and $80 for "use new machine." The optimal act is "use old machine" with an expected profit of $160. The $160 expected-profit amount is placed above the relevant choice point. Again, we choke off the nonoptimal act; this time, however, it is "use new machine."

Continuing back through the tree (to the left), we encounter another chance point. The chance outcomes at this point are the readings from the testing device. But we have probabilities associated with each of the possible readings; thus, an expected profit can be computed at this chance point.

It turns out that the single expected profit we obtain here is the expected profit *using* the additional information. But how is this expected profit obtained? It is obtained first by multiplying the probability of a "good-quality reading" (which is .80) by the best expected profit given a "good-quality reading" (which is $240). To this product we add that obtained by multiplying the .20 probability of getting a "poor-quality reading" by the best expected profit given a "poor-quality reading" (which is $160). Summing the two products of our multiplications gives us an expected profit of $224 (at that chance point before receiving either of the readings). This is the expected profit *using* this additional information. We summarize the above steps as follows:

$$
\begin{pmatrix} \text{Expected} \\ \text{profit} \\ \text{using} \\ \text{additional} \\ \text{information} \end{pmatrix} = \begin{pmatrix} \text{probability} \\ \text{of one} \\ \text{particular} \\ \text{test} \\ \text{outcome} \end{pmatrix} \begin{pmatrix} \text{the best} \\ \text{expected} \\ \text{profit} \\ \text{given} \\ \text{this test} \\ \text{outcome} \end{pmatrix} + \begin{pmatrix} \text{probability} \\ \text{of} \\ \text{another} \\ \text{test} \\ \text{outcome} \end{pmatrix} \begin{pmatrix} \text{the best} \\ \text{expected} \\ \text{profit} \\ \text{given} \\ \text{this test} \\ \text{outcome} \end{pmatrix}
$$

$$
= \begin{pmatrix} \text{probability} \\ \text{of a} \\ \text{"good-} \\ \text{quality} \\ \text{reading"} \end{pmatrix} \begin{pmatrix} \text{the best} \\ \text{expected} \\ \text{profit given} \\ \text{a "good-} \\ \text{quality} \\ \text{reading"} \end{pmatrix} + \begin{pmatrix} \text{probability} \\ \text{of a} \\ \text{"poor-} \\ \text{quality} \\ \text{reading"} \end{pmatrix} \begin{pmatrix} \text{the best} \\ \text{expected} \\ \text{profit given} \\ \text{a "poor-} \\ \text{quality} \\ \text{reading"} \end{pmatrix}
$$

$$
= (.80)($240) + (.20)($160)
$$
$$
= $192 + $32
$$
$$
= $224
$$

We can think of this expected profit using the additional information in the following way: On the average we will receive $224 in profit by following the path of obtaining this additional information.

But we can expect to obtain $208 profit without any additional information at all. (Recall that the best expected profit under prior information is $208.) Thus, getting a reading from this perfect test will increase our expected profit by only $16: $224 − $208 = $16.

We would say that the additional information is "worth" only $16 to us. Indeed, this is what we call the *value* of the additional information. Properly, we should refer to it as the *"expected value* of additional information" because the $16 represents the amount of additional profit per decision period (average profit) that would be obtained in the long run using the perfect additional information.

If this additional information costs $10, it would be desirable to obtain it (under the maximization-of-expected-profit criterion). However, if it would cost $20, it would be preferable to make the decision (on which machine to use) under prior information alone even though the uncertainty is greater.

SELECTING THE BEST ACT AFTER OBTAINING ADDITIONAL INFORMATION FROM AN IMPERFECT PREDICTOR

The procedure to be followed in getting information from an *imperfect* predictor (and using it in a decision) is essentially the same as that which we used for a perfect predictor above. Additional information that is not always correct obviously does not lead to a state of perfect knowledge; thus, given a prediction from an imperfect predictor, the prior probabilities are revised, not completely to 0.00 or to 1.00 (that is, not to certainty), but usually to values somewhat closer to 0.00 and 1.00. Generally, we can say that good, but imperfect, predictors reduce uncertainty; however, they do not fully remove the uncertainty such as a perfect predictor does.

Posterior Probabilities from the Reverse Tree

In the case of a perfect predictor above, we asserted that by definition a perfect predictor leads to posterior probabilities of 0.00 or 1.00. However, for imperfect predictors the necessary posterior probabilities can be obtained only by the use of Bayes' formula or by following the reverse-tree procedure (which embodies Bayes' formula).

However, before proceeding directly to the reverse probability tree for an imperfect predictor, let us see how the initial and reverse probability trees for a perfect predictor would look in the machine example even though they were not necessary in order to obtain the posterior probabilities.

In Figure 5-4 we have the initial probability tree. When the state has been good-quality materials (in the shipment), the reading from the testing device has always been a "good-quality reading." When the state has been poor-quality materials, the reading has always been a "poor-quality reading."

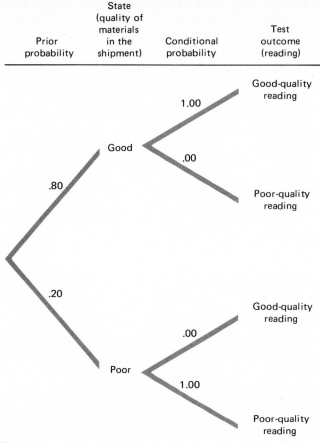

Figure 5-4 Initial probability tree for the perfect testing device (a perfect predictor).

Table 5-1 Joint and Marginal Probabilities for the Perfect Testing Device (a Perfect Predictor)

Test outcome (reading)	State (quality of materials in the shipment)		Marginal probability
	Good	Poor	
"Good-quality reading"	(.80)(1.00) = .80	(.20)(0.00) = 0	.80 + 0 = .80
"Poor-quality reading"	(.80)(0.00) = 0	(.20)(1.00) = .20	0 + .20 = .20
			1.00

In Table 5-1 we show the joint and marginal probabilities related to the initial probability tree of Figure 5-4. Recall from Chapter 4 that the marginal probabilities provide the probabilities for the first set of branches of the reverse tree. The reverse tree for the perfect testing device is shown in Figure 5-5.

Also in Chapter 4 we developed the procedure for obtaining the posterior probabilities in the reverse tree. Recall that each posterior-probability computation (there are four of them in this example) involves dividing a marginal probability into a joint probability in the same row. Let us illustrate the computation of one of these posterior probabilities.

$$P\left(\begin{array}{c|c}\text{good-quality} & \text{good-}\\ \text{materials in} & \text{quality}\\ \text{the shipment} & \text{reading}\end{array}\right) = \frac{P\left(\begin{array}{c}\text{good-}\\ \text{quality}\\ \text{materials}\end{array}\right)\cdot P\left(\begin{array}{c|c}\text{good-} & \text{good-}\\ \text{quality} & \text{quality}\\ \text{reading} & \text{materials}\end{array}\right)}{P\text{ (good-quality reading)}}$$

$$= \frac{(.80)(1.00)}{.80}$$

$$= 1.00$$

Thus, given this "good-quality reading," the prior probability of good-quality materials has been revised upward from .80 to 1.00. This posterior probability of 1.00 appears in the upper section of the reverse probability tree in Figure 5-5. The reverse tree in Figure 5-5 in effect was incorporated into the lower section of the decision tree in Figure 5-3 which was used in the first part of this chapter to determine the expected profit using a perfect predictor.

In Figure 5-3 you can see that a choice point was introduced after each of the possible readings from the testing device. The marginal probabilities shown in Table 5-1 (and in Figure 5-5) also provide the probabilities of the test readings (.80 for a "good-quality reading" and .20 for a "poor-quality reading"). The posterior probabilities from the reverse tree in Figure 5-5 provide the appropriate conditional probabilities of the states of quality of the raw materials.

Thus, although we did not need to obtain the reverse tree for the perfect predictor to assign the probabilities at the chance points in Figure 5-3, we can illustrate their computation by using the results of the bayesian reverse-tree method shown in Figure 5-5. As indicated earlier, the analysis of the use of an imperfect predictor requires this reverse-tree procedure.

Let us now examine this procedure with reference to an imperfect testing device (imperfect predictor) to be considered for use in the same machine decision problem. All aspects of the problem shall remain the same except that now the value of an imperfect predictor rather than of a perfect predictor is to be analyzed.

First, the initial probability tree for the imperfect testing device is shown in Figure 5-6. On the first set of branches are shown the same prior probabilities of the states: .80 on good-quality materials and .20 on poor-quality materials.

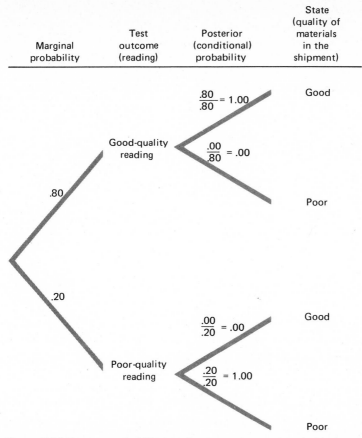

Figure 5-5 Reverse probability tree for the perfect testing device (a perfect predictor).

On the branches of the second section of the tree (moving to the right) appear the two sets of conditional probabilities. When the state has been good-quality materials, the testing device has given a "good-quality reading," not 100 percent of the time but 60 percent of the time. Thus, .60 is the probability (conditional) assigned to the receipt of a "good-quality reading" given that the state of the materials is of good quality. Given that same state, the conditional probability of receiving a "poor-quality reading" (an incorrect reading) is .40. This conditional probability, too, is based on the relative frequency of this reading given this state.

The other set of conditional probabilities is based on the relative frequency of each reading given the state of poor-quality materials. Here, we see that, given this state, the relative frequency of a "poor-quality reading" has been 90 percent. Only 10 percent of the time has an incorrect "good-quality reading" been received given the state of poor-quality materials.

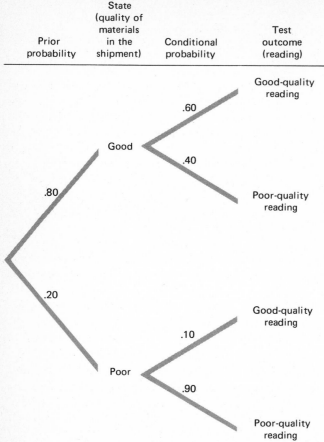

Figure 5-6   Initial probability tree for the imperfect testing device (an imperfect predictor).

From the initial probability tree for the imperfect testing device we obtain the joint and marginal probabilities shown in Table 5-2. Again, the marginal probabilities from Table 5-2 provide the probabilities for the first set of branches in the reverse probability tree shown in Figure 5-7.

As before, the posterior probabilities in Figure 5-7 are each obtained by dividing a joint probability by a marginal probability in the same row (in Table 5-2). Let us illustrate one of the computations.

$$P\left(\begin{array}{c}\text{good-quality} \\ \text{materials in} \\ \text{the shipment}\end{array}\middle|\begin{array}{c}\text{poor-} \\ \text{quality} \\ \text{reading}\end{array}\right) = \frac{P\left(\begin{array}{c}\text{good-} \\ \text{quality} \\ \text{materials}\end{array}\right) \cdot P\left(\begin{array}{c}\text{poor-} \\ \text{quality} \\ \text{reading}\end{array}\middle|\begin{array}{c}\text{good-} \\ \text{quality} \\ \text{materials}\end{array}\right)}{P\text{ (poor-quality reading)}}$$

$$= \frac{(.80)(.40)}{.50}$$

$$= \frac{.32}{.50}$$

$$= .64$$

Thus, the receipt of a "poor-quality reading" has reduced the prior probability of the state of good-quality materials from .80 to the posterior probability of .64. The other three posterior probabilities in Figure 5-7 are similarly obtained.

Once the reverse probability tree for a predictor is obtained, its value can be studied by incorporating it into the larger decision tree, such as the one in Figure 5-3. In Figure 5-3 the use of a perfect predictor was studied. Here we want to do the same for an imperfect predictor. Thus, in Figure 5-8 we incorporate the reverse probability tree of Figure 5-7 into the machine decision problem. The only changes in Figure 5-8 compared with Figure 5-3 are in the marginal and posterior probabilities in the lower section of the tree.

To obtain the expected profit using the additional information from this imperfect testing device we start (as before) at the extreme right of Figure 5-8 and work back through the lower section of the tree. First, we compute the expected profits of $198.40 (for "use old machine") and $233.60 (for "use new machine") posterior to a "good-quality reading." We move the best expected profit, $233.60, back to the appropriate choice point.

Posterior to a "poor-quality reading," we compute expected profits of $185.60 (for "use old machine") and $182.40 (for "use new machine"). The expected profit of $185.60 is higher and is moved to the appropriate choice point.

Finally, to get the expected profit using this additional information, we multiply the .50 marginal probability of getting a "good-quality reading" (where one can expect $233.60 in profit) by the expected profit of $233.60, and add it to the product of the .50 marginal probability of getting a "poor-quality reading" (where one can expect $185.60 in profit) and the expected profit of $185.60. This gives us an expected profit of $209.60: .50($233.60) + .50($185.60) = $209.60. We place this $209.60 amount next to the appropriate chance point in Figure 5-8

Table 5-2 Joint and Marginal Probabilities for the Imperfect Testing Device (an Imperfect Predictor)

Test outcome (reading)	State (quality of materials in the shipment)		Marginal probability
	Good	Poor	
"Good-quality reading"	(.80)(.60) = .48	(.20)(.10) = .02	.48 + .02 = .50
"Poor-quality reading"	(.80)(.40) = .32	(.20)(.90) = .18	.32 + .18 = .50
			1.00

leading to the test outcomes. We call this expected profit "the expected profit using this additional information."

How much is a reading from this imperfect device worth? In order to obtain its expected value we need only compare the expected profit using the additional information with the best expected profit not using it. Clearly, it has an expected value of $1.60: $209.60 − $208 = $1.60.

Therefore, if the cost of using this testing device is greater than $1.60, the preferred alternative is to go ahead and make the decision (on which machine to use) on the basis of prior information alone. If the cost is less than $1.60, the preferred act is to obtain the additional information before deciding. If the cost is $1.60, each alternative is equally preferable.

SUMMARY

1 We can obtain the value (the expected value) of additional information (such as that from tests, surveys, and samples) before being committed to obtaining them.

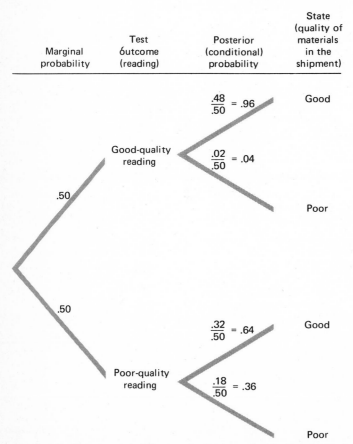

Figure 5-7   Reverse probability tree for the imperfect testing device (an imperfect predictor).

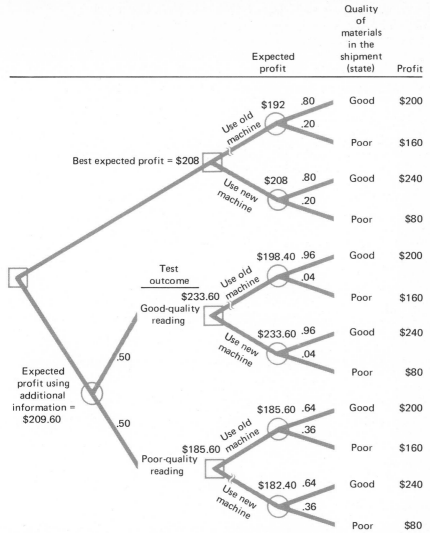

Figure 5-8 Obtaining the expected profit *using* additional information from an imperfect predictor.

2   After we obtain a specific prediction (such as a specific test outcome), we revise our prior probabilities on the events to posterior probabilities on those events. The best act to take after receiving additional information typically will depend upon the specific prediction (the specific test outcome) obtained.

3   The essential idea in determining the value (the expected value) of additional information is, first, to find the best expected profit *not* using the additional information (that is, under prior information only). Second, obtain the expected profit *using* the additional information. The difference between the two expected profits is *the expected value of additional information*.

4   Even though a test, survey, or sample has some (expected) value, it may

not be worthwhile to obtain it because its cost may exceed its expected value. Thus, at times it may be more profitable to make the decision under our existing uncertainty rather than under less uncertainty.

PROBLEMS

5-1 Consider again the packaging-machine example discussed in this chapter. Suppose, now, that past shipments have been of good quality with a relative frequency of only .60 instead of .80. Thus, the prior state of knowledge is represented by a .60 probability on the receipt of good-quality materials and a .40 probability on the receipt of poor-quality materials.

    a   Under this different prior state of knowledge, what is the expected profit *using* a perfect predictor? In obtaining your answer, construct a tree that shows the decision problem under prior information and also using a perfect predictor.

    b   What, now, is the expected value of perfect information?

    c   Does the change in the expected value of perfect information make sense? Explain.

5-2 Let us continue with the packaging-machine example with the new prior probabilities as indicated in Problem 5-1.

    a   Under this prior state of knowledge what is the expected profit *using* the imperfect testing device discussed in this chapter? (*Note:* The conditional probabilities of the test outcomes as shown in Figure 5-6 are still valid. In obtaining your answer, construct a tree of the problem that shows the decision under prior information and also using the imperfect testing device. Remember to obtain a new reverse tree and incorporate it into the larger decision tree.)

    b   What is the expected value of the additional information from this imperfect testing device?

    c   Do your answers to *a* and *b* appear to be reasonable compared with those obtained for a perfect predictor in Problem 5-1? Explain.

    d   If a reading from this imperfect testing device costs $10, should it be obtained? Explain.

5-3 It is common in real-world problems for changes in production costs to occur because of such factors as higher raw-material costs or the cost of improved facilities. Total costs are commonly divided into those that vary as output varies (variable costs) and those that remain fixed as output varies (fixed costs). In the case of variable costs, however, the input unit cost (the raw material cost per ton, for example) is assumed to remain constant. Higher output levels simply require more of, say, the raw materials; and thus raw-material cost is higher, at higher output levels. In this problem, however, we are assuming an increase in the unit cost of raw materials.

    Suppose that we go back to the packaging-machine example discussed in this chapter (with the original prior probabilities) and assume an increase in raw-material unit cost that has the effect of reducing by one-half the profit consequences of each act-event combination.

    a   After this raw-material-cost increase has occurred, what is the optimal act and its expected profit under prior information only?

    b   Now what is the expected profit *using* a perfect predictor?

    c   What is the expected value of perfect information? Has it changed because of the cost change? Explain.

    d   From your answer in *c*, what can you say about the expected value of an *imperfect* predictor?

    e   Compute the expected value of the imperfect testing device (discussed in this chapter) after this raw-material-cost increase. Compare your computed expected value with your answer in *d*.

5-4   Consider again the original packaging-machine example discussed in this chapter. Instead of a raw-material-cost increase, suppose that there is an increase in fixed cost because of an improvement in the facilities. This has the effect of reducing the profit of each act-event combination by $100.

    a   After this fixed-cost increase, what is the optimal act and its expected profit under prior information only?

    b   What is the expected profit *using* a perfect predictor?

    c   What is the expected value of perfect information?

    d   From your answer in *c*, what can you say about the expected value of an *imperfect* predictor?

    e   Compute the expected value of the imperfect testing device (discussed in this chapter) after this fixed-cost increase. Compare your computed expected value with your answer in *d*.

    f   Discuss the general effect on the value of information of the two different types of cost increases illustrated in Problems 5-3 and in this problem.

5-5   In Problem 2-10 a decision had to be made on whether or not to drill for oil in a particular region. In Problem 2-10 the decision had to be made under prior (existing) knowledge.

      Now suppose that we consider the use of additional information (specifically, seismological information) that has been found to be helpful in oil exploration. We refer loosely to this technique as using a "seismic device."

      In a later problem we shall focus upon a more common imperfectly predicting seismic device, but first in this problem let us find out what a perfect seismic device would be worth. By a perfect seismic device we mean that when there was oil the device always predicted that oil would be encountered. When there was no oil, it predicted this correctly.

    a   What is the expected profit *using* a perfect predictor (a perfect seismic device)? In obtaining your answer, construct a tree of the entire decision problem.

    b   What is the expected value of perfect information (expected value of a prediction from the perfect seismic device)?

    c   Explain why the expected value of perfect information is the value obtained in *b*.

    d   From your answer in *b* indicate in your own words what an imperfect seismic device would be worth. Explain.

5-6   Let us now see what an imperfect seismic device is worth in the oil-drilling decision in Problem 5-5.

      This seismic device has been in use for some time and so a record of its performance as a predictor of oil is available. This record was indicated in Problem 4-9 in which an initial and a reverse tree were constructed. Thus, in this problem, please refer back to the data in Problem 4-9, particularly to the probabilities in the reverse tree.

    a   What is the expected profit *using* this imperfect predictor? Construct a tree of the entire decision problem. Incorporate the appropriate reverse tree into the larger decision problem.

    b   What is the expected value of this imperfect predictor?

c   Compare the expected value of this imperfect predictor obtained in *b* with the expected value of a perfect predictor obtained in Problem 5-5*b*.

d   If the imperfect seismic device costs $20,000 for a prediction, is it worthwhile to obtain it before making the decision on whether or not to drill?

5-7   Now let us see how a change in the prior probabilities in the oil-drilling example in Problems 2-10, 5-5, and 5-6 affects the expected value of additional information.

Suppose that drilling operations are contemplated in a different (and more promising) region. In this region 25 percent of the drillings have encountered oil. Thus, the prior probability of encountering oil is .25 instead of .10 (as it was in Problem 5-6). The prior probability of encountering no oil is .75.

a   What is the optimal act and its expected profit under prior information?

b   What is the expected profit *using* a perfect seismic device?

c   What is the expected value of a perfect seismic device?

d   What is the expected profit using the imperfect seismic device of Problem 5-6? (*Note:* Do not round the probabilities or expected profits. Use fractions where appropriate.)

e   What is the expected value of the information from the imperfect seismic device?

f   Describe in your own words the answers obtained in *a*, *b*, *c*, *d*, and *e*.

5-8   Let us go back to the oil-drilling decision in Problem 5-6 with the original prior probabilities and profit consequences. But now let us assume that drilling costs have increased by $30,000. This cost increase, in turn, decreases the profit consequences associated with drilling whether or not oil is found. Under these new profit consequences obtain the following:

a   The optimal act and its expected profit under prior information.

b   The expected profit *using* a perfect predictor.

c   The expected value of perfect information.

d   The expected profit *using* the imperfect seismic device referred to in Problem 5-6.

e   The expected value of a reading from the imperfect seismic device.

f   Should the information from the imperfect seismic device be obtained if it costs $20,000?

g   Describe in your own words the meaning of the answers to *a*, *b*, *c*, *d*, *e*, and *f*.

5-9   In Problems 2-7 and 2-8 an agricultural decision on whether or not to apply an insecticide was examined. At that time the decision under prior information was studied. then in Problem 4-11 we saw how the detection of larvae could be used as an imperfect predictor of subsequent infestation. Let us refer again to the reverse tree that we obtained in Problem 4-11 and incorporate it into our evaluation of using this additional information (the larvae information) before making the decision on whether or not to apply the insecticide.

a   Construct a tree of the decision problem under prior information alone and also of making the decision after obtaining the larvae information. Incorporate the reverse tree from Problem 4-11 into the large tree of this problem.

b   What is the expected not revenue *using* the larvae information? (Recall that we interpret net revenue here as total revenue of an output amount less any insecticide cost.)

c   What is the expected value of the larvae information?

d   If the cost of getting the larvae information is $20, should it be obtained before making the decision on whether or not to apply the insecticide to 100 acres?

5-10   In Problem 2-4 we considered the bicycle maker's decision with respect to expanding his production facilities by building either a large plant or a small plant. We assumed that the state of the market for the product was either good or fair, with prior probabilities of .50 and .50.

The profit consequences of building the small plant are estimated to be $500,000 if the market is good and $100,000 if the market is fair. If the large plant is constructed, the profit is estimated to be $700,000 if the market is good and −$200,000 (a loss) if it is fair.

Now suppose that a market-survey procedure is available that has been in use for some time in such market-demand studies. Its record as a predictor was given in Problem 4-13.

a Construct a tree that represents the decision under prior information and also using the market-survey information. (Remember to incorporate the reverse tree into the relevant section of the larger decision tree.)

b What is the expected profit *using* the market-survey information?

c What is the expected value of the survey information?

d If the market survey costs $20,000, is it worthwhile to obtain it before making the decision on which size plant to build?

5-11 Suppose that the bicycle maker in Problem 5-10 has very little time to choose between making the construction decision on the basis of prior information alone or after getting market survey information. Suppose that there is not even enough time for analysis such as that undertaken in Problem 5-10.

a Would the computation of the expected value of perfect information be helpful? Obtain it and discuss its possible value.

b On the basis of your answer in a, would you encourage the bicycle maker to delay his construction decision until he could get the expected value of the market-survey information (as obtained in Problem 5-10) providing the survey information is known to cost $20,000? Explain.

5-12 A bank has a request for a $3,000 loan from a customer. A decision must be made on whether to grant the request. If the loan is made, there is the possibility that the customer will default in repayment of the loan. For this size of loan (and for this type of customer) there tends to be a $500 loss consequence if default occurs. On the other hand, if the loan is repaid as planned (that is, there is no default) the profit is $250.

An alternative use of the $3,000 in funds is to purchase a government bond for which there would be a profit of $200 that is considered to be certain.

a If 400 out of 4,000 recent customers of this type have defaulted, should the loan be made if this is the only information available? (*Note:* Use the maximization-of- expected-profit criterion.)

b There is also the possible alternative of obtaining a credit rating on such a customer before making the decision on the loan. Suppose the recent record of of the credit-rating service for 4,000 customers is given as follows (in absolute frequencies):

State	Frequency with which this credit rating was given		
	A	B	C
Default	20	60	320
No default	1,080	1,400	1,080

       In view of the record of the credit-rating service, would the receipt of a credit rating on a customer ever result in a decision different from that under prior information only? Explain. (Use three-digit probabilities in the computations.)

c What is the expected value (the expected gain) of getting a credit rating on a customer before making the lending decision?

d What is the most that should be paid for the credit-rating service per customer?

e Examine the posterior probabilities in relation to the prior probabilities and discuss the reasons for the direction and magnitude of the revisions.

Chapter 6

Using Additional Information from a Sample: What Is It Worth?

Now we shall examine the way in which we can apply the ideas of the last chapter to those situations where the additional information we might obtain is through *sampling*.

Sampling is a common way of getting more information about many different things. Usually, in the more technical discussions, it refers to obtaining a *random selection* of a part of the items from a population of some sort and then observing a characteristic of each item in the sample. (*Note:* By random selection we mean that each item in the population has an equal chance of being selected in the sample.)

For example, we might take a sample from a shipment of products (a population) and then observe each unit sampled to see whether or not it is defective. A common use of a sample result is to consider it as an indicator of this characteristic (say, the proportion defective) in the entire population.

Very roughly, we can say that a sample with a very large number of defective products (in relation to the size of the sample) indicates that the entire shipment has a high proportion of defective products. To cite another example, a sample of potential buyers from a market for a new product may be obtained to learn more about the state of this market. Again very roughly, a large number in the sample who want to buy the product indicates a good market for the product (that is, the entire market has a high proportion of persons wanting to buy the new product).

What we wish to do in this chapter is to refine and develop the foregoing ideas and to tie the sampling alternatives into a decision problem. After all, obtaining additional information of any type is usually considered because some decision is to be made where it may be of some value.

In the case of uncertain product quality, a decision may have to be made on accepting the shipment or refusing it under the present terms. In the case of an uncertain market for a new product, the decision may be whether or not to introduce it throughout a large market. In both these cases, sampling can be used to reduce some of the uncertainty facing the decision maker and thus reduce the probability of decision error.

In sampling, as in other ways of gaining additional information, we can choose to make a particular decision under prior (existing) information or wait to make the decision until additional information has been obtained.

In this chapter, where we focus on sampling as a means of obtaining additional information, we shall see that a sample of a particular size in a particular situation has some specific *expected value* (that is, it has some worth). This expected value can be obtained even before being committed to any sampling at all.

Should the cost of the sampling be greater than its expected value, there would be no gain in taking the sample. However, in some situations the expected value of the sample is greater than its cost, and thus there could be a net gain from sampling.

To obtain the expected value of a sample, we first compute the *expected profit using the additional information* for a sample of a particular size and then subtract from it the maximum expected profit under prior information only. This is the *expected value of additional information* for that sample size. It is often called the "expected value of sample information."

Thus the following definition holds. (Aside from the sampling interpretation, it is the same definition that we used in the previous chapter.)

$$
\begin{array}{c}
\text{Expected value} \\
\text{of additional} \\
\text{information from} \\
\text{a sample of a} \\
\text{particular size}
\end{array}
=
\begin{array}{c}
\text{expected profit} \\
\text{using the} \\
\text{additional} \\
\text{information}
\end{array}
-
\begin{array}{c}
\text{maximum expected} \\
\text{profit under} \\
\text{prior informa-} \\
\text{tion only}
\end{array}
$$

Often samples of different sizes can be considered, and each sample size essentially involves a separate path of gaining additional information. After all, a very large sample should improve our state of knowledge much more than an extremely small sample. A large sample usually turns out to be a different (and better) predictor than a small one.

Thus we shall see near the end of this chapter that before any actual sampling takes place we can compute the expected value of additional information for each of various sample sizes; and then, by comparing these expected values with their corresponding costs, we shall be able to select the sample size that is best for that particular decision situation.

A MARKETING DECISION PROBLEM: SHOULD A NEW PRODUCT BE INTRODUCED?

Real-world decision problems are often exceedingly complex. Therefore, in order to see in a fairly clear way how some of the important concepts apply to real-world problems, we use some very simplified versions of them.

But the procedures we illustrate with the simplified examples generally extend to the larger real-world problems, too. Although the concepts and procedures in this chapter (as well as those discussed throughout the book) apply to various areas (such as finance, marketing, and production operations), we choose a marketing decision problem for purposes of illustration here.

Suppose our problem is one of deciding whether or not to introduce for sale throughout a large national market a new product (say a new type basketball shoe). There is considerable uncertainty with respect to the state of the market for the new product.

This uncertainty regarding the state of the market in turn gives rise to considerable uncertainty with regard to the profit if the product is introduced. There is prior information that is available, but the possibility also exists for obtaining additional information by surveying potential buyers (through sampling).

First, however, let us examine the decision under prior information only (that is, without sampling). Later, we shall investigate to see if we would be better off by sampling the potential buyers before making the decision on introducing the product.

Making the Decision under Prior Information Only

There are two acts from which to choose in this decision problem: "introduce the new product" or "do not introduce the new product." In Figure 6-1 we represent these two acts at the appropriate choice point.

When it comes to the relevant events in this problem we have simplified matters considerably. The relevant events are the possible states of the market for the new product. We are assuming that there are just two states of the market.

It can be a good market for the new product, or it can be a poor market. More states would perhaps make the example more realistic, but they would complicate the computations. Regardless, the basic procedures we discuss here would be the same.

Note, too, in Figure 6-1 that we additionally describe each state of the market by the approximate proportion of the potential buyers (say, basketball players) who would purchase the new product. If it is a good market, approximately 60 percent of the players would buy; whereas if it is a poor market, the

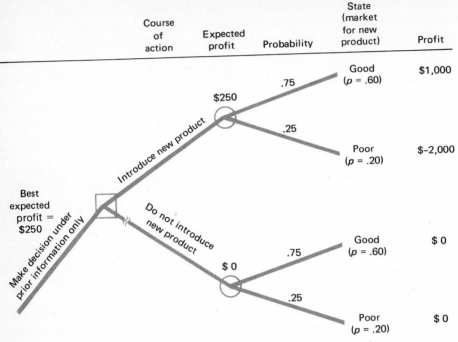

Figure 6-1 The marketing decision under prior (existing) information only.

proportion would be only 20 percent. We often refer to these proportions by the lowercase letter p.

Either of these two states of the market could occur with each of the two acts. Thus, the act-event combinations for the decision problem are four (as can be seen in Figure 6-1).

And what about the profit consequences of the act-event combinations? As seen in Figure 6-1, the additional profit is $1,000 for the decision period if the new product is introduced and the market for it is good. However, if it is introduced and the market for it is poor, a loss (negative profit) of $2,000 would occur. The additional profit is $0 for the act "do not introduce the new product" regardless of the state of the market. No revenues would be forthcoming, and no costs would be incurred.

Something is already known about the state of the market for this product. The results of previous studies for similar products and the direct experience of persons working in this market may be typical sources of information that are available. True, knowledge with respect to this market may have to be based on intuitive judgments, but it is not knowledge to be disregarded. We have seen in the previous chapter (as we shall see here again) that the use of prior knowledge is essential in determining whether or not additional information is likely to be worthwhile to obtain.

The existing knowledge with regard to this market is represented by a probability of .75 assigned to the existence of a good market for the product and a probability of .25 for a poor market. Thus, prior information indicates that a good market for this product is quite likely.

Using these assigned prior probabilities to the states, we compute an expected profit for each of the acts. As seen in Figure 6-1, the best act (using the maximization-of-expected-profit criterion) is "introduce the new product." It has an expected profit of $250. The alternative act "do not introduce the new product" has an expected profit of $0.

Although we find that under prior information the introduction of the new product is expected to be profitable, might it not be even more profitable to obtain additional information about the market before deciding on the product introduction?

Let us proceed with our analysis of the use of the additional information and find out. First, let us see what a perfect predictor would be worth, and then what a sample of some size (an imperfect predictor) would be worth.

The Value of a Perfect Predictor

In our example it is possible (just from the analysis under prior information) to estimate what a perfect predictor would be worth to us.

Although under prior (existing) information we would introduce the new product, it would involve a 25 percent chance of the market being poor. This, in turn, if it were to occur, would result in a $2,000 loss.

However, if a perfect predictor is available (and, of course, if we wait for the prediction before making our decision), it would be possible to choose the decision "do not introduce" if the market is poor.

Thus, instead of a 25 percent chance of incurring a $2,000 loss, we would have a 25 percent chance of a profit consequence of $0. This would raise our expected profit from $250 to $750: $.25($0) + .75($1,000) = 750. Thus, the (expected) value of a perfect predictor in this situation is $500, the difference between the expected profits of $250 and $750.

More formally, however, in Figure 6-2 we compute the expected profit using a perfect predictor (along the lines that we followed in the preceding chapter). In the marketing decision problem of this chapter we find the expected profit using a perfect predictor to be $750 (as we indicated informally above). Thus, the expected value of a perfect predictor is $500: $750 - $250 = 500.

The Value of an Imperfect Predictor: What Is a Sample Worth?

It is useful to think of sample outcomes as predictors of the populations from which they came. But, of course, usually they are not perfect predictors. They are imperfect predictors.

Thus, when we view sample outcomes as imperfect predictors, the ideas of the preceding chapter are seen to apply to sampling as well as to gaining additional information from imperfect predictors generally. Throughout the remainder of this chapter we shall see how those procedures apply to sampling. To be sure, sampling is a large field of probability and statistics, but some of its essential ideas can be illustrated in this brief introduction.

In order to obtain the expected profit using a predictor of any type, we have followed the practice (as in the lower section of Figure 6-2) of first setting down the possible predictions that can be obtained. Then we have inserted a decision point just posterior to each possible prediction. Each act represented at each decision point in turn leads (usually) to a chance point and the possible states with their associated posterior probabilities and profit consequences.

As we have indicated before, this sequence of predictions, acts, and states makes a lot of sense. If we are to obtain additional information, we want to wait

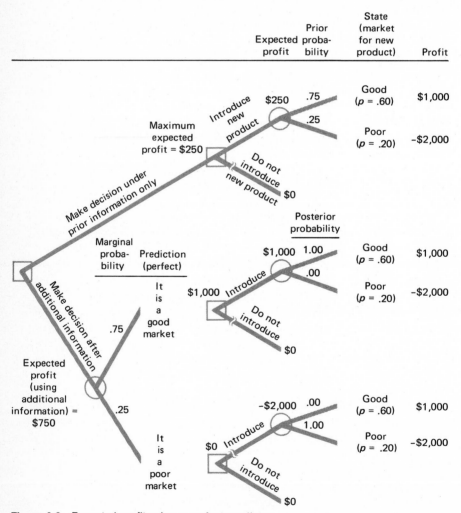

Figure 6-2 Expected profit using a perfect predictor.

until it is available, then update (revise) our probabilities, and then make the decision of primary concern.

After inserting the marginal and posterior probabilities (from the initial- and reverse-tree computations that are done on the side), we begin at the right side of the tree (as before) by computing an expected profit at each chance point. Moving left to the choice points, we pick the best expected profit and move this expected profit back to a point just above the appropriate decision point. Then each of these (best) expected profits is multiplied by the (marginal) probability leading to it. Summing all of these separate probability and profit multiplications gives us the expected profit using the additional information. For the perfect predictor in Figure 6-2 we see it to be $750: .75($1,000) + .25($0) = $750.

How is the above procedure modified for the determination of the expected profit using a sample of some particular size? Very little. The primary difference is that we treat each sample outcome as a separate prediction.

In order to get the full picture before us, let us take a look at the tree diagram in Figure 6-3 in which we obtain in our marketing example the expected profit using the information in a sample of 2 potential buyers from the market for the new product. We find this expected profit to be $448.80. Since $250 is the best expected profit under prior information, we conclude that the expected value of the information from a sample of 2 is therefore $198.80: $448.80 − $250 = $198.80. But let us go back to the beginning and summarize more explicitly the way we lay out the trees, such as the one that appears in Figure 6-3.

To obtain the lower section of the tree in Figure 6-3 (as well as comparable sections for other and larger sampling problems), we perform three main steps that we summarize below. In previous paragraphs we performed these steps more informally, but now it is useful to be more explicit in our procedure.

Step 1 below specifies the general sequence of sample outcomes, acts, states, and consequences. Step 2 outlines the probabilities to be obtained; step 3 summarizes the procedure in "moving back through the tree" that gives us the expected profit using the particular additional information.

Step 1: Construct a section of the main decision tree (that represents obtaining additional information) by laying out from left to right the sequence of sample outcomes, acts, states, and consequences of the act-event (act-state) combinations. (Illustrations that follow are from the marketing example in Figure 6-3.)

a *Possible sample outcomes*
   Illustration: For a sample of 2 in our marketing example, the possible sample outcomes are:
   "0 out of 2 buys the product"
   "1 out of 2 buys the product"
   "2 out of 2 buy the product"

b *Possible acts after each sample outcome*
   Illustration:
   "Introduce the new product"
   "Do not introduce the new product"

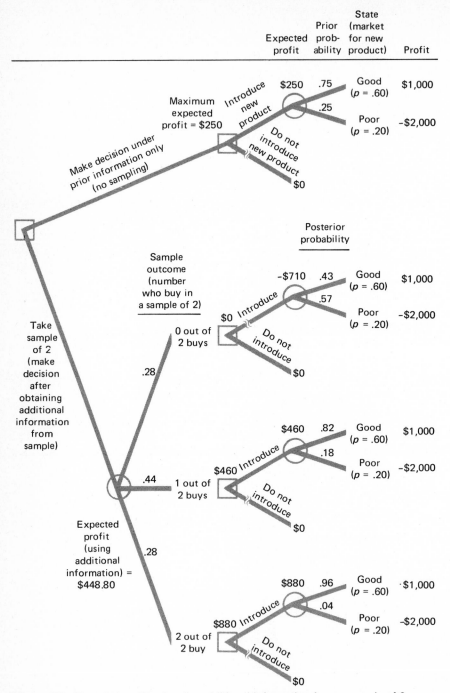

Figure 6-3 Expected profit using the additional information from a sample of 2.

    c   *Possible states*
       Illustration:
          "Good market for the new product"
          "Poor market for the new product"

    d   *Possible act-event combinations and their consequences*
       Illustration:
          "Introduce new product and good market":
          $1,000
          "Introduce new product and poor market":
          −$2,000
          "Do not introduce the new product and
          good market": $0
          "Do not introduce the new product and
          poor market": $0

Step 2: Obtain the marginal probabilities of the sample outcomes and the posterior probabilities of the states; then insert them at the appropriate places in the main decision tree constructed in step 1. (The marginal and posterior probabilities should be computed away from the main tree to avoid confusion.) As before, this step has three elements: *(a)* the construction of an initial probability tree; *(b)* the formation of a joint and marginal probability table; and *(c)* the construction of a reverse probability tree.

    a   *Constructing the initial probability tree*
       Illustration: For a sample of 2 in our marketing example, the initial probability tree is shown in Figure 6-4. Moving from left to right, we represent first the possible states: a good market (with a proportion of .60 who buy) and a poor market (with a proportion of .20 who buy). The sample outcomes for a sample of 2 are three: "0 out of 2 buys," "1 out of 2 buys," or "2 out of 2 buy." The probability of each of these sample outcomes is obtained first by assuming we are sampling from a good market (where $p = .60$) and then assuming that we are sampling from a poor market (where $p = .20$). Thus each sample-outcome probability is a conditional probability. It is conditional in the sense that one is assuming that he or she is sampling from a particular population with a known p-value and given sample size. How do we get the probabilities for the sample outcomes that appear in Figure 6-4? They do not come from the record of predictions as was the case in the previous chapter. They can be computed as we shall see below.[1] The simplest way to get them when such a small sample is involved is to construct still another probability tree (on the side) to guide the computations. This is done in Figure 6-5.
       Observe in the upper section of Figure 6-5 we compute the probabilities of the sample outcomes providing the sample comes from a good market (with a proportion who buy of .60). The lower section of Figure 6-5 provides a tree for the computation of the probabilities of these same sample outcomes provided

---

    [1]In more advanced discussions they are called *binomial probabilities*. Extensive binomial probability tables are available.

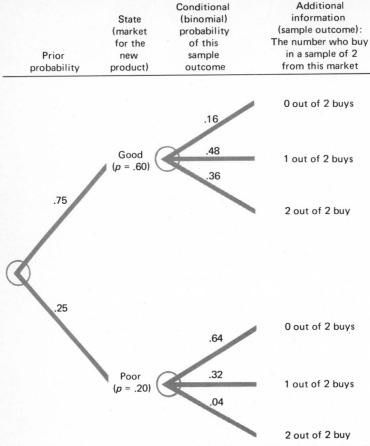

Prior probability	State (market for the new product)	Conditional (binomial) probability of this sample outcome	Additional information (sample outcome): The number who buy in a sample of 2 from this market

Figure 6-4 Initial probability tree when obtaining additional information from a sample of 2 potential buyers.

one is sampling from a poor market (with a proportion who buy of .20). One can see that any of the three sample outcomes can be obtained from either of the two markets (populations), but of course the probabilities of the sample outcomes should be (and are) different depending on the market from which one is obtaining the sample.

Thus, in the upper section of Figure 6-5 we see that each person sampled from that market has a probability (to us) of .60 of buying the new product. If we were to sample two persons, the probability of both of them buying is obtained by multiplying their separate probabilities. This is .36, as seen in Figure 6-5: $(.60)(.60) = .36$. The other probabilities are similarly obtained by multiplying through the tree. In the lower section of Figure 6-5 we compute the probabilities of the same sample outcomes providing we were to take a sample of two persons from a poor market (where $p = .20$). Here the probability (to us) of each person buying is .20. And from this market the probability of "2 out of 2 buying" is .04: $(.20)(.20) = .04$. Again, the remaining probabilities are obtained by multiplying

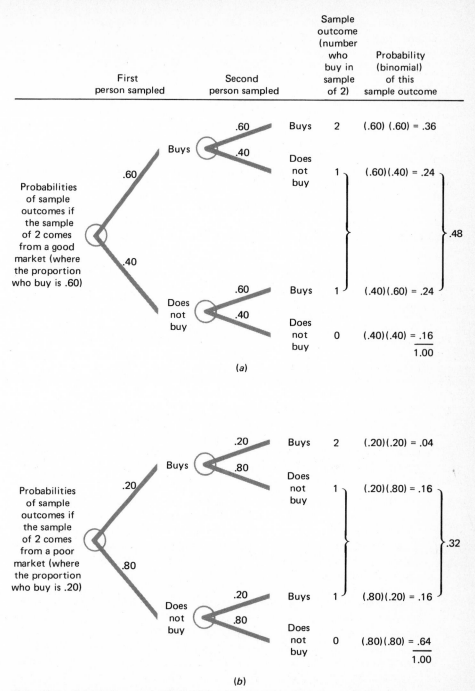

Figure 6-5   Calculation of the probabilities (binomial) of sample outcomes when the sample of 2 comes *(a)* from a good market and *(b)* from a poor market. The probabilities are obtained here by "multiplying through the trees."

Table 6-1   Joint and Marginal Probabilities for Obtaining Additional Information from a Sample of 2 Potential Buyers

Sample outcome	State of the market for the new product		Marginal probability (probability of sample outcome)
	Good ($p = .60$)	Poor ($p = .20$)	
0 out of 2 buys	(.75)(.16) = .12	(.25)(.64) = .16	.12 + .16 = .28
1 out of 2 buys	(.75)(.48) = .36	(.25)(.32) = .08	.36 + .08 = .44
2 out of 2 buys	(.75)(.36) = .27	(.25)(.04) = .01	.27 + .01 = .28
			1.00

through the tree. In both the good and poor markets the probability of "1 out of 2 buying" is obtained by the summing of the appropriate probabilities as seen in Figure 6-5. For example, if the sample comes from a good market, the probability of "1 out of 2 buying" is .48, the *sum* of the separate probabilities of .24 and .24. Once these conditional probabilities of the sample outcomes are obtained, they are inserted on the appropriate branches of the initial tree in Figure 6-4.

b   *Forming a joint and marginal probability table*
Illustration: Multiplying through the initial probability tree in Figure 6-4 provides us with the joint probabilities in the main section of Table 6-1. For example, the cell in the upper-left corner of Table 6-1 has a joint probability of .12. This is the probability of the joint occurrence of a good market and "0 out of 2 buy" in a sample of 2: (.75)(.16) = .12. As before, the summing of the joint probabilities in each row gives us the marginal probabilities (that is, the unconditional probabilities of each sample outcome).

c   *Constructing the reverse probability tree*
Illustration: From the joint and marginal probabilities in Table 6-1 we can obtain the necessary marginal and posterior probabilities for the reverse tree in our marketing example (that appears in Figure 6-6). The marginal probabilities from Table 6-1 go directly on the first set of branches (from the left) in Figure 6-6. The posterior probabilities of the states are obtained from the joint and marginal probability table as in the previous chapter.

For example, the probability of a good market, given a sample outcome "0 out of 2 buy," is obtained by dividing the joint probability of .12 (that is, the probability of the joint occurrence of a good market and "0 out of 2 buy") by the (marginal) probability of that particular sample outcome, .28.

Thus, the (posterior) probability of a good market (given that "0 out of 2 buy") is .12/.28 or .43 (approximately). The remaining posterior probabilities in Figure 6-6 are similarly obtained.

When all the marginal and posterior probabilities are computed, they are then placed in the appropriate positions in the main decision tree (in Figure 6-3), which also has the acts and consequences represented. We should have a set of probabilities for each chance point in the main decision tree. [*Note:* If in the

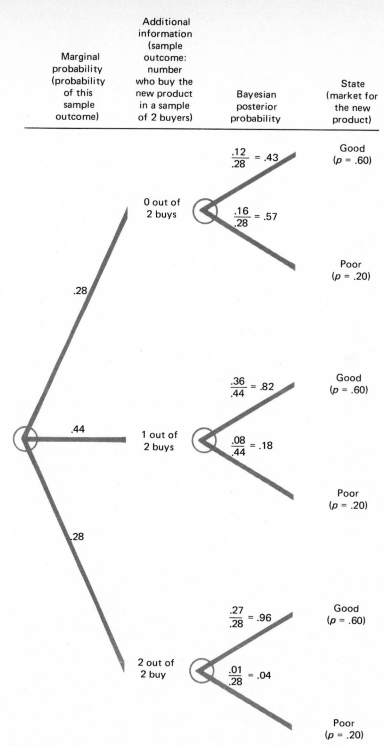

Marginal probability (probability of this sample outcome)	Additional information (sample outcome: number who buy the new product in a sample of 2 buyers)	Bayesian posterior probability	State (market for the new product)
		$\dfrac{.12}{.28} = .43$	Good ($p = .60$)
.28	0 out of 2 buys	$\dfrac{.16}{.28} = .57$	Poor ($p = .20$)
.44	1 out of 2 buys	$\dfrac{.36}{.44} = .82$	Good ($p = .60$)
		$\dfrac{.08}{.44} = .18$	Poor ($p = .20$)
.28	2 out of 2 buy	$\dfrac{.27}{.28} = .96$	Good ($p = .60$)
		$\dfrac{.01}{.28} = .04$	Poor ($p = .20$)

Figure 6-6 The reverse probability tree when we are obtaining additional information from a sample of 2 potential buyers.

computations we round or approximate the probabilities, we want to be sure that they sum exactly to 1. If they do not, we should adjust the probabilities so that they do sum exactly to 1. If in the present case the posterior probability of a good market (given that "0 out of 2 buy") is approximated at .43. The posterior probability of a poor market (given that same sample outcome) should be .57.]

Step 3: Move back through the main decision tree from left to right. *Illustration:* At the extreme right side of Figure 6-3 we compute an expected profit at each of the chance points. For example, after the sample outcome "0 out of 2 buy" the chance point associated with the act "introduce the new product" has a negative expected profit, − $710: .43($1,000) + .57(−$2,000) = − $710. After the *same* sample outcome, the expected profit associated with the act "do not produce the new product" is $0.

When we have computed an expected profit at each of these chance points we move back (to the left) to the decision points and place ourselves at these decision points one at a time.

At each of these decision points we reverse our view for a moment and look forward (to the right) to the expected profit associated with each of the acts (of course, here we have only the two acts). From the set of expected profits we choose the best one. At the same time we identify the act with the best expected profit as the act to take if in the actual sampling we get the sample outcome "0 out of 2 buy." Thus, in our example, the two expected profits given this sample outcome are −$710 and $0. The best is obviously $0, and so the best act given "0 out of 2 buy" is "do not introduce the new product."

We repeat this procedure for each of the other decision points. In our example, the other best expected profits are $460 and $880. After obtaining each of the best expected profits, we place each of them just above the appropriate decision points. For example, we place the $0 expected profit just above the decision point following the sample outcome "0 out of 2 buy." Finally, we multiply each of these expected profits by the probability of getting to the point where we can expect that profit. This means that we multiply the expected profit of $0 by the marginal probability of .28, the expected profit of $460 by the marginal probability of .44, and the expected profit of $880 by the marginal probability of .28.

Then, summing the products of these multiplications gives us the *expected profit using* the information from a sample of 2. It is $448.80 as seen in Figure 6-3.

But we want to know, too, the *expected value of* this sample information. That is, we want to know how much better our expected profit would be by taking this sample of 2.

Under prior information the maximum expected profit is $250. Since the *expected profit using* the sample information is $448.80, the *expected value of* the sample information is the difference, $198.80: $448.80 − $250 = $198.80.

What Is the Best Sample Size?

We have just illustrated in our marketing example the steps to be followed in obtaining the expected value of sample information. First, we found that the

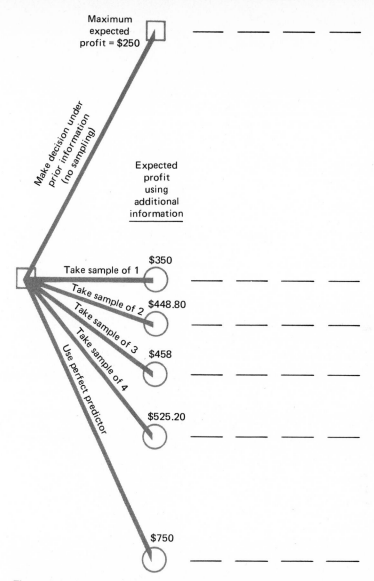

Figure 6-7 A partial decision tree of the sampling problem showing the expected profit using additional information from samples of four different sizes (and a perfect predictor).

expected profit using the information from a sample of 2 is $448.80. Then, since the best expected profit under prior information is $250, the expected value of additional information from a sample of 2 is $198.80.

But would not a larger sample help us more and have even a higher expected value? Would not a larger sample permit us to reduce further our probability of decision error and thus increase our expected profit using the information? Yes,

Table 6-2   Finding the Best Sample Size

Sample size	Expected profit using additional information from sample	Expected value of additional information from this sample	Sampling costs ($75 per unit sampled)	Expected net gain from this sample
1	$350.00	$100.00	$ 75.00	$25.00
2	448.80	198.80	150.00	48.80*
3	458.00	208.00	225.00	−17.00
4	525.20	275.20	300.00	−24.80
.				
.				
.				
Perfect predictor	750.00	500.00		

generally this is the case. Besides, we can determine how these expected values change as we vary the sample size.

We have gone ahead and computed the expected profit using the information from several different sample sizes. The results are shown in Figure 6-7. Each sample size involves taking a different path of obtaining additional information. It can be seen in Figure 6-7 that larger samples give rise to higher expected profits (using the associated sample information).

Also, since the best expected profit under prior information in all cases is $250, the expected value of sample information for the various sizes is also greater for larger samples. These results are shown in the first three columns of Table 6-2.

Also in Table 6-2 we see that although larger samples have larger expected values, they do not have as large an expected value as a perfect predictor has. Although if we were to continue to increase the size of the sample, ultimately we would approach the expected value of a perfect predictor which is $500.

But additional information usually costs something, and in order to determine which sample size actually is the best to take depends also on how much the various samples cost.

In our marketing example we are assuming that it costs $75 to sample each person. In Table 6-2 we have included a column that shows the total costs of each sample size. Also, in Table 6-2 for each sample size we subtract the sampling costs from the expected value of sample information. This gives us the *expected net gain* for each sample size.

The expected net gain for each sample size appears in the extreme right column of Table 6-2. The sample size with the maximum expected net gain is the best sample size (providing it is greater than $0). In our example we see that the best sample size is 2 with an expected net gain of $48.80. Larger samples yield more information and higher expected profits using the additional information, but when we take into account the larger costs of the larger samples the net gain is less.

SUMMARY

1 To obtain the expected value of the additional information from a sample, we proceed as we did in the previous chapter. We identify the best expected profit under prior information and then compute the expected profit *using* the additional information. The difference between the two expected profits gives us the *expected value of additional* (sample) *information*.

2 Larger samples reduce uncertainty further, but the reduction in uncertainty may cost more than it is worth. For each sample size we can compute an expected value of additional (sample) information.

3 The best sample size is the one that has the highest *expected net gain*. The expected net gain for a sample of a particular size is obtained by subtracting the sampling cost for that sample size from its expected value.

PROBLEMS

6-1 Consider again the marketing decision problem discussed in this chapter. Suppose that there is more uncertainty regarding the state of the market prior to any sampling than that indicated in the discussion. A good market and a poor market are now considered *equally likely*.

    a Under this different prior state of knowledge, what is the optimal act under prior information?

    b What is the expected profit *using* a perfect predictor?

    c What is the expected value of perfect information?

    d Does the change in the expected value of perfect information (due to the change in prior information) make sense? Explain.

6-2 With the new prior state of information indicated in Problem 6-1, let us see what a sample of 2 persons from the product market will be worth.

    a Construct a tree of the problem showing the decision under prior information and also after the sample outcome has been observed. Remember to obtain a new reverse tree and incorporate it into the larger decision tree.

    b What is the expected profit *using* the information from a sample of 2 persons?

    c What is the expected value of the sample information from 2 persons?

    d Compare your answer in *c* with the expected value of perfect information obtained in Problem 6-1c. Also, compare it with the expected value of sample information obtained in this chapter ($198.80). Explain the basis for any differences.

    e If it costs $75 to sample each person, is it worthwhile to take the sample? Explain your answer.

6-3 **a** With the prior information in Problems 6-1 and 6-2, would it be worthwhile to take a sample of 1 person if the sample costs $75? Construct a new tree showing the decision under prior information and also after the sample outcome of one person has been obtained. Remember to incorporate a new reverse tree into the larger decision tree.

    b Discuss the basis for your answer in *a*. Is it reasonable? [*Note:* Our assumption of only two states of the market makes this problem quite simplified, but its simplicity illustrates why sampling can have value: It can reduce decision error. Of course if additional information does not lead to a change in your decision (from the prior decision), it does not have any value. At least it has no value in terms of that decision.]

6-4 In Problems 2-1 and 2-2 a timber-products firm had the problem of deciding whether to produce plywood or regular lumber from logs that were acquired periodically. Recall that uncertainty got into the problem because a decision on which product to make from the logs had to be made before the quality of the logs was known.

In Problem 2-2 we examined the decision under prior information. The prior probability of the logs being of good quality was .50, and the probability of them being of poor quality was also .50. The profit consequences of the act-event combinations were given in Problem 2-2 and are to be used in this problem, too.

a Construct a tree of the problem representing the decision under prior information and also using a perfect predictor.

b What is the expected profit *using* a perfect predictor?

c What is the expected value of perfect information?

d Explain why a perfect predictor has the value obtained in *c*. Does it change one's decision in this problem? What would a perfect predictor be worth if the prior state of knowledge was one of certainty?

6-5 Continue with Problem 6-4. Now additional information on the quality of the logs can be obtained from an imperfect predictor before the decision is made on which product to make from them. A random sample of the logs in a batch can be taken early enough to use this information in making the product decision. Each log in the sample is tested for its quality and is classified as being good or defective. The "defective" classification refers to a poor-quality log that is not preferred in the production of either of the products. A "good" log is desirable in the production of either of the products.

The event of primary interest is the state of an entire batch of logs. Earlier we referred to each of the batches of logs being in one of two possible states, good quality or poor quality. Suppose that in a good-quality batch the typical proportion of defective logs is .20. (Let us refer to this proportion by the small letter p: $p = .20$.) In a poor-quality batch suppose the proportion defective is .40 ($p = .40$).

Now let us consider taking a random sample of two logs from an incoming batch of logs. We shall receive the test outcome on the quality of the logs sampled and then make the decision on which product to make.

a Construct a tree of the problem that represents the decision under prior information and also after the sample results are available.

b What is the probability of a good-quality batch of logs if 1 log out of 2 in the sample is found to be defective? Intuitively, which product do you think should be made?

c Given that 1 log out of 2 in the sample is defective, the production of which product will maximize expected profit? Compare this with your answer in *b*.

d What is the expected profit *using* the information from a sample of 2 logs from the incoming batch?

e What is the expected value of sample information (the sample of 2 logs)? Explain why it is worth this amount, and compare it with the expected value of perfect information obtained in 6-4*c*.

6-6 In Problem 4-12 we dealt with a sampling-type problem that we shall now use to illustrate general sampling procedures. Recall from Problem 4-12 that there were a large number of identical-looking earthen jars in a room. Each jar contains 10 balls. In each of the jars some of the balls are red and the rest are green. Some of the jars hold balls most of which are red, the others most of which are green. You are told that 80 percent of the jars contain mostly red balls, whereas the remaining 20 percent contain mostly green balls. Thus, this is known before any balls are drawn (that is, before any samples are taken) from any of the jars.

Suppose now we incorporate a decision element into the problem that did not appear in Problem 4-12. In Problem 4-12 we focused upon revising the prior probabilities of .80 and .20 in light of the additional information obtained from drawing a ball from the unidentified jar that was selected at random.

In this problem let us focus on making a decision on the basis of prior information alone. In subsequent problems we shall examine the making of the decision after obtaining additional information such as that obtained from drawing a ball (or balls) from the unidentified jar.

The two acts from which to choose in this problem are of a verbal type. Act 1 is "say the unidentified jar selected at random contains balls most of which are red." Act 2 is "say the unidentified jar selected at random contains balls most of which are green." If the statement you choose is correct, there is a profit; if it is wrong, there is a loss. The consequences of the act-event combinations are as follows: If you choose act 1 (that is, you say it is a mostly red jar) and it is such a jar, the profit is $300; if it is a mostly green jar, it is $-$900. If you choose act 2 (that is, you say it is a mostly green jar) and it is such a jar, the profit is $1,000; if it is a mostly red jar, it is $-$200.

a   Construct a tree diagram of the problem of making the decision under prior information.

b   Under prior information what is the optimal act and its expected profit?

6-7   a   In Problem 6-6 what is the expected profit *using* a perfect predictor?

b   What is the expected value of perfect information? Explain the basis for its value in this decision problem.

c   What is the expected value of perfect information in Problem 6-6 if, instead of being told that 80 percent of the jars contain balls most of which are red and 20 percent most of which are green, you were told that these percentages are *reversed?* (Now 20 percent of the jars contain balls most of which are red.) Explain why your answer is different from that obtained in *b*.

6-8   Now we can sample before making the decision discussed in Problem 6-6. In addition to the original prior probabilities you are now informed that each of the "mostly red" jars contains 6 red and 4 green balls. Each of the "mostly green" jars contains 1 red and 9 green balls. We can also refer to the jars by the proportion of balls that are red. That is, the mostly red jars have 60 percent of the balls red ($p = .60$), and the mostly green jars have only 10 percent that are red ($p = .10$).

a   Construct a tree representing the decision (taking act 1 or act 2 defined in Problem 6-6) under prior information and also making the decision after the outcome of one draw from the unidentified jar is known. Construct a reverse probability tree on the side (or use the one you constructed in Problem 4-12) and incorporate it into the larger decision tree. In constructing the initial and reverse trees, refer to the sample outcomes each by the *number* of red balls observed.

b   What is the expected profit *using* the information from one draw from the unidentified jar?

c   What is the expected value of one draw from the unidentified jar? What is the basis for its value? Compare it with your answer Problem 6-7*b*.

d   What is the expected value of one draw from the unidentified jar if you are informed that 20 percent of the jars contain balls most of which are red and 80 percent contain balls most of which are green? Explain the basis for your answer and why your answer is different from that obtained in c.

6-9 Let us continue with Problem 6-8c and see what would happen if we take a sample of 2 (that is, if we draw 2 balls from the unidentified jar) before making our decision to take act 1 or act 2.

   a   Construct a tree representing the decision under prior information and also after we obtain the outcome from the sample of 2 balls. Do this in conjunction with the following part b. Refer to the type of jar (the state) as a population with a proportion red (that is, with $p = .60$ or $p = .10$) and the sample outcomes as 0, 1, or 2 red balls.

   b   Construct a reverse probability tree (on the side) and incorporate it into the larger decision tree in a. To obtain the conditional probabilities of the sample outcomes in the initial probability tree, construct another probability tree (also, on the side) representing the sampling from a population where the proportion of red balls is .60 ($p = .60$) and then where the proportion of red balls is .10 ($p = .10$).

   c   Give a verbal interpretation of the revision of the prior probabilities after observing the possible outcomes from a sample of 2.

   d   What is the expected profit *using* the information from a sample of 2?

   e   What is the expected value of the information from a sample of 2?

   f   Compare your answer in e with the expected value of the information from a sample of 1 obtained in Problem 6-8c and the expected value of perfect information obtained in Problem 6-7b. Explain the basis for any differences in your answers.

6-10 Suppose the sampling costs are $110 for each item in the sample (for each ball drawn) in Problem 6-9.

   a   Does it pay to sample at all?

   b   Compute the expected net gain for the sample sizes of 1 and 2. From this set of two sample sizes, which is optimal?

6-11 With respect to a component part in its competitive-model compact car, a manufacturer is faced with a choice between buying batches of components from a supplier either under a guarantee arrangement or under a no-guarantee arrangement. The batches of components vary in the proportion of the units that are defective. The proportion defective tends to be either .10 or .60, but it cannot be known in advance.

Each defective unit must be reworked before it can be used. The rework cost is estimated to be $4 per unit. Thus, a batch with the higher proportion of defective units involves substantially higher rework costs.

Under the no-guarantee arrangement the cost of a batch of 200 units is $1,000. The additional rework cost must be borne by the car manufacturer, and these costs cannot be known in advance. But it is known that 40 percent of the past batches have had a .10 proportion defective, and 60 percent have had a .60 proportion defective.

Under the guarantee arrangement the cost is $1,300 for a batch of 200 units. Under this arrangement, any rework costs for more than 10 percent of the components will be assumed by the supplier of the components. Thus, the cost of this alternative can be known in advance. In addition to the $1,300, it is known that rework costs of $80 will be incurred (but no more than $80).

   a   Construct a tree representing the decision on which arrangement to choose

under prior information. From the data given above, obtain the cost consequences for each act-event combination.

b What is the optimal act and its expected cost under prior information?

c Construct a tree representing the decision on which arrangement to choose
using a perfect predictor. What is the expected cost *using* a perfect predictor?

d What is the expected value of perfect information? Discuss the basis for its
value.

6-12 Continue with Problem 6-11. Suppose now that a sample from a new shipment can
be taken before choosing the guarantee or no-guarantee arrangement offered by the
parts supplier.

a Construct a tree representing the decision (on the guarantee arrangement)
under prior information and also making the decision after the outcome of a
sample of 1 unit from the new shipment is known. Construct a reverse
probability tree on the side and incorporate it into the larger tree.

b What is the expected cost *using* the information from a random sample of just
one of the parts of the new shipment?

c What is the expected value of sample information (if the sample size is 1)?
Compare your answer with the expected value of perfect information obtained
in 6-11*d*. Explain the basis for any difference.

6-13 Continue with Problems 6-11 and 6-12. Now suppose a sample of 2 units can be
taken from the new shipment before making the decision on which guarantee
arrangement to take.

a Construct a tree of the decision under prior information and also after a sample
of 2 units has been obtained. Construct a reverse probability tree on the side
and incorporate it into the larger decision tree. Obtain the conditional probabilities of the sample outcomes (0, 1, or 2 defective) in the initial probability tree by
constructing still another probability tree on the side that represents the possible sample outcomes from a shipment with a .10 proportion defective ($p = .10$)
and another from a shipment with .60 proportion defective ($p = .60$).

b What is the expected cost *using* the information from a sample of 2?

c What is the expected value of sample information when the sample size is 2?

d Compare your answer in *c* with that obtained in Problem 6-11*d* for a perfect
predictor and with that obtained in Problem 6-12*c* for a sample of 1 unit.

6-14 a If in Problems 6-11, 6-12, and 6-13 the sampling cost is $2 per unit in addition to
a fixed charge of $10, would it pay to sample at all? Compute the expected
net gain for a sample of 1 unit and for a sample of 2 units.

b If sampling is worthwhile, what is the optimal sample size if you consider only
the sample sizes of 1 and 2? Discuss the reason for your answer.

c To find the expected value of sample information for a sample of 3 units
involves heavier computation. Therefore, if you have some computational
assistance, obtain the expected cost *using* the information from a sample of 3
units and then the expected value of sample information for a sample of 3 units.

d Obtain the expected net gain for the sample sizes of 1, 2, and 3 units.

e What is the optimal sample size if you consider only the sample sizes of 1, 2,
and 3? Explain the basis for your answer.

Chapter 7

Opportunity Losses and Utilities in Decision Making under Uncertainty

In the first part of this chapter we shall focus on the cost of errors in our decision making, particularly those errors due to our uncertainty. True, we have discussed aspects of this topic in earlier chapters, but now we shall look at decision errors in a slightly different way. It turns out to be a very useful task, as we shall see shortly.

In this connection, the concept of *opportunity loss* is discussed. This concept refers to losses in the opportunity for greater attainment of an objective (such as profit) because of our failure to take the most profitable act. We shall see that under conditions of uncertainty the chance of incurring opportunity losses cannot be avoided entirely.

The second part of this chapter is concerned with those situations in which the criterion we have been using so far (the maximization of expected profit) is not satisfactory. When a decision maker prefers to avoid risk (or in some instances to seek it), the maximization-of-expected-profit criterion usually is not a satisfactory one. What, then, can we do?

It turns out that procedures in *modern utility theory* are useful in such cases, and, furthermore, they provide a framework for a general theory of decision making under uncertainty of very wide applicability. This general theory has relevance far beyond our primary concern here, which is decision making involving monetary consequences.

OPPORTUNITY LOSSES: THE COST OF DECISION ERROR

We indicated above that in this chapter we shall look at decision making under uncertainty in a different way. Here we focus on the mistakes (the errors) that we might make in our decisions and their cost to us.

In a loose sense, we are now looking at decisions under uncertainty with the idea of finding out how much better we could do if the uncertainty were not present. This gives us a measure of the cost of the uncertainty in terms of its interference with attaining the highest possible levels of our objective (such as the highest profit). The concept of *opportunity loss* refers to this cost (or loss) due to our failure to take the best act.

Opportunity Losses under Certainty

Although we are concerned primarily with decision making under uncertainty in this part of the book, the simplest illustration of opportunity losses comes from examples in decision making under *certainty*.

A slight modification of our packaging-machine problem in Chapter 2 provides a clear example. Recall that we had to make a decision on using either the old or the new machine to package products for shipment.

But in the earlier discussion there was uncertainty with regard to the quality of the materials at the time a decision had to be made on which machine to use. This uncertainty, in turn, gave rise to uncertainty regarding the profit consequences for each act.

Suppose, however, that we now know for sure (with certainty) that the materials are of good quality. This new decision problem can be represented by the tree shown in Figure 7-1. It is a very simple problem, too, because there is only one possible profit consequence for each act. This makes it easy to choose the best act. We merely select the one with the highest profit consequence. The best act is "use new machine" with a profit of $240. Obviously, it is better than the act "use old machine" with a profit of $200.

But our purpose is to illustrate opportunity losses. Recall that an opportunity loss represents a loss in the opportunity for greater attainment of our objective (here, it is profit).

Thus, in Figure 7-1 we have an opportunity loss for each act. For the act "use old machine" we would realize $200 in profit. But this $200 profit is $40 less than the $240 profit that could have been realized if the act "use new machine" had been taken. *This $40 difference is the opportunity loss for the act "use old machine."* We call it a "cost" of decision error because that is the cost in profit if that act is taken rather than the most profitable act.

The best act under certainty will always have an opportunity loss of $0. If the most profitable act is taken, no greater profits are foregone (are lost), and therefore the opportunity loss is $0. (*Note:* Opportunity losses are never negative. No profits are lost if we choose the most profitable act.)

Thus, if the consequences of the alternative acts are represented in terms of opportunity losses, a criterion for the selection of the best (most profitable) act is

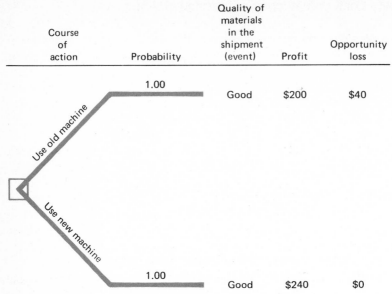

Course of action	Probability	Quality of materials in the shipment (event)	Profit	Opportunity loss
Use old machine	1.00	Good	$200	$40
Use new machine	1.00	Good	$240	$0

Figure 7-1 Opportunity losses in a decision under certainty.

to select the act with the *minimum* opportunity loss. Of course in our example in Figure 7-1 we have just the two acts and the two opportunity losses of $40 and $0.

The minimum of the two opportunity losses obviously is $0 and is associated with the most profitable act "use new machine." Thus, either the maximization-of-profit criterion or the minimization-of-opportunity-loss criterion can be used to select the best profit act. (*Note:* This is useful to know in verifying or checking computations, too.)

But the main point of opportunity losses is that the opportunity loss of the most profitable act (here, "use new machine") is *a measure of the cost of uncertainty.*

Of course in this example we have assumed conditions of certainty, and so we would expect the cost of uncertainty to be $0 (because, of course, there is no uncertainty). It is $0 for the most profitable act as seen in Figure 7-1. However, in decision making under uncertainty the most profitable act in terms of expected profit will always have an (expected) opportunity loss greater than $0.

This is so because under conditions of uncertainty we cannot be sure of the actual consequence of each act. Therefore, we cannot avoid the possibility of decision error and an opportunity loss. As long as there is some probability of incurring an opportunity loss (even though the probability is small), the expected opportunity loss will be greater than $0.

Opportunity Losses under Uncertainty

Let us return to the original packaging-machine problem of Chapter 2 where there is uncertainty with regard to the quality of the materials. We repeat this problem in Figure 7-2, but now include opportunity losses, too.

In Figure 7-2 we have an opportunity loss for each act-event (act-state) combination. Just as we have a profit for each act-event combination, we also have a "loss of profit" (an opportunity loss) for each act-event combination.

In computing the opportunity losses in Figure 7-2, we assume *temporarily* that a particular event (state) occurs, such as "good-quality materials." Then, with this event given, we identify the best profit amount associated with the given event "good-quality materials." The profit amounts are $200 and $240. It is $200 if the act "use old machine" is taken, whereas it is $240 if the act taken is "use new machine."

Of these two profit amounts, clearly $240 is the maximum. Thus, if we take the act "use old machine" (given this event) and get only $200 profit, the opportunity loss is $40: $240 − $200 = $40. The profit for this act (given "good-quality materials") is $200, which is $40 less than the $240 profit that would be realized if the act "use new machine" is taken with this event.

If we take the act "use new machine" (given this event), the profit is $240. The opportunity loss for this act-event combination is $0 because no higher profits would be possible (given this event).

Now let us assume temporarily that the other event "poor-quality materials" occurs. The profit amounts associated with this event are $160 (with the

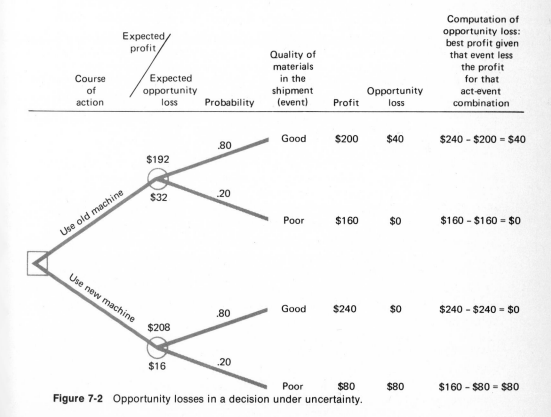

Figure 7-2 Opportunity losses in a decision under uncertainty.

act "use old machine") and $80 (with the act "use new machine"). The maximum profit here is obviously $160.

Thus, if we take the act "use old machine," the opportunity loss is $0 (there is no profit that is better). However, if the act taken is "use new machine," the opportunity loss is $80: $160 − $80 = $80. The profit for this act-event combination is $80, and the profit "lost" is $80 because the best act ("use old machine" with a profit of $160) was not taken.

In our packaging-machine example we now have both a profit outcome and an opportunity-loss outcome for each act-event combination (as seen in Figure 7-2). Since we have probabilities for each of these outcomes, we can compute an expected profit and also an expected opportunity loss for each act.

We have computed expected profits many times before whereby we multiply each profit amount by its probability of occurrence and add the products of the multiplications. As seen in Figure 7-2, we record for the act "use old machine" the expected profit of $192 above the appropriate chance point. For the act "use new machine" we place the expected profit of $208 above the appropriate chance point for that act.

We compute an *expected opportunity loss* for each act in the same way that we compute an expected profit for each act. The probabilities of the profit outcomes are also the correct probabilities of the opportunity-loss outcomes.

Thus, as seen in Figure 7-2, for the act-event combination "use old machine" and "good-quality materials," the $40 opportunity loss has a probability of .80 (the same probability as the $200 profit). The opportunity loss of $0 for the act-event combination "use old machine" and "poor-quality materials" has a probability of .20 (the same probability as the $160 profit).

The expected opportunity loss for the act "use old machine" is simply the expected value of another random variable (opportunity loss) whereby we multiply the $40 opportunity loss by its .80 probability which gives us $32. The $0 opportunity loss is multiplied by the probability of .20 and gives us a product of $0. Adding these two products gives us an expected opportunity loss of $32: $32 + $0 = $32. We place this $32 expected opportunity loss just below the chance point associated with taking the act "use old machine."

Similarly, for the other act "use new machine" the opportunity loss of $0 is multiplied by its probability of .80, giving us a product of $0. The opportunity loss of $80 is multiplied by its probability of .20, giving us a product of $16. Adding the two products gives us an expected opportunity loss of $16: $0 + $16 = $16. We place this $16 expected opportunity loss just below the chance point associated with the act "use new machine."

Thus for each act we have an expected opportunity loss. But what does it mean? Essentially, we can think of it this way: If we repeatedly took the act "use old machine," our average profit would tend toward $192 per decision and our *average profit lost* (expected opportunity loss) would be $32 (because of our failure at times to take the most profitable act). Eighty percent of the time we would be making a decision error, and it would cost us $40 in profit each time.

If we took the act "use new machine," our average profit would tend toward $208 and our average profit lost (expected opportunity loss) would be $16. For this act the .20 probability of decision error is less, but the $80 cost of the error (if it occurs) is greater. The small probability contributes to the smaller expected opportunity loss.

We can see that whatever act we take under uncertainty we expose ourselves to the chance of decision error and opportunity loss. The expected opportunity loss for each act gives us a measure of this loss of profit.

Also from Figure 7-2 we can see that the act with the minimum expected opportunity loss is the act with the maximum expected profit. This will always be the case for such problems. Thus, to obtain the best profit act, we can alternatively search for the act with the lowest expected opportunity loss.

Note, too, in Figure 7-2 that the expected opportunity loss of the best act is not $0. It is $16. Under uncertainty it cannot be $0 because even when we take the best act, profits may be lost because of a wrong decision. In this problem the lowest "average loss of profit" is $16 per decision.

Thus, if the best we can do is to lose only $16 in profit per decision (because of our uncertainty), we could say that our uncertainty is costing us $16 per decision. If that is what the uncertainty is costing us, the removal of the uncertainty must be worth the same amount, $16.

The removal of the uncertainty is what a perfect predictor achieves. Thus, we can also say that a perfect predictor in this decision situation would be worth $16.

Notice what we have just done. We have obtained the expected value of a perfect predictor (the expected value of perfect information) with very little effort. All that we needed was the expected opportunity loss of the best act. Thus, we have the following:

$$
\begin{array}{c}
\text{Expected} \\
\text{opportunity} \\
\text{loss of} \\
\text{the best act}
\end{array}
=
\begin{array}{c}
\text{expected} \\
\text{value of} \\
\text{perfect} \\
\text{information}
\end{array}
$$

The important practical value of this shortcut is that we obtain the expected value of perfect information directly from the prior probabilities and the opportunity losses. There is no need (as there is in the case of all imperfect predictors) to undertake the analysis and computation of the expected profit using a predictor (in the lower section of the tree as we did in Chapters 5 and 6) and then to observe the difference between it and the expected profit under prior information only.

Once again, the most general relationship regarding perfect and imperfect predictors is the following:

$$
\begin{array}{c}
\text{Expected} \\
\text{value of} \\
\text{additional} \\
\text{information}
\end{array}
=
\begin{array}{c}
\text{expected} \\
\text{profit} \\
\text{using the} \\
\text{additional} \\
\text{information}
\end{array}
-
\begin{array}{c}
\text{expected} \\
\text{profit} \\
\text{under prior} \\
\text{information} \\
\text{only}
\end{array}
$$

The above relationship holds for all predictors whether they are perfect or imperfect. What we have discussed in this chapter is the point that for the perfect predictor (and the perfect predictor only) we can obtain its expected value by a shortcut method involving prior analysis only.

In the Chapter 5 discussion we obtained this very $16 expected value of perfect information (in this packaging-machine problem) by the longer method. A review of that section will illustrate the advantage of the shortcut method we have discussed here.

Another practical point is this: Even though in real problems only imperfect predictors are available, a rough idea of what a good imperfect predictor is worth can be obtained by computing the expected value of a perfect predictor from the prior analysis, as we have done.

Of course the imperfect predictor will be worth less than the perfect predictor, but we can easily determine the expected value of perfect information and then say that an imperfect predictor will definitely not be worth more than this amount. Of course it will actually be worth something less. Therefore, if the cost of an imperfect predictor is equal to or greater than the expected value of perfect information, the use of any imperfect predictor would not be justified under the maximization-of-expected-profit criterion. Its expected value would be less than its cost.

USING UTILITIES IN DECISION MAKING UNDER UNCERTAINTY

In our discussions of decision making under uncertainty so far we have used primarily the maximization-of-expected-profit criterion. But as we get closer to real-world decision problems, we find that there are some difficulties encountered in its direct use. Now is the time to examine these difficulties and become acquainted with the main ways to overcome them.

Difficulties Encountered Using the Maximization-of-Expected-Profit Criterion

Unless we are quite sure that the maximization-of-expected-profit criterion is appropriate for the person or organization faced with making a decision, we should be very careful in its use. In this way it is just one of the many elements and assumptions of the model that should be subjected to the usual tests of real-world fit or validity.

We should recall, too, that there is much that is implicit in any model or procedure. Of course this statement applies to the use of the maximization-of-expected-profit criterion as well as to other procedures.

What is implicit in the use of this criterion is that each additional dollar of profit is assumed to be of equal "attractiveness" or "subjective worth" to the decision maker. Thus, if for some act the possible profit outcomes range from $0 to $100, the computation of an expected profit implicitly gives just as much weight (subjective worth) to the first dollar of additional profit as is given to the ninety-ninth dollar of additional profit. That is, each dollar of additional profit is assumed to have the same attractiveness or "subjective value" to the decision maker.

Thus, to use this criterion freely, the decision maker should have no greater preference for the first additional dollar than (say) for the ninety-ninth additional dollar.

Consequently, in fairly simple decision problems it is not surprising to find that persons who have a greater preference for the first additional dollars of profit (than for subsequent additional dollars of profit) *do not* make choices in accord with the maximization-of-expected-profit criterion.

Indeed, it is common for persons with limited financial resources to choose acts that would not be the best in terms of expected profit. For such persons, we shall see, it would be clearly inappropriate to use the maximization-of-expected-profit criterion for larger and more complex decision problems.

Therefore, some other criterion is needed that reflects the perhaps unique subjective values for additional dollars of profit for each decision maker. The criterion must make sense to the decision maker, too; and when applied to a small decision problem that he or she can fully comprehend, the criterion must select the same act as the person does intuitively (without the use of the criterion).

The Maximization-of-Expected-Utility Criterion

Fortunately, others have gone this way before and have developed procedures in *modern utility theory* that provide a criterion for such decision problems. It is called the *maximization-of-expected-utility criterion.*

There is an elusiveness to some aspects of this procedure primarily because of the subjective values for the profit consequences that it attempts to capture. But the representation of subjective considerations is a difficult undertaking. And there is no other way because the important consequences of act-event combinations in a deeper and more realistic sense are always of a subjective nature.

Roughly, how does the procedure work? First, we obtain for each profit outcome a *utility value* that reflects the person's underlying preferences for the profit outcomes. We shall discuss shortly the way in which this is done. (In one sense the utilities obtained are values of still another random variable defined on the same basic events.)

Second, for each act we compute an *expected utility.* An expected utility of an act is obtained just as expected profits are obtained for acts except that the probability of each profit outcome is now multiplied by its associated utility instead of the profit. Again, the products of the multiplications are added, and the sum is the expected utility of that act.

Third, we examine the expected utility of each act and select the act with the highest expected utility. We then say that this is the best act for the decision maker for whom the utilities were derived.

Different persons, of course, have different underlying preferences for additional profit amounts; and, thus, for the very same decision problem with the same profit outcomes (and probabilities), a different person would typically indicate another set of utility values. Consequently, for another person the expected utility of each act typically would be different and, in turn, the best act (the one with the maximum expected utility) may well be different.

Let us illustrate the use of this criterion by taking the packaging-machine example from previous chapters and see what the best decision is for a person whose utility values for the profit outcomes have already been derived.

Later we shall see how these utility values are derived, but let us make one comment right now on the utility values. The utility values for a person usually range from 0.00 to 1.00. Another range of values could be used, but this range is perhaps the simplest with which to work and has been the most widely used.

Thus, let us assign the following utility values to the different profit outcomes for the packaging-machine problem as shown in Figure 7-3. A utility value of .97 is assigned to the $200 profit outcome, a utility of .92 to the $160 profit outcome, a utility of .99 to the $240 profit outcome, and a utility of .75 to the $80 profit outcome.

Next, we compute the expected utility for each act. For the act "use old

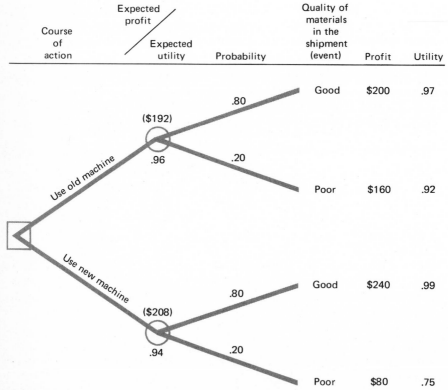

Figure 7-3 One set of utility values associated with the profit outcomes in the machine example.

machine'' the utility of .97 is multiplied by the .80 probability, and the utility of .92 is multiplied by the .20 probability. Adding the two products of the multiplications gives us an expected utility of .96 as follows:

$$\begin{matrix} \text{Expected} \\ \text{utility} \\ \text{of ``use} \\ \text{old machine''} \end{matrix} = .80\,(.97) + .20\,(.92)$$

$$= .96$$

And, for the other act:

$$\begin{matrix} \text{Expected} \\ \text{utility} \\ \text{of ``use} \\ \text{new machine''} \end{matrix} = .80\,(.99) + .20\,(.75)$$

$$= .94$$

Thus, the best act for this person by the maximization-of-expected-utility criterion is ''use old machine'' (which has the highest expected utility). Note that this is *not* the act with the maximum expected profit. (We show in Figure 7-3 the expected profit for each act in parentheses above the appropriate chance point.)

The use of the maximization-of-expected-profit criterion would have selected the other act ''use new machine.'' This act, however, is not the best act when the decision maker's underlying preferences for the profit outcomes are taken into account (as they are through the use of the utilities).

The important point, however, is that the procedures using the maximization-of-expected-utility criterion can be applied to decision problems of considerable size and complexity. As we have noted before, the formal procedures are not limited in the way that our intuitive processes are.

But we need utilities to attach to the profit outcomes. In the next section we discuss how we obtain them.

Obtaining the Utility Values for a Decision Maker

The general idea of the procedure by which we obtain utility values for the profit outcomes is to *create* a small decision problem under uncertainty for the decision maker. His or her decision regarding this small problem (perhaps arrived at by intuitive means) will reveal something about that person's underlying preferences for profit outcomes.

It may seem strange to create *more* uncertainty for the decision maker than the individual already has, but it actually serves as a means of achieving in large decision situations the selection of acts that are more likely to be in accord with the person's true preferences.

From the decision on this small problem we can obtain for the decision maker a utility value for a particular profit amount. A series of such small decision problems will provide a sufficient number of utility values for what we really have in mind—the larger and more complex decision problems which would overwhelm the decision maker's intuition (if utility procedures are not used).

Let us now describe in more detail the six steps by which these utility-values for a decision maker can be obtained.

Step 1. Construct a simple two-act decision problem under uncertainty, such as the one shown in Figure 7-4. Act 1 must have two profit outcomes, and act 2 must have only one. Act 1 involves uncertain profit outcomes, whereas act 2 has a single (certain) profit outcome.

The two profit outcomes for act 1 should have a range that encompasses any possible profit outcome for which "real" decisions are anticipated by the decision maker.

For the packaging-machine example a range of $0 to $250 would be adequate, but it should be made large enough for all decision problems that might arise.

Step 2. Assign a profit amount to the only outcome of act 2. The profit amount assigned is one selected *between* the extreme profit outcomes of act 1.

For the packaging-machine example this means we select a profit amount between $0 and $250. Suppose we select $50. (This can be done somewhat arbitrarily, but to obtain useful results, they should not lie close to either of the extreme profit values.)

Step 3. Assign a probability of 1.00 to the highest profit of act 1 and a probability of 0.00 to the lowest profit outcome of that act.

In our example in Figure 7-4 it is a probability of 1.00 on the $250 profit and 0.00 probability on the $0 profit.

Then, we have the decision maker begin to make a series of decisions as we alter the probabilities. First, we ask the person to indicate which act he or she prefers with the probability assignments of 1.00 and 0.00.

This first decision, however, is essentially a trivial one because it would involve (in the example we are using) asking the decision maker to make a choice: $250 for sure or $50 for sure. Suppose the choice is act 1, as expected.

We continue with the series of decisions leaving everything the same except the probabilities on act 1. Suppose we proceed by lowering from 1.00 to .90 the probability on the highest profit outcome (here, $250). The probability of .90 on the $250 profit implies a probability of .10 on $0 profit. (These changes in the probabilities can be larger or smaller.)

Now if the decision maker still shows a preference for act 1, we decrease the .90 probability to a still lower level. Suppose we reduce it to .80 and then ask for a choice.

If he or she still prefers act 1, we reduce the probability on the higher profit outcome ($250) still further. We continue to decrease this probability (in steps) until the *decision maker says he or she does not prefer one act over the other.* At this point we say that the person shows an "indifference" between the two acts.

It is at this point of indifference between the acts that the probability

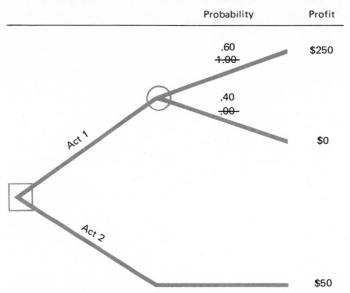

	Probability	Profit

.60
~~1.00~~
$250

.40
~~.00~~
$0

Act 1

Act 2

$50

Figure 7-4   A small problem presented to the decision maker in order to derive a utility value for a particular profit outcome ($50).

assignments are very important. Suppose they are .60 on $250 and .40 on $0 (as shown in Figure 7-4). These probabilities play a crucial role in the steps that follow.

Step 4. From the decision made in step 3, we now shall see how we can obtain a utility value to assign to the $50 (certain) profit outcome in act 2.

How does this work? We summarize it in Figure 7-5. First, we assign a *utility* of 1.00 to the highest profit outcome of act 1 (here it is $250). Then, we assign a utility of 0.00 to the lowest profit outcome of act 1 (here it is $0, but it could be a positive or a negative profit instead of $0).

As we said before, the utility values of 1.00 and 0.00 are indeed somewhat arbitrary; other numbers could be used, but they are the simplest ones with which to work.

Now, with utility values associated with the profit outcomes of act 1 we can compute for act 1 an *expected utility*. It is .60 and is obtained as follows:

$$\text{Expected utility of act 1} = (\text{probability})\begin{pmatrix}\text{utility}\\\text{for }\$250\end{pmatrix} + (\text{probability})\begin{pmatrix}\text{utility}\\\text{for }\$0\end{pmatrix}$$

$$= .60\,(1.00) + .40\,(0.00)$$
$$= .60$$

We place this expected utility of .60 under the chance point associated with act 1 shown in Figure 7-5.

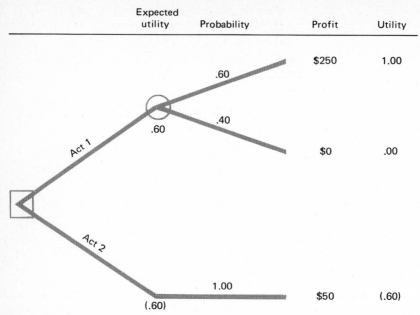

Figure 7-5 Obtaining a .60 utility value for the $50 profit outcome.

Now comes the most important part of this step. Since the decision maker showed an equal preference for act 1 and act 2 (when the probabilities for the act 1 outcomes were .60 and .40), it follows that the number that represents the expected utility for one of the acts (act 1) can be used to represent the expected utility for taking the other act (act 2). We have an expected utility for one of the acts. It is for act 1 and is .60.

Because act 2 was indicated to be equally preferable to act 1, we can use the same .60 to represent the expected utility of act 2. We indicate this in Figure 7-5 by placing the .60 expected utility in parentheses at the end of the branch representing act 2.

Now the final point: Since act 2 has but the single $50 profit outcome, the .60 expected utility of act 2 implies that the utility of $50 is .60.

More formally, we obtain the .60 utility of $50 profit as follows:

$$\text{Expected utility of act 2} = (\text{probability})\ (\text{utility for \$50})$$

We now know that the expected utility of act 2 is .60. Thus, we substitute .60 into the left-hand side of the above expression. We also know that the probability on the right-hand side is 1.00 and so we substitute 1.00 for the probability of the single outcome.

Table 7-1   Utility Values for Various Profit Outcomes that Were Derived for a Decision Maker

Profit outcome	Utility value for profit outcome
$ 0	.00
50	.60
100	.80
150	.90
250	1.00

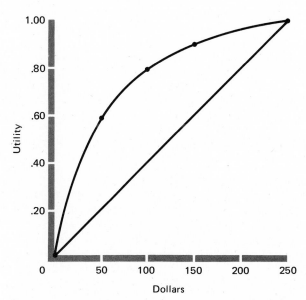

Figure 7-6 Drawing a smooth curve through the points gives a concave utility-for-profit graph.

.60 = (1.00) (utility for $50)

Then, multiplying the right-hand side and rearranging the terms, we have the following:

Utility for $50 = .60

We record in parentheses this .60 utility value in the appropriate column in Figure 7-5.

Step 5. We record in a table (such as in Table 7-1) the .60 utility for the profit outcome of $50. We also place in the table utility values of 1.00 for $250 profit and 0.00 for $0 profit.

Utility values for profit amounts other than $50 are obtained by repeating the above steps with the certain profit outcome set alternatively at amounts other than $50. In our example we have set the (certain) profit outcome of act 2 first at $100 and then at $150. For each of these amounts we repeated all of the steps The results are recorded in Table 7-1. A utility of .80 was obtained for $100 profit and a utility of .90 for $150 profit.

Step 6. Construct a utility graph from the utility-for-profit data obtained in the previous steps (such as that in Table 7-1). Profit is customarily plotted on the horizontal axis and utility on the vertical axis.

Plotting the associated pairs of profit and utility values, we obtain the five points (represented by the large dots) in Figure 7-6.

We then draw a smooth curve through the five points in Figure 7-6. Of course, the more points we have the better. We now have for the decision maker a *utility graph* for profit.

For another person we would no doubt obtain different points and thus a different utility graph.

Using the Utility Graph to Make Larger Decisions

Having obtained for a decision maker a utility graph for profit, we are able to use it in larger and more complex decision problems. We illustrated such a use earlier in the packaging-machine example shown in Figure 7-3. Of course it is still a small decision problem, but it can be used to illustrate the procedure.

The utility values assigned to the profit outcomes in a larger real-world problem would come from a utility graph such as the one in Figure 7-6. First, we observe what the possible profit outcomes in the real-world problem are. In Figure 7-3, for example, they are $200, $160, $240, and $80.

We then go to the utility graph as in Figure 7-6, specifically to the points on the horizontal (profit) axis that correspond to the profit outcomes of our real-world decision problem.

For example, we identify the point on the horizontal axis corresponding to $200 of profit and then go up to the graph and observe its "height" (the utility value associated with that profit). We see that is is approximately .97. And for $160, $240, and $80 we find the approximate utility values to be .92, .99, and .75, respectively. We can actually obtain from the utility graph in Figure 7-6 an approximate utility value for any profit amount between $0 and $250.

Finally, we associate a utility value with each profit outcome and compute the expected utility for each act, such as is done in Figure 7-3. There, we find that the act with the maximum expected utility is "use old machine."

Once again, remember that this procedure can be applied to decision problems with many alternative acts and many profit outcomes for each act. It is in such large problems that sole reliance on intuitive decision making can be hazardous. Often there can be much gain in rational decision making through the use of the procedures we have discussed.

A Note on Risk Aversion

We have remarked that each decision maker has perhaps unique preferences for profit outcomes. Thus, for each decision maker, a different utility graph is likely to be obtained by the procedure described above.

Although each of us would perhaps have a different utility graph, there are three general classes of utility graphs:

1 Those that are *concave;* such graphs are associated with *risk-averse* decision makers.
2 A *straight-line* graph; this graph is associated with *risk-neutral* decision makers.
3 Those that are *convex;* such graphs are associated with *risk-seeking* decision makers.

Risk-Averse Decision Makers   Utility graphs of the curved-type obtained in Figure 7-6 are called *concave.* In such concave graphs the utility values increase as profit amounts increase, but the slope of the graph is decreasing over the entire range of possible profit amounts.

Thus, the rate of increase in utility is higher for the first dollar of profit than for any other dollar of profit in that range. (In some discussions we would refer to this as an illustration of the "diminishing marginal utility for money.")

Such a concave utility graph is associated with a *risk-averse* decision maker. This term is easy to misinterpret. It does *not* mean that the decision maker avoids (is averse to) all uncertainty in decision making; it simply means that he or she is not inclined to take acts involving some uncertainty *unless* the expected profits of the acts involving such uncertainty are considerably higher than those of the alternative acts yielding a certain profit outcome.

We would describe the curved utility graph in Figure 7-6 as that of a risk-averse decision maker. This person is not inclined to take an act involving some uncertainty unless such an act has an expected profit considerably higher than that of an act with a certainty profit outcome. This is illustrated by the tree in Figure 7-5 (which shows the decision maker's indifference between the two acts).

If in Figure 7-5 we compute the expected profit for act 1, we get $150: .60 ($250) + .40 ($0) = $150. Now this decision maker has said that he or she was indifferent between act 1 (with an expected profit of $150) and act 2 (with a certain profit of $50). This implies that if act 1 had an expected profit greater than $150, it would be chosen over act 2. Thus, the decision maker will take the "risky" act if the expected profit is high enough.

But we would also have to say that this person is quite risk-averse. The expected profit of act 1 (when he or she showed an indifference between it and act 2) is quite high compared with the certain profit outcome of act 2 ($150 compared with $50).

A decision maker with less risk aversion would indicate an indifference between act 1 and act 2 when the expected profit of act 1 is lower than the $150. In terms of the associated utility graphs they would be less concave (less curved) and would lie closer to the *straight-line* graph that is also shown in Figure 7-6. Thus, we can visualize utility graphs that become flatter and flatter and approach the straight-line graph in Figure 7-6.

Risk-Neutral Decision Makers   As the utility graphs become straight lines, risk aversion disappears, and we refer to the decision maker with such a utility graph as being *risk-neutral*.

A risk-neutral decision maker would be indifferent between act 1 and act 2 (in Figure 7-5) when the expected profit of act 1 is $50, the same as the certain profit outcome of act 2. To him, $50 for certain is no more preferable than an act involving uncertainty with an expected profit of $50.

Furthermore, for such a decision maker, there is really no need to bother with utilities at all in the real-world decision problems because in this case the maximization-of-expected-profit criterion would always select the very same act as that selected by the maximization-of-expected-utility criterion.

Risk-Seeking Decision Makers   The final class of utility graphs is perhaps the least common. A *convex* utility graph is essentially the opposite of one that is concave.

In a convex utility graph the rate of increase in utility is lower for the first dollar of profit than for any other dollar of profit (in the range considered). The entire graph lies below the straight-line utility graph.

A decision maker with such a utility graph is referred to as a *risk-seeker*. This term refers to a decision maker who prefers acts involving uncertainty where the expected profit of such acts is *less* than the certain profit outcome of an alternative act.

In terms of Figure 7-5 this would mean that the decision maker would have a preference for act 1 with an expected profit of, say, $25 over the $50 for certain from act 2.

There are degrees of risk seeking among decision makers, too. Where there is a very strong desire to attain the very highest profit amount (in the range given) the utility graph derived would tend to be quite convex. We would characterize such a decision maker as an extreme risk seeker (at least in the range of profit outcomes considered).

SUMMARY

1   An *opportunity loss* of an act-event combination refers to the amount of the "loss" (or deficiency) in the attainment of an objective because of the failure to take the best act.

2   In decision making under *certainty* no opportunity loss should occur, whereas in decision making under *uncertainty* it is not possible to avoid the chance of opportunity losses.

3 The *expected opportunity loss* of an act can be viewed as the future average loss in the attainment of an objective because of the failure to take the best act.

4 Under conditions of uncertainty all courses of action involve expected opportunity losses greater than $0. This is true even if some of the acts have certain profit outcomes.

5 The best course of action in terms of maximization-of-expected-profit can also be obtained by identifying the act with the minimum expected opportunity loss. The expected opportunity loss of the best act is a measure of the *expected cost of uncertainty*.

6 A perfect predictor removes the uncertainty with respect to the occurrence of a particular event. Thus, the value of a perfect predictor is equal to the expected opportunity loss of the best act under prior (existing) information.

7 The maximization-of-expected-profit criterion may not be appropriate for direct use by some decision makers. In these cases it is necessary to use the *maximization-of-expected-utility criterion*. The latter is the most general criterion for decision making.

8 In order to use the maximization-of-expected-utility criterion in large problems, a utility-for-profit graph must be obtained for the decision maker. It is derived by constructing a small decision-under-uncertainty problem of a special type and obtaining the decision maker's preferences with regard to various alternatives.

9 Three general classes of utility-for-profit graphs are obtained: concave graphs (associated with *risk-averse* decision makers); a straight-line graph (associated with *risk-neutral* decision makers; and convex graphs (associated with *risk-seeking* decision makers).

PROBLEMS

7-1 In the decision under certainty in Figure 7-1,

    a Suppose that an increase in the cost of raw materials occurs which, in turn, decreases the profit outcomes of each act by 50 percent. Do the opportunity losses also change? If so, why do they change?

    b What is the effect upon the opportunity losses if there is a fixed-cost increase of $100 that decreases each profit outcome by $100? Discuss.

7-2 In the packaging-machine example discussed in this chapter (and illustrated in Figure 7-2), suppose the prior probability of receiving a good-quality shipment decreases from .80 to .60. Also, the probability of receiving a poor-quality shipment increases from .20 to .40.

    a What is the best act under the maximization-of-expected-profit criterion?

    b What is the best act under the minimization-of-expected-opportunity-loss criterion? Why does this criterion identify the act with the maximum expected profit?

    c What is the expected value of perfect information from your expected-opportunity-loss computations in *b*? Explain why the expected opportunity loss of the optimal act under prior information provides the expected value of perfect information.

    d Compare your answer in *c* with the expected value of perfect information obtained in 5-1*b* for the same packaging-maching problem.

7-3 Let us continue examining the packaging example with the new prior probabilities provided in Problem 7-2. Suppose that a raw-material unit-cost increase reduces the profit of each act-event combination by 50 percent.
   a Obtain the new profit consequence of each act-event combination.
   b Obtain the new opportunity loss for each act-event combination.
   c What is the expected value of perfect information after the raw-material cost increase?
   d Compare your answer obtained in *c* with that obtained in Figure 7-2. Explain the basis for the change in the expected value of perfect information due to the raw-material cost increase.

7-4 In Problem 5-10 we examined a bicycle maker's decision on whether to build a small plant or a large plant in order to provide additional production facilities. Using the data in Problem 5-10,
   a Obtain an opportunity loss for each act-event combination.
   b Determine the expected value of perfect information (obtained by computing the expected opportunity losses). Compare it with that obtained in Problem 5-11*a* by the longer method.

7-5 The timber-products firm in Problem 6-4 had to decide whether to produce plywood or regular lumber from a new batch of logs. Using the data in Problem 6-4, determine the following:
   a An opportunity loss for each act-event combination.
   b The expected value of perfect information using the opportunity losses. Compare it with that obtained in Problem 6-4*c*.

7-6 Let us examine again the oil-drilling decision in Problem 5-5.
   a What are the opportunity losses for the act-event combinations?
   b Interpret the opportunity losses obtained in *a*.
   c Obtain the expected value of perfect information from the opportunity losses. Compare this value with that obtained in Problem 5-5*b*.
   d Obtain from prior information alone the expected profit *using* a perfect predictor.

7-7 In Problem 5-9 an agricultural decision on whether or not to use an insecticide was examined. Use the data from Problem 5-9 to obtain the following:
   a An opportunity loss for each act-event combination.
   b The expected value of perfect information from the opportunity losses.

7-8 A car maker's decision on whether to choose a guarantee arrangement or not from a supplier was examined in Problem 6-11. Using the data from Problem 6-11, obtain the following:
   a The opportunity loss for each act-event combination.
   b The expected value of perfect information from the opportunity losses. Compare this value with that obtained in Problem 6-11*d*.
   c From prior information alone determine the expected cost *using* a perfect predictor.

7-9 In the packaging-machine example represented in Figure 7-3, suppose the probability of receiving good-quality materials decreases from .80 to .60. Also, the probability of receiving poor-quality materials increases from .20 to .40.
   a Given the utility values for the profit outcomes as shown in Figure 7-3, obtain for each act an expected utility based on the new probabilities.
   b Which act is optimal in terms of expected utility? Discuss the relationship of this example to the one in Figure 7-5.

7-10   Consider the decision maker whose utility-for-profit graph is shown in Figure 7-6. Suppose he or she is now faced with an investment-decision problem where a choice must be made of one of three alternatives in which to invest a given amount of funds. The alternative investments with their possible profit outcomes and associated probabilities are as follows:

Investment 1		Investment 2		Investment 3	
Profit outcomes	Probability	Profit outcomes	Probability	Profit outcomes	Probability
$ 10	.07	$180	.06	$130	.46
175	.32	90	.29	150	.23
125	.61	140	.65	110	.31

    a   Construct a decision tree of the problem.
    b   Identify the investment alternative with the maximum expected profit.
    c   Using the utility graph in Figure 7-6, obtain an approximate utility value for each profit outcome.
    d   Compute an expected utility for each act and indicate which act is best for this decision maker in terms of expected utility.
    e   Is the best act in *d* also the act with the maximum expected profit? Explain the reasons for any differences.

7-11   A decision maker in a simplified problem is faced with choosing one of two alternative courses of action. One alternative involves a certain profit outcome of $10,000. The other alternative involves two possible profit outcomes of $50,000 and $0, with probabilities of .70 and .30, respectively.
    a   If the decision maker is indifferent between the two alternatives, what can we say about the decision maker's utility for profit? Is the expected profit for each act the same? If not, what does this indicate?
    b   If a utility value of 1.00 is assigned to the $50,000 chance outcome and 0.00 to the $0 outcome, what can we conclude regarding the utility of $10,000 if indifference between the above alternatives is shown? Plot on graph paper the utility values for $0, $10,000, and $50,000. Freehand or using a French curve, draw a smooth curve (or a straight line) through the three points. Of what further use is such a graph?
    c   If *another* decision maker did not indicate indifference between the above alternative acts until the probability of $50,000 was reduced to .20, what can we say about the decision maker's utility graph for profit? In obtaining your answer, plot on graph paper the utility values for $0, $10,000, and $50,000. Draw a smooth curve (or a straight line) through the three points.
    d   If a third decision maker did not indicate indifference between the two acts until the probability of $50,000 was reduced to .05, what can we say about this decision maker's utility graph for profit? Plot on graph paper the utility values for $0, $10,000, and $50,000. Draw a smooth curve (or a straight line) through the three points.
    e   Discuss the presence of risk aversion or its absence in the three decision makers.

7-12 In Problems 2-1, 2-2, and 6-4 a timber-products firm had the problem of deciding whether to produce plywood or regular lumber from logs with uncertain quality. Using the probabilities and the profit outcomes from those previous problems, let us examine which act is best (under prior information) if the following utility values for profit were derived for the decision maker.

Profit outcomes	Utility
$ 0	.00
5,000	.30
15,000	.70
35,000	.95
50,000	1.00

a Plot on graph paper the utility values for each profit outcome. Freehand or using a French curve, draw a smooth curve (or a straight line) through the above points.

b Construct a tree representing the timber-products decision under prior information (as in Problems 2-1 and 2-2). From the smooth utility graph obtained in a, associate an approximate utility value for each profit outcome.

c Compute an expected utility for producing plywood and an expected utility for producing regular lumber. Which is optimal?

d Compare your answer in c with your answer in Problem 2-2c where the act with the maximum expected profit was selected. When we used the maximization-of-expected-profit criterion, what implicit assumptions did we make regarding utility and different profit amounts? Discuss.

7-13 In Problems 2-10 and 5-5 a decision was to be made on whether or not to drill for oil in a particular region. Let us use the probabilities and profit outcomes from those previous problems and examine the same decision from the points of view of three different firms (three different decision makers). Thus, we have three different utility-for-profit schedules as shown below (that have been derived by the methods discussed in this chapter).

Decision maker 1		Decision maker 2		Decision maker 3	
Profit	Utility	Profit	Utility	Profit	Utility
−$ 50,000	.00	−$ 50,000	.00	−$ 50,000	.00
275,000	.50	0	.25	200,000	.10
600,000	1.00	100,000	.60	400,000	.35
		300,000	.90	550,000	.75
		600,000	1.00	600,000	1.00

a Plot on graph paper the utility values of each profit outcome for each of the decision makers. Freehand or using a French curve, draw smooth curves (or straight lines) through the points associated with each decision maker.

b   Construct a tree representing the drilling decision under prior information (as in Problem 2-10). From the smooth utility graphs obtained in a, associate for each decision maker an approximate utility value for each profit outcome.

c   Compute for each decision maker an expected utility for the act "drill" and an expected utility for the act "do not drill."

d   Which act is optimal for each decision maker? Discuss underlying reasons for differences in the optimal act and why for some decision makers the maximization-of-expected-profit criterion may not fit adequately.

Part Three

An Approach to Decision Making under Certainty: Linear-Programming Analysis

Chapter 8

Linear Programming and Decisions

In this part of the book we shall examine some of the characteristics of perhaps the most widely used quantitative procedure for the analysis of real-world decision problems under conditions of *certainty*. This procedure is known as *linear programming*.

As in the first part of the book, we shall focus on some simple problems in order to gain familiarity with the procedures. Remember that the procedures we illustrate in the small problems generally extend to the larger real-world problems.

BACKGROUND FOR LINEAR PROGRAMMING

There are elements in each of our lives that have connections to some of the concepts and ideas in linear programming. Of course the procedures of linear programming are quite formal and explicit, but by making note of the connections to things familiar, our understanding of linear programming may be facilitated and strengthened.

Each day we find ourselves "doing things." We spend our time and use the resources at our disposal in various ways. At work, we are producing goods, rendering services, and learning. In private life, typically, we are consuming and enjoying things (often with some additional production of goods), doing things for others, and learning. It appears that we all try to spend our time and use our resources in the best way that we can.

In the terminology of linear programming we would say that each day we are "engaging in various activities." The term "activity" essentially has a meaning analogous to "doing something." Thus, the term is very broad and can encompass many things. However, our attention shall be focused primarily on the activities of producing goods, rendering services, and the like.

In real life a problem of making the best decision often arises in choosing a set of activities in which to engage because it is common for some of the activities to compete with each other for the limited time or scarce resources available. Also, some of the activities may contribute more to an objective than other activities.

But if particular elements of a problem can be quantified, linear programming can be used to facilitate the choosing of a best program of activities.

Linear programming is a procedure by which a choice can be made of the best set of activities in which to engage when the possible activities from which to choose are very numerous and the scarce resources (or restrictions) are many. In this book we shall illustrate these main procedures by focusing primarily on the problems faced by business firms in choosing some set of products to make (that is, different production activities in which to engage).

We shall not include in our discussions important aspects of communication and organizational behavior that are related to the implementation of the chosen program (course of action) and the exercise of the necessary control and influence in order to realize the program. Another point is that linear programming need have nothing to do with computer programming; although, in fact, computers and the already-written programs of the major computer manufacturers typically are used in solving large practical problems.

Perhaps linear programming can best be viewed simply as a decision-making procedure where many of the relationships are represented by straight lines (or by piecewise linear segments). In this way it has some connections with the traditional straight-line, break-even analysis. But the traditional break-even analysis is of very limited use when there are numerous production activities and many limits on these production activities imposed by scarce resources, budgets, laws, and so forth. Also, it should be said that, in contrast to the usual break-even analysis, linear programming is generally oriented toward the determination of a best course of action, particularly in situations where our intuition is inadequate due to the complexity of the real situation.

That more formal methods, such as linear programming, can effectively supplement and often improve upon the decisions made by the more traditional intuitive methods is quite widely known. Examples can be found in virtually every area. Some of the more obvious applications are in the areas of planning the production of the types and amounts of goods or services, the planning of the amounts and quality of resources (human, physical, and financial), the planning of the technology to be used in production, and the planning of the location or expansion of facilities.

In summary, it can be said that there are important applications of linear programming in management, economics, finance, accounting, marketing, transportation, and decision making pertaining to the operation of virtually any private or public organization. Some of these applications will be suggested by examples in the text used to illustrate the methods. The problems at the end of each chapter provide some insight into various other applications.

AN ILLUSTRATIVE PROBLEM

Let us now look at a very simple example and see how a decision might be studied informally. Then, let us examine how linear-programming analysis might be used in arriving at a decision.

A Lawn-Mower–Golf-Cart Example

A firm makes two products, lawn mowers and golf carts, but it is limited in its output activities by two scarce resources, labor and a lawn-mower assembly facility.

The lawn-mower assembly facility has a capacity of 50 lawn mowers per day and is used only in the lawn-mower production activity. Each lawn mower uses one unit of this capacity. This and other relevant data are shown in Table 8-1.

Table 8-1   Data Table for the Lawn-Mower–Golf-Cart Example

	Rate of profit and rate of resource use		
	Product 1 (lawn mowers)	Product 2 (golf carts)	Resource capacity or availability
Profit	$40 (profit per unit)	$50 (profit per unit)	
Resource 1 (lawn-mower assembly facility)	uses 1 unit of the capacity	uses 0 units of the capacity	50 units of capacity
Resource 2 (labor)	uses 1 hour of labor	uses 2 hours of labor	80 hours available

Regarding the other scarce resource (labor), there are 80 hours available each day. Both the lawn-mower and golf-cart production activities use the labor resource. Each lawn mower requires one hour of labor whereas each golf cart uses two hours.

Each lawn mower contributes $40 to total profit (before fixed costs), and each golf cart contributes $50 to total profit (also, before fixed costs).

If total profit on all activities is to be maximized, what is the best product (or combination of the products) to produce?

How would you proceed? In Part Two of the book, we looked at decision problems in terms of four elements of good decision procedures. Let us see how those procedures might be applied here.

1 *The alternative courses of action:* Here we are to consider producing only lawn mowers, only golf carts, or any possible combination of the two products. This opens up the possible courses of action to a very, very large number. The decision tree, although conceptually helpful here, gets unwieldy with such a large number of alternative courses of action to consider. As we shall see, the procedures of linear programming provide an efficient method of handling such numerous courses of action and for solving such problems.

2 *The possible consequences of each course of action:* First, since we are assuming conditions of certainty, there is only one possible consequence for each course of action. Nevertheless, since the courses of action are so numerous, the computation of the profit consequences of all the courses of action is overwhelming. Later, we shall see that the solution procedures of linear programming provide an efficient method for computing (or taking into account) the profit consequences of all the many possible courses of action.

3 *The degree of uncertainty associated with each of the profit consequences:* Since we are assuming certainty (in the model at least), there is only one consequence for each course of action. Therefore, implicitly each consequence has a probability of 1.00.

4 *The criterion to be used in selecting a course of action:* The maximization of total profit has been suggested in the problem as the objective. This objective, as well as others, can easily be represented in the linear-programming analysis. The course of action (that is, the particular combination of the two products) that will yield the maximum total profit can be obtained by the linear-programming procedures.

An Informal Analysis of the Problem

Before putting the problem in the usual linear-programming form, let us informally consider several selected programs. Suppose that we consider the three programs depicted in Figure 8-1: Program 1 (produce golf carts only), Program 2 (produce lawn mowers only), and Program 3 (produce one of the many possible combinations of lawn mowers and golf carts, say 40 lawn mowers and 20 golf carts). We shall examine whether or not each program is feasible in terms of the resource limitations and then determine its total profit.

Program	Total profit

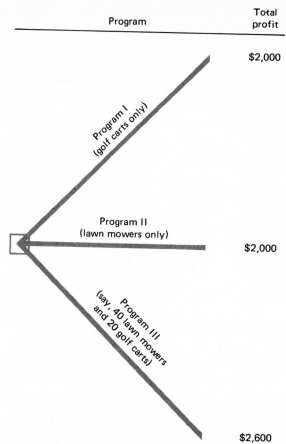

Program I (golf carts only) — $2,000

Program II (lawn mowers only) — $2,000

Program III (say, 40 lawn mowers and 20 golf carts) — $2,600

Figure 8-1 The three alternative programs considered.

PROGRAM 1 (produce golf carts only)

Resources

1   Lawn-mower assembly facility: No restriction is imposed by this resource. It would not be used in this program at all.

2   Labor: This resource imposes a restriction. Only 80 labor-hours are available. Each golf cart uses 2 hours of labor. Therefore, an output limit of 40 golf carts is imposed by this resource.

   Summary: In terms of *all* the resources, a maximum of 40 golf carts can be produced.

Total profit

A maximum of 40 golf carts can be produced. The unit profit on golf carts if $50. Thus, total profit for this program is $2,000: $50 × 40 golf carts = $2,000. (*Note:* This is total profit before the fixed costs are deducted. If we knew the fixed costs we would deduct them from the $2,000. But we can determine the best program without knowing them since incorporating the fixed costs involves subtracting a constant amount from each total-profit amount computed. Thus, linear programming, and other procedures, too, leave out the fixed costs from the analysis and then incorporate them later.)

PROGRAM II (produce lawn mowers only)

Resources
1 Lawn-mower assembly facility: This resource imposes a restriction. The facility has a capacity of 50 lawn mowers. This is the maximum output possible.
2 Labor: This resource imposes a restriction, also. Only 80 hours are available, and lawn-mower production requires 1 hour of labor per unit of output. Thus, the production of 80 lawn mowers is the maximum amount possible in terms of this resource.

Summary: In terms of *all* the resources, a maximum of 50 lawn mowers can be produced.

Total profit
A maximum of 50 lawn mowers can be produced. Profit per lawn mower is $40; thus, total profit for this program is $2,000, too: $40 × 50 lawn mowers = $2,000.

PROGRAM III (produce 40 lawn mowers and 20 golf carts)

Resources
1 Lawn-mower assembly facility: This resource has a capacity of 50 lawn mowers and is not used in golf-cart production. Thus, the program is within the limit of this resource.
2 Labor: The production of 40 lawn mowers would require 40 hours of labor since each unit requires 1 hour of labor. The production of 20 golf carts also would require 40 hours because each golf cart would require 2 hours of labor. Summing the labor hours required by each product in this program gives us 80 hours, which is the exact amount available.

Summary: In terms of all of the resources, this program of 40 lawn mowers and 20 golf carts is feasible.

Total profit
The program of 40 lawn mowers (with a unit profit of $40) and 20 golf carts (with a unit profit of $50) gives us a total profit of $2,600: $40 (40) + $50 (20) = $2,600.

Of the three programs considered, Program 3 (40 lawn mowers and 20 golf carts) is obviously the most profitable. However, we have no basis for concluding that we have identified the most profitable program of all that are possible (feasible) in terms of scarce resources. Actually, it turns out that the maximum-profit-feasible program is 50 lawn mowers and 15 golf carts. The total profit of this program is $2,750, better than any of the three programs we considered. We shall see that the linear-programming procedure will identify this particular program for us. But first the problem has to be put into the standard linear-programming form.

The Linear-programming Formulation of the Problem

The general form of a linear-programming problem is characterized by a series of "statements" that describe the essential elements of a problem. To be sure, these statements ultimately have to be in the form of equations (or inequalities), but they can be expressed verbally as well.

There are two types of statements. One type pertains to the objective, and the other, to obstacles or limitations in attaining unlimited levels of the objective. Usually, there is a single statement pertaining to the objective but many statements with regard to the limitations.

It was indicated earlier that the major concept (or term) in linear-programming analysis is the concept of an *activity*. Its potential application is very extensive. In business problems a typical interpretation is that an activity pertains to the production of a particular product. Of course there may be many activities that may be engaged in (that is, many different products or services may be produced). The *level* of a particular activity typically refers to the *amount of output* of the product associated with that activity. Actually, it is the best level of each of the activities (taken together) that we are seeking. Of course, the best program in terms of the given objective (such as the maximization of total profit) is expressed in terms of levels of the various activities (such as the output levels of the various products).

The Objective   Engaging in each of the activities in a problem usually has some effect upon the stated objective (such as total profit). The top row of our data table (Table 8-1) summarizes this. Product 1 output activity (lawn mowers, in our example) contributes to total profit at one rate ($40 in this case), and product 2 output activity (golf carts) may contribute to total profit at another rate (here, $50). These data permit us to make a statement in the following form:

Total profit = $40 × (output of product 1) + $50 × (output of product 2)

Representing the level of output of product 1 (lawn mowers) by x_1 (read as "x-sub one") and the level of output of product 2 (golf carts) by x_2, we have the following statement that describes the way in which the activities contribute to the specified objective.

Total profit = $40x_1 + \$50x_2$

Thus, the total profit for any program considered can be obtained simply by substituting the output levels of that program for the appropriate values of x_1 and x_2 and then summing the resulting profit amounts from the various activities. For a program of 40 lawn mowers and 20 golf carts, the x_1-value is 40 and the x_2-value is 20. Thus, the total profit is $2,600:

$$\$40\ x_1 + \$50\ x_2 = \$40\ (40) + \$50\ (20) = \$2,600$$

The Limitations on Attaining the Objective: The Constraints In business problems the typical limitations that arise in the attainment of the stated objective are imposed by scarce resources. Usually, the limitation imposed by each resource is represented by a separate statement (that is, by a separate equation or inequality). From our data table (Table 8-1) we see that the resource 1 row shows the use of this resource by the various product-output activities and also shows the capacity of the resource. Similarly, the resource 2 row shows the use of that resource by the same product-output activities and the availability of that resource.

When we use an equation we are saying that the sum of the terms on the left-hand side of the equality sign must be equal to those on the right-hand side. However, in the case of inequalities, sometimes we are saying that the left-hand side must be "less than" the right-hand side; whereas at other times, we are saying that the left-hand side must be "greater than" the right-hand side.

In the lawn-mower–golf-cart example we have only "less-than" inequalities. "Less-than" inequalities are designated by the symbol $<$, whereas "greater-than" inequalities are designated by the symbol $>$. Inequalities may be combined with equations, and this is commonly done in linear programming. Thus, the symbol for "less than or equal to" is given by $\leq$. The symbol for "greater than or equal to" is given by $\geq$.

In our example, resource 1 (the lawn-mower assembly facility) has a capacity of 50. Each unit of product 1 (lawn mowers) uses one unit of this capacity. Product 2 output (golf carts) does not use resource 1 at all. This information pertaining to resource 1 can be represented by the following statement (also, it corresponds to the data in the resource 1 row of Table 8-1):

Use of resource 1 per unit of product 1	Output of product 1		Use of resource 1 per unit of product 2	Output of product 2		Capacity or availability of resource
1	x_1	+	0	x_2	$\leq$	50 (resource 1: lawn-mower assembly facility)

More compactly, we have:

$$1x_1 + 0x_2 \leq 50 \text{ (resource 1: lawn-mower assembly facility)}$$

Thus, we are saying that the sum of the terms on the left-hand side of this inequality must be equal to or less than 50. The economic meaning is this: The left-hand side represents the total use of resource 1 by various output programs (various values of x_1 and x_2), and the total use of resource 1 cannot exceed its capacity, which is 50. For example, a program of 40 lawn mowers and 20 golf carts would use resource 1 at less than full capacity since the left-hand side sums to 40, whereas the right-hand-side amount is 50: $1 (40) + 0 (20) \leqslant 50$.

Labor is the only other given resource limitation in our problem. It is used by both of the product-output activities, 1 hour of labor for each lawn mower and 2 hours of labor for each golf cart. The total amount of labor available per day is 80 hours. This limitation can be expressed by the following separate statement pertaining to resource 2 (also, it corresponds to the data in the resource 2 row of Table 8-1):

Use of resource 2 by unit of product 1	Output of product 1		Use of resource 2 by unit of product 2	Output of product 2		Capacity or availability of resource
1	x_1	+	2	x_2	$\leqslant$	80 (resource 2: labor-hours)

And, more compactly, we have:

$1x_1 + 2x_2 \leqslant 80$ (resource 2: labor-hours)

Here we are saying that the sum of the terms on the left-hand side of this inequality must be equal to or less than 80. The economic meaning is that the total use of resource 2 (labor) by various output programs cannot exceed the availability of resource 2, which is 80 hours. For example, a program of 40 lawn mowers and 20 golf carts uses all of the hours of resource 2 that are available: $1 (40) + 2 (20) \leqslant 80$. The left-hand side is equal to the right-hand side. The nice thing about representing the resources by inequalities (combined with equations) is that we can specify that a resource may be used at less than full capacity if it is more profitable to do so.

Then, in the usual linear-programming formulation, the statement pertaining to the objective (the objective function) is set apart from the statements regarding the use of resources and their limitations (the constraint inequalities) as follows:
Maximize:

Total profit $= \$40x_1 + \$50x_2$

Subject to the following constraints:

$1x_1 + 0x_2 \leqslant 50$ (resource 1: lawn-mower assembly facility)
$1x_1 + 2x_2 \leqslant 80$ (resource 2: labor-hours)

Since this example involves only two activities, we can represent the problem graphically, too. Let us graph the constraint functions individually and then combine them later.

The first constraint inequality is:

$1x_1 + 0x_2 \leq 50$ (resource 1: lawn-mower assembly facility)

First, we graph the *equation* portion of the constraint function: $1x_1 + 0x_2 = 50$. Setting x_2 to 0, we find that the x_1-value (the x_1-intercept) is 50. There is no x_2-intercept. (Setting x_1 to 0 does not give us an x_2-value.) The graph of the equation is the perpendicular straight line intersecting the x_1-axis at 50, as shown in Figure 8-2. Whatever the value of x_2, the x_1-value will be 50.

Next, we indicate the direction of the inequality by attaching small arrows to the straight-line graph and orienting them in the proper direction. This constraint inequality is a "less-than" inequality (the amount on the left-hand side must sum to an amount less than the amount on the right-hand side); thus, we orient the arrows to the left, as shown in Figure 8-2.

Any program corresponding to a point *on* the straight line is feasible in terms of the equation, and any program corresponding to a point *to the left* of the graph of the equation is feasible in terms of the inequality. We indicate this feasible area for resource 1 (lawn-mower assembly facility) by the shaded area in Figure 8-2.

Point A, for example, corresponds to a program of 20 lawn mowers and 60 golf carts: $(x_1, x_2) = (20,60)$. This program is feasible in terms of resource 1 (the lawn-mower assembly facility). Thus, if we substitute these values for x_1 and x_2 into the constraint inequality, we will obtain a true statement, or, we could say that the inequality is satisfied: $1 (20) + 0 (60) \leq 50$. The left-hand side sums to 20 and is less than or equal to 50.

We should take notice here that this particular inequality represents only the limitation that resource 1 imposes upon output of the two products and nothing

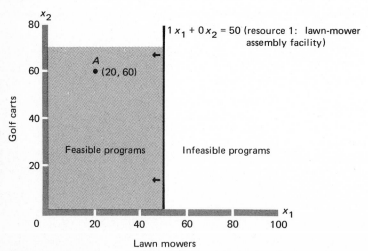

Figure 8-2 A separate graph of the first inequality constraint (resource 1: the lawn-mower assembly facility).

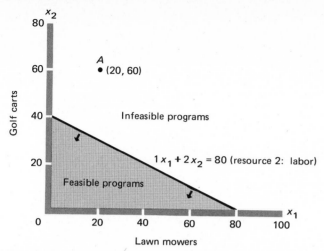

Figure 8-3   A separate graph of the second inequality constraint (resource 2: labor).

more. It says nothing about the limitations imposed by other resources, nor does it represent something that is quite obvious to us, namely, that the production of lawn mowers or golf carts cannot be less than 0. Therefore, after listing all the constraint inequalities, it is common to specify that the levels of the activities can only be 0 or something greater than 0. (This is sometimes referred to as the "nonnegativity restriction.")

Let us graph the second constraint inequality:

$$1x_1 + 2x_2 \leq 80 \text{ (resource 2: labor)}$$

Its graph is shown in Figure 8-3. First, we graph the equation portion. The x_1-intercept of the equation is 80 (by setting x_2 to 0 and solving). The x_2-intercept is 40 (by setting x_1 to 0 and solving). Since the equation is of linear form, we connect the two intercepts with a straight line. The inequality is a "less-than" inequality, and so the arrows are pointed in the appropriate direction. The feasible area in terms of this constraint inequality is shaded, too.

We see from Figure 8-3 that the program corresponding to point A, (x_1, x_2) = (20, 60) is *infeasible* in terms of resource 2 (labor). Thus, we would say that this program is infeasible in terms of the resource constraints taken all together. A program that is infeasible in terms of a single constraint makes the program infeasible.

We combine the graphs of both the constraint inequalities in Figure 8-4. The area that is "overlapped" by the shaded areas pertaining to *every one* of the constraint inequalities is termed the *feasible region* for the whole problem. (Also, we are not allowing the consideration of negative values of x_1 and x_2.)

Therefore, only points in the double-shaded area are termed feasible programs. Included, of course, are the programs represented by points on the

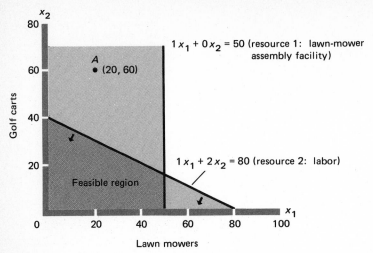

Figure 8-4 A graph of the feasible region of programs obtained by plotting both of the inequality constraints.

boundary of the feasible region. It is from this set of feasible programs on the boundary that an optimal feasible program will come. But to identify an optimal feasible program we need to take into account the objective function.

Recall that in this problem the objective function to be maximized is:

$$\$40x_1 + \$50x_2 = \text{total profit}$$

The objective function, in some respects, is to be contrasted with the constraint functions. First, it is an equation and not an inequality. Second, it does not have a given (and fixed) right-hand-side amount. No particular profit amount

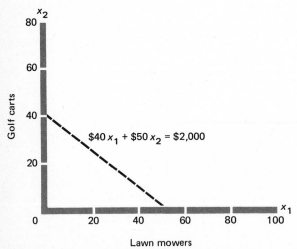

Figure 8-5 A graph of the profit objective function where a $2,000 total profit is assumed.

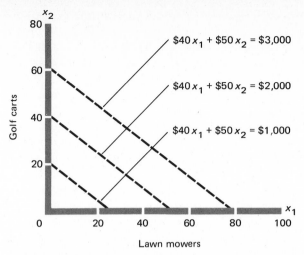

Figure 8-6 Graphs of the objective function for total profit amounts of $1,000, $2,000, and $3,000.

is given, and the instruction is to obtain the highest total profit possible within the limits imposed by the constraints.

Thus, as we graph the objective function as given, we must note that it corresponds to a whole family of graphs—a different one for each total profit amount assumed. Each graph will have the same slope, however, so that they will all be parallel to one another.

Let us arbitrarily assume some profit amount in order to get a graph. Suppose that we assume a total profit amount of $2,000. Then in Figure 8-5 we plot the equation:

$$\$40x_1 + \$50x_2 = \$2,000$$

Setting the x_2 to 0, we obtain the x_1-intercept of 50. This means that the (50, 0) program generates $2,000 in total profit. Next, we set x_1 to 0 to obtain the x_2-intercept of 40. At this intercept, the program is (0, 40). This program has a total profit of $2,000, too. Since the equation is of linear form, we connect the two intercepts with a straight line—a dashed line because we want to distinguish clearly the objective function from the constraint functions. Every point on that dashed line represents a program that generates a total profit of $2,000.[1]

---

[1]Remember that in plotting an objective function with a total profit equal to the product of the two coefficients (here, it is $2,000 = $40 × $50) the x_2-*intercept* will be equal to the x_1-*coefficient* (here, 40) and the x_1-intercept will be equal to the x_2-coefficient (here, 50). Thus, a quick way to plot an objective function is to observe the coefficients, identify the x_2- and x_1-intercepts (here, 40 and 50), and then connect the intercepts with a straight (dashed) line.

Also, to plot the same objective function closer to the origin, we can simply divide each coefficient by a number (such as 2), identify the intercepts, and then connect with a straight (dashed) line the x_2- and x_1-intercepts (here, they would be 20 and 25). Of course the total profit associated with this plot of the objective function would be much less (here, only $1,000).

We plot the objective function for several total-profit amounts in Figure 8-6. When larger total-profit amounts are assumed, the graph moves further from the origin. We should note that every point on a single graph of an objective function (with a given total profit amount) corresponds to programs that would generate the same total profit (sometimes they are called "iso-profit" lines).

In Figure 8-7 we superimpose two graphs of the objective function upon the graphs of the constraint inequalities. The graphs of the constraint functions are, of course, fixed, but the objective function is not. In a sense we can think of our being able to "move" the objective function outward from the origin (in the "optimizing" direction). As we do so, it is associated with higher total profit amounts.

Our aim here is the maximization of total profit, and so graphically we can think of the basic linear-programming problem as one of trying to move the objective function out as far as possible and still stay within the feasible region.

In Figure 8-7 the program with the highest total profit corresponds to the last point intersected by the objective function as it is moved outward. This last point corresponds to the program of 50 lawn mowers and 15 golf carts, or $(x_1, x_2) =$ (50, 15). The total profit is $2,750, which is considerably higher than the best profit program discovered by the informal methods discussed earlier. We say that the program (50, 15) is the *optimal feasible program* with a maximum total profit of $2,750.

An important principle of linear programming is illustrated in Figure 8-7. It turns out that if all the constraints in a problem are linear inequalities (and the objective function is an equation of linear form), an optimal feasible program will always "be at" a corner point of the feasible region. Since there will always be a finite number of corner points (because there will always be a finite number of variables and constraints), the problem of searching for an optimal feasible

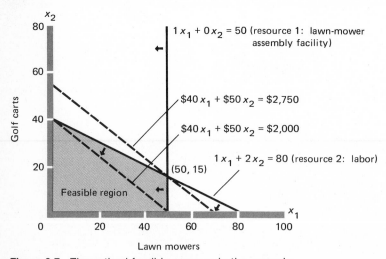

Figure 8-7   The optimal feasible program in the example.

program is reduced to one of examining the total profit of the programs corresponding to the corner points of the feasible region of a problem. Of course this is not a simple task if the problem is large, but the "simplex method" of solution (to be discussed in Chapter 10) and the existence of modern electronic computers make the solving of such problems widely practicable.

ASSUMPTIONS OF LINEAR PROGRAMMING

You will recall from Chapter 1 in our general discussion on "models and reality" that in order to use a model well we must know its many assumptions and how it fits the particular real situation of interest. Only then can we begin to determine the amount of confidence to place in the results, that is, in its prediction or indicated optimal course of action.

Although in some ways there appears to be a roughness in the linear (or piecewise linear) approximations to reality found in linear programming, they are in a total sense usually less crude than those used in many of the older (calculus-based) procedures. In the older procedures, various difficulties are frequently encountered. For example, the handling of numerous resources results in an aggregation of quite different resources to an uncomfortable degree. In linear programming, on the other hand, the relative ease in representing numerous resources in the model permits much of the character of the real situation to be captured. Because so many constraints can be handled, particular facilities, machines, or bottlenecks can each be represented in the analysis, often without excessive cost or complication. Furthermore, limits imposed upon activities or resources (for example, by social, economic, environmental, or resource policies) can easily be handled in a linear-programming model.

Thus, before proceeding further, it is well to examine some of the meanings and the importance of the main assumptions of linear programming: linearity (or proportionality), additivity, divisibility, and certainty.

Linearity (or Proportionality)

The assumption of *linearity* sometimes is also referred to as the "proportionality" assumption. In a linear-programming model we represent such factors as the rate of profit for each activity and the rate of resource use by each activity. Let us examine this in more detail.

Linearity in the Objective Function If we assume the rate of profit to be constant as the level of the associated product-output activity rises or falls, we have a linear relationship between the level of that activity and the total profit generated from that activity.

For example, in the lawn-mower production activity the constant unit profit was assumed to be $40. As we increase the level of lawn-mower output, the total profit from *lawn-mower production* rises by $40 for each unit. When we plot this relationship for various output levels (for various values of x_1), we get the graph shown in Figure 8-8a.

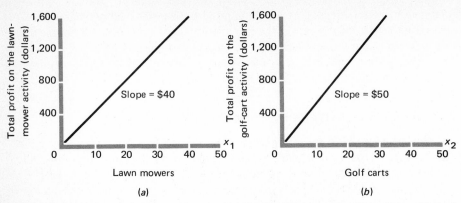

Figure 8-8 *(a)* Total profit from various levels of lawn-mower production activity; *(b)* total profit from various levels of golf-cart production activity.

Note that the linearity assumption here refers only to the level of each activity and the associated total profit from that same activity considered by itself. The slope of the graph in Figure 8-8*a* is $40, an amount equal to the constant unit profit.

The reason for describing this assumption as the proportionality assumption is clear when it is seen that if output is increased by 100 percent (say from 10 units to 20 units) as shown in Figure 8-8*a* the total profit on this activity also increases by the same proportion, from $400 to $800.

In Figure 8-8*b* the relationship between golf-cart output and its total profit is graphed. For this product-output activity the slope of the total-profit graph is seen to be $50.

Linearity in the Constraints   In the case of the resource-constraint functions, the linearity arises because of the assumed constant rate of use of each of the resources by each activity. For example, each lawn mower produced uses 1 hour of the labor-hours available. A graph of this relationship is shown in Figure 8-9*a*. The total use of labor by the lawn-mower production activity is directly proportional to the level of that activity. Doubling the level of an activity, for example, doubles the total use of a resource by that activity.

Similarly, in Figure 8-9*b* we see represented the case of the golf-cart production activity with its twice-as-high rate of use of this resource. The slope of the graph of the total use of labor by golf-cart production in Figure 8-9*b* is seen to be 2, whereas in Figure 8-9*a* it is 1.

Modification in the Linearity Assumption   We shall see in a later chapter that a slight modification in the basic linear-programming model permits the use of these procedures to study some problems of a nonlinear type, too. It turns out that many real-world nonlinear relationships can be represented adequately by *piecewise linear* graphs. Problems involving these piecewise linear relations can then be solved by linear programming. This greatly enlarges the use of linear-programming methods.

Additivity

The word *additivity* implies a reference to the addition of elements or components. As seen in the objective function for the lawn-mower–golf-cart problem, there is an adding together of the total profits from each of the different activities: $\$40x_1 + \$50x_2 =$ total profit.

This provides a total profit amount for a particular program of outputs of lawn mowers and golf carts. Such addition implies that there is no effect upon the unit profit of any activity from changes in the level of any other activity. For example, it is assumed that changes in lawn-mower output do not affect the unit profit on golf-cart production and that changes in golf-cart output do not affect the unit profit on lawn-mower production.

Analogously, the total use of resources by the activities is assumed to be additive. The rates of use of resources are assumed to be not affected by changes in the levels of other activities.

The linearity (proportionality) premise considered earlier referred to the assumption that a rate of profit (or rate of resource use) by an activity remained constant as the level of that *same* activity changed. Here, we are referring to the assumption that changes in the level of a given activity do not affect the rates of profit or resource use by any of the *other* activities.

Divisibility

In the basic linear-programming model the variables (the activity levels) are assumed to be "continuous" variables (not "discrete" variables). Recall from your algebra that this means that within some interval the variable can take any one of an infinite number of values. If one thinks of the interval in terms of a segment on a straight line (a continuum), the line conceptually could be subdi-

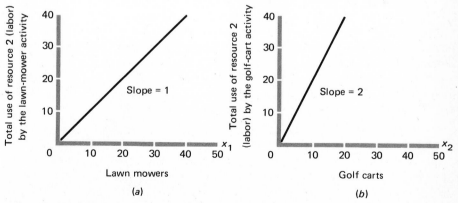

Figure 8-9 *(a)* Total use of resource 2 (labor) by various levels of the lawn-mower production activity; *(b)* total use of resource 2 (labor) by various levels of the golf-cart production activity.

vided into smaller intervals without end. One could say the interval is infinitely divisible.

This divisibility assumption greatly facilitates the search for an optimal feasible solution, as we shall see in Chapter 10, but it does result in solutions with fractional (noninteger) values. Because in many real-world problems only whole-number (integer) solutions can be implemented, some questions arise as to the best whole-number solution (program). There exist methods known as "integer linear programming" to deal with this problem when this aspect is of sufficient importance. But in many cases it is sufficient to solve the problem without concern for the fractional solution and then round the solution values to the nearest whole number. We shall examine integer programming briefly in Chapter 14.

Certainty

The coefficients and constants in the linear-programming model are assumed to be known and fixed. These coefficients and constants represent such items as unit profits, rates of resource use, and resource capacities or availabilities.

Thus, by assigning a single fixed value to each coefficient or constant we are assuming that it does not vary either due to chance or choice. We are assuming in the model that for the period under study the following are certain: the unit profits, the rates of resource use, and the resource capacities or availabilities.

Even though linear-programming models in the usual form are *certainty* (deterministic) models, this does not mean that all of the relevant conditions in reality must be fixed or certain in order to use these procedures. It simply means that *in the model* there are no chance variations such as those we observed in earlier sections. As we shall see, however (in the next chapter), the study of the effects upon the attainment of objectives from the variation of such items as resource capacities (either due to chance or choice) can be effectively studied by linear-programming procedures.

SUMMARY

1 Linear programming is perhaps the most widely used quantitative procedure for the analysis of practical, complex decision problems under conditions of certainty.

2 Linear programming provides a procedure to choose a best program of activities given that limitations exist on engaging in these activities (such as those imposed by scarce resources).

3 The main concept in linear programming is that of an *activity*. This is a very broad concept and helps make linear programming widely applicable. In a typical business application the making of a particular product is viewed as an activity. Usually, a firm produces a number of different products, and the making of each product is viewed as a separate activity. The amount of each product made (or that might be made) is referred to as the *level* of that activity. In a large real-world problem the number of different activities considered may be in the hundreds or even in the thousands.

4 In the usual linear-programming formulation of a decision problem there is a statement about the objective (the objective function) and a number of statements regarding the resource limitations or other restrictions (the constraints).

5   The *objective function* specifies the objective (or goal) that is sought and how each of the activities contributes to this objective.

6   Each scarce resource typically is represented by a separate inequality *constraint*. It is common for many different resources to impose limitations on the levels of the activities in which we can engage. Usually, the capacity (or availability) of each resource, and the use of it by each of the activities, is represented by a separate constraint inequality. Consequently, the constraint inequalities may be quite numerous (in the hundreds or thousands) in a large real-world problem.

7   Each resource constraint specifies what levels of activities are feasible in terms of that particular resource. Usually, the resource constraints are in the form of "less-than-or-equal-to" inequalities because in real-world problems we wish to represent the possibilities of not using the resource at all, using it partially, or using it at its capacity, whatever in a total sense is most profitable.

8   A *feasible* program of activities is one which satisfies every one of the constraints. *Infeasible* programs are programs of activities that are not possible (at least as we have described them). If a particular program does not satisfy every one of the constraints specified, the program is termed infeasible.

9   A typical objective function specifies the rate at which each activity contributes to an objective (such as profit) but does not specify a particular total profit amount that must be attained.

10   The *linearity* (or *proportionality*) assumption means that in the objective function each activity contributes to the stated objective at a constant rate irrespective of the level of the activities. In the constraints this means that each activity uses each resource at a constant rate regardless of the level of the activities. This assumption appears much more restrictive than it turns out to be in real-world applications because nonlinear relationships usually can be approximated adequately by piecewise linear graphs and solved by the usual linear-programming methods.

11   The *additivity* assumption is a valid one if in the reality being represented the level of one activity does not significantly affect the unit profit in another activity. Similarly, in the constraints the rate of use of a resource by one activity is assumed not to be affected by the level of another activity.

12   The *divisibility* assumption often results in fractional (non-integer) optimal programs being selected by the linear-programming procedure.

13   The *certainty* assumption means that (in the model) the coefficients and constants are known and remain fixed at their assumed values. In the objective function each coefficient represents a unit profit on each activity. In the constraints each coefficient refers to a rate of use of a resource. Each right-hand-side constant in the constraints typically refers to a resource capacity or availability.

PROBLEMS

8-1   A firm has two fixed resources that impose limits on its production activities. For a particular period of time it has 30 hours of resource 1 available and 80 hours of resource 2. Suppose that the firm considers making only two products and desires to know the maximum-profit program. It has the following additional data:

Product 1:   Unit profit = $60
              Use of resource 1 per unit of output = 1
              Use of resource 2 per unit of output = 2

Product 2:   Unit profit = $20
              Use of resource 1 per unit of output = 0
              Use of resource 2 per unit of output = 1

a   Form a data table for the problem such as that shown in Table 8-1.
b   Formulate the objective function in the form of an equation.
c   Formulate a "less-than" constraint inequality for resource 1 and also one for resource 2. Combine these inequalities with the objective function in *b* and represent the problem in the standard linear-programming formulation.
d   Representing product 1 output on the horizontal axis and product 2 on the vertical axis, obtain a graph (using graph paper) of the resource 1 inequality. Indicate on the graph the area representing feasible programs in terms of resource 1.
e   Obtain a graph of the resource 2 inequality. Indicate on the graph the area representing feasible programs in terms of resource 2.
f   Superimpose one of the resource-inequality graphs in *d* and *e* upon the other. Indicate on this graph the feasible programs (the feasible region) in terms of *both* resource 1 and resource 2.
g   On the graph obtained in *f*, label product 1 and product 2 outputs (the coordinates) associated with each corner point of the feasible region.
h   On the graph obtained in *f*, plot the objective function formulated in *b* for some arbitrary profit amount such as $1,200. (The profit amount $1,200 is the product of the two profit coefficients.) Therefore, the x_2-intercept will be 60, the same value as the $60 coefficient of x_1 in the objective function. Similarly, the x_1-intercept will be 20, the same value as the $20 coefficient of x_2.) With a clear plastic ruler "move" the objective function "outward" until it intersects the last corner point of the feasible region. Identify the last corner point by its coordinates.
i   What is the best feasible program and its total profit? Give a verbal interpretation of this result. If fixed costs for the period are $1,000, what is the maximum total (net) profit?

8-2 In the making of backpacks and raincoats, a firm has a limited number of sewing machines and a limited number of persons to operate them and perform other tasks. Expressed in terms of hours available for a period of time, there are 160 sewing-machine-hours available and 240 labor-hours. Each product when finished is packed in boxes with 24 items to a box. The identification of the maximum-profit program is desired. The following additional data have been compiled:

Backpacks: Profit per box = $48
              Hours of sewing-machine time required per box = 4
              Hours of labor required per box = 4

Raincoats: Profit per box = \$32
Hours of sewing-machine time required per box = 2
Hours of labor required per box = 4

a   Form a data table for the problem as is done in Table 8-1.
b   From the information in the data table formulate the problem in the usual linear-programming form with an objective function and resource inequality constraints.
c   Graph the objective function and the constraint inequalities on the two product axes. In plotting the objective function, merely connect the x_2-intercept of 48 with the x_1-intercept of 32 identified from an inspection of the \$48 coefficient for x_1 and the \$32 coefficient for x_2.
d   At each corner point of the feasible region label the associated coordinates (the output of each product). Solve for the coordinates by simultaneous equations if necessary. See the section in the next chapter on obtaining the coordinates of a corner point if you need to review this procedure.
e   What is the optimal feasible program and its total profit?

8-3   With a limited capacity of its processing facilities and a limited amount of trained labor a dairy-foods processor is attempting to identify the program of ice-cream and cheese outputs that will be most profitable for a particular period. The processed products are packed in 200-pound cases. Each case of ice cream generates \$8 in profit, and each case of cheese generates \$12. The following resource-constraint inequalities have been formulated. Ice-cream output (in numbers of cases) is represented by the variable x_1, and cheese output (in numbers of cases) is represented by the variable x_2.

$$x_1 + 2x_2 \leq 80 \text{ (processing-facility capacity)}$$
$$2x_1 + 2x_2 \leq 120 \text{ (labor-hours)}$$

a   Formulate the profit objective function and graph it together with the constraint inequalities on the product axes.
b   From inspection of your graph obtained in *a*, which corner point of the feasible region will be intersected last as the objective function is moved outward? Use simultaneous equations to obtain the exact coordinates. See the section in the next chapter on obtaining the coordinates of a corner point if you need to review this procedure.
c   What is the optimal feasible program and its total profit?
d   How much in total profit would be lost if an all-cheese or an all-ice-cream program was implemented?

8-4   Let us look at an elementary version of a production decision that might face a car manufacturer in terms of its assembly operations.
    The assembly facilities are such that they can be used for assembling cars of regular size or those of small size. The capacity of the assembly facilities can be expressed as 600 small-size cars per week. Thus, each small-size car uses 1 unit of the total capacity. Regular-size cars use the assembly capacity as expressed above at *twice* the rate of the small-size cars. Use x_1 to represent the output of regular cars and x_2 to represent the output of small-size cars.
    Additionally, there are only 1,600 hours of a special type of labor available

each week. Each car of either type uses 4 hours of this labor. The unit profit on regular-size cars is $320; on small-size cars it is $240.

a Form a data table for the car manufacturer.

b Formulate the problem in standard linear-programming form.

c Graph the objective function and the constraint inequalities on the two product axes. (In plotting the objective function, merely connect the x_2-intercept of 320 with the x_1-intercept of 240 identified from an inspection of the $320 coefficient for x_1 and the $240 coefficient for x_2.)

d What is the optimal feasible program and its total profit?

8-5 Sometimes the capacity of a resource or facility is expressed in terms of 100 percent, and the use of the capacity in making a unit of a product is expressed in terms of the percent of the total capacity used.

Suppose that a food processor has a processing facility and its total capacity is expressed as 100 percent. However, this facility can be used in making two different products. Product 1 uses 2 percent of the capacity for each unit produced, whereas product 2 uses 4 percent of the capacity for each unit produced.

Additionally, there is a limited number of labor-hours available for the period. The total hours available are 160. Each product uses 4 hours of labor per unit of output. The processor desires to know the most profitable program of the two products. The unit profit on product 1 output is $4. It is $2 for product 2.

a Form a data table for the food processor's decision problem.

b Formulate the problem in standard linear-programming form.

c Graph on the product axes the inequality constraints and the objective function.

d At each corner point of the feasible region obtained in c, insert the coordinates (the programs of output).

e What is the optimal feasible program and its total profit? Explain in your own words why the corner point you identified as optimal represents a more profitable program than any of the other corner points.

8-6 A small-vehicle manufacturer is faced with a very limited capacity in its assembly facility for small, motorized, industrial vehicles. This facility can accommodate only 120 such vehicles per week. It is very specialized and is used only in the assembly of these vehicles. Let us represent this output by the variable x_1.

The manufacturer also makes motorcycles. Their production does not place any demand at all on the assembly facilities for industrial vehicles. However, the amount of labor available for the period imposes a limit on motorcycle production and on industrial vehicle production as well. There are 360 hours of labor available per week. Each motorcycle requires 4 hours of labor, whereas each industrial vehicle uses only 2 hours.

The manufacturer desires to know the maximum-profit program for the week and indicates that the unit profit is $120 for each industrial vehicle and $160 for each motorcycle.

a Form a data table for the problem and then place it in standard linear-programming form.

b Plot on the two product axes the inequality constraints and the objective function.

c What is the optimal feasible program and its total profit?

8-7 A firm is attempting to determine the most profitable program of production. It makes two products and finds that two resources are effectively limiting its production activities. Resource 1 has a capacity of 24 for the period, whereas resource 2 has an availability of 40. Other relevant data are summarized below.

Product 1: Unit profit = $40
            Use of resource 1 per unit of output = 4
            Use of resource 2 per unit of output = 4

Product 2: Unit profit = $20
            Use of resource 1 per unit of output = 4
            Use of resource 2 per unit of output = 20

a Form a data table for the problem.
b Formulate the problem in standard linear-programming form.
c On the two product axes, graph the inequality constraints and the objective
     function.
d What is the optimal feasible program and its total profit? If fixed costs for the
     period are $110, what is the optimal total (net) profit?

8-8 A farm contains 600 acres of cropland that can be used in the production of either
corn or soybeans. The effective limitations on production are imposed by the land
acreage and the amount of labor available during the production period. The labor
available during this period is 2,000 hours.

   Each acre of land devoted to corn production requires 4 hours of labor and, of
course, also 1 acre of cropland. Each acre devoted to soybean production requires 2
hours of labor and 1 acre of land.

   Suppose there is the desire to identify the most profitable program of corn and
soybean production that is feasible. The price per bushel of corn is estimated to be
$2; for soybeans it is $5. Yields per acre are estimated to be 100 bushels for corn and
20 bushels for soybeans. There is an estimated $50 cost of seed, fuel, and fertilizer
for each acre devoted to corn production. This cost for each acre devoted to
soybean production is $20.
a Form a data table in which product 1 is interpreted as *acres* devoted to corn
     production and product 2 as *acres* devoted to soybean production. Profit per
     acre for each use must be computed from the above data.
b Formulate the problem in the standard linear-programming form.
c Graph on the product axes (acres devoted to each product) the constraint
     inequalities and the profit-objective function.
d What is the optimal feasible program and its total profit? Give a verbal
     description of the program.

8-9 A given real-world decision problem often can be formulated in more than one way.
To illustrate this, consider again the data provided in Problem 8-8. Now let us
formulate the problem in such a way that product 1 output represents *bushels* of
corn produced and product 2 represents *bushels* of soybeans produced. The
coefficients in the objective function and the constraints will have to be computed
and assigned carefully.
a Form a data table with this alternative interpretation.
b Formulate the problem in standard linear-programming form.
c Graph the problem on the product axes (bushels of corn and bushels of
     soybeans).
d Obtain the optimal feasible program of output and its total profit. Can you
     determine from this program how many acres should be devoted to each
     product? How? Interpret the program verbally and relate it to the optimal
     feasible program obtained in Problem 8-8d. If fixed costs for the period are
     $24,000, what is the optimal (net) profit?

8-10   There are three resources that effectively impose limits on product 1 and product 2 output activities. Resource 1 has a capacity of 1,200, resource 2 a capacity of 400, and resource 3 a capacity of 60. The identification of the most profitable program is desired. The following additional data have been collected.

Product 1:   Unit profit = $40
Use of resource 1 per unit of output = 20
Use of resource 2 per unit of output = 4
Use of resource 3 per unit of output = 0

Product 2:   Unit profit = $120
Use of resource 1 per unit of output = 20
Use of resource 2 per unit of output = 20
Use of resource 3 per unit of output = 4

a   Form a data table for the problem.
b   Formulate the problem in the standard linear-programming form.
c   Graph the objective function and constraint inequalities on the product-output axes.
d   What is the optimal feasible program and its total profit?
e   From your inspection of the graph obtained in *c*, what can be said about the utilization of resource 3 capacity if the optimal feasible program is implemented?

8-11   A manufacturer of automotive parts is interested in identifying the most profitable program of products to produce in a particular period. Pistons and axles are the two products currently produced. Each unit of output is defined as 100 pistons or 100 axles. Piston production generates $24 per unit; whereas the production of axles yields $36 per unit.

Output of the products is limited by the capacities of three types of machines used in production: cutting machines, grinding machines, and polishing machines. The hours available for the period on the cutting machines are 400, on the grinding machines 320, and on the polishing machines 160. The use of each type of machine per unit of output is given as follows.

Pistons: Use of cutting machine per unit of output = 8
Use of grinding machine per unit of output = 8
Use of polishing machine per unit of output = 2

Axles: Use of cutting machine per unit of output = 8
Use of grinding machine per unit of output = 4
Use of polishing machine per unit of output = 4

a   Form a data table for the problem.
b   Formulate the problem in standard linear-programming form.
c   Graph the problem on the two product axes.
d   What is the optimal feasible program and its total profit?
e   Which, if any, resources are idle (or partly idle) under the optimal feasible program obtained in *d*? Explain why it can be the most profitable to choose a program that does not fully use every resource?

8-12 Consider again the decision problem of the automotive-parts manufacturer in Problem 8-11. Now there is consideration given to producing a third product, too. This third product is a type of connecting rod. It has a unit profit of $20 (assume that there are 100 rods in a unit). Also, its production uses all three machines but at different rates. For each unit produced, 4 hours of cutting-machine time are required, 2 hours of grinding-machine time, and 2 hours of polishing-machine time.

    a Form the data table for this problem.

    b Formulate the problem in standard linear-programming form.

    c Looking at your data table and the linear-programming formulation, *estimate* the optimal feasible program and its total profit. In Chapter 10 we shall learn the "simplex method" which permits us to solve this problem and others that are too large to be graphed.

Chapter 9

Analysis for the Planning of Facilities, Equipment, and Other Resources: A Graphic Introduction to Sensitivity Analysis and Parametric Programming

In the previous chapter we became acquainted with the main concepts of linear programming. We saw that when a problem is formulated in this way a best program of activities can be identified (for example, a most profitable set of product outputs). This procedure can be of great help in decision making that involves many possible activities and numerous resource constraints (as well as other types of constraints).

BACKGROUND FOR SENSITIVITY ANALYSIS AND PARAMETRIC PROGRAMMING

In Chapter 8 we made a number of assumptions. Some of these assumptions pertained to the fixed capacities of resources, the fixed rates of use of these resources by the activities, and, also, the fixed rates of profit from the various activities. In the previous chapter we wanted to obtain the best profit program in light of these fixed and known elements (that is, the given coefficients in the objective function and the constraints, as well as the right-hand-side constants in the constraints).

In this chapter we look beyond the identification of the best program of activities given the fixed coefficients and constants. Now we shall focus on the ways in which we can get answers to the following questions that involve *changes* in the previously fixed coefficients or constants. Thus, what had been fixed or constant now changes or can be changed to other amounts.

1   What would our best profit be if one of our resource capacities was *larger* (or smaller) than it is at the present time? We may be able to expand facilities, acquire more equipment, or dispose of facilities or equipment.

2   What would our best profit be if the rate of profit on an activity (a product output) *increased* above what it is at the present time (or decreased in amount)? The price of the product may be expected to rise (or fall) and, in turn, cause unit profit on the output activity to increase (or decrease).

3   What would our best profit be if the rate of use of a resource in an activity *decreased* below what it is at the present time (or increased)? It may be possible to train persons in a new technique that allows them to use less time to complete a task connected with a particular product-output activity. On the other hand, morale factors may increase the average amount of time it takes to complete a task.

The Lawn-Mower–Golf-Cart Example

Let us illustrate each of the above points in terms of the familiar lawn-mower–golf-cart problem that we examined in the last chapter. (*Note:* As we make a change in the original problem, we go back to the original problem again before making another change.)

An Increase in the Capacity of the Lawn-Mower Assembly Facility   Suppose that we want to know how much the total profit would increase if we enlarged the capacity of the lawn-mower assembly facility from its present 50 units per day to 60.

The way in which we obtain the answer is, first, to solve the new problem with the new capacity (60 as the right-hand-side constant instead of 50). We obtain a new optimal program and a new total profit. Then, we compare the total profit of the new best profit program with the old best profit program.

The amount of the difference between the two maximum total-profit amounts is attributable to the increase in the lawn-mower assembly facility. Obviously, this is of value in planning for such facility expansion because the additional profit from the expansion would be crucial in determining whether the expansion costs would be covered by the additional profit.

In Figure 9-1 we have the lawn-mower–golf-cart example with both the original 50-unit capacity for the lawn-mower assembly facility and also the proposed 60-unit capacity. The original best profit program was 50 lawn mowers and 15 golf carts, with a total profit of $2,750.

The new best profit program is 60 lawn mowers and 10 golf carts. The last corner point of the feasible region intersected by the objective function as we move it away from the origin (in the optimizing direction) is where $x_1 = 60$ and $x_2 = 10$. The total profit of this program is $2,900: $40(60) + $50(10) = $2,900.

The difference between the original (best) total profit and the new (best) total

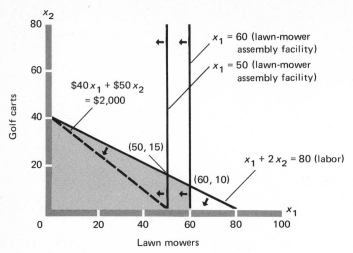

Figure 9-1   The lawn-mower–golf-cart example with an increase in the capacity of resource 1 (the lawn-mower assembly facility).

profit is $150: $2,900 − $2,750 = $150. Thus, the effect of the expansion of the facilities upon total profit is to increase them by $150 per day (of course this assumes everything else holds constant that is assumed to be fixed).

What we have shown is a simple illustration of the way in which linear programming can be used in the analysis for decisions regarding the expansion of facilities or the acquisition of additional equipment. Of course any real-world problem is much more complex than this one, but the basic ideas regarding the potential role of linear programming in such decision problems is illustrated by this example.

An Increase in the Unit Profit of Golf Carts   If the price of golf carts is expected to rise, the profit per golf cart, in turn, may be expected to increase by a comparable amount. This, of course, would follow only if the variable costs per golf cart remain unchanged.

But in order to illustrate some useful analysis of the effects of an increase in the unit profit of one of the products (one of the activities), let us assume that the unit profit of golf carts increases by a large amount, say from $50 to $100.

To study the effect of this unit-profit change, we solve the new linear-programming problem. Everything is the same as in the original problem except that the *second* coefficient in the objective function is now $100 instead of $50.

In Figure 9-2 we have the original problem represented along with the new problem. The only change is in the objective function. The original problem had the objective function, $40x_1 + $50x_2 =$ total profit, and as it moved outward from the origin it intersected last the corner point $(x_1, x_2) = (50, 15)$.

The new objective function is $40x_1 + $100x_2 =$ total profit, and has a much flatter slope as seen in Figure 9-2. We plotted the $4,000 total-profit graph for the new objective function. (When x_2 was set to 0, we found the x_1-intercept to be 100. When x_1 was set to 0 the x_2-intercept was found to be 40. We connected the two intercepts with a dashed line, as shown in Figure 9-2.)

Once we have the new objective function graphed, we can take a clear plastic ruler and "move it outward" (that is, plot successively higher values of the objective function). When we do this in Figure 9-2 we see that the new objective function intersects last a different corner point. It is the corner point where $x_1 = 0$ and $x_2 = 40$, right on the objective function we graphed. No other feasible program will generate a higher total profit under the new unit profit for golf carts. The new program is comprised of 40 golf carts and no lawn mowers at all. The amount of the total profit is $4,000: \$40(0) + \$100(40) = \$4,000$.

What have we just done? We have found out that an increase in the unit profit of golf carts from \$50 to \$100 will increase total profit by \$1,250: $\$4,000 - \$2,750 = \$1,250$.

Of course to obtain this \$1,250 increase in total profit it will be necessary to shift from a program of 50 lawn mowers and 15 golf carts to a program of 0 lawn mowers and 40 golf carts. The old program (50, 15) is still feasible with the new unit profit on golf carts, but it simply is not now the most profitable program.

A Decrease in the Rate of Use of Labor in the Golf-Cart Production Activity Suppose that a new technique has been developed in the making of golf carts whereby the amount of labor time needed for each golf cart has been cut in half.

However, in order for persons to learn the new technique, special training is required. The training will incur additional costs, and thus it would be very useful to get an advance measure of the effect of the training on total profit. If the gain in

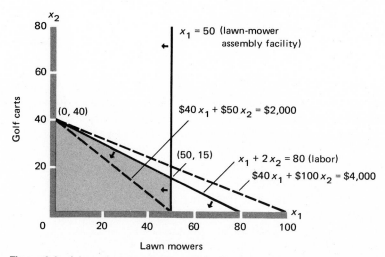

Figure 9-2 A large increase in the unit profit on the golf-cart production activity.

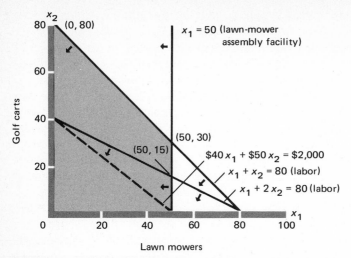

Figure 9-3   An increase in the productivity of labor in making golf carts.

total profit would at least cover the additional costs involved in the training of the relevant personnel, it would appear desirable to implement the training program.

In the original problem, each golf cart required 2 hours of labor. Now, after the training, it is assumed that only 1 hour of labor is required for each golf cart.

Once again, we have a new linear-programming problem to solve. In Figure 9-3 we have both the original problem and the new problem represented. The only change is that we have a new graph for the labor resource.

The original labor-resource inequality was $x_1 + 2x_2 \leq 80$. Now it is $x_1 + x_2 \leq 80$. The only change is in the coefficient for x_2 which represents the rate of use of the labor resource by the golf-cart production activity. In plotting the equation we find that the x_1-intercept stays at 80. However, the x_2-intercept shifts from 40 to 80. As shown in Figure 9-3, the feasible region after the training is much larger than it was before.

With the new problem represented, we go to our objective function, $40x_1 + \$50x_2 = $ total profit, and move it outward. As we do this, we see that the old optimal feasible program of 50 lawn mowers and 15 golf carts is no longer a corner point of the feasible region and definitely is not the most profitable program. As seen in Figure 9-3, the most profitable program is at $x_1 = 0$ and $x_2 = 80$. This last corner point intersected has a total profit of $4,000: \$40(0) + \$50(80) = \$4,000$.

Thus, we can get a measure of the effect of this reduction in the rate of use of labor in golf-cart production by comparing this $4,000 total profit with the $2,750 total profit in the original problem. The difference is $1,250: \$4,000 - \$2,750 = \$1,250$. Additional profit of $1,250 per day would be forthcoming if the training was undertaken. By taking into account the training cost, a decision could be made on whether or not the cost should be incurred.

ELEMENTARY SENSITIVITY ANALYSIS

In most real-world problems the unit profits from the activities, the rates of resource use by the activities, and the capacities of the resources are not as fixed and constant as is assumed in the usual linear-programming model.

Thus, we often have some justifiable uneasiness as to whether an optimal feasible program obtained from solving a linear-programming problem is actually the best one (or even whether it is actually feasible). Also, as shown in the previous section, some changes in the coefficients and right-hand-side constants may be under our control. Sometimes, we may wish merely to identify those coefficients or constants which, if changed, would affect our optimal program and total profit.

Thus, we may wish to know the "things" to which the optimal program we have obtained is "sensitive." More specifically, we may want to identify those coefficients and constants, which, if they were to change from their currently assumed values, would alter the optimal program. This is undertaken in *sensitivity analysis*.

Most simply, we can think of a one-unit change occurring in each coefficient or right-hand-side constant (one coefficient or constant at a time) and then solving the new problem. If the optimal program in the new problem is different from that in the original problem, we say that the original optimal program is "sensitive" to changes in that particular coefficient or right-hand-side constant. Let us illustrate this in terms of the lawn-mower–golf-cart example.

Sensitivity Analysis of the Lawn-Mower–Golf-Cart Problem

In the lawn-mower–golf-cart problem, let us increase individually each coefficient and constant by 1 unit and then solve the new problem to see if the optimal program changes.

In this small problem we can identify (in a graph) the coefficients and constants to which the optimal program is sensitive, but this, of course, cannot be done in larger problems. Also, our analysis will prepare us for the final section of this chapter which is essentially an extension of this sensitivity analysis. In another later chapter, we shall return to sensitivity analysis for a study of further aspects of the procedure.

Obtaining the Coordinates of a Corner Point A look at the original lawn-mower–golf-cart problem in Figure 8-7 or 9-1 will show that the last corner point of the feasible region intersected by the objective function (as it is moved outward) is at $(x_1, x_2) = (50, 15)$ with a total profit of $2,750.

Graphically, we identified the corner point as the optimal one, but how did we get the exact x_1- and x_2-values? In this case they can perhaps be read directly from the graph, but this is not always possible. Therefore, we should spend a moment right here to see how for such small problems we can obtain the exact coordinates (the program) that correspond to the optimal corner point.

First, any corner point is determined by an intersection of two straight lines. The corner point is a point that is common to both lines. The coordinates of this point (at the intersection) are referred to as the "solution" to the two equations; that is, the coordinates (of the point in common) when substituted into each equation "satisfy" each equation. By the term "satisfy" we simply mean that it makes each equation a true statement.

In our original lawn-mower–golf-cart example, the optimal corner point is determined by the equation portions of the two resource inequalities. Thus, the coordinates of the optimal corner point can be obtained by solving the two relevant equations simultaneously.

To do this we first set down the equations as follows (leaving the unit and zero coefficients implicit):

$$x_1 \qquad = 50 \text{ (lawn-mower assembly limit)}$$
$$x_1 + 2x_2 = 80 \text{ (labor-hour limit)}$$

Usually, we would then try to eliminate one of the unknowns (x_1 or x_2) in one of the equations by multiplying one of the equations by an appropriate number and then adding the two equations term by term. However, in this case our first equation already has only one unknown, and so the first step of eliminating one of the unknowns from one of the equations is not necessary. But once we have the value for one of the unknowns, we simply record its value and then substitute it back into one of the equations to find the value of the other unknown.

Thus, in the first equation above, we see that $x_1 = 50$. Next, we substitute 50 for x_1 in the second equation as follows:

$$x_1 + 2x_2 = 80 \text{ (labor-hour limit)}$$
$$50 + 2x_2 = 80$$
$$2x_2 = 30$$
$$x_2 = 15$$

Therefore, the optimal corner point of the original problem that we identified in the graph in Figure 9-1 has the coordinates $x_1 = 50$ and $x_2 = 15$, or simply, $(x_1, x_2) = (50, 15)$.

Sensitivity of the Optimal Program to Changes in the Resource Capacities (The Right-Hand-Side Constants)   As we indicated earlier, the most direct way of identifying whether or not an optimal program is sensitive to a change in a resource capacity is to increase the capacity by 1 unit (or decrease it by 1 unit) and then solve the newly created problem.

For an illustration, let us increase the lawn-mower assembly capacity by 1 unit (that is, from 50 to 51). From the graph of the new problem in Figure 9-4a we see that the optimal corner point shifts slightly and indicates to us that our original optimal program is sensitive to this resource-capacity change.

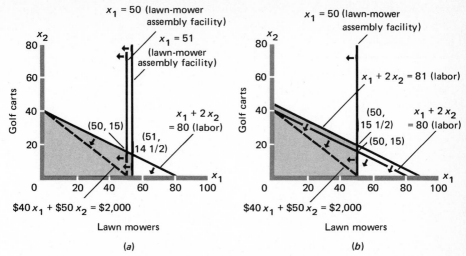

Figure 9-4 *(a)* A 1-unit increase in the capacity of resource 1 (lawn-mower assembly facility) and *(b)* a 1-unit increase in the availability of resource 2 (labor hours).

The new optimal corner point, however, is still determined by the equation portions of the two resource inequality constraints. But one of the equations (the one pertaining to the lawn-mower assembly facility) now has a larger right-hand-side amount. Thus, from the graph in Figure 9-4*a* we see that the optimal corner point is determined by the two following equations:

$$x_1 = 51 \text{ (lawn-mower assembly limit)}$$
$$x_1 + 2x_2 = 80 \text{ (labor-hour limit)}$$

We have a value of 51 for x_1, and so we substitute 51 for x_1 in the second equation and then solve for x_2.

$$x_1 + 2x_2 = 80$$
$$51 + 2x_2 = 80$$
$$2x_2 = 29$$
$$x_2 = 14\tfrac{1}{2}$$

Thus, the coordinates of the optimal corner point of the new problem are $x_1 = 51$ and $x_2 = 14\tfrac{1}{2}$. Since this optimal program is different from the original optimal program, we conclude that the original optimal program is sensitive to this resource-capacity change.

We can proceed to increase the other resource amounts by 1 unit individually and then determine whether or not the optimal program of the new problem is different from the original optimal program. Let us now increase by 1 unit the right-hand-side amount of our only other resource, labor.

From the graph of this new problem in Figure 9-4*b* we identify the optimal corner point as being determined by the equation portions of the two resource inequalities. They are as follows:

$$x_1 = 50$$
$$x_1 + 2x_2 = 81$$

Substituting 50 for x_1 in the second equation, we have:

$$50 + 2x_2 = 81$$
$$2x_2 = 31$$
$$x_2 = 15\frac{1}{2}$$

Thus, the coordinates of our new optimal program are $x_1 = 50$ and $x_2 = 15\frac{1}{2}$. Our original optimal program is sensitive to this resource amount, too.

Sensitivity of the Optimal Program to Changes in the Unit Profits of the Activities

If we increase by $1 the unit profit for lawn mowers (the coefficient of x_1 in the objective function), we obtain a new objective function as follows:

$$\$41x_1 + \$50x_2 = \text{total profit}$$

The graph of this new problem is shown in Figure 9-5a, and it is seen that the small change in the unit profit has the effect of changing the slope of the objective function only slightly. Thus, the optimal program to this new problem is the very same program as the optimal program to the original problem. Thus, we say that

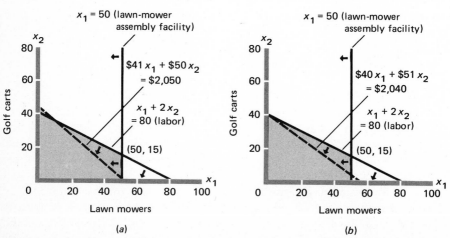

Figure 9-5 (a) A $1-increase in the unit profit on lawn mowers and (b) a $1-increase in the unit profit on golf carts.

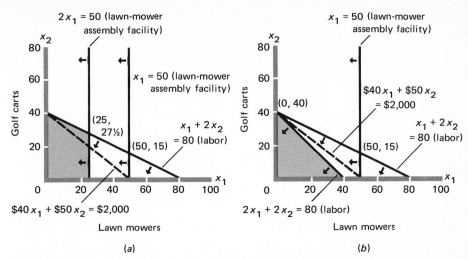

Figure 9-6 *(a)* A 1-unit increase in the rate of use of resource 1 in making lawn mowers; *(b)* a 1-unit increase in the rate of use of resource 2 in making lawn mowers.

the original optimal program is *not* sensitive to a $1 change in the rate of profit on lawn mowers.

Similarly, the original optimal program is not sensitive to a $1 increase in the rate of profit on the golf-cart production activity, either. That new problem has the following objective function:

$$\$40x_1 + \$51x_2 = \text{total profit}$$

The graph of this new problem is shown in Figure 9-5*b*.

Sensitivity of the Optimal Program to Changes in the Rates of Use of Resources   In our lawn-mower–golf-cart example the original optimal program is sensitive to every one of the rates of use of the resources.

In Figure 9-6*a* we have a unit increase in the rate of use of the lawn-mower assembly facility by the lawn-mower production activity. In Figure 9-6*b* we have a unit increase in the rate of use of labor in the lawn-mower production activity. In an earlier section of this chapter we examined a unit decrease in the rate of use of labor by the golf-cart production activity and found that the optimal program changed as a result. The graph of that new problem appears in Figure 9-3.

ELEMENTARY PARAMETRIC PROGRAMMING

We have now acquired enough background to examine the main elements of the procedure called *parametric programming*. The term results because each coefficient in the objective function or the constraints, as well as each right-hand-side constant in the constraints, is also termed a *parameter*.

In previous sections of this chapter we studied the effects of changes in each type of parameter that appears in the usual linear-programming problem. Parametric programming essentially involves an extension of these ideas that we have already discussed in this chapter.

The systematic variation of a parameter over a broad range of values and the accompanying analysis of the effects on the optimal program and its value (total profit) are undertaken in *parametric-programming analysis.*

In its more elementary form, only one parameter at a time is varied; however, the simultaneous variation of two or more parameters is sometimes desired in the study of real-world problems. In this book we shall focus only upon individual parameter variation, but the procedures extend to the simultaneous variation of two or more parameters. Computer programs, too, are widely available that allow parametric-programming analysis to be undertaken with considerable ease in large practical problems.

Variation of Resource Capacities over a Broad Range   Suppose that we vary the capacity of our lawn-mower assembly facility from 0 all the way to 100 and examine the effect this has on our optimal program and its total profit.

The present capacity of the facility is 50, and earlier in this chapter we observed that the optimal program (given this capacity of 50) is 50 lawn mowers and 15 golf carts. The total profit was found to be $2,750.

In Table 9-1 we record this optimal program and its total profit in the row associated with the capacity of 50. In a previous section, too, we solved the

Table 9-1   Varying the Lawn-Mower Assembly Capacity over a Broad Range

	Lawn-mower assembly capacity	Optimal program (x_1, x_2)	Total profit of optimal program, $\$40x_1 + \$50x_2$	Rate of increase in total profit or the marginal contribution to profit (also, the slope of the total-profit graph in Figure 9-7)
	0	(0, 40)	$2,000	—
	1	(1, 39½)	2,015	$15
	2	(2, 39)	2,030	15
	.			
	.			
	.			
(current)	50	(50, 15)	2,750	15
	51	(51, 14½)	2,765	15
	.			
	.			
	.			
	80	(80, 0)	3,200	15
	81	(80, 0)	3,200	0

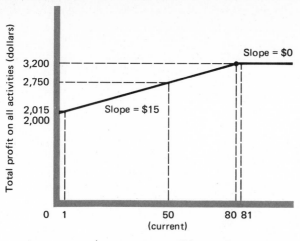

Figure 9-7 The effect on total profit of varying the capacity of resource 1 (lawn-mower assembly facility) over a broad range.

problem when the capacity was 51. We record that optimal program and its total profit as well.

But now our concern is directed toward a variation of this parameter over a much larger interval (from 0 to 100) and particularly toward its effect upon our objective (here, maximum total profit). What we desire is a statement (or a graph) showing the relationship of this parameter variation to our total profit objective.

Generally, we would suspect that increasing the lawn-mower assembly capacity would increase optimal total profit, but often we want a quantitative statement of that relationship. This is what is accomplished in parametric-programming analysis. It provides information such as that shown in Table 9-1 and the corresponding graph in Figure 9-7. Our aim right now is to discuss in an elementary way just how we obtain the data in Table 9-1 and the graph in Figure 9-7 that show specifically how optimal total profit changes as the lawn-mower assembly capacity is varied upward from 0 to 100.

In this discussion let us use Figure 9-8 to gain a clearer understanding of the procedure. Bear in mind that we are now allowing the once-fixed, lawn-mower assembly capacity to vary. In Figure 9-8 we have left as a benchmark the capacity limit when it was 50 but have also "moved" the capacity limit to other amounts such as 0, 1, 80, and 81.

We start by solving the new linear-programming problem when the lawn-mower assembly capacity is 0. With the aid of the graph in Figure 9-8, we see that if we have this capacity at 0 this constraint equation will be superimposed right on the vertical axis. This leaves as the feasible "region" only the programs (the points) lying on the vertical axis from the origin (0, 0) to the corner point (0, 40).

Given our objective function, we see that the last corner point it intersects as it moves outward is (0, 40). Thus, this is the optimal program when the lawn-

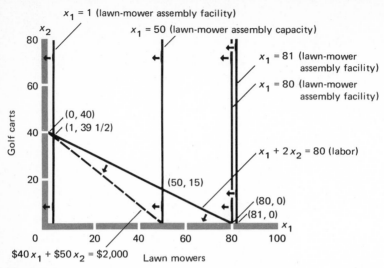

Figure 9-8 Solving the new linear-programming problems in order to obtain the slopes of the total-profit graph of the resource 1 variation (variation of the lawn-mower assembly facility).

mower capacity is 0. The total profit is $2,000: $40(0) + $50(40) = $2,000. We record this in Table 9-1 and plot this total profit against the 0 lawn-mower assembly capacity in Figure 9-7. This is a point on the vertical axis where the total profit is $2,000.

Next, we increase the lawn-mower capacity *by 1 unit* (from 0 to 1). Then, we solve this new problem. With the aid of the graph in Figure 9-8, we see that the optimal corner point must be $(1, 39\frac{1}{2})$ with a total profit of $2,015. We record this optimal program and its total profit in Table 9-1 and plot in Figure 9-7 this total profit against the lawn-mower assembly capacity of 1.

We have just done something of considerable importance. We have obtained the *change in total profit for a unit change* (from 0 to 1) *in the lawn-mower assembly capacity*. We refer to this change also as the "marginal contribution to profit" of this resource. We record this total-profit *increase* in the extreme-right column of Table 9-1. Also, in Figure 9-7 we associate a slope-value of $15 with the first straight-line segment of the total-profit graph. Recall that the slope of a straight-line segment is defined as the change in the value of the variable on the vertical axis (here, total profit) as the value of the variable on the horizontal axis (here, lawn-mower assembly capacity) increases by 1 unit.

If we continued to increase this parameter by 1 unit at a time, we would find that over some range the total profit would increase at a constant rate. (In Table 9-1 we increase the assembly capacity to 2 units and note another $15 increase in total profit.) Thus, we are on a straight-line segment of the total-profit graph. But how much can this parameter increase before a "breakpoint" is encountered and also another linear segment with a new slope?

At this stage of our discussion we answer this question with the aid of the graph in Figure 9-8. We see from the graph that we can increase the lawn-mower assembly capacity unit by unit (from a capacity of 1), and our optimal program for each capacity amount will "crawl" down the line representing the fixed labor-resource limit until it intersects the horizontal axis. It turns out that because of the linearity in linear-programming problems, we can be assured that as the optimal program crawls in the same "direction," total profit will be increasing at a constant rate until the direction of the "moving" optimal corner point changes. This occurs when an axis is reached or when the limit of some fixed resource constraint is encountered that prevents the optimal corner point from continuing to move in the direction in which it has been moving as the parameter has been increased.

A change in the direction of movement of our optimal corner point will occur in our example when the lawn-mower assembly limit line intersects the horizontal axis at (80, 0). At that point, too, in our parameter variation the lawn-mower assembly limit is 80. This we see from the graph in Figure 9-8. We solve this new problem and find the optimal program to be (80, 0) with a total profit of $3,200. This total profit is recorded in Table 9-1 and is plotted against a capacity of 80 in Figure 9-7. The first (and only) breakpoint will be at a capacity of 80.

Once a point such as (80, 0) is reached, we increase the parameter (here, the lawn-mower assembly capacity) by 1 unit and then solve the newly created problem. This new problem has a lawn-mower assembly capacity of 81, and the optimal program with this new capacity is (80, 0) with a total profit of $3,200. We record this total profit in Table 9-1 and plot the total profit for a capacity of 81 in Figure 9-7.

We see that increasing the capacity from 80 to 81 did not increase total profit at all. This is simply because the labor constraint did not permit any more than 80 lawn mowers to be produced. Therefore, the slope of this linear segment of the total-profit graph is $0. Additional increases in the lawn-mower assembly capacity beyond 80 (and, of course, through 100 and beyond) would yield no increases in total profit.

We can do a similar parametric-programming analysis of the other resources (the other right-hand-side amounts). Here we have just one other resource, labor. But let us vary it, too, over a broad range (from 0 to 100) and observe the effect upon total profit from all of the activities.

First, we graph the problem as in Figure 9-9. Once again, we plot the present labor-hour limit of 80 for purposes of reference even though our analysis involves its variation from 0 to 100.

We start with 0 labor-hours and solve this new problem. The only feasible program now is (0, 0) right at the origin, where no lawn mowers and no golf carts are produced at all. Of course it is also the optimal program with a total profit of $0. This is recorded in Table 9-2 and plotted in Figure 9-10.

Next, we increase the labor-hours by 1 unit (1 hour) and solve that new problem. We have a very small feasible region for this new problem, but from the graph in Figure 9-9 we can see that the optimal program lies right on the horizontal axis where it is intersected by the labor-limit line. (Note also that the

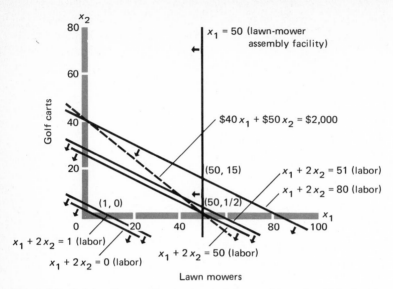

Figure 9-9 Solving the new linear-programming problems to obtain the slopes of the total-profit graph of the resource 2 variation (labor hours available).

lawn-mower assembly limit is now fixed at 50 and when the labor hours available are so few the lawn-mower assembly limit does not affect the feasible region.)

The equation portion of the labor constraint is now $x_1 + 2x_2 = 1$. Since x_2 is 0 at the x_1-intercept, x_1 must be 1 at this corner point: $x_1 + 2(0) = 1$. Since the optimal program is $(x_1, x_2) = (1, 0)$, we have a new total profit of $40: $40(1) +

Table 9-2   Varying Over a Broad Range the Labor-Hours that are Available

	Labor-hours available	Optimal program (x_1, x_2)	Total profit of optimal program, $40x_1 + 50x_2$	Rate of increase in total profit or the marginal contribution to profit (also, the slope of the total-profit graph in Figure 9-10)
	0	(0, 0)	$ 0	—
	1	(1, 0)	40	$40
	.			
	.			
	.			
	50	(50, 0)	2,000	40
	51	(50, ½)	2,025	25
	.			
	.			
	.			
(current)	80	(50, 15)	2,750	25

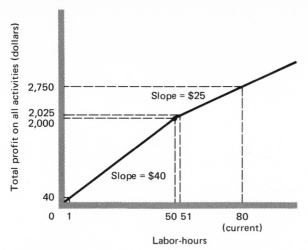

Figure 9-10   The effect on total profit of varying the availability of resource 2 (labor hours) over a broad range.

$50(0) = \$40$. We record this total profit in Table 9-2, and plot it against 1 hour of labor in Figure 9-10.

We have obtained the optimal total profit when the labor-hours are 0 and when they are 1. The increase in total profit is $40 due to this labor-hour increase, as shown in Table 9-2. This increase in total profit with a unit increase in the labor resource gives us the slope of the first linear segment of the total-profit graph for the labor-resource variation.

How long will this slope of $40 continue? Let us look at the graph of the problem in Figure 9-9. The optimal program will crawl along the horizontal axis as the labor-hours are increased up to the point where x_1 is 50, that is, the program (50, 0). If labor-hours are increased further, the optimal program will move *up* the vertical lawn-mower assembly limit line. Thus, this shift in the direction of the optimal corner point corresponds to a breakpoint in our total-profit graph and a new slope-value when the labor-limit line intersects the horizontal axis where x_1 is 50.

This point on the horizontal axis may be described by the ordered pair $(x_1, x_2) = (50, 0)$, and when we substitute these values into the labor resource equation we have:

$$x_1 + 2x_2 = \text{labor-hours}$$
$$50 + 2(0) = \text{labor-hours}$$
$$\text{labor-hours} = 50$$

Therefore, this corner point corresponds to the program $(x_1, x_2) = (50, 0)$, and the labor-hours associated with the labor-constraint equation when it intersects this point are 50 hours. This labor equation is plotted in Figure 9-9.

Once we reach the place where the optimal corner point begins to move in a new direction, we want to increase the parameter we are varying (here, labor-hours) by 1 unit and then solve that new problem.

Recall from above that when the labor-hours are 50, the optimal program is $(x_1, x_2) = (50, 0)$ with a total profit of $2,000. Then, when we increase the labor hours to 51, we have a new problem to be solved. The new problem includes the labor resource equation $x_1 + 2x_2 = 51$ (labor-hours). We plot this equation in Figure 9-9 and observe the new optimal corner point.

The new optimal program is $(x_1, x_2) = (50, \frac{1}{2})$ which has a total profit of $2,025. Thus, the fifty-first hour of labor would increase total profit only by $25 (the fiftieth hour of labor increased profit by $40). We record this in Table 9-2 and plot it in Figure 9-10.

We are now on a new linear segment of our total-profit graph and, of course, are interested in the interval of labor-hours over which this $25 slope will hold. From Figure 9-9 we can see that this slope will continue until some other constraint (not represented in the model) imposes a limit. In a later chapter, we shall see that in solving large problems there is a method for obtaining this range without the use of a graph.

The Variation of a Unit Profit over a Broad Range What we have done with respect to the right-hand-side constants we can also do to the coefficients of the objective function (or the coefficients of the constraints). It is more common to vary the objective-function coefficients; therefore, let us select one of the unit profits in our lawn-mower–golf-cart example and vary it over a broad range. Suppose we choose the lawn-mower activity and vary its unit profit from $0 to $100.

In the original lawn-mower–golf-cart example the unit profit on lawn mowers was $40 and in Table 9-3 we record this unit profit on lawn mowers and the associated optimal total profit on all activities.

With the aid of the graph in Figure 9-11, we note that the unit profit on lawn mowers can increase by $1 (or decrease by $1), and the optimal program will remain at (50, 15). However, total profit does change by $50 for each $1 change in the unit profit of lawn mowers. Thus, we are on a linear segment of a total-profit graph with a slope of $50. The completed graph appears in Figure 9-12, but let us discuss the way in which we can obtain such a graph.

First, let us set the unit profit on lawn mowers at $0 and then solve that problem. The graph of this objective function will be parallel with the horizontal axis as seen in Figure 9-11. (Using the coefficients to obtain the intercepts, we have an x_1-intercept of 50 and an x_2-intercept of 0.) The optimal program is at (0, 40) with a total profit of $2,000. We record this in Table 9-3 and also plot the total profit against the $0 unit profit on lawn mowers in Figure 9-12. At this unit profit of $0, all of the total profit is being generated by the golf-cart production activity.

As before, we want the slope of the total-profit graph in Figure 9-12. We can get this slope by solving the new problem as we increase the unit profit on lawn mowers from $0 to $1. But this leaves the graph of the objective function in

Table 9-3 Varying over a Broad Range the Unit Profit on Lawn Mowers

Unit profit on lawn mowers c_1	Optimal program (x_1, x_2)	Total profit on optimal program $c_1 x_1 + \$50 x_2$	Rate of increase in total profit (also, the slope of the total-profit graph in Figure 9-12)
$ 0	(0, 40)	$2,000	
1	(0, 40)	2,000	$ 0
.			
.			
.			
24	(0, 40)	2,000	0
25	(0, 40) or (50, 15)	2,000	0
26	(50, 15)	2,050	50
.			
.			
.			
(current) 40	(50, 15)	2,750	50
41	(50, 15)	2,800	50
.			
.			
.			
100	(50, 15)	5,750	50
101	(50, 15)	5,800	50

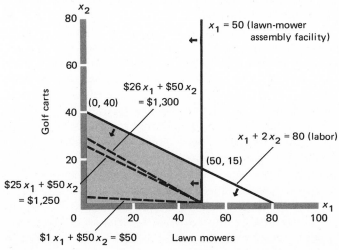

Figure 9-11 Solving the new linear-programming problems to obtain the slopes of the total-profit graph of the variation of the unit profit on product 1 (lawn mowers).

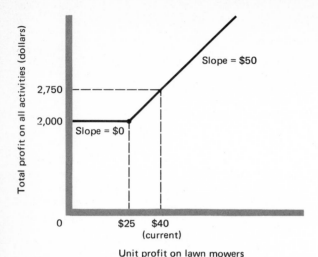

Figure 9-12   The effect on total profit of varying the unit profit on product 1 (lawn mowers) over a broad range.

Figure 9-11 virtually the same. (The x_1-intercept is 50 and the x_2-intercept is 1.) Thus, the program (0, 40) is still the optimal one. The total profit is still the same, too, at \$2,000. Thus, we are on a linear segment of the total-profit graph where the slope is \$0.

How long does the slope of \$0 continue? It will continue until another corner point of the feasible region becomes optimal. In this case the slope of the objective function will have to change considerably before the optimal program shifts from (0, 40) to (50, 15). Actually, the unit profit on lawn mowers will have to increase to \$25 before a shift will take place.

When the unit profit on lawn mowers is \$25, the objective function in Figure 9-11 will simultaneously intersect the corner point (0, 40) and the corner point (50, 15), as well as all the points on the boundary between those two corner points. Thus, we have two optimal corner points that yield the same total profit of \$2,000. (We have this situation when the slope of one of the constraint equations is the same as the slope of the objective function. Thus, in this situation the ratio of the two coefficients in the constraint equation involved is equal to the ratio of the coefficients of the objective function. In our example, the coefficient 2 of x_2 in the labor equation constraint is twice as large as the coefficient 1 of x_1 in that same equation. The coefficient \$50 of x_2 in the objective function is also twice as large as the coefficient \$25 of x_1 in the objective function.)

However, if we increase the unit profit on lawn mowers to \$26, only the (50, 15) corner point is optimal, and total profit rises by \$50. Thus, we are now on a linear segment of the total-profit graph with a slope of \$50. As we view Figure 9-11 we can see that increases in the unit profit of lawn mowers will leave the (50, 15) corner point the optimal program up through a \$100 unit profit.

SUMMARY

1 *Sensitivity analysis* and *parametric programming* focus on the effect of changes in the coefficients and constants that were fixed in an original problem. Some of these changes may be under our control, such as the expansion of facilities. Other changes may be beyond our control and sometimes change because of unknown factors (chance).

2 Sensitivity analysis is primarily concerned with the sensitivity of the optimal program of the original problem to changes in the coefficients and constants from what they were in the original problem. Identification of those coefficients and constants whose change affects the optimal program is sought.

3 Parametric-programming analysis involves the variation of one or more of the coefficients or constants over a broad range. The effect of such parameter variation upon the objective (such as maximum total profit) is of primary interest.

PROBLEMS

9-1 Consider again Problem 8-1. Let us now increase the amount of resource 1 that is available from its current amount of 30 to 31 (leaving the resource 2 amount unchanged).

  a Graph the new problem on the product axes, and identify the corner point of the feasible region associated with the new optimal feasible program.

  b What is the new optimal feasible program and its total profit?

  c Comparing the optimal total profit for the original problem obtained in Problem 8-1*i* with that obtained above, how much does another unit of resource 2 (the thirty-first unit) add to total profit?

9-2 Let us go back to the original Problem 8-1 and increase *individually* by 1 unit the amount of resource 2 that is available (from 80 to 81).

  a Graph this new problem on the product axes, and identify the corner point of the feasible region associated with the optimal feasible program.

  b What is the optimal feasible program and its total profit?

  c Comparing the optimal total profit for the original problem obtained in Problem 8-1*i* with that obtained above, how much does another unit of resource 2 (the eighty-first unit) add to total profit?

9-3 Suppose that in Problem 8-1 we vary the amount of resource 1 over a broad range, specifically from 0 to 50. We are particularly concerned with the effect of such variation upon the best total profit that can be obtained with various amounts of resource 1.

  a Set the resource 1 amount at 0, and graph the new problem on the product axes.

  b What is the optimal feasible program and its total profit with the resource 1 amount of 0?

  c Record in a table (as in Table 9-1) the optimal program and its total profit with a resource 1 amount of 0.

  d Increase the resource 1 amount by 1 unit (from 0 to 1) and graph this new problem. What is the new optimal program and its total profit? Record this in your table (as in Table 9-1).

  e How much did the first unit of resource 1 add to total profit? What is the slope of the first linear segment of the graph of optimal total profit as resource 1 is varied (a graph such as in Figure 9-7)?

f As the resource 1 amount is increased further, the increase in optimal total profit will be at the same rate until the "direction" of movement of the optimal solution changes or until such movement is halted. From an inspection of your graph of the problem and the possible movement of the resource 1 constraint outward, what is the last program (pair of coordinates) and its total profit associated with this halt or change in direction? What is the resource 1 amount associated with this program? This resource 1 amount is associated with a breakpoint in the total-profit graph. Record these results in your table for the resource 1 variation.

g To the resource 1 amount obtained in *f,* add one more unit of the resource. How much does it increase optimal total profit? Record the optimal program and its total profit (also, the increase in total profit) in your table for the resource 1 variation.

h Complete a graph of optimal total profit as the resource 1 amount is varied from 0 to 50. Indicate on the graph the slopes of the linear segments of the graph.

i Indicate on the horizontal axis of your total-profit graph obtained in *h* the current (original) resource 1 amount of 30. What is the marginal contribution to profit of resource 1 (the slope of the total-profit graph) in the vicinity of 30? What is the range over which the resource 1 amount can vary and still have the same marginal contribution to profit?

9-4 In Problem 8-1 let us now vary the other resource amount (resource 2) over a broad range, leaving the resource 1 amount fixed at its original 30 units. Suppose we vary the resource 2 amount from 0 to 100.

a Set the resource 2 amount at 0 and graph the new problem on the product axes. Obtain the new optimal feasible program and its total profit. Record the results of this resource 2 variation in a table as in Table 9-2.

b Increase the resource 2 amount from 0 to 1 and graph this new problem. Obtain the new optimal feasible program and its total profit. Record the results in your table of the resource 2 variation. Be sure to include the *increase* in optimal total profit due to the 1-unit increase in the resource 2 amount. This is equal to the slope of the first linear segment of the total-profit graph of the resource 2 variation.

c In which direction (and on which axis) does the optimal feasible solution move as the resource 2 amount is increased beyond 0 and 1? What is the last of the optimal solutions in this first direction of movement? What is the resource 2 amount associated with this last optimal solution? This resource 2 amount is associated with a breakpoint in the total-profit graph of resource 2 variation. Record the optimal solution, its total profit, and the associated resource 2 amount in your table of the resource 2 variation.

d When the last optimal solution is reached in a particular line of movement of optimal solutions in such parametric variation as in *c,* increase the associated resource amount by 1 more unit and then solve that new problem. What is the new optimal solution and its total profit if resource 2 is increased by 1 more unit? What is the marginal contribution to profit (and slope of the total-profit graph) associated with this new direction of movement of the optimal solutions? How far does it extend? Record the results in your table of the resource 2 variation.

e   Using your table of the resource 2 variation, complete a total-profit graph for the resource 2 variation. Label the slopes of the linear segments and indicate the current (original) resource 2 amount of 80.

9-5   For the maker of backpacks and raincoats in Problem 8-2 vary resource 1 (sewing-machine-hours) individually from 1 to 250 to study the effect of more or fewer sewing machines upon total profit (this total profit amount, however, does not include the cost of more sewing machines).

a   Form a table of your resource 1 (sewing-machine-hours) variation as in Table 9-1.

b   From your table of the resource 1 variation obtain a total-profit graph of this variation. Label the slopes of the linear segments and indicate the current (original) resource 1 amount.

c   What is the range over which the resource 1 amount can vary with its marginal contribution to profit holding at the value associated with the current (original) resource 1 amount?

9-6   In Problem 8-2 vary the other resource (resource 2: labor-hours) individually from 0 to 350.

a   Obtain a total-profit graph of this resource 2 variation. Label the slopes of the linear segments and indicate the current (original) resource 2 amount.

b   What is the current marginal contribution to profit of resource 2? Over what range of resource 2 amounts will it hold at that value?

9-7   a   For the dairy-foods processor in Problem 8-3 vary the resource 1 amount individually from 0 to 200. Obtain a total-profit graph of the resource 1 variation. Label the slopes and indicate the current resource 1 amount.

b   In Problem 8-3 vary the other resource (resource 2) individually from 0 to 200. Obtain a total-profit graph of the resource 2 variation. Label the slopes and indicate the current resource 2 amount.

c   From your parameter variations in a and b, what is the current marginal contribution to profit of resource 1? Of resource 2? Over what range of resource amounts will each of them hold?

9-8   a   In Problem 8-4 let us vary for the car manufacturer the labor-hours available from 0 to 2,500. Obtain a total-profit graph of this resource variation. Label the slopes and indicate the current labor-hours available.

b   In Problem 8-4 vary the other resource (the capacity of assembly facilities) from 0 to 1,000. Obtain a total-profit graph of this resource variation. Label the slopes and indicate the current capacity.

c   From your parameter variations in a and b, what is the marginal contribution to profit of each resource at its current amount? Over what range of resource amounts will each of them hold? Explain.

9-9   a   To what parameters is the optimal solution for the food processor in Problem 8-5 sensitive?

b   In Problem 8-5 vary the labor-hours available from 0 to 250. Obtain a total-profit graph of this resource variation.

c   In Problem 8-5 vary the capacity of the processing facility from 0 to 150 percent. Obtain a total-profit graph of this resource variation.

d   From your parameter variations in b and c, what is the marginal contribution to profit of each resource at its current amount? Over what range of resource amounts will each of them hold?

9-10   a   For the small-vehicle maker in Problem 8-6 vary the labor-hours available from

0 to 500. Obtain a total-profit graph of this resource variation. Label the slopes and indicate the current labor-hours available.

b In Problem 8-6 vary the other resource (the capacity of the industrial vehicle assembly facility) from 0 to 200. Obtain a total-profit graph of this resource variation. Label the slopes and indicate the current capacity.

c From your parameter variation in *a* and *b*, what is the marginal contribution to profit of each resource at its current amount? Over what range of resource amounts will each of them hold?

9-11 Let us consider again the agricultural decision in Problem 8-8.

a Is the optimal solution sensitive to an individual 1-unit change (a $1 change) in the profit per acre of either corn or soybeans? Explain.

b In Problem 8-8 vary individually the profit per acre from corn production from $0 to $200. Form a table of this parameter variation as is done in Table 9-3.

c From your table in *b* obtain a total-profit graph of this unit-profit variation as in Figure 9-12. Label the slopes and indicate the current unit-profit amount.

d Over what range of unit-profit amounts in corn production will the current (original) solution remain optimal?

9-12 Suppose we are interested in studying the relationship of corn prices (per bushel) to the agricultural production decision in Problem 8-8. Use the data in Problem 8-8 and that which you derived in Problem 9-11. From Problem 9-11 you obtained the profits per acre in corn production that were associated with shifts in the optimal program. Identify the corn prices (per bushel) that result in these particular profits per acre.

a Is the optimal production program sensitive to a 1-cent change in corn prices?

b Vary individually the corn price from $.50 per bushel to $3.00 per bushel. Form a table of this variation that includes unit profit from corn production and total profit from both corn and soybean production.

c From your table in *b* obtain a total-profit graph of the corn-price variation. Indicate the slopes in terms of 1-cent changes in corn prices. Identify on the graph the current corn price as it was given in the original data in Problem 8-8.

d Obtain a graph showing the amount of corn produced in relation to the corn price. Soybeans may still be produced, but we want to examine only the corn-price–output relation. It is customary in plotting supply graphs to place product price on the vertical axis and output on the horizontal axis.

Chapter 10

Solving Larger Problems: An Elementary Discussion of the Simplex Method

Most of the problems encountered in Chapters 8 and 9 involved but two activities (two product-output activities). This permitted the problems to be solved graphically or, at least, to be solved with the aid of a graph. However, most real-world problems involve more than two activities (also, more than a couple of resource constraints) and thus require solution procedures that are not as limited as the graphic methods.

The main solution procedure used in linear-programming problems is the *simplex method*. Widely available computer programs employ this procedure, and it is the aim of this chapter to set down the elements of this method as clearly as possible.

The simplest and perhaps most common linear-programming problem is where some objective (such as profit) is to be maximized but where the available resources impose limits on the levels of the profit-generating activities. This is the type of problem to which we shall apply the simplex method in this chapter. In chapters that follow we shall indicate how minor modifications in these procedures extend the use of the simplex method to a wide variety of problems.

In order to attach some meaning to the steps in the simplex method, we shall first examine some of the mathematical ideas on which it is based.

BACKGROUND FOR THE SIMPLEX METHOD

Let us use a simple little example to illustrate some of the ideas and concepts connected with the simplex method. Suppose that a *single* product is to be produced with a unit profit of $8. A limit on its output is imposed by the capacity of a machine used in its production. Each unit of output requires 2 hours of machine time. There are only 40 machine-hours available each week.

We can formulate the problem as a profit-maximization problem subject to the single resource constraint. In this problem we have but one decision variable, x_1, the amount of product output. If we choose to maximize total profit per week, subject to the machine-hours available per week, we have the following formulation. (Recall that we assume throughout the book that the decision variables cannot take negative values.)

Maximize: Total profit $= \$8x_1$
Subject to the following constraint: $2x_1 \leq 40$ (machine-hours available)

This problem is really a trivial one, as can be seen in Figure 10-1a, but it is useful in that it provides a simple illustration of the simplex-solution procedure, which, in turn, can be applied to complicated problems involving many products and many resources.

The limited number of machine-hours available, 40 hours, restricts the output of the product to 20 units because each unit uses 2 machine-hours in its production. Thus we indicate in Figure 10-1a by point M the limit on product output (x_1) imposed by the machine. The single point M represents an x_1-value of 20 that satisfies the equation $2x_1 = 40$. This point simply represents the limit on product output due to the machine.

The arrow attached to point M is oriented toward the origin indicating that output levels less than 20 will be permissible because in our original problem the machine constraint was expressed in the form of a "less-than" inequality.

We can see in Figure 10-1a that the maximum-profit solution is an output of 20 units. We can think of moving the objective function, total profit $= \$8x_1$, from the origin where total profit $= \$0$ to point M where total profit $= \$160$. No higher profit is possible. We see that the optimal feasible solution is $x_1 = 20$, where total profit $= \$160$. Thus, we have a little problem for which we already know the answer, but let us see how the simplex method leads us to the same solution.

A typical linear-programming problem includes "less-than" inequality constraints, as does our example. This is so because it is highly desirable in real situations to be able to represent some limit on the activities imposed by the capacity or limited availability of a resource and, at the same time, to allow the use of the resource at less than full capacity should it be more profitable to do so. In most real-world problems it turns out that the most profitable program does not fully use every one of the resources available.

However, the presence of inequality constraints in our models creates some difficulties in obtaining solutions to problems that are too large to be graphed. If

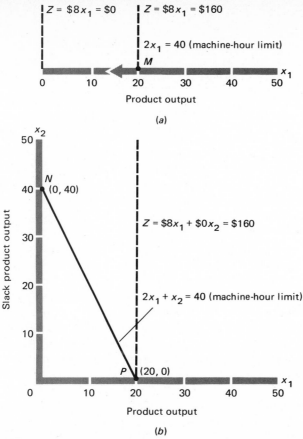

Figure 10-1 The graphs of the problem represented *(a)* by an inequality and *(b)* by an equation with a slack variable added.

the constraints were *equations* rather than *inequalities,* it would be far simpler to solve the problem. Could we, then, arbitrarily remove the inequality signs in a given set of constraints, thus leaving us with a set of equations? No, because the reality would not be represented as was desired. Doing this would force us to find a solution (program) that *used fully* every one of the resources (that is, satisfied every one of the equation constraints). As indicated above, in most real-world problems this usually is not the most profitable solution, and, besides, it simply may not be feasible. In the latter case, our set of equations would have no solution that would satisfy every one of the equations.

Fortunately, there is a little mathematical procedure that permits inequalities to be converted to equations without doing any injustice to the reality we are trying to represent. However, it does require that *a new variable be added to each "less-than" inequality.* Thus, in our example the single constraint $2x_1 \leqslant 40$ can be converted to an equation by adding a new variable x_2 as follows:

Product- output variable		Slack variable	
$2x_1$	$+$	$1x_2$	$= 40$ (machine-hours)

We call this new variable a *slack variable* for good reason. It will take up any "slack" in the use of the machine. We can think of it as a fictitious product-output activity which takes up any slack; that is, it utilizes any unused capacity of the machine after our real product-output amount has been attained. For example, if the real product output is 0, the slack variable will take a value of 40. Thus we can say that 40 units of the fictitious product could be "produced." Since the slack variable x_2 has a coefficient of 1 in the constraint equation above, this means that only 1 hour of machine time would be "used" for each unit of the slack product. With 40 machine-hours available, 40 of these fictitious units could be "produced." But the important point is that we have obtained the equation $2x_1 + x_2 = 40$, which represents the restriction on product output imposed by the machine just as well as the inequality of $2x_1 \leqslant 40$.

Thus the graph of the equation $2x_1 + x_2 = 40$, as shown in Figure 10-1b, represents the same physical constraint imposed by the machine as the inequality graph (with the arrow) in Figure 10-1a. Point N in Figure 10-1b corresponds to the origin in Figure 10-1a. At point N, 40 units of the fictitious slack product could be produced and none of the real product. The important point, however, is that this "program" of 0 units of real product output is now satisfying the equation $2x_1 + x_2 = 40$ in place of satisfying the inequality $2x_1 \leqslant 40$.

We can see the optimal feasible program in Figure 10-1b, too. It is at point P. Point P corresponds to point M in Figure 10-1a. As the objective function intersects point P, total profit is $160, as it is, too, at the corresponding point M in Figure 10-1a. The fictitious slack product has a unit profit of $0. (Of course it would not actually be produced at all). Likewise, it can be seen that as the objective function intersects the origin in Figure l0-1a the total profit is $0, just as it is at the corresponding point N in Figure 10-1b. Moreover, we might note right here that the simplex-solution procedure in such problems can be thought of as a procedure in which we move from the solution where total profit is $0 to a solution where it is larger. Ultimately, the solution with the maximum total profit is reached. In our example this can be illustrated in Figure 10-1b where we move from point N where total profit is $0 to point P where it is $160. We can always think of points O and M in our original inequality graph as corresponding to the points N and P.

The main disadvantage of the addition of slack variables to the constraints is that the number of variables in the model increases. Some difficulties in solving problems are thereby created. Typically, it makes the number of variables in a problem greater than the number of equations. Perhaps you recall from your algebra that if you have as many linearly independent equations as you have variables, a solution can be obtained (that is, if one exists).

One of the main ideas in the simplex method is to reduce the number of variables in a problem until they are equal to the given number of equations. That is, just enough of the variables are set equal to 0 to permit a solution to be obtained from the resulting equations.

When we set a variable to 0 this means that for a brief period in the computations the level of that activity remains at 0. That is, the product is not considered to be produced at all. Obviously, which variables are set to 0 could make a lot of difference. In a particular instance, it might well be that the variables we had set to 0 (those that in our analysis we have shut down) represented the most profitable product-output activities. Therefore, if we took the solution of the problem so reduced as the solution to implement in the real situation, we would not be putting into effect the most profitable solution or program. Some way is needed to avoid this.

The way this difficulty is avoided is by repeatedly setting a different set of variables equal to 0 until all possibilities have been exhausted. Each time the resulting equations are solved, a different solution is provided. Thus, more than one solution to the original problem is obtained. Of course, we want to find out which one of them is best.

Let us illustrate what has been said by referring to our example where the single constraint is $2x_1 \leq 40$. After adding the slack variable, we have the equation $2x_1 + x_2 = 40$. The number of variables that we have is two, whereas the number of equations is only 1. Thus, the variables exceed the equations by one. Therefore, we need to set one variable at a time to 0. The order does not matter here, but let us set x_1 to 0 first and then solve the resulting equation (usually there will be more than one remaining equation). The result is as follows:

$$2x_1 + x_2 = 40$$
$$2(0) + x_2 = 40$$
$$x_2 = 40$$

Thus, the solution of the reduced problem (involving only the one variable here) is simply $x_2 = 40$. (The value of x_1 is 0 since we set it to that value).

Second, x_2 is set to 0. We obtain the following second solution: $x_1 = 20$. (Here x_2 is 0 since we set it to 0.)

$$2x_1 + x_2 = 40$$
$$2x_1 + 0 = 40$$
$$x_1 = 20$$

We now have two feasible solutions pertaining to the original problem.[1] The first is: $x_1 = 0$; $x_2 = 40$. The second solution is: $x_1 = 20$; $x_2 = 0$. In relation to our

---

[1] Later we shall call these the two *basic* feasible solutions of the problem.

objective, the maximization of profit, which one of these two feasible solutions is optimal? By substituting each solution individually into the objective function we can find out. The first solution gives us a total profit of $0.

$$
\begin{aligned}
\text{Total profit} &= \$8x_1 + \$0x_2 \\
&= \$8(0) + \$0(40) \\
&= \$0
\end{aligned}
$$

The second solution has a total profit of $160 and obviously is the better of the two solutions.

$$
\begin{aligned}
\text{Total profit} &= \$8x_1 + \$0x_2 \\
&= \$8(20) + \$0(0) \\
&= \$160
\end{aligned}
$$

We have just examined the main algebraic steps in the simplex method. As we discuss the simplex method later, we shall see that the steps we have taken will be done more systematically.

Some technical terms from linear algebra are associated with particular steps in the above discussion and should be noted. Those variables that are *not* set equal to 0 to obtain a solution are referred to as *basic variables* and are said to be in the "basis." The resulting solution is referred to as a *basic solution*. If none of the solution values of the basic variables is negative, we have a *basic feasible solution*. We desire the most profitable solution or program. Thus, we can substitute each basic feasible solution into the objective function and obtain the total profit for each of these solutions. The solution with the maximum profit value is the *optimal basic feasible solution*. It should be noted, too, that those variables that are set equal to 0 each time are referred to as *nonbasic variables*.

The basic solutions and their associated total profits are summarized in Table 10-1. Also shown is the correspondence between the basic solutions and points on the graphs in Figure 10-1*a* and *b*.

THE SIMPLEX METHOD

Let us break into two parts our discussion on using the simplex method to solve real-world problems. The first part will deal with the preparation of a problem for the simplex computations. The second part will deal with the simplex steps to be taken in obtaining an optimal program.

Preparatory Steps

There are a few *preparatory steps* to be completed before a problem can be solved by the simplex method. They are as follows:

1 *Put the problem in standard linear-programming form.* (Usually this includes an objective function and inequality constraints.)

Table 10-1   Basic Solutions and Their Values

Variables set equal to 0 (nonbasic variables)	Resulting equations (in basic variables)	Basic solution	Basic solution in Figure 10-1b	Corresponding point in original problem in Figure 10-1a	Total profit of basic solution (or program) $Z = \$8x_1 + \$0x_2$
Setting x_1 to 0	$x_2 = 40$	$x_1 = 0$ $x_2 = 40$	N	O	$\$8(0) + \$0(40) = \$0$
Setting x_2 to 0	$2x_1 = 40$	$x_1 = 20$ $x_2 = 0$	P	M	$\$8(20) + \$0(0) = \$160^*$ *maximum

2 *Add a slack variable to each "less-than" inequality constraint.* (This step will be extended later for various types of problems.)

3 *Rearrange the terms in the objective function* so that all the terms are on the left-hand side leaving a right-hand side of 0.

4 *Bring the objective function down with the constraints* leaving the maximization instruction implicit.

5 *Construct a simplex table* with column headings from left to right, such as the following, for a two-product and two-resource example.

    a   Basic variables (to be identified when the first table is completed)

    b   Total-profit variable, Z

    c   Product 1 output, x_1

    d   Product 2 output, x_2

    e   Slack variable, x_3 (introduced for resource 1)

    f   Slack variable, x_4 (introduced for resource 2)

    g   Right-hand-side constants (initially, resource capacities)

6 *Lift the coefficients and right-hand-side constants from the equations* and place them in their appropriate positions in the simplex table.

7 *Identify the basic variables* with a left-hand-margin designation.

The first step is not discussed further in this chapter. It is, of course, a difficult and important one whereby elements in reality are selected to be represented in a model by variables, constants, inequalities, or equations. Briefly, this was discussed in Chapter 1. We shall consider it in later chapters, too.

The second step is illustrated by our example with the single inequality constraint representing machine-hours. In its original form we had the following:

Maximize: Total profit = $\$8x_1$
Subject to: $2x_1 \leqslant 40$ (machine-hours)

Adding a slack variable, we convert the inequality to the following equality constraint. Also, the new slack variable is placed in the objective function. It is given a \$0 unit-profit coefficient because it would not add or subtract anything to total profit. (Again, we should say that actually it would not be produced at all.)

Maximize:　Total profit $= \$8x_1 + \$0x_2$
Subject to:　$2x_1 + x_2 = 40$ (machine-hours)

The more formal simplex method involves the use of tables and a set of rules in solving for basic feasible solutions. Each table usually represents one basic feasible solution. Recall from our earlier discussions that an optimal feasible solution will always "be at" a corner point of the original feasible region defined by the inequalities. The basic feasible solutions correspond to these corner points.

Having obtained one basic feasible solution, we want to know if it is the most profitable one. In previous discussions we have determined this by substituting each basic feasible solution into the objective function. Actually, this same evaluation of each basic feasible solution can be done very easily in the simplex table by bringing down the objective function and including it among the constraint equations, then determining the total profit at the same time we obtain the basic feasible solution. Bringing it down to the top row and leaving the maximization instruction implicit gives us the following. (We also use the letter Z to represent total profit and drop the dollar signs on the unit-profit coefficients.)

$Z = 8x_1 + 0x_2$ (total profit)
　　$2x_1 + x_2 = 40$ (machine-hours)

A more convenient form is obtained when all the terms in the objective function appear on the left-hand side. Of course this changes the signs on the unit-profit coefficients as follows: (A -0 is equal to a $+0$, and so subsequently we shall simply use a $+0$.)

$Z - 8x_1 - 0x_2 = 0$
　　$2x_1 + x_2 = 40$

The problem is now ready to be transferred to a simplex table. To make it as clear as possible, let us set down the 1 and 0 coefficients explicitly and label the variables as follows: (We treat total profit as an unknown or as a variable Z. We now make its coefficient of 1 explicit in the objective function, and, since it did not appear in the constraint equation originally, we give it a coefficient of 0.)

Total-profit variable		Product-output variable		Slack variable		Right-hand-side constants
$1Z$	$-$	$8x_1$	$+$	$0x_2$	$=$	0
$0Z$	$+$	$2x_1$	$+$	$1x_2$	$=$	40

Table 10-2 The First Simplex Table for the Problem

Total profit variable Z	Product-output variable x_1	Slack variable x_2	Right-hand-side constants RHS
1	−8	0	0
0	2	1	40

The first simplex table for this problem is comprised of just the two foregoing equations. Only the coefficients and the right-hand-side constants appear in the main part of the table, as shown in Table 10-2. However, it is easy to link each coefficient with its associated variable because we have the variables listed at the head of each column of coefficients. Also, the equality signs are dropped and left implicit. We shall use the column heading RHS for all the constant amounts that appear on the right-hand side of the equality sign.

It turns out that the optimal basic feasible solution will appear in the RHS column of the *final* simplex table. In the top row of the RHS column the total profit (or Z-value) of the optimal basic feasible solution will appear. Actually, every completed table provides in the RHS column a basic feasible solution with the associated Z-value. This is illustrated by the very first simplex table for our problem shown in Table 10-2. Implicitly, in Table 10-2 the variable x_1 is set to 0, which leaves a Z-value of $0 and an x_2-value of 40. Bringing the equations out of Table 10-2 and setting them down explicitly (also, dropping those terms with 0 factors), we have the following:

$$Z = 0$$
$$x_2 = 40$$

Thus, when the column of coefficients of a variable is in a particular form we can read its solution value in the RHS column. This "particular" form is such that the column of coefficients for the variable has a single coefficient of 1, with all the remaining coefficients 0. In Table 10-2 we see that the coefficients of x_2 are in this form, and the solution value for x_2 appears in the RHS column in the same row as the "1" appears. Thus we see that the solution value for x_2 is 40.

In effect, Z is treated as a variable, too. It always has its "coefficient" 1 appearing in the top row under the Z heading. All other entries in the Z column are 0 and always remain 0 from one table to the next. Thus, the Z-value for every basic feasible solution is given at the top of the RHS column (which is what we want). In a profit-maximization problem, such as the one we have in this example, the Z-value is $0 in the first table and increases from table to table (that is, from one basic feasible solution to another) until a maximum is obtained.

As we look at Table 10-2 we can see that now we have two equations represented in table form. We have added to our constraint equation the objective function which included another variable, that is, the "variable" Z. Thus, we have two equations and three variables which require that one of the variables at a time is set to 0. (Actually, there is one exception. Because we always want to know the value of Z for every basic feasible solution, we never set Z to 0.)

It turns out that in using the procedure we have discussed (that is, adding slack variables, rearranging the objective function, and forming the first simplex table) an initial basic feasible solution is automatically obtained. Thus, one variable is implicitly set to 0 (it is x_1) and the other two variables that are not set to 0 (x_2 and Z) are *automatically* in the proper form (a coefficient of 1 and the rest 0) which permits their solution values to be read from the RHS. Therefore, by merely looking at the initial table in Table 10-2, we can extract the first basic feasible solution: $x_1 = 0$ (its coefficients are not in the proper form and is 0) $x_2 = 40$, and $Z = \$0$.

In order to identify easily those rows (equations) in the simplex table in which the unit coefficient of a basic variable appears (and thus the row in which its solution value appears in the RHS), we list the basic variables at the left margin of the table. For example, in Table 10-2 at the left margin of the second row (equation) we could list x_2, indicating that it is a basic variable whose solution value is found in the RHS column in that same row. This we do in Table 10-3. The top row in Table 10-2 is associated with the basic variable Z. The coefficient of 1 for this variable remains fixed for the entire series of simplex tables (solutions) since it never is set to 0. In Table 10-3 we identify Z as the basic variable in the top row. Also, let us refer to the initial simplex table as Simplex Table I.

The Simplex Steps

The main idea of the simplex method is to move from one basic feasible solution to another until a maximum-profit basic feasible solution is obtained. We have an *initial* basic feasible solution in Table 10-3. But we need some systematic way to determine if the current solution is optimal and, if it is not optimal, a procedure for setting a different variable to zero, getting a new solution, and so forth. Let us begin by setting down the main steps to be followed in the simplex method *after* we get an initial basic feasible solution such as in Table 10-3.

  1 *Apply an optimality test.* Is this basic feasible solution optimal?
  2 *Select an incoming basic variable.* Which variable (product output) now set to 0 should be brought in for consideration?

Table 10-3   Simplex Table I with the Basic Variables Identified

Basic variables	Total-profit variable Z	Product-output variable x_1	Slack variable x_2	Right-hand-side constants RHS
Z	1	-8	0	0
←x_2	0	②	1	40

3 *Select an outgoing basic variable*. Which variable (product output) not set to 0 should be set to 0 (that is, taken out of current consideration)?

4 *Obtain a new basic feasible solution*. With the new set of basic variables, obtain a new basic feasible solution. Then return to step 1 to apply the optimality test to the new solution.

Optimality Test   To see if the current basic feasible solution is the best one, we simply examine the coefficients in the top row of the current simplex table. If any of the coefficients are *negative,* we have not yet reached a maximum-profit solution. In Table 10-3 we clearly see that in our small problem we have not obtained an optimal solution because we have a -8 coefficient for x_1.

Selection of the Incoming Variable   The variable (product output) currently set to 0 that would increase profit at the fastest rate (if it were brought in for consideration) is the one whose coefficient is the *most* negative. Thus we select the new (incoming) basic variable by using this rule. In Table 10-3 there is but a single negative coefficient (-8) in the top row, and so it is also the most negative. Thus, the variable x_1 is the incoming variable for the next table. We insert an inward-pointing arrow just below the column heading of this variable.

Selection of the Outgoing Variable   One of the current basic variables in a simplex solution, such as that in Table 10-3, must be set to 0 in the subsequent simplex table so that another basic feasible solution can be examined. The general idea in making this selection is to make as much "room" as we can for the new (most profitable) activity that is being brought in for consideration. We can get a rough measure of this by *dividing each of the coefficients in the incoming variable column* (here, the x_1-coefficients) *into the RHS-value in the same row*. (There are these exceptions: The coefficient in the top Z row of the column is never divided into its RHS, and we never divide by 0 or any negative number.) In a typical problem this still gives us a large set of ratios. We choose the *minimum* of these eligible ratios. The minimum of these ratios is associated with a particular coefficient of the incoming variable. This coefficient is referred to as the "pivot element" for computing the next simplex table. It will always be in the column of coefficients of the incoming variable. The pivot element will also be in a particular row (or equation) of the table. This row is the one with the minimum ratio. And this row is associated with a particular variable in the current basic feasible solution, as indicated in the left-hand margin. Loosely, we can think of this activity (variable) as the one that if removed would make the most room for the to-be-considered activity (the incoming basic variable). We indicate this with an outward-pointing arrow at the left margin of the outgoing variable.

In our small example there is only the single coefficient of 2 to be divided into the RHS-value in the same row (40). Thus we obtain the single ratio: 40/2. It is also the minimum, and so the coefficient 2 is identified as the pivot element.

Table 10-4   The New Set of Basic Variables for Simplex Table II

Basic variables	Total-profit variable Z	Product output-variable x_1	Slack variable x_2	Right-hand-side constants RHS
Z				
(new) x_1				

We follow the convention of enclosing it with a dashed circle as shown in Table 10-3. We note at the left margin in Table 10-3 that the basic variable associated with the row containing the pivot element is x_2. Thus we identify x_2 as the outgoing variable by inserting the outward-pointing arrow.

Obtaining the New Basic Feasible Solution   After selecting the incoming and outgoing basic variables, we are ready to obtain the new basic feasible solution. The new solution is obtained entirely from operations on the rows of the previous table. It is in this step that most of the computational work is to be done.

The first thing to do in developing the second simplex table (Simplex Table II) is *to list the new set of basic variables*. Always, there will be but *one* substitution. It is good practice first to list the basic variables for the next simplex table as is done for Simplex Table II in our example in Table 10-4. Usually, the list is larger than the one we have here. The order of the variables in the new Simplex Table II should be the same as in the previous Simplex Table I with the one incoming variable substituted for the outgoing variable. In our example we substitute x_1 for x_2.

Next, we begin obtaining the new solution values. *We focus on the pivot element and the row (equation) in which it appears. We perform an operation on it and also use it to perform operations on all the other rows (equations) to obtain the new table (the new basic feasible solution).*

We need to obtain the elements for the new Simplex Table II, as shown by

Table 10-5   The First Step in Obtaining the New Simplex Table II: Dividing the Row in the Old Simplex Table I Containing the Pivot Element by the Pivot Element 2

Basic variables	Total-profit variable Z	Product-output variable x_1	Slack variable x_2	Right-hand-side constants RHS
Z	1	−8	0	0
(old) ←x_2	0	②	1	40
	$(0 \div 2 = 0)$	$(2 \div 2 = 1)$	$(1 \div 2 = \frac{1}{2})$	$(40 \div 2 = 20)$

Table 10-6 Part of the New Simplex Table II After Dividing Through the Old Pivot-Element Row of Simplex Table I by the Pivot Element 2

Basic variables	Total-profit variable Z	Product-output variable x_1	Slack variable x_2	Right-hand-side constants RHS
Z				
(new) x_1	0	1	$\frac{1}{2}$	20

the vacant sections in Table 10-4. To do so, we work from Simplex Table I in Table 10-3. We start developing Simplex Table II by focusing on the pivot-element row (the second row) of Simplex Table I. Because we want the pivot element to be converted to 1 in the new table, we simply divide the elements in the pivot-element row by the pivot element. Here it is 2, and so we divide *every* element in the second row of Simplex Table I by 2. This step is seen in Table 10-5. We take this result and place it as the second row of the Simplex Table II, as shown in Table 10-6. Thus, one row of the new table has been completed from the old table.

Recall that all other elements in the column of the pivot element (as they appear in Simplex Table I) must be eliminated. To do this we *multiply or divide the old pivot element by some "correct" number and add the result to or subtract it from the element that we are trying to eliminate* (that is, get to 0). Any multiplication or division operation we make on the pivot element has to be done also on all the other elements in that same row. Similarly, when we try to eliminate a coefficient in a particular row of the pivot-element column, we must add or subtract *all the corresponding elements* (or the resulting product or quotient from an operation on the corresponding element in the old pivot-element row). Let us illustrate this with our example. We see from Simplex Table I in Table 10-3 that the -8 in the top row of the pivot-element column must be eliminated. We want to eliminate it by an operation on the pivot element (in the second row in Table 10-3). We do this by multiplying the old pivot-element row

Table 10-7 Multiplying Each Element in the Pivot-Element Row in the Old Simplex Table by 4 as a First Step in Eliminating -8 in the Top Row

Basic variables	Total-profit variable Z	Product-output variable x_1	Slack variable x_2	Right-hand-side constants RHS
Z	1	-8	0	0
(old) ←x_2	0	(2)	1	40
	$(0 \times 4 = 0)$	$(2 \times 4 = 8)$	$(1 \times 4 = 4)$	$(40 \times 4 = 160)$

Table 10-8   Obtaining the New Top Row for Simplex Table II by Adding the Old Pivot-Element Row, Multiplied by 4, to the Old Top Row in Simplex Table I

Basic variables	Total-profit variable Z	Product-output variable x_1	Slack variable x_2	Right-hand-side constants RHS
Z	1 $(1 + 0 = 1)$	-8 $(-8 + 8 = 0)$	0 $(0 + 4 = 4)$	0 $(0 + 160 = 160)$
(old) $\leftarrow x_2$	0 $(0 \times 4 = 0)$	$\widehat{2}$ $(2 \times 4 = 8)$	1 $(1 \times 4 = 4)$	40 $(40 \times 4 = 160)$

by 4, giving us the elements shown in Table 10-7. These elements are then added to the corresponding elements in the top row of the old Simplex Table I as shown in Table 10-8. This gives us the top row for the new Simplex Table II. Our new (and fully completed) Simplex Table II appears in Table 10-9.

Optimality Test of the New Solution   Given the new basic feasible solution, is it an optimal one? The test is to see if there are any negative elements in the Z row. There is none, indicating that we have reached an optimal basic feasible solution.

Of course for our example we had expected this very optimal solution: $x_1 = 20$; $x_2 = 0$ (this variable was implicitly set to 0 for this solution); and $Z = \$160$.

We summarize the steps in the simplex method as follows:

1   *Optimality test:* Are there any negative elements in the Z row? If there is none, an optimal solution has been attained. If there are negative elements, an improved basic feasible solution is possible.

2   *Select incoming basic variable:* Identify the most negative element in the Z row. The variable associated with this coefficient is the incoming variable. (*Note:* In the cases where there is a tie for the most negative element, select any one of the associated variables as the incoming variable and proceed as usual. For example, we may select the variable with the smallest subscript.)

3   *Select outgoing basic variable:* Divide the elements of the incoming-variable column into their respective right-hand sides (except when the elements

Table 10-9   The New Simplex Table II

Basic variables	Total-profit variable Z	Product-output variable x_1	Slack variable x_2	Right-hand-side constants RHS
Z	1	0	4	160
(new) x_1	0	1	$\frac{1}{2}$	20

Table 10-10   A Summary of the Steps in Obtaining Simplex Table II from Simplex Table I

Basic variables	Z	Product-output variable x_1	Slack variable x_2	RHS	Operation on the pivot-element row and this row that obtains the corresponding row in the next table
Table I		↓			
Z	1	−8	0	0	We must replace −8 with 0. Thus, to obtain the top row in the next table, we multiply each element in the pivot-element row by 4 and add the result to the corresponding elements in this row.
←x_2	0	②	1	40	We must convert the pivot element 2 to 1. Thus, to obtain the second row in the next table, we divide each element in this row by the pivot element 2.
Table II					
Z	1	0	4	160	There are no negative elements in this row. This table contains the optimal feasible solution:
x_1	0	1	½	20	$Z = 160$ $x_1 = 20$ $x_2 = 0$ (was implicitly set to 0)

are 0 or negative or a member of the Z row). The minimum of the eligible ratios identifies in the left margin the outgoing variable. The element associated with this minimum ratio is called the pivot element. (*Note:* Here, too, ties may occur. Again, merely select any one of tied minimum ratios and proceed as usual.)

4 *Obtain new basic feasible solution:* Convert the pivot element to 1 and eliminate all other elements in the incoming-variable column by appropriate operations on the old pivot element. Then go back to step 1.

The application of the foregoing steps to our example is shown in a more compact form in Table 10-10. The appropriate operation on a particular row of Simplex Table I is shown in order to obtain the desired corresponding row in Simplex Table II. A form such as this is found useful in working problems of the type found at the end of this chapter.

SOLVING A LARGER PROBLEM BY THE SIMPLEX METHOD

In Chapters 8 and 9 we illustrated some of the main linear-programming concepts with a lawn-mower–golf-cart example. We solved graphically for the most profitable program of production of the two products given the existence of two resource constraints. Now let us solve this same problem by the simplex method. First, let us state the problem as it appeared in Chapter 8.

Maximize:
$$Z = \$40x_1 + \$50x_2 \text{ (total profit)}$$
Subject to:
$$x_1 \leq 50 \text{ (lawn-mower assembly facility)}$$
$$x_1 + 2x_2 \leq 80 \text{ (labor-hours)}$$

In Figure 10-2 we show again the graph of the problem and its optimal solution: $x_1 = 50$; $x_2 = 15$; and $Z = \$2,750$. Thus, the production of 50 lawn mowers and 15 golf carts would generate the greatest total profit.

Continuing with the preparatory steps for the simplex method, we add the necessary slack variables and rearrange the terms in the objective function. Adding a slack variable to each "less-than" constraint inequality gives the following equations:

Product-output variables		Slack variables		Right-hand-side constants	
x_1	$+$	x_3	$=$	50	(lawn-mower assembly facility)
$x_1 + 2x_2$	$+$	x_4	$=$	80	(labor-hours)

We rearrange the terms in the objective function which gives us $Z - 40x_1 - 50x_2 = 0$. Including it with the constraint equations gives us the following (which in effect gives us the first simplex solution or Simplex Table I).

Total-profit variable	Product-output variables		Slack variables		Right-hand-side constants	
Z	$-40x_1 - 50x_2$			$=$	0	(total profit)
	x_1	$+$	x_3	$=$	50	(lawn-mower assembly facility)
	$x_1 + 2x_2$		$+ x_4$	$=$	80	(labor-hours)

Lifting the coefficients from this formulation and identifying the basic variables as x_3, x_4, and Z in the left-hand margin gives us Simplex Table I, as shown in the top section of Table 10-11. The first basic feasible solution is read directly from the right-hand-side column: x_1 and x_2 were implicitly set to 0 for this solution; $x_3 = 50$; $x_4 = 80$; and $Z = \$0$.

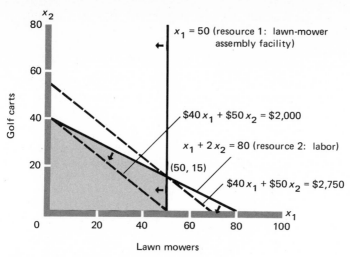

Figure 10-2 The lawn-mower–golf-cart problem.

Because in Simplex Table I negative elements appear in the top row, we proceed to select an incoming and an outgoing variable and then to obtain a new basic feasible solution. As shown in Table 10-11, three basic feasible solutions are obtained before the optimal one is reached.

There are four basic feasible solutions to this problem; however, the simplex method requires the solving of only three of them to obtain the best one. Thus, one of them was implicitly skipped. A look at Figure 10-2 indicates that it was the basic feasible solution corresponding to the corner point $(x_1, x_2) = (50, 0)$ that was "jumped over." In quite large problems it has been estimated that by the simplex method only about one-fourth of all basic feasible solutions are solved in obtaining an optimal one. This, in part, accounts for its widespread use.

SUMMARY

1 The main solution procedure for practical linear-programming problems is the *simplex method*. Most computer manufacturers have already-written computer programs that one can use for solving problems.

2 "Less-than" inequality constraints are converted to equations by the addition of a *slack variable* for each such inequality. The resulting equation constraints lend themselves to a straightforward solution procedure.

3 *Basic variables* are those not set to 0 to obtain a solution. The resulting solution is called a *basic solution*. If none of the solution values is negative, it is called a *basic feasible solution*. A basic feasible solution with the maximum profit is called an *optimal basic feasible solution*.

4 The *preparatory steps* in solving a problem by the simplex method are:

    a Put in the standard linear-programming form.

    b Add a slack variable to each "less-than" constraint inequality.

Table 10-11   The Simplex Solution to the Lawn-Mower–Golf-Cart Problem

Basic variables	Z	Product-output variables		Slack variables		RHS	Operation on the pivot-element row and this row that obtains corresponding row in the next table
		x_1	x_2	x_3	x_4		
Table I			↓				
Z	1	−40	−50	0	0	0	Multiply the pivot-element row by 25 and add the result to this row
x_3	0	1	0	1	0	50	Leave this row as it is
							Divide this row by the
← x_4	0	1	②	0	1	80	pivot element 2
Table II		↓					
Z	1	−15	0	0	25	2,000	Multiply the pivot-element row by 15 and add the result to this row
← x_3	0	①	0	1	0	50	Divide this row by the pivot element 1
x_2	0	½	1	0	½	40	Divide the pivot-element row by −2 and add the result to this row
Table III							
Z	1	0	0	15	25	2,750	Optimal feasible solution: $Z = 2,750$
x_1	0	1	0	1	0	50	$x_1 = 50$
							$x_2 = 15$
x_2	0	0	1	−½	½	15	$x_3 = 0$ (set to 0)
							$x_4 = 0$ (set to 0)

    c Rearrange the terms in the objective function so that the right-hand side is 0.

    d Bring the objective function down with the constraints.

    e Construct a simplex table with appropriate column headings.

    f Lift the coefficients and right-hand-side amounts from the equations and place them in their appropriate positions in the simplex table.

    g Identify the basic variables with a left-hand-margin designation.

5 The *computational steps* in the simplex method are:

    a Make an optimality test.

    b Select an incoming variable.

    c Select the outgoing variable.

    d Obtain a new basic feasible solution.

    e Go back to step *a* and make an optimality test. The cycle is repeated until an optimal feasible solution is found.

PROBLEMS

10-1   Represent graphically, as is done in Figure 10-1a, the following problem involving a single product output and a single resource-constraint inequality. Show the maximum-profit solution (or program).

Maximize: $Z = \$12x_1$ (total profit)
Subject to: $4x_1 \le 20$ (machine-hours)

10-2   Convert the inequality constraint in Problem 10-1 to an equation, put the problem in the standard linear-programming formulation with the new equation constraint, and show graphically the maximum-profit solution to the converted problem.

10-3   Obtain the basic solutions and their values for Problem 10-2.

10-4   Rearrange the terms in the objective function in Problem 10-2 for entry into the first simplex table. Solve Problem 10-2 by using the simplex tables.

10-5   The following problem involves two products and two resource-constraint inequalities. Solve for the maximum-profit solution graphically.

Maximize: $Z = \$24x_1 + \$36x_2$ (total profit)
Subject to: $4x_1 + 4x_2 \le 400$ (labor-hours)
               $2x_1 + 4x_2 \le 240$ (machine-hours)

10-6   Convert the inequlity constraints in Problem 10-5 to equations and solve for all the feasible and infeasible basic solutions and their values. Identify the optimal basic feasible solution.

10-7   Rearrange the terms in the objective function in Problem 10-6 and solve for the maximum-profit solution using the simplex tables. Compare with your graphical solution in Problem 10-5.

10-8   Solve Problem 8-1 by the simplex method. Compare your solution with that obtained graphically in Problem 8-1.

10-9   Solve the backpack-raincoat problem in Problem 8-2 by the simplex method. Compare with your graphic solution.

10-10   For the dairy-foods processor in Problem 8-3 obtain the optimal feasible program by the simplex method. Compare with your graphic solution.

10-11   Obtain the optimal program and its total profit for the car maker in Problem 8-4. Compare with your graphic solution.

10-12   The optimal program for the small-vehicle manufacturer was obtained graphically in Problem 8-6. Solve the same problem by the simplex method.

10-13   **a**   Solve Problem 8-7 by the simplex method. Interpret the optimal solution.
         b   Examine your graph of the problem and explain the presence of a slack variable in the optimal solution. To what resource is it connected? Explain.

10-14   Obtain the optimal agricultural-production program in Problem 8-8 by the simplex method. Compare the solution with that obtained graphically.

10-15   For the automotive-parts manufacturer in Problem 8-11 solve the optimal production program by the simplex method. Compare the solution with that obtained graphically.

10-16   When the automotive-parts manufacturer considers the production of the third product (connecting rods) in Problem 8-12, we have no graphical solution in two dimensions.
         a   Solve the problem by the simplex method.
         b   Interpret the optimal feasible solution and its total profit.

Chapter 11

More on the Simplex Method

In the previous chapter we solved by the simplex method a common-type, linear-programming problem, that is, one in which an objective (such as profit) is maximized and resource constraints impose upper limits on the levels of the activities. Therefore, in this chapter we assume that you are able to solve by the simplex method linear-programming-maximization problems with "less-than" inequality constraints.

Although the type of linear-programming problem that we have studied so far is common, many problems exist in practical work where a slightly different formulation is desired in order to represent the real situation. These alterations in the formulation widen the applicability of linear programming, although at the same time they require some modifications in the solution procedures of the simplex method.

ALTERATIONS IN THE FORMULATION OF THE CONSTRAINTS AND THE OBJECTIVE FUNCTION

First, constraints may not always be of the type that impose only upper limits upon the activities. In some instances it may be desirable to represent by a constraint a *lower limit* upon activities. For example, in some operations it may be necessary to maintain a minimum work force. We shall see in this chapter that this condition can be represented by a *"greater-than"* inequality constraint.

At other times, we may wish to have some condition *exactly* fulfilled. For example, sometimes it may be necessary to use a resource exactly at its stated capacity. In a case such as this the condition can best be represented by an *equation* constraint.

Therefore in real-world problems it is not uncommon for the constraints to be comprised of a mixture of three types of functions: equations, "less-than" inequalities, and "greater-than" inequalities.

The major aim of this chapter is to help us gain familiarity with simplex-method procedures for solving problems with such constraints. Of course some modifications in the simplex method will be necessary, but they are really quite minor. To simplify matters, though, we shall consider very simple examples of each alteration in the formulation. We shall examine each alteration by itself (such as the presence of a "greater-than" inequality constraint) and then discuss the necessary modifications in the simplex method in order to solve such a problem. Later in this chapter, we shall illustrate the solution of a problem that has a mixture of all three types of constraints.

Another alteration in the formulation of linear-programming problems is needed when an objective is to be *minimized* instead of maximized. A fairly common objective in real-world problems is that of cost minimization. Thus, one of the modifications in the simplex method that we shall examine in this chapter is that of minimizing the value of an objective function, instead of maximizing it.

Modifications in the Simplex Method

In this section we shall separately examine each alteration in the linear-programming formulation and then discuss the necessary modifications in the solution procedure of the simplex method.

Equality Constraints   We observed in the previous chapter how the simplex method begins with a basic feasible solution and proceeds to another basic feasible solution until an optimal one is found.

In the last chapter we worked only with problems that had "less-than" inequalities (resources with upper limits on their availability or capacity). Such constraints are illustrated by the one represented in Figure 11-1a. With such constraints we can always start the series of basic feasible solutions at the origin of the problem as it was first formulated. In these cases the the origin (x_1, x_2) = (0, 0) represents a feasible program and is one of the corner points of the feasible region of the original problem. Of course in the initial basic feasible solution by the simplex method the slack variables have values other than 0, but the decision variables are all at 0.

A special problem arises in the formulation of the problem when some constraints are either in the form of equations or "greater-than" inequalities. The problem is that the origin (0, 0) is *not* in the original feasible region. As shown in

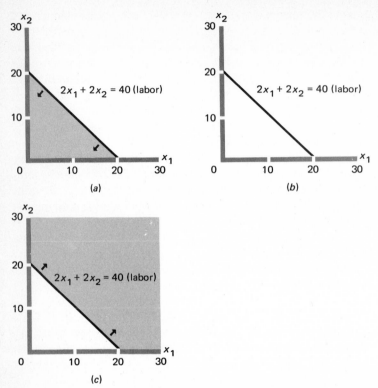

Figure 11-1 *(a)* A "less-than" inequality constraint; 40 hours or less of labor must be used; *(b)* an equation constraint: exactly 40 hours of labor must be used; and *(c)* a "greater-than" inequality constraint: 40 hours or more of labor must be used.

Figure 11-1*b*, the feasible region for the problem with a single equation constraint does not include the origin. Only points on the line represent feasible programs.

We shall discuss the "greater-than" inequality constraints in more detail later, but we can see from Figure 11-1*c* that the shaded feasible region corresponding to a single "greater-than" inequality constraint does not include the origin either. Thus, this special problem arises when a linear-programming formulation includes either of these types of constraints.

Let us look in more detail at the problem created by the presence of an equation constraint. Since the origin $(0, 0)$ is not in the feasible region, we cannot begin our solution procedure there, as we did in the last chapter, with problems containing only "less-than" inequality constraints. In that chapter we merely had to add a slack variable to each "less-than" inequality constraint and we had an initial basic feasible solution. It is not so simple now.

How is our solution procedure modified to handle the equation constraints? You might say that we "pretend" to have a larger problem than we actually have. We pretend that we have activities in which we can engage (the making of products, for example) *in addition* to those originally specified in the linear-programming formulation.

The levels of these additional activities are then represented *not* by slack variables (because there is no slack in the resource capacity) but by *artificial* variables. We add *one artificial variable to each equality constraint* much as we added a slack variable to each "less-than" inequality constraint in the last chapter.

This simple device permits us to get started with an initial basic feasible solution (to the new artifically enlarged problem). However, to be assured that the artificial variable we have added does not show up in the optimal basic feasible solution at the end, we must place the artificial variable in the objective function, too, and assign to it a very low unit profit (specifically, a large negative unit profit). In this respect artificial variables are different from slack variables. Slack variables implicitly are given coefficients of 0 in the objective function.

An Example with a Single Equation Constraint   Suppose we illustrate what we have just said with a simple little example. It is a one-product example that is trivial in a real-world sense, but it can be useful to illustrate clearly what we do when equation constraints appear in a problem.

We have the following:

Maximize: Total profit = $10x_1$
Subject to: $2x_1 = 40$ (labor-hours)

The decision variable x_1 represents the output of chairs (one unit corresponds to 50 chairs). The operation involves the assembling (bolting) of the chair parts. Each unit of output (50 chairs) generates $10 in profit and uses 2 hours of labor. There are 40 hours of labor available each day.

But this labor constraint is in the form of an *equation*. In this form it means that the 40 hours of labor that are available *must* be used each day (no more and no less than 40 hours).

A graph of the problem is shown in Figure 11-2a. The feasible region is comprised of the single point on the horizontal axis. Only when x_1 is 20 is the equation constraint satisfied. Since this point is the only point in the feasible region, it is also the optimal solution. Substituting the x_1-value of 20 into the objective function $Z = \$10x_1$ gives a total profit of $200: $10(20) = $200.

In order to use the simplex method, we must add an artificial variable to each equation constraint. Since we have an equation constraint in our example, let us do just that. At the same time, we must include the artificial variable in the objective function with a large negative-valued coefficient to be sure that it is driven out of the solution once it performs its task of getting us started with the simplex-solution procedure.

Thus, we have the following formulation: (The decision variable is represented by x_1, and the artificial variable by x_2.)

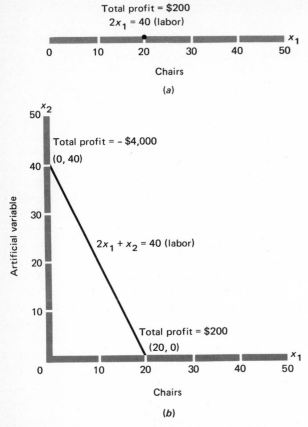

Figure 11-2 Graphs of the problem represented *(a)* by an equation and *(b)* by an equation to which an artificial variable has been added.

Maximize: $Z = \$10x_1 - \$100x_2$ (total profit)
Subject to: $2x_1 + x_2 = 40$ (labor-hours)

In Figure 11-2*b* we have plotted this enlarged problem. Now, the feasible region is comprised of the points on the line segment from (0, 40) on the vertical axis to (20, 0) on the horizontal axis. These points on the axes are also the only corner points of the feasible region (the line). Substituting each pair of coordinates into the objective function $Z = \$10x_1 - \$100x_2$ gives us total profits of $\$-4,000$ and $\$200$ as shown in Figure 11-2*b*. Thus, from this graph, too, we see that the optimal feasible solution is $x_1 = 20$, with a total profit of $\$200$.

Proceeding toward a simplex solution, we bring down the objective function with the constraint and move the terms to the left-hand side as follows:

$Z - 10x_1 + 100x_2 = 0$ (total profit)
$\qquad 2x_1 + \quad x_2 = 40$ (labor-hours)

Next, we move the equations to the simplex table, as shown in Table 11-1, just as we did in the previous chapter. Everything proceeds just as before, but there is a bit of tidying up we must do because of our artificial variable.

In the problems of the last chapter the next step would be to begin our usual simplex-computation procedure by listing the current basic variables in the appropriate row of the extreme left-hand column. Usually, after doing this, we can read the initial basic feasible solution and its value (profit) in the right-hand-side column.

In our present problem in Table 11-1, the coefficients of Z are in their usual proper form so that Z is listed as the first basic variable (the coefficient 1 is in the top row of the Z coefficients).

The listing of the second basic variable is not so easy. We would expect it to be the artificial variable x_2 (as indicated by the parentheses around it in Table 11-1), but its coefficients are not in the proper form. There is a coefficient of 100 in the top row that must be eliminated (changed to 0) in order for the coefficients of x_2 to be in their proper form. Therefore, we have a little extra work to do before we can get started on the usual simplex computational procedure.

We can eliminate the 100 simply by multiplying the second row (every element) by -100 and then adding the result (element by element) to the top row. Thus, we obtain the first simplex table in Table 11-2. This basic feasible solution corresponds to the (0, 40) point in Figure 11-2b with a total profit of $-\$4,000$. From that graph we can see that the next basic feasible solution will be at (20, 0) with a total profit of $\$200$. In the second table of Table 11-2 we obtain this very solution and see that it is optimal.

In summary, when equation constraints are encountered in problems, we must add a separate artificial variable to each equation constraint before moving the problem to a simplex table. Recall that whenever artificial variables are added they must be included in the objective function with a coefficient that assures its being driven from any optimal basic feasible solution.

A Minimization Problem

Our aim here is to illustrate the modifications in the simplex procedures that are necessary when a problem is formulated as a minimization problem.

Table 11-1 Placing the Chair Problem in Simplex-Table Form

Basic variable	Z	Decision variable x_1	Artificial variable x_2	RHS	Operation that obtains the corresponding row in the next table
Z	1	-10	100	0	Multiply second row by -100, add result to this row
(x_2)	0	2	1	40	Leave this row as it is

Table 11-2   The Basic Feasible Solutions (in the Simplex Method) to the Chair Problem

Basic variable	Z	Decision variable x_1	Artificial variable x_2	RHS	Operation on the pivot-element row and this row that obtains the corresponding row in the next table
Table I		↓			
Z	1	−210	0	−4,000	Multiply the pivot-element row by 105 and add to this row
← x_2	0	⟨2⟩	1	40	Divide this row by the pivot-element 2
Table II					
Z	1	0	105	200	Optimal solution: Z = 200
x_1	0	1	½	20	x_1 = 20 x_2 = 0

Suppose we continue with the chair problem that has the same single labor-hour constraint. Also, it is still an equation constraint. But the objective function is now a cost-objective function, and it is to be minimized. Therefore, the coefficient in the objective function represents the cost of the materials for each unit of output. This unit cost is $14. Thus, we have the following:

Minimize: Total cost of materials = $14x_1$
Subject to: $2x_1 = 40$ (labor-hours)

The feasible region for this problem is the same single point shown in Figure 11-2a. We noted earlier that it was also the most profitable solution. Since it is the only feasible solution, it has to be the one with the lowest cost. Thus, we know in advance that the optimal feasible solution is $x_1 = 20$, with a total cost of $280. But let us use it to illustrate the procedures that apply to larger problems.

With such an equation constraint we must add (as discussed above) an artificial variable to the equation constraint and also include it in the objective function.

But now the objective function is a cost-objective function and the coefficients represent unit costs. In the simplex procedure we shall see that lower unit costs are preferred to higher unit costs. Thus, in our assignment of a coefficient to the artificial variable, we must assign to it a *very high* unit cost (a large positive number) in order to assure its being driven out of the solution. (Recall that in the profit-maximization problem discussed earlier a large negative profit was assigned to the coefficient of the artificial variable.) If we somewhat arbitrarily select a value of $100 for the coefficient for the artificial variable, we have the following. (*Note:* In solving larger problems we should assign an extremely large value to the coefficient of the artificial variable. Unfortunately, for hand computations, it is very burdensome.)

Minimize: $Z = \$14x_1 + \$100x_2$ (total cost of materials)
Subject to: $2x_1 + x_2 = 40$ (labor-hours)

The feasible region for this problem is comprised of points on the line shown in Figure 11-2*b*. Now, however, the total cost of the basic feasible solutions is of interest. For the corner point at (0, 40) the total cost is $4,000. The total cost of the other basic feasible solution (20, 0) is $280 (and is optimal).

Then, bringing down the objective function with the constraint and moving the terms to the left-hand side, we have:

$$Z - 14x_1 - 100x_2 = 0 \text{ (total cost of materials)}$$
$$2x_1 + x_2 = 40 \text{ (labor-hours)}$$

In Table 11-3 we have the problem in simplex-table form. Listing the basic variables in the left-hand column, we have Z first and x_2 as a possibility if we eliminate the -100 in the top row. We can eliminate the -100 by multiplying the second row by 100 (every element) and then adding the result to the top row (element by element). This gives us the first simplex table in Table 11-4. This first simplex table has the initial basic feasible solution to the cost-minimization problem: $(x_1, x_2) = (0, 40)$ with a total cost of $4,000.

Once we obtain such an initial basic feasible solution, we apply the "optimality test": Is this basic solution optimal?

Recall from the last chapter that in maximization problems we look for any *negative* coefficients in the top row. If any coefficient is negative we identify the most negative one and select the associated variable as the incoming variable.

Table 11-3 Placing the Cost-Minimization Chair Problem in Simplex-Table Form

Basic variable	Z	Decision variable x_1	Artifical variable x_2	RHS	Operation that obtains the corresponding row in the next table
Z	1	−14	−100	0	Multiply the second row by 100 and add the result to this row
(x_2)	0	2	1	40	Leave this row as it is

Table 11-4 The Basic Feasible Solutions (in the Simplex Method) to the Cost-Minimization Chair Problem

Basic variable	Z	Decision variable x_1	Artificial variable x_2	RHS	Operation on the pivot-element row and this row that obtains the corresponding row in the next table
Table I		↓			
Z	1	186	0	4,000	Multiply second row by −93, add result to this row
←x_2	0	②	1	40	Divide this row by the pivot-element 2
Table II					
Z	1	0	−93	280	Optimal solution: Z = 280
x_1	0	1	½	20	x_1 = 20
					x_2 = 0

Then we proceed to obtain a new basic feasible solution, test it for optimality, and so forth, until no negative coefficients appear in the top row.

Now, however, we are faced with a minimization problem. How does that modify our procedure? Only in one way. In the optimality test we now look for any *positive* coefficients in the top row. If any positive coefficients appear (those values in the RHS and Z columns are not eligible) we do not have an optimal solution.

To select the incoming basic variable, we identify the *most positive* coefficient in the top row. The variable associated with this coefficient is selected as the incoming variable.

Applying this modified optimality test to the initial basic feasible solution in Table 11-4, we see that there is just one positive coefficient in the top row. It is 186. Therefore, we select x_1 as the incoming variable.

The procedure for selecting the outgoing variable and the subsequent steps in obtaining a new solution are *exactly the same* as they are for maximization problems (the minimum ratio determines the pivot element just as in maximization problems as discussed in the last chapter). In our little example in Table 11-4 we obtain the optimal feasible solution in the second table. We see, too, that it is the same solution obtained from the graph earlier.

"Greater-Than" Inequality Constraints

The last of the modifications in the simplex procedure that we shall discuss in this chapter is the modification required because of the presence of "greater-than" inequality constraints. These constraints appear in the linear-programming formulation because there is some lower limit to be imposed upon the activities.

Note that this type of an inequality involves only a lower limit. Thus, programs that satisfy this lower limit are feasible in terms of such a constraint. The graph of a single "greater-than" constraint inequality appears in Figure 11-1c. Points in the shaded region correspond to programs (solutions) that overfulfill the minimum condition specified.

Programs represented by points in the shaded region of the "less-than" inequality in Figure 11-1a are feasible but do not fully use the resource amount specified (40 labor-hours). In our simplex-solution procedure we introduce slack variables to take up any slack in the use of the resources.

In the case of the "greater-than" inequality constraint above, the programs represented by points in the shaded area use more than the amount of the resource specified in the formulation (40 labor-hours). When represented by a "greater-than" inequality constraint only programs that use 40 hours of labor or more are feasible.

Thus, programs that use more than 40 hours of labor are overfulfilling the requirement of using at least 40 labor-hours. Therefore, we have the opposite of a slack condition. It is one of overfulfillment. Consequently, in our simplex procedure we add a *surplus* variable (a negative slack variable) to absorb any excess resulting from the overfulfillment of the minimum condition.

To illustrate this, let us create the following modified chair problem in which the labor constraint is such that 40 hours of labor must be used. Also, we shall minimize the total costs of materials again. Thus, we have the following formulation:

Minimize: Total costs of materials $= \$14x_1$
Subject to: $2x_1 \geqslant 40$ (labor-hours)

The graph of the problem is shown in Figure 11-3. The feasible region is comprised of points on the horizontal axis from the x_1-value of 20 to the right. The program with the minimum total cost obviously is that where $x_1 = 20$. The total cost of this solution is $280.

Let us use this example to illustrate the necessary modifications in the simplex procedure when a constraint is of the "greater-than" type.

We add a surplus variable (a negative slack variable) to each "greater-than" inequality as follows: (Let us use x_2 to designate the surplus variable. Note that its coefficient is -1.)

Minimize: $Z = \$14x_1$ (total cost of materials)
Subject to: $2x_1 - 1x_2 = 40$ (labor-hours)

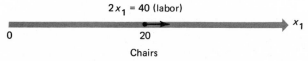

Figure 11-3   A "greater-than" inequality constraint.

But right here we see trouble ahead because of the -1 coefficient for the surplus variable x_2. When we get to the simplex table, such coefficients must be positive; and there is no way to get them positive without making our right-hand-side value negative (and our nonnegativity condition mentioned above does not allow us to let the right-hand-side values become negative. This nonnegativity condition does not apply to the total profit or total cost of a solution that appears at the top of the right-hand-side column).

The way out of this dilemma is also to add an artificial variable to each such equation obtained from a "greater-than" inequality. This is the general rule: *To each "greater-than" inequality first add a surplus variable (with a -1 coefficient), and then add an artificial variable.*

Our addition of an artificial variable requires (as before) that we include it in the objective function with a large coefficient with the appropriate sign (a positive sign in a minimization problem and a negative sign in a maximization problem).

Surplus variables are like slack variables in this respect: They do not have to be included in the objective function (implicitly, their coefficients are given values of 0).

Thus, applying this procedure to our chair problem we have the following. (*Note:* x_1 is our decision variable, x_2 our surplus variable, and x_3 our artificial variable.)

Minimize: $Z = \$14x_1 + \$100x_3$ (total cost of materials)
Subject to: $2x_1 - x_2 + x_3 = 40$ (labor-hours)

It is difficult to get a graph of this problem in three dimensions, so let us go directly to the simplex procedure. We bring the objective function down with the constraints and move the terms in the objective function to the left-hand side. This gives us the following:

$Z - \$14x_1 \qquad\quad - \$100x_3 = 0$ (total cost of materials)
$\qquad 2x_1 - x_2 + \quad x_3 = 40$ (labor-hours)

We now move the problem to the simplex table as shown in Table 11-5. Immediately we see the same difficulty that we encountered before. The coeffi-

Table 11-5 Placing the Chair Problem (with a "Greater-Than" Inequality Constraint) in Simplex-Table Form

Basic variable	Z	Decision variable x_1	Surplus variable x_2	Artificial variable x_3	RHS
Z	1	−14	0	−100	0
(x_3)	0	2	−1	1	40

Table 11-6   The Basic Solutions (in the Simplex Method) of the Chair Problem with a "Greater-Than" Inequality Constraint

Basic variable	Z	Decision variable x_1	Surplus variable x_2	Artificial variable x_3	RHS
Table I		$\downarrow$			
Z	1	186	−100	0	4,000
← x_3	0	⟨2⟩	−1	1	40
Table II					
Z	1	0	−7	−93	280
x_1	0	1	−½	½	20

cient that we added to the artificial variable x_3 in the objective function gives us a non-0 value in the top row whereas it should be 0.

We accomplish this elimination of the coefficient as before and obtain the first simplex table in Table 11-6. This is the initial basic feasible solution. The second (and optimal) basic feasible solution appears in the second table. Of course it is the very optimal solution that we expected from our graphic solution of the original problem in Figure 11-3.

An Example with All Three Types of Constraints

Let us check to see how well we have learned the modifications in the simplex procedures discussed above. Suppose we examine an example in which we have three constraints: a "greater-than" constraint inequality, a "less-than" constraint inequality, and a simple equation constraint.

The Example   Our example is an extension of the chair problem discussed above, but now we have two decision variables and three constraints. The first decision variable, x_1, refers again to the output of chairs, but now we shall designate x_1 as the output of chairs by bolting the parts together.

The second decision variable, x_2, refers to the output of chairs by welding the parts together. Both the bolting process and the welding process use some labor and involve some welding.

Chairs assembled by the bolting process require some welding, but chairs made by the welding process use it more heavily. Each unit of chairs assembled by the bolting process requires 2 hours of labor and 2 hours of welding-equipment time. Each unit made by the welding process requires 2 labor-hours and 4 hours of welding-equipment time.

There are 60 hours of welding-equipment time available. This is an upper limit. All the time available need not be used.

In this problem we have the somewhat unusual requirement that 40 hours or more of labor must be used. The 40 hours is a lower limit.

Also, there is the requirement that a total of 25 units of output be produced.

This requirement does not specify how the units are to be assembled, only that 25 units must be produced (no more and no less than 25).

Profit per unit by the bolting process is $10 and by the welding process, $12. The objective is to determine a program of production that satisfies all three types of constraints and maximizes total profit.

The Formulation   We represent the problem in linear-programming form as follows:

Maximize: Total profit $= \$10x_1 + \$12x_2$
Subject to: $2x_1 + 2x_2 \geqslant 40$ (labor-hours)
                   $2x_1 + 4x_2 \leqslant 60$ (equipment-hours)
                   $x_1 + x_2 = 25$ (units of output required)

A graph of the problem is shown in Figure 11-4. The feasible region is comprised of the points on the line segment from (20, 5) to (25, 0). Moving the profit-objective function in the optimizing direction (outward from the origin), we find that the optimal feasible solution is (20, 5) with a total profit of $260.

Looking at the constraints in the formulation above, we see all three types of constraints. To the "greater-than" inequality we must add both a surplus variable and an artificial variable; to the "less-than" constraint we must add a slack variable; and to the equation constraint we add an artificial variable. Then, for each artificial variable we have added in the constraints, we must insert a large negative coefficient in the objective function. (If it were a minimization problem, the large coefficients we add would have a positive sign.)

Doing this gives us the following. (*Note:* x_1 and x_2 are the decision varia-

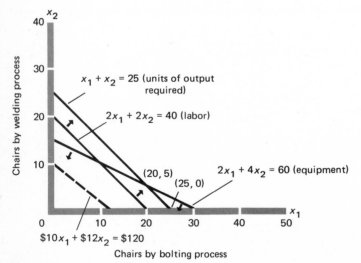

Figure 11-4   The chair-example that includes all three types of constraints.

Table 11-7 Placing the Chair Example in Simplex-Table Form

Basic variables	Z	Decision variables x_1	x_2	Surplus variable x_3	Artificial variable x_4	Slack variable x_5	Artificial variable x_6	RHS
Z	1	−10	−12	0	100	0	100	0
(x_4)	0	2	2	−1	1	0	0	40
x_5	0	2	4	0	0	1	0	60
(x_6)	0	1	1	0	0	0	1	25
Z	1	−210	−212	100	0	0	100	−4,000
x_4	0	2	2	−1	1	0	0	40
x_5	0	2	4	0	0	1	0	60
(x_6)	0	1	1	0	0	0	1	25
Z	1	−310	−312	100	0	0	0	−6,500
x_4	0	2	2	−1	1	0	0	40
x_5	0	2	4	0	0	1	0	60
x_6	0	1	1	0	0	0	1	25

bles; x_3 is a surplus variable; x_4 is an artificial variable; x_5 is a slack variable; and x_6 is an artificial variable.)

Maximize:
$$Z = \$10x_1 + \$12x_2 \quad - \$100x_4 \quad - \$100x_6 \quad \text{(total profit)}$$
Subject to:
$$2x_1 + 2x_2 - x_3 + x_4 = 40 \text{ (labor-hours)}$$
$$2x_1 + 4x_2 \qquad\qquad + x_5 = 60 \text{ (equipment-hours)}$$
$$x_1 + x_2 \qquad\qquad\qquad + x_6 = 25 \text{ (units required)}$$

Bringing down the objective function and moving the terms to the left-hand side we have the following:

$$Z - 10x_1 - 12x_2 \qquad +100x_4 \quad + 100x_6 = 0$$
$$2x_1 + 2x_2 - x_3 + x_4 \qquad\qquad = 40$$
$$2x_1 + 4x_2 \qquad + \qquad x_5 \qquad\qquad = 60$$
$$x_1 + x_2 \qquad\qquad\qquad + \quad x_6 = 25$$

Moving to the simplex table, we have the first table in Table 11-7. The list of basic variables is Z, (x_4), x_5, and (x_6). The artificial variables x_4 and x_6 have coefficients in the top row that must be eliminated before our simplex computations can begin. Let us remove them one at a time.

We can remove the 100 in the top row of the x_4 column by multiplying the second row (in the first table in Table 11-7) by −100 and adding the result to the top row. This gives us the second table in Table 11-7.

The coefficient 100 in the x_6 column is removed similarly. Now we multiply the fourth row by −100 in Table 11-7 and add the result to the top row. This

Table 11-8 The Basic Solutions (in the Simplex Method) of the Chair Example

Basic variables	Z	Decision variables x_1	Decision variables x_2	Surplus variable x_3	Artificial variable x_4	Slack variable x_5	Artificial variable x_6	RHS
Table I			↓					
Z	1	−310	−312	100	0	0	0	−6,500
x_4	0	2	2	−1	1	0	0	40
←x_5	0	2	④	0	0	1	0	60
x_6	0	1	1	0	0	0	1	25
Table II		↓						
Z	1	−154	0	100	0	78	0	−1.820
←x_4	0	①	0	−1	1	−½	0	10
x_2	0	½	1	0	0	¼	0	15
x_6	0	½	0	0	0	−¼	1	10
Table III				↓				
Z	1	0	0	−54	154	1	0	−280
x_1	0	1	0	−1	1	−½	0	10
x_2	0	0	1	½	−½	½	0	10
←x_6	0	0	0	½	−½	0	1	5
Table IV								
Z	1	0	0	0	100	1	108	260
x_1	0	1	0	0	0	−½	2	20
x_2	0	0	1	0	0	½	−1	5
x_3	0	0	0	1	−1	0	2	10

eliminates the second bothersome coefficient and gives us the third table in Table 11-7 which also is the initial basic feasible solution shown in the first table in Table 11-8.

This being a maximization problem, we look for any negative coefficients in the top row and select the most negative as the incoming variable. From here on, we proceed as usual for all types of problems. The remaining steps for this problem are summarized in Table 11-8.

The optimal program corresponds to the graphic solution obtained in Figure 11-4. However, our optimal simplex table (in Table 11-8) includes x_3 in the optimal solution. This is the surplus variable we introduced to take up any possible surplus with respect to the minimum labor requirement.

Thus, in our optimal solution we apparently are overfulfilling the minimum labor requirement. We can see from Figure 11-4 that this is indeed so. The point representing our optimal solution, $(x_1, x_2) = (20, 5)$, lies not on the labor constraint line (the equation), but beyond it.

SUMMARY

1 Some conditions impose upper limits upon the activities in which we can engage. *"Less-than"* inequalities can represent such limitations.

2 Other conditions impose lower limits (minimum requirements) with respect to the activities. *"Greater-than"* inequalities can represent such limitations.

3 Still other situations may impose the condition that some requirement be *exactly* fulfilled. *Equations* can represent such requirements.

4 In some problems an objective (such as total profit) is to be maximized, whereas in others the objective (such as total cost) is to be minimized. Either maximization problems or minimization problems may have each type of constraint in a given problem.

5 The *preparatory* steps in solving problems by the simplex method also need to include instructions regarding the presence of "greater-than" inequality constraints and equation constraints. They are summarized as follows:

    a To each *"less-than"* inequality constraint, add a *slack* variable.

    b To each *equation* constraint, add an *artificial* variable.

    c To each *"greater-than"* inequality constraint, add both a *surplus* variable (a negative slack variable) and an *artificial* variable.

Additional note: The addition of slack or surplus variables does not require their inclusion in the objective function. However, each *artificial* variable added, whether to an equation or "greater-than" inequality, must be included in the objective function with a very large coefficient to drive it out from the optimal solution. If it is a maximization problem, the coefficient should be a *large negative* value. If the problem is of the minimization type, the coefficient should be a *large positive* value.

6 The *computational* steps of the simplex method remain essentially unchanged when "greater-than" inequalities and equations appear in the original formulation. The one important change in minimization problems is that in the optimality test we look for any *positive* elements in the top row. Of course, in the selection of the incoming variable, we look for the most positive element in the top row.

PROBLEMS

11-1 The objective to be maximized is represented by $Z = 8x_1 + 4x_2$. There is a single equation constraint that must be satisfied: $4x_1 + 4x_2 = 16$.

    a Graph the problem on the x_1- and x_2-axes. As the objective function moves outward from the origin, what is the first feasible program encountered? What is the last? Which is the best?

    b Solve for the optimal feasible program and its value by the simplex method. Compare with your graphic solution.

11-2 Suppose that the objective in Problem 11-1 is to be minimized instead of maximized. The same equation constraint must be satisfied.

    a Graph the problem on the x_1- and x_2-axes. As the objective function is moved toward the origin (from a location some distance from the origin), what is the first feasible program encountered? What is the last? Which is the best?

    b Solve for the optimal feasible program and its value by the simplex method. Compare with your graphic solution.

11-3 The following objective function is to be minimized: $Z = 8x_1 + 8x_2$. A minimum condition must be satisfied that is represented by the following "greater-than" inequality constraint: $8x_1 + 4x_2 \geq 32$.

    a Graph the problem on the x_1- and x_2-axes and obtain the optimal feasible solution and its value graphically.

    b Obtain the optimal feasible solution and its value by the simplex method.

11-4 The objective function $Z = 2x_1 + 4x_2$ is to be maximized. Two inequality constraints must be satisfied. There is a "less-than" inequality constraint, $2x_1 + 2x_2 \leqslant 8$, and a "greater-than" inequality constraint, $2x_1 \geqslant 2$.

    a Graph the problem on the x_1- and x_2-axes. Obtain the optimal feasible solution graphically.

    b Solve for the optimal feasible solution and its value by the simplex method. Compare it with the solution obtained graphically in a.

11-5 For a particular period the total funds available to a bank for making loans and purchasing securities is $10 million. The rate of return on loans is 10 percent; on securities it is 6 percent. The bank wishes to identify the combination of loans and securities that will maximize total revenue, providing some specific conditions are also satisfied. These conditions are as follows:

Total-funds constraint: The total amount of loans made and securities purchased must not exceed $10 million.

Securities constraint: The total amount of securities purchased must be $3 million or more.

    a Let x_1 represent the amount devoted to loans and x_2 the amount devoted to securities. Formulate the problem in the standard linear-programming form.

    b Graph the problem on the x_1- and x_2- axes. Solve for the optimal feasible program and its value graphically.

    c Solve the problem by the simplex method. Compare your solution with that obtained graphically.

11-6 Suppose that the car manufacturer in Problem 8-4 wants to test the market for its new small-size car. To do this, it is decided that at least 250 cars must be produced for the decision period.

    a Add the necessary constraint to the resource constraints of Problem 8-4 and obtain a new linear-programming formulation.

    b Graph the problem on the product axes. Obtain the optimal feasible program and its total profit graphically.

    c Obtain the optimal feasible program and its value by the simplex method.

    d How much in total profits are lost for the decision period because of the new constraint?

11-7 A firm has an advertising budget of $7,200. It wishes to allocate the $7,200 to two media, newspapers and television, so that total exposure is the greatest. Each page of newspaper advertising is estimated to result in 60,000 exposures, whereas each minute of television time is estimated to result in 120,000 exposures. Each page of newspaper advertising costs $900, and each minute of television time costs $1,200. An additional condition that the firm has specified is that at least two pages of newspaper advertising be used and at least 3 minutes of television time.

    a Formulate the problem in standard linear-programming form. Represent the number of pages of newspaper advertising by x_1 and the number of minutes of television time by x_2. The advertising budget is to be represented by a "less-than" inequality constraint. Total exposures are to be maximized.

    b Graph the problem on the x_1- and x_2-axes. Solve for the optimal feasible program and its value graphically. Interpret the solution.

    c Solve the problem by the simplex method. Compare the solution with that obtained graphically.

11-8 For a particular period a firm has 280 machine-hours and 320 labor-hours available. It produces two products and desires to know the maximum-profit program. Additionally, it has obtained the following data:

Product 1: Unit profit = $14
           Use of machine-hours per unit of output = 4
           Use of labor-hours per unit of output = 2

Product 2: Unit profit = $4
           Use of machine-hours per unit of output = 2
           Use of machine-hours per unit of output = 4

    a Put the problem in standard linear-programming form and solve graphically.

    b Suppose that the firm establishes a minimum-level-of-employment policy whereby it decides to use as a minimum 200 labor-hours for the decision period. Formulate this minimum condition as a "greater-than" inequality constraint and include it with the other constraints in *a*. Graph the new problem and solve for the optimal feasible program and its total profit. Has the optimal program changed because of the new constraint? What is the effect upon optimal total profit?

    c Solve the new problem in *b* by the simplex method. Compare this solution with that obtained graphically.

11-9 There is a type of linear-programming problem often referred to as the "diet-type" problem. In a common form, different minimum nutritional requirements are specified. These requirements can be fulfilled by various foods (or inputs), and there is the desire to satisfy these minimum requirements at the lowest possible total cost.

    Suppose in a particular situation there is a minimum mineral requirement of 12 units and a minimum vitamin requirement of 16 units, both of which must be fulfilled. Two different foods (food 1 and food 2) are considered as a means of fulfilling these minimum requirements. The cost of each food and the rate of contribution of each food toward the fulfillment of each minimum requirement is as follows:

Food 1: Cost per ounce = $0.24
           Contribution per ounce toward the fulfillment of the
             mineral requirement = 2 units
           Contribution per ounce toward the fulfillment of the
             vitamin requirement = 4 units

Food 2: Cost per ounce = $0.16
           Contribution per ounce toward the fulfillment of the
             mineral requirement = 2 units
            Contribution per ounce toward the fulfillment of the
             vitamin requirement = 2 units

    a Formulate as a linear-programming problem in order to find the least-cost program of the two foods that satisfies both requirements. Represent the amount of food 1 by x_1 and the amount of food 2 by x_2.

    b Solve the problem graphically that you formulated in a. Interpret the solution.

    c Solve the problem in a by the simplex method. Compare this solution with that obtained graphically.

11-10 **a** Solve the following problem graphically:

$$\text{Maximize:} \quad Z = 8x_1 + 4x_2$$
$$\text{Subject to:} \quad 4x_1 \qquad\quad \leqslant 8$$
$$4x_2 \geqslant 12$$
$$4x_1 + 4x_2 = 16$$

    b Solve the problem in a by the simplex method.

11-11 Suppose in Problem 11-10a that the objective function is to be minimized instead of maximized.

    a Obtain the optimal feasible program and its value graphically.

    b Solve the problem by the simplex method.

Chapter 12

Sensitivity Analysis and the Dual Linear-Programming Problem

We discussed sensitivity analysis briefly in Chapter 9. In that chapter we observed that its primary focus is upon the coefficients and constants of a linear-programming problem and how a change in some of these elements can affect the optimal program. A specific aim of this analysis is to identify those coefficients and constants that would alter the optimal program if they were to have values different from those originally assumed.

Such analysis can yield great benefit in studying many real-world problems because some of the coefficients or constants in such problems often do not hold at the values we have assumed. There may be influences on these coefficients and constants that are unknown to us. Of course, changes in them may also be under our own control.

Once we identify those coefficients or constants whose changes affect the optimal program, we often want to know just how they change the optimal program and particularly how much they affect the objective we seek (such as maximum total profit). This was illustrated in Chapter 9 in terms of the lawn-mower–golf-cart example.

Sensitivity analysis (and parametric programming, too) is closely related to the *dual linear-programming problem*. We shall describe the dual problem more fully later in this chapter, merely noting at this point that every linear-programming problem can be formulated in a specific alternative way. This alternative formulation, in essence, still represents the same real-world problem and uses the same data. It can be solved by the simplex method, too.

Let us illustrate as simply as we can some of the main practical uses of the dual problem, delaying a discussion of the more technical aspects until later in the chapter.

VARIATION OF THE RIGHT-HAND-SIDE CONSTANTS AND THEIR CONNECTION TO THE DUAL LINEAR-PROGRAMMING PROBLEM

A commonly used part of sensitivity analysis and parametric programming that is helpful to examine in connection with the dual linear-programming problem is the variation of the right-hand-side constants. The right-hand-side constants usually represent resource capacities or availabilities.

In Chapter 9 we illustrated such parameter variation and obtained the graphs of optimal total profit associated with a broad range of right-hand-side amounts (resource capacities or availabilities). In Figure 12-1a we repeat the total-profit graph for the individual variation of resource 1 (the lawn-mower assembly facility) capacity from 0 to 100. In Figure 12-1b we repeat the analogous total-profit graph for the individual variation of resource 2 (the labor-hours available) from 0 to 100.

Note in Figure 12-1a the current lawn-mower assembly capacity of 50 and the optimal total profit of $2,750. Also, the current amount of labor-hours available is 80 and is associated with an optimal total profit of $2,750. Thus, $2,750 is the optimal total profit when the right-hand-side amounts are 50 and 80.

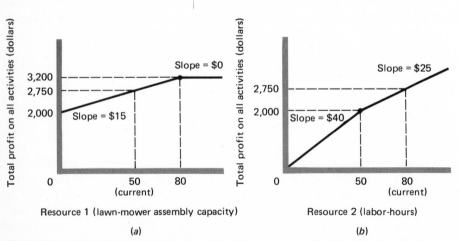

Figure 12-1 The effect upon total profit of the individual variation of (a) the amount of resource 1 (the lawn-mower assembly facility) and (b) the amount of resource 2 (labor-hours available).

Table 12-1   Optimal Simplex Table for the Original Lawn-Mower–Golf-Cart Problem

Basic variable	Z	Output of product 1 x_1	Output of product 2 x_2	Slack variable for resource 1 x_3	Slack variable for resource 2 x_4	RHS
Z	1	0	0	→15	→25	2,750
x_1	0	1	0	1	0	50
x_2	0	0	1	$-\frac{1}{2}$	$\frac{1}{2}$	15

Marginal contribution to profit ($15) of resource 1 (lawn-mower assembly facility)

Marginal contribution to profit ($25) of resource 2 (labor)

Each total-profit graph was obtained by individually varying each right-hand-side amount.

The change in total profit from an individual unit increase in each right-hand-side amount was obtained in Chapter 9 and gives us the slope of each total-profit graph in the vicinity of the current right-hand-side amounts (as shown in Figure 12-1).

A unit increase in the lawn-mower assembly capacity (resource 1) increased total profit by $15 and gives us the slope of $15. A unit increase in the labor-hours available (resource 2) increased total profit by $25 and gives us the slope of $25.

As we noted before, this increase in total profit from a unit increase in a resource amount is also called the *marginal contribution to profit* of that resource. Thus, in our lawn-mower–golf-cart example the marginal contribution to profit of resource 1 (lawn-mower assembly capacity) is $15, whereas it is $25 for resource 2 (labor-hours).

If a unit increase in a resource amount contributes more to total profit than it costs, normally it would be worthwhile to increase its capacity or availability. For example if an additional hour of labor would cost $5 but would add $25 to total profit, an increase in the amount of the labor resource obviously would be worthwhile.

In Chapter 9 we obtained the slopes of each total-profit graph (the marginal contributions to profit) for each of our two resources represented in the problem by increasing each resource amount by 1 unit, solving the new linear-programming problem, and observing the difference in the two optimal profits.

It turns out that our final simplex table for the original lawn-mower–golf-cart problem contains these very marginal contributions to profit (and slopes of the total-profit graphs) for an individual unit change in each resource amount. The final simplex table for that problem appeared originally in Table 10-11. We have repeated it in Table 12-1. In Table 12-1 we have added notes indicating the location of the marginal contribution to profit of each resource represented in the problem. The marginal contribution to profit of resource 1 (lawn-mower assembly facility) appears in the top row of the column associated with the slack variable x_3 that was introduced to take up any slack in resource 1.

Analogously, the marginal contribution to profit of resource 2 (labor) is found in the top row in the column associated with the slack variable x_4 that we introduced to take up any slack in resource 2.

Recall that the marginal contribution to profit of each resource is also equal to the slope of each of the associated total-profit graphs for an individual unit change in the resource amount. Thus, an important practical point is this: When we solve the original lawn-mower–golf-cart problem by the simplex method, the final simplex table gives us not only the optimal program of lawn mowers and golf carts (and the maximum profit) but also *the changes in optimal total profit that would occur if each of the resource amounts was increased individually by 1 unit*.

In other words, a proper interpretation of our final simplex table saves us much work in obtaining these marginal contributions to profit of each resource (the slopes of the total-profit graphs for each resource).

RANGE ANALYSIS: THE RANGE OF THE RESOURCE AMOUNT OVER WHICH THE INDICATED MARGINAL CONTRIBUTION TO PROFIT WILL HOLD

From our final simplex table in a linear-programming problem we can know the marginal contributions to profit of increasing individually by 1 unit each of the resource amounts represented in the problem. We readily see that for problems with many different resources this constitutes a big savings in computation time and cost.

Thus, in terms of the total-profit graphs in Figure 12-1a and b, the final simplex table (in Table 12-1) indicates that at our current resource 1 and resource 2 amounts the maximum total profit is $2,750. If the resource 1 amount (lawn-mower assembly capacity) is increased individually by 1 unit, maximum total profit will go to $2,765: $2,750 + $15 = $2,765. If the resource 2 amount (labor-hours) is increased individually by 1 unit, maximum total profit will go to $2,775: $2,750 + $25 = $2,775.

But the obvious next question is this: How *much* can we increase or decrease each resource capacity (or availability) individually and know that the marginal contribution to profit will hold at $15 (for resource 1) or $25 (for resource 2)?

In Chapter 9 we discussed this question and obtained this information with the aid of the original graph of the linear-programming problem. However, the method that we discussed (and used to obtain the graphs in Figure 12-1) does not extend to the larger practical problems with numerous activities (that is, with many dimensions).

Fortunately, it turns out that the final (optimal) simplex table provides us with this very information: *the ranges over which the indicated marginal contributions to profit will hold.*

However, the range values are not in the table ready to be picked out; we must do a little work to get them. The procedure for finding the range of resource capacities (or availabilities) over which the indicated marginal contribution to profit will hold focuses upon the elements in the slack-variable columns. For example, resource 1 is associated with the slack variable x_3. The marginal contribution to profit of resource 1 ($15) appears in the top row of that column. *The remaining elements in the same x_3 column are used to obtain the range of resource 1 amounts over which the $15 marginal contribution to profit will hold.*

The remaining elements in the x_3 column are 1 and $-\frac{1}{2}$. As shown in Table 12-2, we divide each of these elements *into* the right-hand-side amount in the same row. The right-hand-side amount of 50 is associated with the element 1. The element $-\frac{1}{2}$ is associated with a right-hand-side amount of 15. Thus, we have the following results. (Note that the algebraic sign is not the one we expect.)

Operation	Interpretation
$50 \div 1 = 50$	This is the amount by which resource 1 (lawn-mower assembly capacity) can be *decreased* before a change in the $15 marginal contribution to profit will occur. Thus, since the current assembly capacity is 50, a breakpoint (or starting point) in the total profit graph will occur at 0 capacity: $50 - 50 = 0$.
$15 \div (-\frac{1}{2}) = -30$	This is the amount by which resource 1 (lawn-mower assembly capacity) can be *increased* before a change in the $15 marginal contribution to profit will occur. Thus, since the current assembly capacity is 50, a breakpoint in the total-profit graph will occur at a capacity of 80: $50 + 30 = 80$.

Again, let us note that the sign is not what we might expect, but the -30 obtained above represents (in absolute value) the amount the resource 1 (lawn-mower assembly) capacity can be *increased* before a breakpoint in the total-profit graph is reached. This means that with the current capacity at 50 an increase in the capacity by 30 (to 80) is possible before a breakpoint will be reached (and a new slope and a new marginal contribution to profit).

This is seen in Figure 12-1a which we obtained by the longer method of Chapter 9. From the final simplex table we cannot say what the new slope (and new marginal contribution to profit) will be. We can only say that the lawn-

Table 12-2   The Optimal Simplex Table Yields the Range of the Resource 1 Capacity (Lawn-Mower Assembly Facility) over Which the $15 Marginal Contribution to Profit Will Hold

Basic variable	Z	Output of product 1 x_1	Output of product 2 x_2	Slack variable for resource 1 x_3	Slack variable for resource 2 x_4	RHS
Z	1	0	0	15	25	2,750
x_1	0	1	0	1	0	50
x_2	0	0	1	$-\frac{1}{2}$	$\frac{1}{2}$	15

$50 \div 1 = 50$
Resource 1 capacity can *decrease* by 50 before the marginal contribution to profit will change from $15.

$15 \div (-\frac{1}{2}) = -30$
Resource 1 capacity can *increase* by 30 before the marginal contribution to profit will change from $15.

mower assembly capacity can go up to 80 before the marginal contribution to profit will change. However, we have just taken a big step. This method of finding the range from the final simplex table extends to large practical problems. Many computer programs that are available incorporate this range analysis into their various options.

The other ratio, 50/1 or 50, gives us the amount that resource 1 can be *decreased* before the marginal contribution to profit will change. This means that if the current resource 1 capacity of 50 is decreased by 50 (to a capacity of 0) a breakpoint will be reached and a new slope and marginal contribution to profit will occur. In our example, as seen in Figure 12-1a, this is associated with a total profit of $2,000.

And what we have done for resource 1 we can do for resource 2. Now, however, our attention shifts to the x_4 column because x_4 is the slack variable associated with resource 2 (labor).

We see in the top row of the x_4 column that the marginal contribution of the labor resource is $25. Following the same method as in the case of the other resource, we divide the remaining coefficients of the x_4 column into the right-hand-side amounts in the same row. This gives us the ratios $50 \div 0$ and $15 \div \frac{1}{2}$ or 30.

The second ratio is positive in sign and indicates that the current resource 2 amount of 80 can be decreased by 30 (to 50) before a new marginal contribution to profit is reached (and, of course a breakpoint in the total-profit graph), usually indicating a new linear segment with a new slope. This is seen in Figure 12-1b which was obtained by the longer method of Chapter 9.

From Figure 12-1*b* we can see there is no breakpoint in the total-profit graph if we increase the amount of resource 2. There it can be seen why we interpret any ratio in which 0 appears in the denominator as an infinite increase in the resource.

In summary, the range analysis shows that the marginal contribution to profit of $25 for resource 2 (labor) will hold from 50 hours up to an infinite number of hours. Practically speaking, however, there will be some limit to this range due to limited resource availabilities or capacities that we have not included in the original formulation.

THE DUAL LINEAR PROGRAMMING PROBLEM
OF THE LAWN-MOWER–GOLF-CART EXAMPLE

Every original linear-programming problem has an associated dual linear-programming problem. The original problem is usually referred to as the *primal linear-programming problem*. As indicated above, the dual formulation of the original problem essentially comes out of the linear algebra underlying linear programming.

However, in a practical sense we can think of the dual problem requiring the interchanging of the rows and columns of our data table associated with the original (primal) problem. This is done for the lawn-mower–golf-cart example in Table 12-3. What had been a row in the primal data table becomes a column in the dual data table.

We now repeat from earlier chapters the standard formulation of our primal lawn-mower–golf-cart problem which is based on the primal data table in Table 8-1.

Table 12-3   Forming the Dual Data Table from a Primal Data Table

Primal Data Table	Rate of profit and rate of resource use		Resource amount (capacity or availability)
	Product 1	Product 2	
Profit	$40	$50	—
Resource 1	1	0	50
Resource 2	1	2	80

Dual Data Table	Resource amount and rate of resource use		
	Resource 1	Resource 2	Profit
Resource amount	50	80	—
Product 1	1	1	$40
Product 2	0	2	$50

Maximize: $Z_x = \$40x_1 + \$50x_2$

Subject to: $x_1 \qquad \leqslant 50$ (Resource 1: lawn-mower assembly facility)

$\qquad\qquad x_1 + 2x_2 \quad \leqslant 80$ (Resource 2: labor-hours)

The dual linear-programming problem is based on the arrangement of the problem in the dual data table in Table 12-3. First, however, we must define a set of new variables $(u_1, u_2, \dots)$ that replace the variables $(x_1, x_2, \dots)$ in our original (primal) problem. These original variables in our example represented outputs of lawn mowers and golf carts. We sought the feasible program of these product outputs that maximized total profit.

In the dual problem the new set of variables is associated with the resources or constraints. In our example, each new variable in the dual problem represents a *marginal contribution to profit* for each resource represented in the original problem. Thus, we create a new variable for each resource constraint that appears in the original (primal) problem.

For example, the first constraint in the original problem represents resource 1 (lawn-mower assembly facility). Related to it we create the variable u_1 in the dual problem.

For resource 2 (labor) we create the new variable u_2. And, in a larger problem, we would continue until we had created a new variable for each resource (each constraint). After all, we will be solving for the marginal contribution to profit for each resource, and, of course, we need a variable to represent the value of each resource.

Thus, we will have as many variables in the dual problem as we had constraints in the primal problem. Also, we will have as many constraints in the dual problem as we had variables in the primal problem. In our lawn-mower–golf-cart example we had two variables (lawn-mower output and golf-cart output), and so we shall have two constraints in the dual problem. Therefore, in the dual problem each constraint pertains to a product output (at least in our example).

Thus, at this point we can set down the following new variables, leaving such elements as the coefficients and right-hand-side amounts to be added later. (*Note:* If our primal problem had three constraints and two variables, we would have three dual variables, u_1, u_2, and u_3, along with two constraints.)

Objective function: $u_1 + u_2$

Subject to the following constraints: $u_1 + u_2$

$\qquad\qquad\qquad\qquad\qquad\qquad\qquad u_1 + u_2$

Specifically, what we need to do is the following:

1 Provide the appropriate maximization or minimization instruction with regard to the objective function.

2 Indicate the direction of the inequality constraints.

3   Assign the appropriate coefficients to the new variables in the objective function and the constraints, and designate the right-hand-side constants.

The Maximization or Minimization Instruction

If a primal problem is a *maximization* problem, the dual is a *minimization* problem. Thus, in our example the dual objective function is to be minimized. (*Note:* If, on the other hand, the primal objective function is to be minimized, the dual of that problem is a maximization problem.)

The Direction of the Constraint Inequalities

If in the primal problem the constraint inequalities are *"less-than"* inequalities, the contraint inequalities in the dual problem will be reversed to *"greater-than"* inequalities. Analogously, if the primal constraints are "greater-than" constraints, the dual constraints will be "less-than" constraints.

Assignment of the Coefficients and Right-Hand-Side Amounts

This step is the most complicated because it involves transposing rows and columns of coefficients. Very roughly, it refers to converting a *column* of values into a *row* of values (or vice versa). This is what is done when a dual data table is formed from a primal data table, as in Table 12-3.

In forming the dual problem from the primal problem, we take the column of right-hand-side values in the primal problem and convert them to the row of objective-function coefficients in the dual problem. In our example, the right-hand-side amounts of 50 and 80 (from top to bottom) become the coefficients (from left to right) in the dual objective function.

Analogously, the first column of coefficients (from top to bottom) in the constraints of the primal problem become the first row of coefficients (from left to right) in the constraints of the dual problem. In our example, this means that the first column of coefficients in the primal constraints, 1 and 1, become the coefficients in the first constraint (first row) of the dual problem: $1u_1 + 1u_2$.

Similarly, the second column of coefficients, 0 and 2 in the primal, become the coefficients of the second constraint in the dual: $0u_1 + 2u_2$.

The above steps give us the following dual formulation of our primal lawn-mower—golf-cart problem.

Minimize: $Z_u = 50u_1 + 80u_2$ (imputed total profit)
Subject to: $u_1 + u_2 \geqslant \$40$ (Product 1: lawn mowers)
             $2u_2 \geqslant \$50$ (Product 2: golf carts)

A graph of the dual problem is shown in Figure 12-2. The optimal feasible solution is seen to be $u_1 = \$15$ and $u_2 = \$25$, with a Z_u-value of $2,750.

First, note that when we solve the dual problem we solve *directly* for what in our original problem we called the "marginal contribution to profit" for each resource (this is the meaning of the dual variables with a profit-maximization

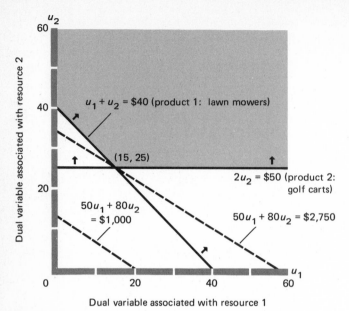

Figure 12-2 The dual linear-programming problem associated with the original lawn-mower–golf-cart problem.

primal problem). Recall that these very same marginal-contribution-to-profit values of \$15 for resource 1 and \$25 for resource 2 were also picked out of the top row of the final simplex table of the primal problem. Thus, in the simplex solution of the primal problem we solved the dual problem, too, implicitly.

It turns out that if we were to solve the dual problem by the simplex method, the solution to the primal problem is obtained from the final simplex table. The values in the top row in the columns of the surplus variables will show the optimal solution of the primal: $(x_1, x_2) = (50, 15)$. (The negative sign is ignored.)

One final point: The value of the optimal solution of the primal (total profit) will always be equal to the value of the optimal solution (imputed total profit) of the dual problem. We use Z_x to refer to the value of the primal objective function and Z_u for the value of the dual objective function. One, of course, is to be maximized and the other minimized. But Z of the optimal feasible solution of the dual problem equals the optimal feasible solution to the primal problem.

The economic meaning of the primal objective function is quite clear. We seek the program of product outputs that maximizes total profit. In the dual problem, however, we search for the program of marginal-contribution-to-profit amounts that minimizes *total imputed profit* to the various resources. It turns out that the minimum total profit that we can impute to (or attribute to) the resources is equal to the maximum total profit that can be generated through the use of the resources in making products or engaging in particular activities.

In our example, u_1 (the marginal contribution to profit of resource 1) has an optimal value of $15, and u_2 (the marginal contribution to profit of resource 2) has an optimal value of $25. Substituting this optimal program into the dual objective function gives us a (grand) total imputed profit of $2,750. Also it gives us a total imputed profit of $750 to resource 1 and a total imputed profit of $2,000 to resource 2.

$$
\begin{aligned}
\text{Total imputed profit} &= 50u_1 + 80u_2 \\
&= 50(\$15) + 80(\$25) \\
&= \$750 + \$2,000 \\
&= \$2,750
\end{aligned}
$$

SUMMARY

1 Every linear-programming problem can be formulated in a specific alternative way. This alternative formulation is called the *dual linear-programming problem*.

2 The *marginal contribution to profit* of each resource refers to the increase in optimal total profit if an additional unit of the resource is available.

3 The marginal contribution to profit of each resource can be obtained by (a) individually increasing each resource by 1 unit, solving the new problem, and observing the difference in the optimal total profits; (b) solving the original (primal) problem by the simplex method and identifying the marginal-contribution-to-profit values from the top row of the final simplex table; or (c) formulating the dual problem and solving directly for the marginal contributions to profit of every resource.

4 The *range analysis* regarding a resource constraint is concerned with identifying the range of the resource amounts over which the current marginal contribution to profit will hold.

5 The range analysis for each resource constraint can be accomplished (a) in small problems by identifying on a graph the resource amount associated with a change in the direction of the optimal solution as the resource amount is varied or (b) in small and large problems by solving the problem by the simplex method and then (in the final table) dividing each element in the appropriate slack-variable column into its associated right-hand-side amount.

6 To obtain the dual data table from a primal data table, the rows and columns must be interchanged.

7 The definition of new (dual) variables ($u_1, u_2, \ldots$), one for each resource constraint in the primal problem, together with the dual data table, forms the main part of the dual formulation of a primal linear-programming problem. Additionally, it is necessary to provide the maximization or minimization instruction with respect to the dual objective function and, also, to indicate the direction (or sense) of the inequalities in the constraints.

8 The dual variables in our discussions so far are to be interpreted as the "marginal contributions to profit" of the resources. In other applications the interpretations are different; however, the interpretation that is most direct and intuitive is this: The optimal dual solution obtains values for the dual variables that are equal to the marginal contribution to the primal objective if each of the right-hand-side amounts is increased individually by 1 unit. Terms such as shadow prices, implicit values, and marginal values are used to refer to these marginal effects upon the primal objective.

    9 The solutions to *both* the primal problem and the dual problem are obtained from solving by the simplex method *either* the primal problem or the dual problem.

PROBLEMS

12-1 Suppose a firm has obtained the following primal data table.

	Product 1	Product 2	Resource capacity or availability
Profit	$8	$2	
Resource 1	2	0	8
Resource 2	2	2	12

    a Formulate the primal linear-programming problem in the standard form.

    b Graph the problem on the x_1- and x_2-axes and solve for the optimal feasible program and its total profit.

    c Using the graph of the problem in *b*, obtain a total-profit graph for the variation of the resource 1 amount over a broad range (from 0 to 30).

    d Using the graph of the problem in *b*, obtain a total-profit graph for the variation of the resource 2 amount over a broad range (from 0 to 60).

12-2 Solve by the simplex method the problem formulated in Problem 12-1*a*. Compare the solution with that obtained graphically in Problem 12-1*b*.

12-3 From the final simplex table in Problem 12-2,

    a Obtain the marginal contribution to profit of each resource. Compare with that obtained in Problem 12-1*c* and *d*.

    b Obtain for each resource the range of resource amounts over which the current marginal contribution to profit will hold. Compare with that obtained in Problem 12-1*c* and *d*. Comment on any differences in the results obtained.

12-4 **a** From the primal data table in Problem 12-1 form the dual data table by representing in columns what had been in rows.

    b From the dual data table in *a* and the primal linear programming formulation in Problem 12-1*a*, form the dual linear-programming problem.

    c Graph the dual linear-programming problem in *b* on the u_1- and u_2-axes. Obtain the optimal feasible solution and its value. Interpret the solution and its value. Compare the dual solution with the marginal contribution to profit of each resource obtained in Problems 12-1*c*, 12-1*d*, and 12-3*a*.

12-5 **a** Solve by the simplex method the dual linear-programming problem formulated in Problem 12-4*b*.

    b Indicate the location of the dual solution and its value on the final simplex table. Is the value of u_1 in the optimal dual solution equal to the marginal contribution to profit of resource 1 obtained in Problems 12-1*c* and 12-3*a*? What about resource 2?

c   Indicate the location of the primal optimal solution in the final simplex table of the dual problem in *a*.

12-6   Consider again the problem first encountered in Problem 8-1, then in Problems 9-1, 9-2, 9-3, 9-4, and again in Problem 10-8.

    a   From the final simplex table in Problem 10-8, obtain the marginal contribution to profit of each resource.

    b   From the final simplex table in Problem 10-8, obtain the range of resource 1 amounts over which the current marginal contribution to profit of resource 1 will hold. Compare the range obtained here with that in Problem 9-3*i*.

    c   From the final simplex table in Problem 10-8 obtain the range of resource 2 amounts over which the current marginal contribution to profit of resource 2 will hold. Compare the range obtained here with that in Problem 9-4*e*.

    d   From the primal data table in Problem 8-1*a* form the dual data table for the problem.

    e   From the dual data table in *d* and the primal linear-programming formulation in Problem 8-1*c*, form the dual linear-programming problem.

    f   Graph the dual problem in *e* on the u_1- and u_2-axes. Obtain the optimal feasible solution and its value. Compare the dual solution with the marginal contribution to profit of each resource obtained in Problems 9-1*c*, 9-2*c*, and 10-8.

    g   Solve by the simplex method the dual linear-programming problem formulated in *e*. Indicate the location of the dual solution and its value on the final simplex table. Also indicate the location of the optimal solution to the primal problem.

12-7   Consider again the maker of backpacks and raincoats in Problems 8-2, 9-5, 9-6, and 10-9.

    a   From the final simplex table in Problem 10-9, obtain the marginal contribution to profit of resource 1 (sewing-machine-hours) and resource 2 (labor-hours).

    b   From the final simplex table in Problem 10-9, obtain the range of sewing-machine-hours over which the current marginal contribution to profit will hold. Compare the range obtained here with that in Problem 9-5*c*.

    c   From the final simplex table in Problem 10-9, obtain the range of labor-hours over which the current marginal contribution to profit will hold. Compare the range obtained here with that in Problem 9-6*b*.

    d   From the primal data table in Problem 8-2*a*, form the dual data table for the problem.

    e   From the dual data table in *d* and the primal formulation in Problem 8-2*b*, form the dual linear-programming problem.

    f   Graph the dual problem in *e* and obtain the dual solution graphically. Compare the dual solution with the marginal contribution to the profit of each resource obtained in Problems 9-5*b*, 9-6*b*, and 10-9.

    g   Solve by the simplex method the dual problem formulated in *e*. Indicate the location of both the dual and primal solutions on the final simplex table.

12-8   Let us look again at the dairy-foods processor in Problems 8-3, 9-7, and 10-10.

    a   From the final simplex table in Problem 10-10, obtain the marginal contribution to profit of resource 1 (processing facility) and resource 2 (labor-hours).

    b   From the final simplex table in Problem 10-10, obtain the range of the processing-facility capacities over which its current marginal contribution to profit will hold. Compare the range obtained here with that in Problem 9-7*c*.

    c   From the final simplex table in Problem 10-10, obtain the range of labor-hours over which its current marginal contribution to profit will hold. Compare the range obtained here with that in Problem 9-7c.

    d   Form the dual problem from the primal problem in Problem 8-3.

    e   Graph the dual problem in d and obtain the dual solution graphically. Compare the dual solution with the marginal contribution to profit of each resource obtained in Problems 9-7c and 10-10.

    f   (Optional)   Solve by the simplex method the dual problem formulated in d. Interpret the dual and primal solutions and the optimal value of the objective function.

12-9   The car manufacturer in Problem 8-4 had to decide on a program of output of regular-size cars and small-size cars. In Problem 9-8 we varied individually the capacity of the assembly facilities (resource 1) and also the labor-hours available (resource 2). In Problem 10-11 we solved the original (primal) problem by the simplex method.

    a   From the final simplex table in Problem 10-11, obtain the marginal contribution to profit of each resource.

    b   From the final simplex table in Problem 10-11, obtain the range of assembly facility capacities (resource 1) over which its current marginal contribution to profit will hold. Compare the range obtained here with that in Problem 9-8c.

    c   From the final simplex table in Problem 10-11, obtain the range of labor-hours (resource 2) over which its current marginal contribution to profit will hold. Compare the range obtained here with that in Problem 9-8c.

    d   Form the dual problem for the car manufacturer from the primal problem in Problem 8-4b.

    e   Graph the dual problem in d and obtain the dual solution graphically. Compare the dual solution with the marginal contribution to profit of each resource obtained in Problems 9-8c and 10-11.

    f   (Optional)   Solve by the simplex method the dual problem formulated in d. Interpret the dual and primal solutions and the optimal value of the objective function.

12-10   Let us consider again the small-vehicle manufacturer encountered in Problems 8-6, 9-10, and 10-12.

    a   From the final simplex table in Problem 10-12, obtain the marginal contribution to profit of each resource.

    b   From the final simplex table in Problem 10-12, obtain the range of resource amounts over which the marginal contribution to profit of each resource will hold. Compare with the ranges obtained in Problem 9-10c.

    c   Form the dual problem from the primal problem in Problem 8-6a.

    d   Solve the dual problem in c graphically. Compare the dual solution with the marginal contribution to profit of each resource obtained in Problems 9-10c and 10-12.

    e   (Optional)   Solve by the simplex method the dual problem formulated in c. Interpret the dual and primal solutions and the value of the objective function.

12-11   The firm in Problems 8-7 and 10-13 makes two different products and is faced with effective limitations from two resources.

    a   From the final simplex table in Problem 10-13a obtain the marginal contribution to profit of each resource. Is the presence of a slack variable in the optimal solution related to the marginal contribution to profit of $0? Explain.

    b   From the final simplex table in Problem 10-13a, obtain the range over which the marginal contribution to profit of each resource will hold.

    c   Form the dual problem from the primal problem in Problem 8-7b.

    d   Solve the dual problem in c graphically. Compare the dual solution with the marginal contribution to profit of each resource obtained in Problem 10-13a.

    e   (Optional) Solve by the simplex method the dual problem formulated in c. Interpret the dual and primal solutions and the value of the optimal solution.

12-12   An agricultural production decision was put into a linear-programming formulation in Problem 8-8b and the primal problem was solved by the simplex method in Problem 10-14.

    a   From the final simplex table in Problem 10-14, obtain the marginal contribution to profit of resource 1 (land) and the marginal contribution to profit of resource 2 (labor).

    b   From the final simplex table in Problem 10-14, obtain the range of land acreages over which its current marginal contribution to profit will hold.

    c   From the final simplex table in Problem 10-14, obtain the range of labor-hours over which its current marginal contribution to profit will hold.

    d   Form the dual data table from the primal data table in Problem 8-8a.

    e   Form the dual problem from the primal problem in Problem 8-8b.

    f   Solve the dual problem in e graphically. Compare the dual solution with the marginal contribution to profit of each resource obtained in Problem 10-14.

    g   (Optional) Solve by the simplex method the dual problem formulated in e. Interpret the primal and dual solutions and the optimal value of the objective function.

12-13   The manufacturer of automotive parts in Problem 8-11 was interested in identifying an optimal program of pistons and axles. Three types of machines (three resources) were used in making each product and effectively imposed limitations on the production activities. The problem was solved by the simplex method in Problem 10-15.

    a   From the final simplex table in Problem 10-15, obtain the marginal contribution to profit of each resource (each type of machine).

    b   From the final simplex table in Problem 10-15, obtain the range over which the marginal contribution to profit of each resource will hold. Use the graph in Problem 8-11c to verify the ranges.

    c   Form the dual data table from the primal data table in Problem 8-11a.

    d   Form the dual problem from the dual data table in c and the primal formulation in Problem 8-11b.

    e   (Optional) With three dual variables there is no graphical solution in two dimensions. Solve by the simplex method the dual problem formulated in c. Interpret the dual and primal solutions and their values.

12-14   Consider again the "diet-type" problem in Problem 11-9.

    a   Formulate the dual linear-programming problem.

    b   Give a verbal interpretation of the newly created dual variables.

    c   Graph the problem on the u_1- and u_2-axes.

    d   Indicate the optimal solution to the dual problem in your graph in c.

    e   Solve the dual problem by the simplex method. Does it correspond to your graphical solution in c and in Problem 11-9c?

Chapter 13

Decision Making When More than One Technique of Production Is Available

In the previous chapters we have for the most part assumed that the various products we might make can each be produced by only one method (by one process). For example, in the production of each lawn mower in the earlier example, 1 hour of labor is used and 1 unit of the assembly capacity is used. This was the case for all the products we considered. Thus, there were no other processes available that used, say, less labor per lawn mower or more labor per lawn mower. In other words, we could say that we considered only one type of technology in the production of each of the products.

Now we are at the place where we should enlarge our view of linear-programming analysis so that we can incorporate other technologies into our analysis. Thus, the main idea of the chapter is that, in reality, products or services can be produced by more than one method (or process), and we wish to incorporate this aspect into our linear-programming analysis, too. It turns out that we can do so quite easily.

But how is it done? Simply *by treating each different process of making a product as a separate "activity."* In making shoes, for example, one process (one activity) might be the making of shoes where the sewing is done mostly by hand. Another process (another activity) might make heavy use of sewing machines.

Thus, in this chapter we focus directly upon what are sometimes called the "techniques" or the "technological" aspects of the activities in which we might engage. Typically, different techniques of production use resources at different rates. Thus, various techniques are associated with different rates of use of the resources.

We shall see that as new techniques are either discovered, made known, or become available to those making the decisions, the optimal programs are subsequently altered and the extent to which objectives can be attained is also affected. We shall examine this in some detail.

MAKING SHOES BY TWO DIFFERENT PROCESSES

In making shoes (just the single product), we can think of making them by different techniques or processes. Let us consider making them by just two different processes, such as we discussed above. More than two processes could be considered in our analysis, but at the beginning let us stay with the simple example in order to illustrate the main ideas of this chapter as clearly as we can. Later, we shall look at an example that involves more than one product, each of which can be produced by more than one process.

Remember that we treat each process as a separate activity, and in our shoemaking example we give the following interpretation to each of the two processes.

Process 1   (Activity 1): Making shoes with heavy use of sewing machines. (Each pair of shoes by this process uses 4 hours of labor and 4 machine-hours.)

Process 2   (Activity 2): Making shoes primarily by a hand sewing method with only limited use of sewing machines. (Each pair of shoes by this process uses 5 hours of labor and 2 machine-hours.)

Let us think of process 1 as the "machine process" in making shoes and process 2 as the "hand process." Of course the hand process does require some machine time, as indicated above, but involves a considerable amount of hand sewing operations.

The *level* of the machine process (process 1) is to be thought of as the number of pairs of shoes produced by that process. The level of output by process 1 is represented by the variable x_1. We represent the level of output by the hand process (output by process 2) by the variable x_2. Thus, in a particular problem involving different processes, the number of variables in its formulation is determined by the number of processes considered.

As in earlier linear-programming problems, a common formulation is one where we are to choose a program (output levels by each process) that maximizes (or minimizes) some objective subject to the limitations imposed by scarce resources or other constraints.

Suppose that in the shoemaking problem there are 60 hours of labor and 36 hours of sewing-machine time available per day. Each pair of shoes can be sold for $60 regardless of the process used in its production.

Given the resource limitations above and the condition that production can be undertaken only by the two processes, what program of output by each process will maximize total revenue? Let us formulate the problem as a linear-programming problem and see.

The linear-programming formulation is as follows:

Maximize: Total revenue $= \$60x_1 + \$60x_2$
Subject to: $4x_1 + 5x_2 \leq 60$ (labor-hours)
                $4x_1 + 2x_2 \leq 36$ (machine-hours)

A graph of the problem appears in Figure 13-1. The optimal feasible program is $(x_1, x_2) = (5, 8)$ with a maximum total revenue of $780. This means that the combination of processes that will result in the greatest total revenue is to produce 5 pairs of shoes by the machine process (process 1) and 8 pairs of shoes by the hand process (process 2). No other combination of the two processes will result in more revenue.

As indicated above, numerous processes of production can be so represented in single linear-programming formulation with the problem being solved by the now-familiar simplex method. Also, the procedures of sensitivity analysis and parametric programming permit useful further study of problems formulated in this way.

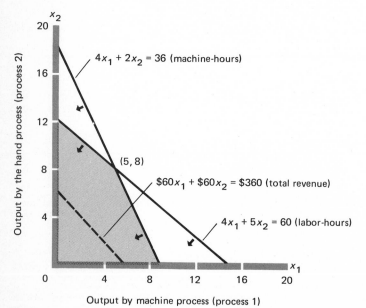

Figure 13-1   The shoemaking problem with two processes of production.

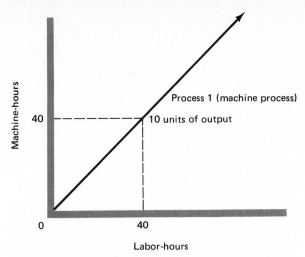

Figure 13-2   Making shoes by the machine process.

Another Way to Represent Processes Graphically

Our understanding of the concept of a process and its relationship to linear programming can be strengthened further if we represent a process in an alternative way to that shown in Figure 13-1.

First, however, let us look at the constraints in the linear-programming formulation of the shoemaking example above. Product output by the machine process (process 1) is represented by the variable x_1.

If we lift out only the x_1 terms (and ignore the x_2 terms associated with process 2), we can make the following statements about the machine process and the resources required for various levels of output by that process.

Process 1
$4x_1$ = labor-hours needed
$4x_1$ = machine-hours needed

The first statement pertains to the labor-hours that would be needed for various possible output levels by the machine process (process 1). For example, when x_1 is 10, the total labor-hours needed to produce 10 pairs of shoes by this process is 40: $4(10) = 40$ labor-hours needed.

The second statement has an analogous interpretation for the machine-hours needed. The *same* program where x_1 is 10 (that is 10 pairs of shoes by this process) requires 40 machine-hours: $4(10) = 40$ machine-hours needed.

A graphic representation of what we have just discussed appears in Figure 13-2. Note that this graph has the resource inputs on the two axes. We have labor-hours on the horizontal axis and machine-hours on the vertical axis. We represent the product output by this process (that is, x_1-values) by points *on the process ray*.

How do we obtain such a process ray? First, we can do so in two dimensions only if we have but two resources. But if we have just the two resource inputs (such as labor-hours and machine-hours), we treat each of these resource inputs as variables and represent their magnitudes on the two axes.

With appropriate scales defined on the two resource axes, we ask the following question (or one similar to it): What amounts of the two resources will be needed to produce, say, 10 pairs of shoes by this process (that is, when x_1 is 10)? We have already determined this above and found it to be 40 labor-hours and 40 machine-hours. We summarize our results as follows:

Process 1	Resource inputs needed	Process 1	Resource inputs needed to produce 10 pairs of shoes by this process
$4x_1$	= labor-hours needed	4(10)	= 40 labor-hours needed
$4x_1$	= machine-hours needed	4(10)	= 40 machine-hours needed

Thus, 40 labor-hours and 40 machine-hours will produce 10 units of output (10 pairs of shoes) by this process. To graph this process ray, we go to 40 on the labor-hour axis and 40 on the machine-hour axis; then, we find the point that represents this pair of resource amounts. Associated with this point is an output of 10 units (10 pairs of shoes).

In such problems the process ray begins at the origin so that it constitutes one point on the ray. We have found one other point by substituting a value of 10

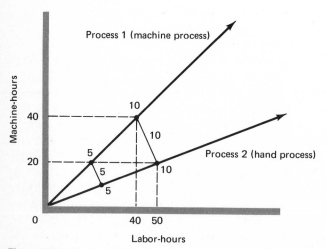

Figure 13-3 Output of shoes by the two processes graphed on the resource-input axes.

for x_1. Thus, if we connect the two points with a straight line and extend it outward, we have the process 1 ray. This graph is shown in Figure 13-2.

Other process rays (for other processes) can be graphed in similar fashion. To do so we simply assume a particular level of output by the process (this means that we assume a value for the relevant product-output variable). For process 1 we assumed an x_1-value of 10. Let us do the same for the hand process (process 2) in the shoemaking example.

If we were to produce 10 pairs of shoes by the hand process (process 2), x_2 would take a value of 10. The x_2-terms in the constraints of the original linear-programming formulation are lifted out, and the substitution of 10 for x_2 is made. This indicates that the following resource inputs are needed to produce the same 10 units by this process.

Process 2	Resource inputs needed	Process 2	Resource inputs needed to produce 10 pairs of shoes by this process
$5x_2$	= labor-hours needed	5(10)	= 50 labor-hours needed
$2x_2$	= machine-hours needed	2(10)	= 20 machine-hours needed

Thus, 50 labor-hours and 20 machine-hours are needed to produce 10 pairs of shoes by the hand process (process 2). This compares with 40 labor-hours and 40 machine-hours needed to produce the same output by the machine process (process 1).

The process 2 ray begins at the origin, also. Thus, we already have that point on our process 2 ray. The second point that we need is at 50 labor-hours and 20 machine-hours, as shown in Figure 13-3. The product output (x_2) at that point is 10 units. A straight line drawn from the origin through this point outward gives us the process 2 ray as shown in Figure 13-3.

Levels of product output by a particular process are represented by points on the associated process ray. Because the rates of use of each of the resources are constant for all levels of output (that is, the constraint coefficients remain fixed), the product-output scale on each process ray will be uniform. For example, in Figure 13-3 the distance from the origin to an output of 5 units is exactly one-half the distance from the origin to an output of 10 units.

Although each process ray will have a uniform product-output scale, typically the scale will be unique to that particular process ray. This means that the distance representing the output from 0 to 10 units on one process ray will differ from the distance representing the output from 0 to 10 units on another process ray. For example, in Figure 13-3 the distance representing the output levels from 0 to 10 units on the process 2 ray is slightly less than the distance on the process 1 ray that represents the output levels from 0 to 10 units by that process. Remember, though, that on each process ray the distances representing such 10-unit intervals are uniform.

Once we have identified some product-output levels on each of the process rays, *we can connect with a straight line the points representing the same output amounts*. This is done in Figure 13-3 for product outputs of 5 and 10 units. All such "equal-product" lines will be parallel with one another.

What does a straight line connecting two points of equal output (for example, 10 units) mean? It means that any point on that line also represents an output of 10 units that can be produced *by some combination of process 1 and process 2*. In other words, part of the output of 10 units would be produced by the machine process and part by the hand process.

But how much is to be produced by each process? Let us illustrate this in Figure 13-4 by selecting (quite arbitrarily) a point that we label *A*. We could have picked another point on this line just as well, but let us work with the one selected.

Point *A* can be "reached" from the origin by "going out" some distance on the process 1 ray and then switching to the process 2 ray. In the example in Figure 13-4 we would produce 6 units by process 1 and 4 units by process 2. The output by process 2 is represented by the linear segment from point *B* to point *A* and has the same slope and output scale of the process 2 ray.

How did we determine that the 10 units of output at point *A* can be obtained by producing 6 units by process 1 and 4 units by process 2? We solved it graphically. Given point *A*, we drew a straight line through point *A*, *parallel* with the process 2 ray. This parallel line intersects the process 1 ray at point *B*.

The output at point *B* (which is 6) identifies the output by process 1. The distance from point *B* to point *A* measured on the process 2 output scale

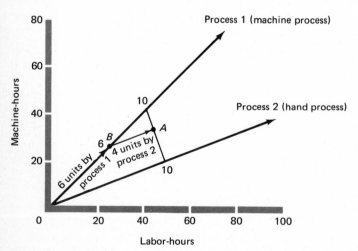

Figure 13-4   Producing 10 pairs of shoes by a combination of the two processes.

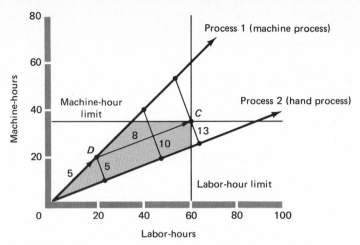

Figure 13-5 The shoemaking problem with the resource limitations.

represents the output by process 2 (it is 4 units). This is a particular combination of the two processes that will produce 10 units of output.

Of course we could have selected a point other than A on the 10-unit line, and another combination of processes would be involved. Also, a lower or higher equal-output line (such as the 9- or 11-unit output line) could have been selected. Points on such different output lines would also call for different combinations of the two processes.

Particular points on the equal-output lines in practical problems are essentially determined by the resource limitations. In a small problem, such as our shoemaking problem, this can be illustrated quite clearly.

Recall from our original linear-programming formulation above that 60 labor-hours and 36 machine-hours were available. If for the decision period these available amounts are fixed, we represent these limits by the resource-limitation lines in Figure 13-5 that are perpendicular to the resource axes.

Thus, labor-hours beyond 60 are not available. And machine-hours beyond 36 are not available. Also, the production of shoes can take place only by the two processes. Thus, the "feasible region" in terms of our representation of the problem in Figure 13-5 is shown by the cone-shaped shaded area.

If in this problem we wish to maximize the *total output* of shoes, we can simply plot additional parallel lines to our 5-unit and 10-unit lines. Since such equal-output lines represent total output, our maximization-of-output problem can be viewed simply as one of identifying the highest equal-output line that is attainable and then determining the combination of processes that will attain that output.

From Figure 13-5 we see that the highest output line attainable is the 13-unit line. This line intersects the feasible region only at point C. Thus, point C is analogous to point A in Figure 13-4. We draw a straight line through point C parallel with the process 2 ray. This parallel line intersects the process 1 ray at D (at 5 units). Thus, the maximum output of 13 units can be obtained by producing 5 units by process 1 and 8 units by process 2 (the distance from D to C as measured on the process 2 ray). Obviously, the total output by this combination of processes is 13.

But suppose we wish to maximize total revenue instead of total output. Then, we associate total-revenue amounts with output levels on each process ray. For example in Figure 13-6 we associate a total revenue of $600 with outputs of 10 units (each unit by each process generates $60 in revenue). When we connect the points on the process rays that represent the same total revenue ($600), we get a line that is superimposed on the output line of 10 units. Thus, this line represents both 10 units of output and $600 in revenue.

If we are to maximize total revenue, we plot successive parallel revenue lines and find that the highest total-revenue line attainable is the $780 line. It is associated with 13 units of output. This highest revenue line intersects the shaded feasible region only at point E. A line drawn through point E parallel to the process 2 ray intersects the process 1 ray at point F (5 units by process 1). The distance from point F to point E (as measured on the process 2 ray) gives us an output of 8 units by process 2. Thus, this combination of processes will maximize total revenue. We see in this problem that it is the same program that maximizes total output.

Something of considerable practical importance should be noted here. We solved this very shoemaking problem in Figure 13-1. In Figure 13-1 we also solved for the combination of these two processes in the shoemaking problem that maximizes total revenue. There, of course, we found the very same optimal solution; $x_1 = 5$ (that is, 5 units by process 1) and $x_2 = 8$ (that is, 8 units by process 2) with a maximum total revenue of $780.

Since the graphic solution obtained in Figure 13-1 is more easily associated

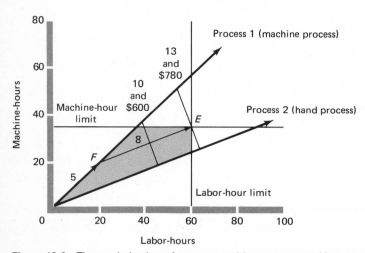

Figure 13-6 The maximization-of-revenue problem represented in terms of the process rays.

with the simplex method, let us focus on that graphic representation of the problem. That representation gives us perhaps a more direct access to the simplex method, which is the standard solution procedure for practical problems with many processes and resource limitations. The process-ray representation widens our view and can extend our applications of linear programming; but ultimately in solving real-world problems, we need to use the simplex method.

Varying the Labor-Hours Available

In Chapter 9 we became acquainted with the methods of sensitivity analysis and parametric programming. We varied the amount of a resource available (or its capacity) and obtained a graph of the total profit that showed the effect of such variation upon the objective: total profit.

An important use of the parameter-variation procedure is in the analysis of the best amount of a resource to make available over a longer time period than that assumed in the original problem. Thus, it is an important aid in resource-planning decisions of all types.

Let us illustrate such a use by varying over a broad range the labor-hours available in the shoemaking example. We can view this labor-resource variation in terms of Figure 13-6 (the perpendicular labor-limitation line will now move), but the parametric-programming procedures of Chapter 9 are more easily applied to this type of problem if we focus on the representation of the problem as it appeared in Figure 13-1.

Suppose in this shoemaking example we vary the labor-hours from 0 to 100. This is directly analogous to the parametric variation that we did in Chapter 9 for the lawn-mower–golf-cart problem. In Chapter 12, duality and the range analysis (both from the final simplex table of the problem) were seen as related procedures that give us the marginal contribution to an objective by a resource (the slopes of the total-profit or total-revenue graphs) as well as the ranges over which they will hold.

Let us use these procedures to study the variation of the labor-hours (from 0 to 100) in the shoemaking example where we seek the combination of processes that will maximize total revenue.

The current labor-hours available are 60. It is this particular right-hand-side amount that is to be varied from 0 to 100. The very simplest method of obtaining the marginal contribution to revenue (the slope of the total-revenue graph) over a particular range of labor-hours requires a graph of the problem such as that in Figure 13-1. Let us start with this method and later shift to methods that, although more complicated, do extend to larger problems.

With the aid of the graph in Figure 13-1 we see that if the labor-hours available are 0, the maximum total revenue is \$0 (the origin is the only feasible corner point). If the labor-hours available are 1, the optimal feasible program is $(x_1, x_2) = (\frac{1}{4}, 0)$, with a total revenue of \$15. We record all of this in Table 13-1.

Thus, the marginal contribution to revenue of the first hour of labor is \$15. And it will continue to be \$15 for additional hours of labor until the optimal solution crawls along the horizontal axis all the way to the point $(9, 0)$. The labor-

Table 13-1 Varying over a Broad Range the Labor-Hours Available

Labor-hours available	Optimal program, (x_1, x_2)	Total revenue of optimal program, $\$60x_1 + \$60x_2$	Rate of increase in total revenue or the marginal contribution to revenue (also, the slope of the total-revenue graph in Figure 13-7)
0	(0, 0)	$ 0	—
1	($\frac{1}{4}$, 0)	15	$15
.			
.			
.			
36	(9, 0)	540	15
37	($8\frac{5}{6}$, $\frac{2}{6}$)	550	10
.			
.			
.			
90	(0, 18)	1080	10
91	(0, 18)	1080	0

hours will be 36 when that point is optimal. How do we know the labor-hours will be 36? Because we know the labor-constraint equation will be intersecting that very point. Thus, from the graph we know that the coordinates of the point are (9, 0). Substituting them into the labor equation and solving for the right-hand-side amount is done as follows:

$$\begin{aligned} 4x_1 + 5x_2 &= \text{labor-hours} \\ 4(9) + 5(0) &= \text{labor-hours} \\ \text{labor-hours} &= 36 \end{aligned}$$

The total revenue for the (9, 0) program is $540.

Now, if we increase the labor-hours further, the direction of movement of the optimal program will change. It will move up the machine limit line all the way to the x_2-axis. To get the rate of increase in total revenue as we move up this line, we need merely increase the labor-hours by 1 hour (from 36 to 37).

We increase the labor-hours from 36 to 37, and a new optimal program ($8\frac{5}{6}$, $\frac{2}{6}$) is obtained. It has a total revenue of $550. Thus the marginal contribution to revenue of the thirty-seventh hour of labor is $10: $550 − $540 = $10. But for how many additional labor-hours will it hold at $10?

From Figure 13-1 we see that the marginal contribution to revenue (and the slope of the total-revenue graph) will be $10 until the optimal solution crawls up the machine-hour limit line all the way to the point (0, 18). At that point the labor-hours will be 90. The labor-constraint equation will intersect the point (0, 18). Thus, we substitute these values into the labor equation and solve for the labor-hours as follows:

$$4x_1 + 5x_2 = \text{labor-hours}$$
$$4(0) + 5(18) = \text{labor-hours}$$
$$\text{labor-hours} = 90$$

Beyond 90 labor-hours no increases in revenue are possible because the machine-hour constraint holds the optimal feasible program at (0, 18). Thus, the slope of the total-revenue graph is $0 for labor-hours beyond 90. All this is summarized in Table 13-1 and is shown in the total-revenue graph in Figure 13-7. From Figure 13-7 we see that the slope of the total-revenue graph (the marginal contribution to revenue of the labor resource) is $15 from 0 hours to 36 hours, $10 from 36 hours to 90 hours, and $0 for hours of labor over 90.

Determining the Best Labor-Resource Amount by Elementary Parametric-Programming Analysis

Suppose we want to determine the best labor-resource amount using the parametric-programming procedures just discussed. We already have obtained the effect that labor-hours between 0 and 100 have on total revenue. What we need to do is to incorporate the cost of the various amounts of labor.

If the cost of each hour of labor is $9 (and constant), we have a straight-line, labor-cost graph (with a slope of $9) as shown in Figure 13-7. To determine the best amount of the labor resource, we look for the maximum *net gain;* that is, we look for the labor amount where the total revenue exceeds the total labor cost by the greatest amount. It appears to be greatest at 90 labor-hours. At that number of labor-hours, the net gain is $270 (total revenue is $1,080 and total labor cost is

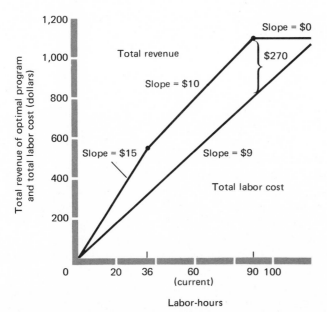

Figure 13-7   Total revenue and total labor cost as labor-hours are varied over a broad range.

Table 13-2 Simplex Tables for the Shoemaking Problem (Including Range Analysis for Resource 1)

Basic variable	Z	Output by process 1 x_1	Output by process 2 x_2	Slack variable for resource 1 x_3	Slack variable for resource 2 x_4	RHS
Table I		↓				
Z	1	−60	−60	0	0	0
x_3	0	4	5	1	0	60
← x_4	0	④	2	0	1	36
Table II			↓			
Z	1	0	−30	0	15	540
← x_3	0	0	③	1	−1	24
x_1	0	1	$\frac{1}{2}$	0	$\frac{1}{4}$	9
Table III						
Z	1	0	0	10	5	780
x_2	0	0	1	$\frac{1}{3}$	$-\frac{1}{3}$	8
x_1	0	1	0	$-\frac{1}{6}$	$\frac{5}{12}$	5

Marginal contribution to revenue ($10) of resource 1 (labor)

Marginal contribution to revenue ($5) of resource 2 (machine-hours)

$8 \div \frac{1}{3} = 24$
resource 1 can *decrease* by 24 hours before the marginal contribution to revenue ($10) will change.

$5 \div -\frac{1}{6} = -30$
resource 1 can *increase* by 30 hours before the marginal contribution to revenue ($10) will change.

$810). Thus, we have illustrated a procedure for determining the best amount of a resource to acquire if all other resources are held at their current amounts.

Determining the Best Labor-Resource Amount Using the Simplex Tables

What we have done in the previous section can also be accomplished using the data in the final simplex table as discussed in Chapter 12. This procedure is especially important because it extends this analysis to large problems where a graph of the entire problem (as in Figure 13-1) is not possible. The procedure is called the *range analysis*.

The marginal contribution to revenue of each resource (the "dual value") is found in the appropriate columns of the top row of the final simplex table. The range analysis involves elements in the same column of the final simplex table. The range analysis shows the range of resource amounts over which the indicated marginal contributions to revenue will hold.

Let us illustrate what we have just said by solving the shoemaking problem by the simplex method as shown in Table 13-2. The $10 marginal contribution to revenue of the labor resource is found in the top row associated with the slack variable x_3 that was introduced to take up any possible slack in resource 1: labor-hours. (The $5 marginal contribution to revenue of the machine resource is found in the slack-variable, x_4-column, but our attention now is only on the labor resource.)

Of particular interest is the range of the $10 marginal contribution to revenue in the final simplex table in Table 13-2. Notice that in that same x_3 (slack-variable) column we have the elements ⅓ and −⅙. If we divide each of these elements into its corresponding right-hand-side amount, we will obtain the range of the $10 marginal contribution to revenue as follows: (Remember that the sign of the value obtained is in a sense opposite to that expected.)

Operation	Interpretation
8 ÷ ⅓ = 24	This is the amount by which the labor resource can be *decreased* before a change in the $10 marginal contribution to revenue will occur. Thus, since the current labor-hours are 60, a breakpoint in the total-revenue graph will occur at 36 labor-hours: 60 − 24 = 36 hours.
5 ÷ (−⅙) = −30	This is the amount by which the labor resource can be *increased* before a change in the $10 marginal contribution to revenue will occur. Thus, since the current labor-hours are 60, a breakpoint in the total-revenue graph will occur at 90 labor-hours: 60 + 30 = 90 hours.

Let us review what we have just done and its connection to variation in the labor resource. We solved the original shoemaking problem by the simplex method. From the final simplex table we found the $10 marginal contribution to revenue of the labor resource. From the range analysis on the final simplex table, we found that the $10 marginal contribution to revenue will hold over the entire range of labor-hours from 36 to 90 (currently it is at 60 hours). This, of course, is exactly the same range of labor-hours for the $10 marginal contribution to revenue that we found in the previous section by the elementary parametric-programming analysis. But the method of this section extends to larger problems.

Thus we know from the range analysis on the final simplex table that at the labor-hours of 36 and 90 we will encounter new marginal contributions to revenue (and new slopes for the total-revenue graph). But what are these new marginal contributions to revenue?

The most direct way to find these new marginal contributions to revenue is to solve *two* new linear-programming problems by the simplex method. One of these new problems will have a labor constraint with 35 hours (at the lower breakpoint of 36 *less 1 hour* so that we can "hop" onto the new linear segment of the total-revenue graph). The other new problem will have a labor constraint of 91 hours (at the upper breakpoint of 90 *plus 1 hour* to get on that new linear segment of the total-revenue graph).

What will these two new problems show? They will show the desired marginal contributions to revenue for the next-lower range and also for the next-higher range.

Table 13-3 Simplex Tables for the New Linear-Programming Problem with Labor-Hours (Resource 1) at 35

Basic variable	Z	Output by process 1 x_1	Output by process 2 x_2	Slack variable for resource 1 x_3	Slack variable for resource 2 x_4	RHS
Table I						
Z	1	−60	−60	0	0	0
← x_3	0	④	5	1	0	35
x_4	0	4	2	0	1	36
Table II						
Z	1	0	15	15	0	525
x_1	0	1	5/4	1/4	0	8¾
x_4	0	0	−3	−1	1	1

Marginal contribution to revenue ($15) of resource 1 (labor)

Marginal contribution to revenue ($0) of resource 2 (machine-hours)

8¾ ÷ ¼ = 35 resource 1 can *decrease* by 35 hours before the marginal contribution to revenue ($15) will change.

1 ÷ (−1) = −1 resource 1 can *increase* by 1 hour before the marginal contribution to revenue ($15) will change.

In Table 13-3 we find the simplex tables for the new linear programming problem with the labor-hours set at 35. The marginal contribution to revenue of the labor resource for this new range is found in the usual top-row position in the x_3 column. It is \$15 in the next-lower range compared with \$10 in the range associated with the original problem.

And what is the range of labor-hours that the \$15 marginal contribution to profit will hold? Once again, our final simplex table will reveal this. We divide the elements ¼ and -1 in the x_3 column into their respective right-hand-side amounts. This gives us the following range of 0 hours to 36 hours.

Operation	Interpretation
$8\frac{3}{4} \div \frac{1}{4}$ = 35 hours	This is the amount by which the labor resource can be *decreased* before a change in the \$15 marginal contribution to revenue will occur. Thus, since the current labor-hours are 35, a breakpoint (or starting point) in the total-revenue graph will occur at 0 labor-hours: 35 − 35 = 0 hours.
$1 \div (-1) = -1$	This is the amount by which the labor resource can be *increased* before a change in the \$15 marginal contribution to revenue will occur. Thus, since the current labor-hours are 35, a breakpoint in the total-revenue graph will occur at 36 hours: 35 + 1 = 36 hours.

What we have just done is to obtain the range of the labor-hours for which the \$15 marginal contribution to profit will hold. It is 0 hours to 36 hours, just as our earlier parametric-programming analysis revealed (with the aid of the graph in Figure 13-1).

The simplex solution to the linear-programming problem that will reveal the marginal contribution to revenue in the range above that which was encountered in our original problem is found in Table 13-4. In the final table (in the top row in the x_3 column) we find that when the labor-hours are 91, the marginal contribution to revenue is \$0. Thus, the slope of the total-revenue graph is \$0 from 90 labor-hours and above.

To summarize, we have obtained the slopes of our total-revenue graph in Figure 13-7 by using the data in the final simplex table together with the range analysis on that data. This procedure permits us to obtain a total-revenue graph for any resource in a large problem that may include numerous processes and many resources. Once again, from Figure 13-7 we see that with a labor-cost of \$9 per hour the net gain is largest when the labor-hours are at 90.

Table 13-4 Simplex Tables for the New Linear-Programming Problem with Labor-Hours (Resource 1) at 91

Basic variable	Z	Output by process 1 x_1	Output by process 2 x_2	Slack variable for resource 1 x_3	Slack variable for resource 2 x_4	RHS
Table I		↓				
Z	1	−60	−60	0	0	0
x_3	0	4	5	1	0	91
←x_4	0	(4)	2	0	1	36
Table II			↓			
Z	1	0	−30	0	15	540
x_3	0	0	3	1	−1	55
←x_1	0	1	(1½)	0	¼	9
Table III						
Z	1	60	0	→0	→30	1,080
x_3	0	−6	0	1	−2½	1
x_2	0	2	1	0	½	18

Marginal contribution to revenue ($0) of resource 1 (labor)

Marginal contribution to revenue ($30) of resource 2 (machine-hours)

TECHNOLOGICAL CHANGE AND ITS EFFECT UPON THE OPTIMAL PROGRAM

Suppose that a more automatic method of making shoes by the machine process is devised whereby only 2½ hours of labor are needed per pair instead of 4 hours. But there is no change in the machine-hours needed for each pair of shoes.

An obvious question is this: What is the effect of this technological change upon the optimal program and its total revenue? To answer this question, we need to solve the new linear-programming problem that is created by this change in the rate of use of the labor resource in production by the machine process.

Thus, we have the following new problem:

Maximize: Total revenue $= \$60x_1 + \$60x_2$
Subject to: $2.5x_1 + 5.0x_2 \leq 60$ (labor-hours)
$4.0x_1 + 2.0x_2 \leq 36$ (machine-hours)

We graph the problem in Figure 13-8 and also in Figure 13-9. The optimal combination of processes is to make 4 units by process 1 and 10 by process 2.

Total revenue of this program is $840, which is $60 higher than the optimal total revenue in the original problem.

Thus, we have found a means of measuring the effect upon total revenue of a change in the technology used in production. The effect upon total revenue for different labor-resource amounts can be obtained, too. From Figure 13-10 we see that after the technological change new marginal contributions to revenue appear and the best amount of labor-hours has changed to $22\frac{1}{2}$. The net gain is greatest when the labor-hours are $22\frac{1}{2}$.

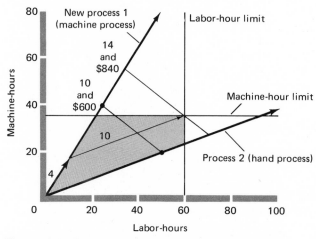

Figure 13-8   A new process in the shoemaking problem.

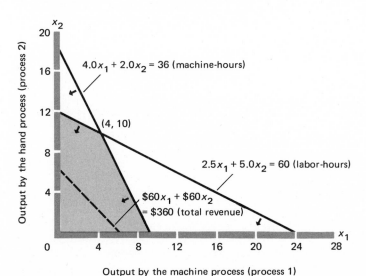

Figure 13-9   Representation on the x_1- and x_2-axes of the shoemaking problem involving the new process.

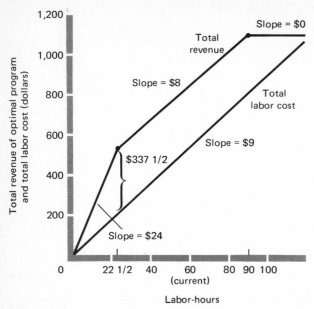

Figure 13-10 Varying the labor-hours over a broad range under the new process.

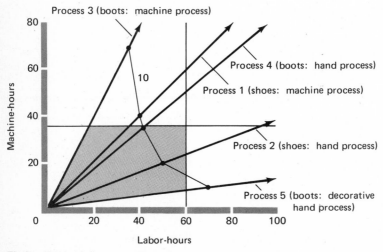

Figure 13-11 A five-process problem.

TOWARD A MORE REALISTIC PROBLEM: MANY PROCESSES

The discussion so far in this chapter has focused on examples with only two processes. Now is the time to illustrate the above procedures with a more realistic problem that includes five different processes.

The example we shall use is an extension of the shoemaking example discussed earlier. We have added three new processes. All the three new processes involve the making of another product: boots. There is a machine process in making boots (process 3) and also a hand process (process 4). In addition, there is a "decorative hand process" in making boots (process 5).

Each pair of shoes by either process 1 or process 2 can be sold for $60, whereas each pair of boots by either process 3 or process 4 has a price of $62. The decorative boots (by process 5) yield a unit revenue of $68. These revenues per unit of output (pairs of shoes or boots) by each process appear as coefficients in the objective function (if we maximize total revenue).

The objective function appears below along with the constraint inequalities that include the rates of use of the labor and machine resources by the new processes as well as the processes that appeared in the earlier problems.

Maximize: Total revenue $= \$60x_1 + \$60x_2 + \$62x_3 + \$62x_4 + \$68x_5$

Subject to: $4.0x_1 + 5.0x_2 + 3.5x_3 + 4.3x_4 + 7.0x_5 \leq 60$ (labor-hours)

$4.0x_1 + 2.0x_2 + 7.0x_3 + 3.1x_4 + 1.0x_5 \leq 36$ (machine-hours)

We cannot represent this problem graphically in the output dimensions as we did in the two-process problems. With five processes and two resources we can only get a graph in the two resource dimensions. We do this in Figure 13-11.

To get the graph of the five process rays, we set each output level individually ($x_1, x_2, \ldots$) to 10 units which determines the amount of labor-hours and machine-hours needed to produce 10 units by that process. Connecting each of these points individually with the origin gives us the process rays and a 10-unit output point on each of the rays. Then, connecting the 10-unit output points on the process rays with a straight line gives us the 10-unit line segments as seen in Figure 13-11.

However, our objective is one of revenue maximization. Remember that we can plot the revenue lines in Figure 13-11, too; but it does get tedious. Therefore, in such problems we would normally go directly to the simplex tables to obtain a solution. With more than two resource constraints we have no other satisfactory solution procedure. (The presence of only the two resource constraints permitted us to get the graph in Figure 13-11, but the usual real-world problem would not permit us to obtain such a graph.)

By the simplex method we find that the optimal feasible program is to produce 4.5 units by process 2 (pairs of shoes by the hand process) and 8.7 units by process 4 (pairs of boots by the hand process). Maximum total revenue is $809.40. No other combination of processes would generate more revenue.

The Best Amount of Labor-Hours
When Five Processes Are Available

The application of the parametric-programming procedures discussed in the first part of this chapter applied to this problem gives us the total-revenue graph in Figure 13-12. With a labor cost of $9 per hour we see from Figure 13-12 that the

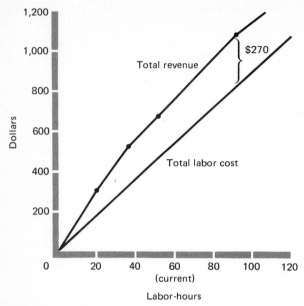

Figure 13-12 Varying the labor-hours over a broad range in the five-process problem.

net gain is greatest when the labor-hours are 90. It is important to note that graphs such as those in Figure 13-12 can be obtained by individually varying the amount of any resource capacity or resource availability. We can still get such a graph for a resource even when the number of different resources (and processes) are in the hundreds or thousands.

SUMMARY

1 In a linear-programming formulation of a problem, the rates of use of the resources by the activities (that is, the coefficients in the constraints) essentially represent the technology available to be used.

2 Each different method or technique of engaging in activities (for example, each method of making a product) involves using the resources at different rates. Each method is referred to as a separate *process*. And each process is treated as a separate *activity*.

3 The *level* of each process (the level of each activity) is represented by a variable such as x_1, x_2, and so forth. This is so even though all the processes involve making the very same product.

4 A real-world problem with numerous variables may involve (a) only one product that can be made by numerous processes, (b) (as in earlier chapters) numerous products each being made by just one process, or (c) a number of products, some of which can be produced by more than one process.

5 A given problem involving two resource constraints and two processes can be graphed in two ways. One graph is in terms of the output dimensions (x_1 and x_2); the other graph is in terms of the resource-input dimensions. The latter graph yields a *process ray* for each separate process. Output by each process is represented by points on the associated process ray.

6 Changes in technology typically affect the rates of use of the resources. Thus, representing a possible technological change by making the appropriate alterations in the coefficients permits an estimate to be made of the effect of such a technological change on maximum total output or other objectives.

7 *Range analysis* and *parametric-programming analysis* are useful in studying problems involving process rays, too. As before, an investigation of the best amount of a resource to acquire can be undertaken through the use of these methods.

PROBLEMS

13-1 An office-furniture maker can assemble metal desks by two different processes. One process (process 1) makes heavy use of welding equipment and is known as the "welding process." The other process (process 2) is called the "bolting process" because most of the parts are bolted together. The bolting process uses the welding equipment but much less than does the welding process.

There is the desire to identify the feasible program (the output by each process) that will result in the greatest total revenue. Two resources impose limitations on product output by either process. There are 180 hours of labor available per day and 100 hours of welding-equipment time. The use of the resources per unit of output by each process is given below. (*Note:* Each unit of output represents 10 desks and results in $1,200 in revenue. The desks produced by each process are considered to be essentially the same product.)

Process 1:   Use of resource 1 (labor) per unit of output = 2 hours
Use of resource 2 (welding equipment) per unit of output = 2 hours

Process 2:   Use of resource 1 (labor) per unit of output = 3 hours
Use of resource 2 (welding equipment) per unit of output = 1 hour

a Form a data table for the problem with the column headings representing separate processes of producing the single product instead of representing different products.
b Formulate the problem in standard linear-programming form.
c On the output axes (x_1 and x_2), graph the inequality constraints and the objective function formulated in *b*.
d From your graphic representation of the problem in *c*, obtain the optimal feasible program and its total revenue. Interpret the program in your own words.
e Solve by the simplex method the problem formulated in *b*.

13-2 From the data in Problem 13-1, graph the two process rays on the resource-input axes. (*Note:* In plotting the process rays, temporarily assume an output of 100 units by process 1 and then 100 units by process 2).
a Connect with a straight line the points on each process ray representing 100 units of output. In your own words, give an interpretation of the points lying on the line you have drawn.
b What is the total revenue associated with each point representing 100 units of

output? Connect these two equal-revenue points with a straight line. Give an interpretation to points lying on this line.

c   Insert the two resource-limitation lines on your process-ray graph and shade the region representing feasible programs. Give an interpretation of the shaded region.

d   From your process-ray graph, obtain the maximum total revenue and the associated optimal feasible program. Interpret your solution and compare it with that obtained in 13-1d and e. Discuss their relationships and the uses of each.

Suppose that the office-furniture maker in Problems 13-1 and 13-2 acquires 60 more hours of welding-equipment time and 60 more hours of labor per day.

a   Formulate the new problem in standard linear-programming form.

b   Graph the new problem on the x_1- and x_2-axes and obtain graphically the optimal feasible program and its total revenue.

c   Graph the new problem on the resource-input axes. Obtain graphically the optimal feasible program and its total revenue in terms of the process-ray graphs. Compare your solution with that obtained in b.

d   Solve by the simplex method the new problem formulated in a. Compare your solution with that obtained in b and c. What are the practical implications of learning to solve such problems by the simplex method?

13-4   A maker of leather products is considering two different processes by which leather belts might be made. The finished belts from one process are considered to be no different from those produced by the other process.

One process (process 1) is referred to as the "mechanized process" because of its heavy use of automatic mechanical equipment. The other process (process 2) is called the "hand process" because of the use of some hand-operated tools.

Two resources impose limitations upon output by either process. There are 120 labor-hours available (resource 1) and 120 hours available on the automatic equipment (resource 2). The rates of use of the two resources by the two processes are as follows: (*Note:* Each unit of output represents 20 belts.)

Process 1:   Use of resource 1 (labor) per unit of output = 2 hours
Use of resource 2 (automatic equipment) per unit of output = 3 hours.

Process 2:   Use of resource 1 (labor) per unit of output = 4 hours
Use of resource 2 (automatic equipment) per unit of output = 2 hours.

a   The leather-products maker wishes to identify the maximum-revenue program. Each unit of output by each process generates $90 in revenue. Form a data table of the problem.

b   Formulate the problem in standard linear-programming form.

c   Graph on the x_1- and x_2-axes the problem formulated in b. Obtain graphically the optimal feasible program and its total revenue.

d   Graph on the resource-input axes the same problem formulated in b. Obtain from this process-ray graph the optimal feasible program and its total revenue. Compare the solution obtained here with that in c.

e   Solve by the simplex method the problem formulated in b. Compare your solution with that obtained in c and d.

13-5 In assembling mobile homes, components are bolted together. The bolting of the parts together can involve heavy use of motor-driven wrenches or hand-operated wrenches. Let us refer to the former process as the "motorized process" and label it process 1. The latter process (process 2) will be called the "hand process," even though some limited use of the motor-driven wrenches occurs in production by this process.

The identification of the maximum-revenue program is desired. Each mobile home generates $2,400 in revenue.

There is a limited amount of labor available (240 hours per day) and also a limited amount of the motorized equipment (120 hours per day). The rates of use of the resources by each process are as follows:

Process 1: Use of resource 1 (labor) per unit of output = 2 hours
Use of resource 2 (motorized equipment) per unit of output = 3 hours

Process 2: Use of resource 1 (labor) per unit of output = 6 hours
Use of resource 2 (motorized equipment) per unit of output = 1 hour

    a Form a data table of the problem.
    b Put the problem in standard linear-programming form.
    c Graph the problem on the x_1- and x_2-axes. What is the optimal feasible program and its total revenue?
    d Graph the problem on the resource-input axes. In terms of the process-ray graphs, what is the optimal feasible program and its total revenue? Compare your solution with that obtained in *c*.
    e Solve by the simplex method the problem formulated in *b*. Compare your solution with that obtained in *c* and *d*.

13-6 A publisher has two processes available for setting type. One process (process 1) heavily uses an automatic typesetting machine and is referred to as the "automatic-typesetting process."

The publisher desires to know the maximum output possible (number of lines) per day given the availability of 24 hours of labor per day and 20 hours of time per day on the automatic-typesetting machine. The rates of use of labor and automatic-equipment time by the two processes are given below. Each unit of output by each process represents 200 lines.

Process 1: Use of resource 1 (labor) per unit of output = 2 hours
Use of resource 2 (automatic-typesetting euipment) per unit of output = 5 hours

Process 2: Use of resource 1 (labor) per unit of output = 4 hours
Use of resource 2 (automatic-typesetting equipment) per unit of output = 2 hours

    a With maximization of total output as the objective, place the problem in the standard linear-programming form. (*Note:* The objective function now involves a summing of the outputs by each of the processes: $x_1 + x_2$ and so forth.)

   b   Graph on the x_1- and x_2-axes the problem formulated in a. Obtain graphically the optimal feasible program and maximum total output.

   c   Graph on the resource-input axes the problem formulated in a. Obtain from the process-ray graphs the optimal feasible program and maximum total output. Compare your solution with that obtained in b.

   d   Solve by the simplex method the problem formulated in a. Compare your solution with that obtained in b and c.

13-7 Solve by the simplex method the office-furniture maker's problem formulated in Problem 13-1b or refer to your final simplex table in Problem 13-1e if you completed it earlier. In this problem we shall obtain the total-revenue graph for labor over a broad range of labor-hours.

   a   From the final simplex table identify the marginal contribution to revenue for each of the two resources.

   b   From the final simplex table, determine the range of labor-hours (resource 1) over which the current marginal contribution to revenue will hold.

   c   Having determined in b the relevant range of labor-hours for the current marginal contribution to revenue, decrease by 1 hour the labor-hours at the lower end point of the range interval and then solve by the simplex method the new linear-programming problem with the new labor-hours. Identify from the final simplex table the marginal contribution to revenue and obtain the new range of labor-hours over which this marginal contribution to revenue will hold.

   d   Let us go back to the original range of labor-hours in b. Now increase by 1 hour the labor-hours at the upper end point of this range interval and then solve by the simplex method this new linear-programming problem. Identify from the final simplex table the marginal contribution to revenue and obtain the range of labor-hours over which this marginal contribution to revenue will hold.

   e   From your work in a, b, c, and d construct a total-revenue graph for labor showing the breakpoints and the slopes of the linear segments. Also, indicate the current labor-hours available.

13-8 Suppose in Problem 13-7 we vary individually the resource 2 amount (welding-equipment hours) over a broad range. Using the range analysis of the optimal simplex tables, obtain a total-revenue graph for the resource 2 variation showing the breakpoints and the slopes of the linear segments.

13-9 If you have not obtained the final simplex table for the leather-goods maker in Problem 13-4e, do so now. Then, we shall obtain the total-revenue graph for various hours of availability of the automatic equipment.

   a   From the final simplex table for the leather-goods maker, identify the marginal contribution to revenue for each of the two resources.

   b   From the final simplex table, determine the range of equipment-hours (resource 2) over which the current marginal contribution to revenue will hold.

   c   Using the results of your range analysis in b, form a new linear-programming problem (and solve by the simplex method) to obtain the marginal contribution to revenue of the equipment for the next-lower range. What is the range of equipment-hours over which this marginal contribution to revenue holds?

   d   Going back to the original range of equipment hours obtained in b, form the new linear-programming problem (and solve by the simplex method) to obtain the marginal contribution to revenue of the equipment over the next-higher

range. What is the range of equipment-hours over which this marginal contribution to revenue holds?

e   From the results obtained in *a, b, c,* and *d*, construct a total-revenue graph for
equipment-hours showing the breakpoints and the slopes of the linear segments.

13-10 If in Problem 3-9 it is estimated that each hour of use of the automatic equipment
costs $25, what is the best amount of automatic equipment to acquire (expressed
in hours)? Superimpose a total-cost-of-equipment-hours graph upon the total-
revenue graph for equipment hours obtained in Problems 13-9*e* and show on the
graph the best amount of equipment-hours. Indicate the current number of equipment-hours.

13-11 For the publisher in Problem 13-6 obtain the final simplex table if you did not do so
in Problem 13-6*d*.

a   From the final simplex table for the publisher, obtain the marginal contribution
to output for each resource. Interpret your answer.

b   From the final simplex table, determine the range of labor-hours (resource 1)
over which the current marginal contribution to output will hold.

c   From the final simplex table, determine the range of automatic-typesetting-
equipment-hours (resource 2) over which the current marginal contribution to
output will hold.

13-12 Suppose a more automatic welding process is developed which is available to the
office-furniture maker encountered in Problem 13-1. This automatic welding process (process 3) uses only 1 hour of labor per unit of output and 4 hours of welding-
equipment time. Additionally, for this future period only 60 hours of labor will be
available, but welding equipment can be used up to 150 hours. All other data
remain as given in Problem 13-1.

a   Form a data table for the new three-process problem.

b   Represent the problem in standard linear-programming form.

c   A two-dimension graph of the problem can be obtained only on the resource-
input axes. Solve the problem formulated in *b* in terms of the process-ray
graphs.

d   Solve by the simplex method the problem formulated in *b*. Compare your
solution with that obtained in *c*.

e   What is the marginal contribution to revenue of each resource now?

13-13 Let us look again at the office-furniture maker considering three different processes in assembling desks in Problem 13-12.

a   Form a dual data table for the problem.

b   From the dual data table, place the problem in the dual linear-programming
formulation.

c   Graph the dual problem on the u_1- and u_2-axes. Obtain the optimal feasible
solution and its Z-value. Compare the optimal u_1- and u_2-values with the
marginal contribution to revenue of resource 1 and resource 2 obtained from
the final simplex table of the primal problem in Problem 13-12*d*.

d   (optional) Solve by the simplex method the dual linear-programming problem
formulated in *b*. Compare your solution with that obtained in *c*.

e   (optional) Obtain from the final simplex table in *d* the optimal solution to the
primal linear-programming problem. Interpret both the primal and dual solutions and their Z-values.

Chapter 14

More than One Objective and Other Decision Problems

In this chapter we shall examine several types of linear-programming problems that have not been discussed directly in the previous chapters. At the outset we shall briefly deal with the main points of each type, and later in the chapter we shall explore each in greater detail.

First we shall examine the situation where there is *more than one objective* to be considered in a decision problem. Up to now we have dealt with different objective functions separately and in different problems, but we have not done so in a single formulation of a particular problem.

For example, in business firms, both high profits and high revenues are usually desired. But programs that have the highest revenue may not also have the highest profit. To obtain higher profit, it may be necessary to sacrifice the attainment of some revenue. Thus, a difficult decision problem can arise when both objectives (profit and revenue) are to be considered simultaneously in selecting a program of activities.

Also, in this chapter we shall discuss the way in which problems that have some *nonlinear* relations can be solved by the simplex method, provided *piece-wise linear graphs* of the relationships are judged to be a satisfactory fit.

A fairly common illustration of the type of nonlinear relation we can deal with is where the unit profit on a product falls at higher output levels because the unit price on the product has to be reduced to sell the output. We shall see that many such nonlinear relations can be satisfactorily represented by a linear-programming formulation of the problem.

In another section of the chapter we shall examine the situation where *one product-output activity uses as an input the output of another product-output activity*. We shall illustrate this interrelationship with our lawn-mower manufacturer who also makes motors. The motors are used as components of the lawn mowers and also are sold as separate units to other firms.

The last section of the chapter examines the special difficulties that arise because of the *divisibility* assumption that is made in the standard linear-programming models. The difficulties arise because it may not be possible to implement a program of activities involving fractional amounts. For example, a fraction of a unit of output simply may not be meaningful or feasible. Often, the optimal solution is simply rounded downward (or toward feasibility) so that a whole-number solution is obtained. However, this procedure does not assure an optimal whole-number (integer) solution and sometimes may deviate substantially from the optimal integer solution. The methods of *integer programming* deal with such problems.

MORE THAN ONE OBJECTIVE

Let us illustrate the problem of decision with more than one objective by using the familiar lawn-mower–golf-cart example discussed in previous chapters.

As originally formulated, total profit was to be maximized subject to two resource constraints, labor-hours and a lawn-mower assembly facility. It was found that the optimal program was 50 lawn mowers and 15 golf carts, with a total profit of $2,750.

But now suppose it is desired that total *revenue* be maximized but under the condition that total profit is at least equal to or greater than some specified amount.

As a first step in illustrating the handling of the two objectives, let us solve the single-objective, revenue-maximization problem that is formulated below. Revenue (price) per unit is $200 on lawn mowers and $600 on golf carts.

Maximize: Total revenue $= \$200x_1 + \$600x_2$
Subject to: $x_1 \qquad\quad \leq 50$ (lawn-mower assembly facility)
$\qquad\qquad x_1 + 2x_2 \leq 80$ (labor-hours)

We graph the problem in Figure 14-1. We also include for reference purposes the profit-objective function from the original problem. With maximization of total revenue as the sole objective, the optimal program shifts to (0, 40) that is, no lawn mowers but 40 golf carts. This is the feasible program with the highest total revenue. The maximum revenue is $24,000. The old optimal-profit program of (50, 15) generates $19,000 in revenue and clearly is not the optimal program when maximization of revenue is the sole objective.

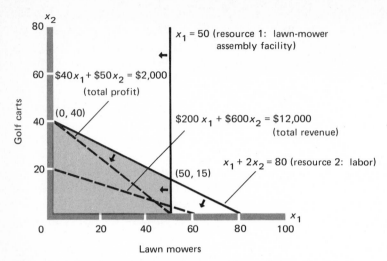

Figure 14-1 The lawn-mower–golf-cart problem with two objectives.

Getting back to the main point of this section, what is the optimal program if we are to combine both the revenue and profit objectives in one formulation of the problem?

This is not an easy question to answer because it depends on such considerations as the decision maker's preference for one objective over the other and how important it is that some minimum level of one or both goals is attained.

Thus, there are various possible linear-programming formulations of a given real-world problem involving more than one objective. But let us proceed with perhaps the simplest formulation in order to get an introduction to some of the procedures that can be used.

Suppose that the decision maker indicates that he or she would like to maximize total revenue (perhaps to keep production and employment levels up and to keep distributors from shifting to other suppliers), but total profit, we are told, must be at least $2,300. Total profit has to be at that level or higher to avoid adverse consequences with respect to stockholders and the possible sale of new securities to finance the expansion of facilities.

How can we formulate the above problem with the two objectives? By selecting one of them for the objective function in the linear-programming formulation and then treating the other objective *as a constraint*.

Since the decision maker indicated the desire to maximize total revenue, we use it as the objective function to be maximized. In that we were given a minimum level of total profit that must be attained, we treat that objective as a constraint. We formulate the problem as follows:

Maximize: Total revenue $= \$200x_1 + \$600x_2$
Subject to: $x_1 \leq 50$ (lawn-mower assembly facility)
$x_1 + 2x_2 \leq 80$ (labor-hours)
$\$40x_1 + \$50x_2 \geq \$2,300$ (total profit)

Notice that we have included among the constraints a "greater-than" inequality that looks like the old profit-objective function. The coefficients are the same, but it is no longer an equation. Also, we have specified a minimum $2,300 profit amount that appears as the right-hand-side constant for this inequality.

In solving this problem by the simplex method, we simply proceed as usual, treating the profit constraint as we would any other "greater-than" inequality constraint. In Chapter 11 we solved linear-programming problems with such inequalities, and of course we can solve this problem by using the procedures discussed there.

This problem we can graph, and we do so in Figure 14-2. Note how the addition of the profit constraint reduces the feasible region to a small, three-cornered, shaded area shown in Figure 14-2. As the revenue-objective function is moved in the optimizing direction (away from the origin) the last corner point intersected is at (20, 30). This is a program of 20 lawn mowers and 30 golf carts.

This program generates the highest total revenue, $22,000. We see in Figure 14-2 that since this program falls on the line representing the profit constraint, the minimum total profit of $2,300 is just satisfied. Thus, we have obtained the optimal feasible program to the problem that we formulated.

PIECEWISE LINEAR PROGRAMMING

In Chapter 8 we discussed the linearity (or proportionality) assumption of linear-programming models. You may recall that the practical meaning of that premise is that all the coefficients in the objective function and the constraints are assumed to remain fixed as different levels of the activities are considered in the analysis.

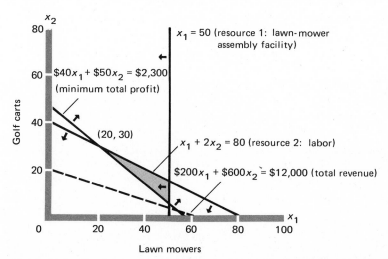

Figure 14-2 The lawn-mower–golf-cart problem with the total-profit objective treated as a constraint.

Thus, in terms of the lawn-mower–golf-cart example, the total profit for the lawn-mower production activity (total profit from this activity alone) will increase at a constant rate as lawn-mower production is increased. This, of course, gives us the usual straight-line relationship between the level of an activity and the total profit on that activity. Analogously, in the constraints there is a straight-line relationship assumed between the level of an activity and the total use of a particular resource by that activity.

What is of special importance in this section is that in those real situations where the single straight-line relationship does not satisfactorily fit, we can substitute for it a *piecewise linear relation*. The piecewise linear segments can be as numerous as we like; however, the more of them we have, the higher the costs will be in solving the problem.

Let us illustrate the use of such piecewise linear relations with the unit-profit coefficient in the objective function of the original lawn-mower–golf-cart example.

Suppose that profit per unit is $40 for smaller outputs of lawn mowers. But, if they are produced in large numbers, the price per lawn mower will have to be cut in order to sell the large amounts produced. To keep it simple for our illustration, suppose that a breakpoint in our total-profit graph for lawn mowers is at 30 units per day. The unit profit is $40 up to (and including) 30 units, but it drops to $20 if over 30 per day are produced.

The total-profit graph for lawn-mower production in Figure 14-3*a* illustrates what we have just discussed. If more linear segments would fit the reality better, we could, of course, make more than the two piecewise linear segments, but let us assume that the two segments will do. Note that the breakpoint in the total-profit graph for lawn mowers is at an output of 30.

The other product-output activity, golf-cart production, is assumed to have

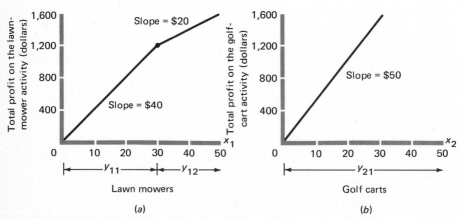

Figure 14-3 In the modified lawn-mower–golf-cart problem *(a)* the piecewise linear total-profit graph on the lawn-mower production activity; *(b)* the simple linear total-profit graph on the golf-cart production activity.

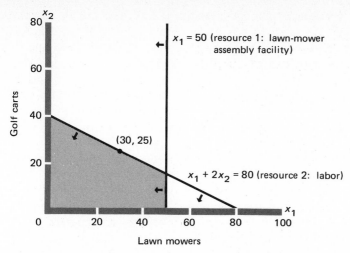

Figure 14-4   The optimal feasible program when the profit from the lawn-mower production activity is piecewise linear.

an unchanged and constant $50 profit per unit at all levels of output. Thus, the unit-profit coefficient in the objective function for this activity remains at $50 for all levels of golf-cart output, as shown in Figure 14-3b. The constraints, also, are the same as in the original problem. We formulate the special piecewise linear-programming problem as follows:

Maximize: Total profit $= c_1 x_1 +$ $\$50 x_2$
Subject to: x_1 ≤ 50 (lawn-mower assembly facility)
            $x_1 + 2x_2 \leq 80$ (labor-hours)

where c_1 is $40 up to and including an x_1-value of 30; $20 where x_1 is greater than 30.

We can graph the constraints as usual in Figure 14-4. However, it would be quite complicated to plot the objective function as we have modified it. Also, the objective function would be piecewise linear and would only give us the solution to our two-product problem. What we want is an illustration of the procedure of solving such piecewise linear problems that extends to the solving of large practical problems. We shall call it the *piecewise linear-programming procedure* (it is one of the procedures of what is sometimes called "separable programming").

Because the unit-profit coefficient for lawn-mower output does not remain constant as the output increases, we cannot solve the problem by the simplex method as it is formulated above. However, we can solve it by the simplex method if we represent the appropriate unit-profit changes by piecewise linear segments.

We do this by breaking up the lawn-mower production activity into two separate activities: (1) lawn-mower production activity up to the breakpoint where lawn-mower output is 30 in the total-profit graph in Figure 14-3a and (2) lawn-mower production activity beyond the breakpoint.

In effect, we are treating the lawn-mower output from 0 through 30 units as one product and the output above 30 units as another product. Thus, we associate one variable (y_{11}) with lawn-mower output from 0 through 30, and another variable (y_{12}) with units of lawn-mower output over 30. In Figure 14-3a we associate the variables y_{11} and y_{12} with their respective output intervals.

We use the letter y to represent the new decision variables to distinguish them from the original decision variables. The first digit in the subscript of the new variables corresponds to the product number (or the original-decision-variable number). For example, in the lawn-mower-golf-cart problem, product 1 is identified as lawn mowers. The second digit in the subscript refers to the particular linear segment with which this variable is associated. Thus, the variable associated with the first linear segment is y_{11} (where the slope is $40).

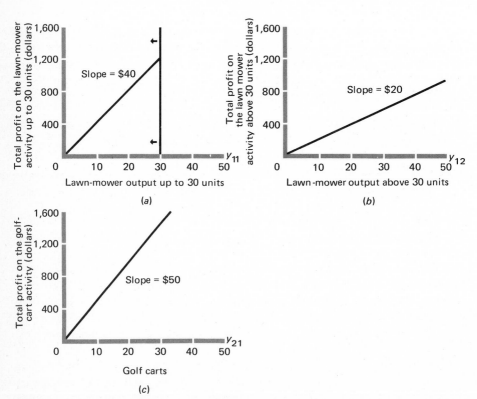

Figure 14-5 The simple linear profit graphs for the new variables: *(a)* lawn-mower output from 0 through 30 units (y_{11}); *(b)* lawn-mower output over 30 units (y_{12}); and *(c)* golf-cart output at all levels (y_{21}).

The second digit of 1 in the subscript refers to the fact that this is the first interval (associated with the first linear segment of the total-profit graph).

The second variable y_{12} is associated with the second linear segment of the total-profit graph for product 1 (lawn mowers). The slope of this linear segment is $20. Thus, the unit profit on product 1 over this interval is $20.

Going to product 2 (golf carts), the first digit in the subscript is 2. But for product 2 we have no breakpoints in our total-profit graph, and so we really have just one interval. Thus, we refer to all output levels of product 2 by the variable y_{21}.

Breaking up the original decision variables as we have illustrated, permits us to formulate the problem in linear-programming form such that it can be solved by the simplex method. For each of the new variables the total-profit relation is linear, as shown in Figure 14-5. However, in Figure 14-5a we show an upper bound on the variable y_{11}. This must be expressed in our linear-programming formulation. Therefore, we add this upper bound to our constraints as shown in the following formulation: (*Note:* such upper bounds must appear on all the new variables except the one associated with the last interval.)

	Lawn-mower production activity x_1 $(y_{11} + y_{12} = x_1)$	Golf-cart production activity x_2 $(y_{21} = x_2)$
Maximize: Total profit $=$	$\$40y_{11} + \$20y_{12}$	$+\$50y_{21}$
Subject to:	$(y_{11} + y_{12})$	$\leqslant 50$ (lawn-mower assembly facility)
	$(y_{11} + y_{12}) + 2(y_{21})$	$\leqslant 80$ (labor-hours)
	y_{11}	$\leqslant 30$ (upper bound)

The decision problem put in this form can now be solved by the simplex method. The optimal program is found to be $y_{11} = 30$, $y_{12} = 0$, and $y_{21} = 25$; the total profit is $2,450.

Since y_{11} and y_{12} were created by breaking up the variable x_1, we now have to add them together to get the solution in terms of x_1 (lawn mowers). Thus, the optimal program in terms of the original variables is $x_1 = 30$, $x_2 = 25$, with a total profit of $2,450.

$$x_1 = y_{11} + y_{12} \qquad x_2 = y_{21}$$
$$= 30 + 0 \qquad\qquad = 25$$
$$= 30$$

This optimal program is shown in Figure 14-4. Note that it is *not* a corner point of the feasible region of the problem graphed in the x_1 and x_2 dimensions.

However, it is a corner point of the feasible region of the newly created problem involving the variables y_{11}, y_{12}, and y_{21}. Unfortunately, it is very difficult to show a graphic solution to that three-dimensional problem, but the solution $(y_{11}, y_{12}, y_{21}) = (30, 0, 25)$ is a corner point of the feasible region in those three dimensions.

ONE PRODUCT OUTPUT AS AN INPUT TO ANOTHER ACTIVITY

In all our previous discussions it has been assumed that the variable resource inputs in the production of a good or service have come directly from other firms. Therefore, no processing or finishing of the inputs was done (prior to their use in making products) that would use some of the scarce resources.

Now it is time to illustrate the situation where one of the firm's product-output activities is also an input to another product-output activity. For example, suppose that instead of producing lawn mowers and golf carts the manufacturing firm produces lawn mowers and small motors, the motors marketed to buyers outside the firm and also used as components (as an input) in the making of lawn mowers.

Therefore, there is the problem of determining how many lawn mowers and motors to produce given the available scarce resources *and* the requirement that a motor must be produced for every lawn mower produced.

This example is a modification of our original lawn-mower–golf-cart problem, with the variable x_2 now representing the output of motors instead of golf carts. The lawn-mower assembly facility and the labor constraints appear here, too. The capacity and availability of these resources is still the same as before, but the rates of resource use in making the motors is different from making golf carts. In making a motor, only 1 hour of labor is used. Thus, there is a modification in that coefficient in the labor constraint. The unit profit on lawn mowers is still \$40, and the unit profit on the motor-production activity is \$20. We have the following formulation of the problem:

$$
\begin{aligned}
\text{Maximize:} \quad & \text{Total profit} = \$40x_1 + \$20x_2 \\
\text{Subject to:} \quad & x_1 \qquad\ \le 50 \text{ (lawn-mower assembly facility)} \\
& x_1 + x_2 \le 80 \text{ (labor-hours)} \\
& -x_1 + x_2 \ge\ 0 \text{ (minimum output of product 2: motors)}
\end{aligned}
$$

The third constraint above is the new one, and so let us discuss it briefly. It represents the use of motors (product 2) in the lawn-mower production activity (product 1). One motor is used in each lawn mower, and so we simply state this by subtracting the number of lawn mowers produced (x_1) from the number of motors produced (x_2) and require that the difference be 0 or more. This is the reason for the -1 coefficient for x_1. Alternatively, we could say that the number of motors produced (x_2) must be equal to or greater than the number of lawn mowers produced (x_1). Thus we can have the following:

$$x_2 \ge x_1$$

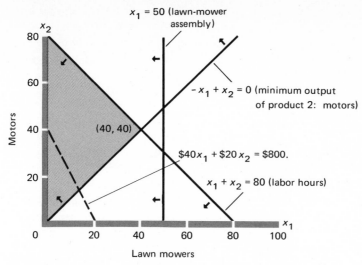

Figure 14–6 A problem in which one product output is an input to another product-output activity.

Rearranging the terms, we have the constraint in the following convenient form:

$$-x_1 + x_2 \geqslant 0$$

We graph the problem in Figure 14-6. The new third constraint equation intersects the origin. When we set x_1 to 0, x_2 must be 0. At an x_1-value of 10, x_2 has a value of 10. Thus, setting x_1 to 10 we have the following:

$$
\begin{aligned}
-x_1 \quad\quad + x_2 &= \;\; 0 \\
(-1)(10) + x_2 &= \;\; 0 \\
x_2 &= 10
\end{aligned}
$$

Given the two points, we draw a straight line through the origin (0, 0) and the second point (10, 10). The constraint is a "greater-than" inequality, and so we orient the arrows in the appropriate direction.

The optimal program is seen to be (40, 40), with a total profit of $2,400. The procedures of the simplex method that we discussed in earlier chapters are, of course, applicable to this type of problem, too.

INTEGER PROGRAMMING

In solving linear-programming problems we have occasionally obtained optimal programs in which some of the outputs are in fractional amounts. But in the real situation it simply may not be possible to implement such a program.

In such cases, one possible alternative is to modify the indicated optimal program by rounding the indicated program levels to the nearest whole number (that is, to the nearest integer). To stay within the feasible region, some care has to be exercised in the direction of the rounding. In most of the problems we have encountered so far, we would usually stay within the feasible region if we rounded the solution to the next-lowest integer.

Unfortunately, however, the rounding procedure does not generally assure us that the resulting integer program is the *best* integer program. In large problems where we do not have a graph of the feasible region, there is need for a procedure that identifies the optimal integer program. These procedures are known as *integer-programming* procedures. We shall not go into the details of these procedures in this book. We shall only describe the integer-programming problem and then solve a problem graphically.

Let us illustrate the integer-programming problem with a small example. Two products are produced with unit profits of $30 for product 1 and $50 for product 2. Two resources impose limitations on the production activities. The usual formulation is as follows:

Maximize: Total profit $= \$30x_1 + \$50x_2$
Subject to: $4x_1 + 5x_2 \leq 20$ (resource 1)
             $2x_1 + 4x_2 \leq 12$ (resource 2)

The graph of the problem is shown in Figure 14-7. We have plotted the constraint equations and the objective function as usual, but additionally we have drawn small circles around the whole-number (integer) programs in the feasible region defined by the two resource constraints.

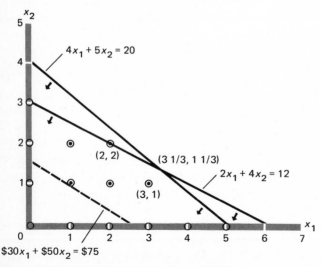

Figure 14-7   An integer-programming problem.

In a more technical sense the feasible programs are comprised only of the integer programs that we have circled. Therefore, the optimal integer program is the last circled point that we intersect as we move the objective function in the optimizing direction (away from the origin).

Thus, the need for a special integer-programming procedure is apparent. To be sure, in some problems the use of the usual simplex procedure with rounding is adequate, especially if the solution values are large and the rounding of them has little effect. But when the program values are small (say 1, 2, or 3) and the unit profits in the objective function are quite large, the need to identify the optimal integer program is clear. Most computer manufacturers include in their computer programs a component on integer programming.

If we were to solve the problem in Figure 14-7 without regard to the integer restriction, we would obtain the program ($3\frac{1}{3}$, $1\frac{1}{3}$), with a total profit of $166.67. This is the optimal program without the integer restriction. But that is not the program we want. We want the optimal integer program.

We could try rounding downward the indicated optimal program ($3\frac{1}{3}$, $1\frac{1}{3}$). This gives us the program (3,1). It has a total profit of $140: $30(3) + $50(1) = $140. We see from the graph in Figure 14-7 that it is feasible, but is it optimal?

If we move our objective function carefully outward from the origin, we will see that the rounding procedure did not identify the optimal integer program. The optimal integer program is (2,2) which has a total profit of $160: $30(2) + $50(2) = $160. The optimal integer program is $20 higher than the integer program obtained from the rounding procedure.

SUMMARY

1 The simplest way to simultaneously consider more than one objective in a linear-programming problem is to treat all the objectives but one as separate constraints. For example, total revenue may be maximized subject to a total-profit constraint as well as the usual resource constraints. However, the minimum level of total profit must be specified.

2 Many problems involving nonlinear relations can be studied using the standard linear-programming procedures (including the simplex method). The nonlinear relations are represented by piecewise linear relations.

3 Sometimes one product-output activity uses as an input the output of another activity. This type of interdependence between activities is easily represented in a linear-programming model.

4 In some real-world decision problems only whole-number (integer) solutions can be implemented. Fractional-valued solutions may not be relevant. Simple rounding procedures may not be adequate for some problems, and then the use of the special techniques of integer programming are necessary.

PROBLEMS

14-1 A firm is giving consideration to two objectives. One is total revenue; the other is total profit. There are two product-output activities. Only one resource imposes an effective constraint on the activities. There are 12 hours of the resource available each day. The rates of use of the resource by the activities and other relevant data are as follows:

Product 1:   Unit revenue = $24
            Unit profit = $4
            Use of resource per unit of output = 2 hours

Product 2:   Unit revenue = $16
            Unit profit = $8
            Use of resource per unit of output = 2 hours

a Suppose total revenue is to be maximized with no reference to the profit objective. Put the problem in standard linear-programming form.

b Graph on the x_1- and x_2-axes the problem formulated in *a*. What is the optimal feasible program and its total revenue?

c Now suppose that total revenue is to be maximized but under the condition that total profit of at least $32 per day be attained. Put this problem in linear-programming form.

d Graph on the x_1- and x_2-axes the problem formulated in *c*. What is the optimal feasible program and its total revenue?

e Solve by the simplex method the problem formulated in *c*. Compare your solution with that in *d*.

f What is the marginal contribution to revenue of the resource? How much would total revenue increase if the minimum total profit specified was decreased by 1 unit to $31? (*Note:* Look for this "marginal contribution to revenue" in the top row of the surplus-variable column introduced because of the "greater-than" profit constraint.) Verify by decreasing the minimum total profit by $1 and solving the new problem. Compare the difference in the optimal total revenues.

14-2 Total profit for a firm is to be maximized subject to a minimum total employment of labor of 18 hours per day and the limitations imposed by two other resources. Resource 1 has a capacity per day of 12 units, and resource 2 has a capacity of 16 units per day. Resource 3 (labor) is available in any amount needed; however, there is the minimum 18-hours-per-day requirement. The following information is available:

Product 1: Unit profit = $10
            Use of resource 1 per unit of output = 4
            Use of resource 2 per unit of output = 4
            Use of resource 3 (labor) per unit of output = 6 hours.

Product 2: Unit profit = $8
            Use of resource 1 per unit of output = 0
            Use of resource 2 per unit of output = 2
            Use of resource 3 (labor) per unit of output = 2 hours

a Put the problem in linear-programming form.

b Graph on the x_1- and x_2-axes the problem formulated in *a*. What is the optimal feasible program and its total profit?

      c   Solve by the simplex method the problem formulated in *a*. Compare your solution with that obtained in *b*.

      d   How much would total profit decrease if the minimum level of employment was raised from 18 hours per day to 19?

14-3 There is just one effective resource constraint for a firm. The resource (facility) has a capacity of 48. There is the desire to identify the maximum-profit program, but the unit profit on product 1 decreases at high-output levels. The following information is available:

> *Product 1:*   Unit profit = $18 from 0 through 6 units
> $12 for more than 6 units
>   Use of resource per unit of output = 4

> *Product 2:*   Unit profit = $8 (for all levels of output)
>   Use of resource per unit of output = 2

      a   Put the problem in standard linear-programming form (designating the change in the coefficients where appropriate).

      b   Make a total-profit graph of the product 1 output activity over a broad range. Designate a new y-variable to correspond to each linear segment of the total-profit graph.

      c   Make a total-profit graph of the product 2 output activity over a broad range. Designate a new y-variable to correspond to each linear segment of the total-profit graph.

      d   Put the problem in linear-programming form in terms of the y-variables.

      e   Solve by the simplex method the problem formulated in *d*. What is the optimal feasible solution and its total profit? What is the meaning of the solution in terms of product 1 and product 2, that is, in terms of x_1 and x_2?

14-4 The maker of small vehicles in Problem 8-6 has encountered a change in the market for industrial vehicles. Although a unit profit of $120 can still be obtained for 75 vehicles per week or less, only $60 profit per unit is attainable if more than 75 units per week are produced. All other data remain unchanged.

      a   Put the problem in standard linear-programming form, designating the coefficient that will change.

      b   Construct a total-profit graph for each product. Designate the output intervals that will be associated with the new y-variables.

      c   Put the problem in linear-programming form in terms of the y-variables.

      d   Solve by the simplex method the problem formulated in *c*. What is the optimal program in terms of the two products? What is the optimal total profit?

14-5 Consider again the firm in Problem 11-7 that wishes to allocate its advertising budget so that exposures to its advertising are maximized. Suppose that any television advertising over 2 minutes for the period results in only 80,000 exposures per minute compared with 120,000 exposures up to (and including 2 minutes) All other data in the problem remain unchanged.

      a   Set down the linear-programming formulation of the problem as in Problem 11-7*a* with the designated change in one of the coefficients in the objective function.

      b   Make total-exposure graphs for each type of advertising (for each activity) and designate the new y-variables and their intervals.

    c   Place the problem in a linear-programming formulation in terms of the new y-variables.

    d   (Optional) Solve by the simplex method the problem formulated in c. What is the solution in terms of the original decision variables?

14-6 A chemical firm makes batteries and flashlights. Both products are sold to buyers outside the firm, but in the manufacture of flashlights, batteries are a required input. The firm wishes to maximize total revenue on the part of its operations that involve these two products.

    A production facility has a capacity of 12 cases of batteries per hour. Labor-hours are available in any amount needed. There is the following additional information:

Product 1 (batteries):   Unit revenue per case = $8
                                    Use of production facility capacity per case = 1

Product 2 (flashlights):   Unit revenue per case = $48
                                      Use of production facility per case = 4
                                      Use of product 1 (cases of batteries) per case of flash-lights = 2

    a   Form a data table for the problem.

    b   Put the problem in standard linear-programming form.

    c   Graph on the x_1- and x_2-axes the problem formulated in b. What is the optimal feasible solution and its total revenue?

    d   Solve by the simplex method the problem formulated in b. Compare your solution with that obtained in c.

14-7 A bank has $50 million in funds that it wants to allocate between loans and the purchase of securities. The return on loans is assumed to be 10 percent, whereas on securities the return is 6 percent. All the funds might be allocated to loans were it not for a number of constraints. For simplicity, suppose there are three constraints upon the lending and the security-purchase activities: a total-funds constraint, a liquidity constraint, and a minimum loan-balance constraint.

    Let us represent the amount of funds devoted to loans by x_1 and the amount used for security purchases by x_2. Then, the total-funds constraint is simply: $x_1 + x_2 \leqslant \$50$ million.

    The liquidity constraint exists because of the need to hold an amount of readily negotiable securities in order to satisfy unforeseen deposit withdrawals. It is the policy of the bank to hold securities in an amount that is at least 25 percent of total assets (loans and securities). This gives us the following constraint:

$$x_2 \geqslant .25(x_1 + x_2)$$

    Carrying out the multiplication on the right-hand side of the above liquidity-constraint inequality gives us $x_2 \geqslant .25x_1 + .25x_2$. Collecting like terms, we have $0 \geqslant .25x_1 - .75x_2$. Rearranging the terms, we have the inequality in a convenient form, which, of course, is equivalent to the first liquidity-constraint inequality above.

$$.25x_1 - .75x_2 \leqslant 0$$

The third and final constraint is the loan-balance constraint. It is based on the policy of the bank that requires that total loans made during the period are at least $15 million. Thus, the loan-balance constraint is simply $x_1 \geq \$15$ million.

   a   Given the return (rate of revenue) on each type of activity and the three inequality constraints specified above, place the problem in standard linear-programming form.

   b   Graph on the x_1- and x_2-axes the problem formulated in a. What is the optimal feasible program and its total revenue?

   c   (Optional) Solve by the simplex method the problem formulated in a. Compare the solution with that obtained in b.

14-8   From your graph in Problem 14-7b or your final simplex table in Problem 14-7c, indicate the effect on total revenue if the total funds available rise by $10 million.

14-9   Consider the following problem:

Maximize: $Z = 80x_1 + 60x_2$
Subject to: $6x_1 + 4x_2 \leq 18$

   a   Graph the problem on the x_1- and x_2-axes. What is the optimal feasible solution and its (total) value without an integer restriction?

   b   By rounding the solution in a toward feasibility (downward), what is the solution obtained and its value?

   c   What is the optimal integer solution and its value? Is it better than that obtained by the rounding procedure?

14-10   Consider the following minimization problem:

Minimize: $Z = 40x_1 + 60x_2$
Subject to: $8x_1 + 10x_2 \geq 40$
$8x_2 \geq 24$

   a   Graph the problem on the x_1- and x_2-axes. What is the optimal feasible solution and its value without an integer restriction?

   b   By rounding the solution in a toward feasibility, what is the solution obtained and its value?

   c   What is the optimal integer solution and its value? Is it better than that obtained by the rounding procedure?

Chapter 15

Transportation-related Decision Problems and the Location of New Facilities

There is a class of linear-programming problems that is comprised of "transportation-related" or "transportation-type" problems. Usually transportation costs are involved in such problems, although there are some in this category that have nothing to do with transportation.

The term "transportation" is associated with all these problems partly because in studying efficient transportation routes a special solution procedure was developed that has become known as the *transportation method* of solving a linear-programming problem. This solution method was developed and used by F. L. Hitchcock and T. C. Koopmans in the early 1940s.

To use this solution procedure, the linear-programming problem has to be of a particular type. This type of problem commonly arises in routing and scheduling decisions as well as in locating new production facilities where transportation factors are significant.

AN EXAMPLE OF TRANSPORTATION-TYPE PROBLEMS

A typical transportation-type problem is illustrated by the following example. A firm makes mattresses for distribution and sale throughout a national market. It has a manufacturing facility on the East Coast and one on the West Coast.

Buyers (distributors) of the mattresses are located throughout the nation. Although it is a very rough approximation, let us think of the buyers as being located in just three market regions: the Eastern region, the Western region, and the Central region.

Mattresses can be made in either the East Coast or West Coast factory and delivered to any or all of the three market regions. Thus, we can think of the problem in terms of the diagram in Figure 15-1 in which we represent by arrows the possible routes the product might take from its origin to its destination.

The main new terms in the transportation-type problem are *origins* and *destinations*. As the term *origin* implies, it is a point where a product originates (for example, where it is manufactured). Each destination is a point where the product can be sent from an origin (for example, where a buyer of the product is located).

In our mattress example we refer to the East Coast factory as origin 1 and the West Coast factory as origin 2. The Eastern market is destination 1, the Western market is destination 2, and the Central market is destination 3. In a more realistic example, we would usually include many more destinations and possibly more origins, too.

The typical decision problem arising in these types of problems is *how much to transport from each origin to each destination*. For our mattress problem in Figure 15-1 we have placed question marks on each of the arrows representing a possible route. The question marks are the "unknowns" or decision variables in this problem.

In the linear-programming problems discussed prior to this chapter, each decision variable represented a product output (or an analogous activity level). Product 1 output, for example, was represented by the decision variable x_1, product 2 output by x_2, and so forth.

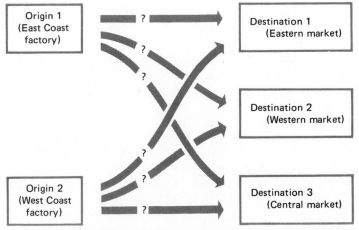

Figure 15-1 The possible routes of shipment in the mattress problem.

In transportation-type problems the level of each "activity" or "output" is the amount to transport from each origin to each destination. We use the variable x to represent these amounts, but we now use a two-digit subscript for easy interpretation of the variables.

For example, the amount to be transported from origin 1 to destination 1 (shown by the top question mark in Figure 15-1) is represented by the variable x_{11}. The first digit in the subscript refers to the origin (here origin 1); the second digit refers to the destination (here, destination 1). Thus, if we speak of x_{23} being 2,000, we mean that 2,000 units are to be transported from origin 2 to destination 3.

Therefore, the decision variables in our mattress problem are six: x_{11}, x_{12}, x_{13}, x_{21}, x_{22}, and x_{23}. There are two origins and three destinations, and so there are six different routes of shipment. The decision problem typically is one of determining a shipping "program" that will minimize total transportation costs.

PUTTING THE PROBLEM IN THE USUAL LINEAR-PROGRAMMING FORM

With six decision variables we cannot graph the problem as we did earlier, but if we place the problem in the usual linear-programming formulation, we can solve it by the simplex method (just as we solved earlier problems). It will be helpful to put it into the usual linear-programming formulation even though discussion of the alternative method of solving this type of linear-programming problem (the transportation method) will be of main concern in this chapter.

Thus, we really have two solution procedures in solving this type of problem: the simplex method and the transportation method. But if a problem can be solved by the transportation method it turns out to be the more efficient procedure and thus the less costly. We should point out, however, that although the two methods appear quite different, their underlying mathematical bases are essentially the same.

To put a problem in the usual linear-programming form, we need to answer the two following questions:

1 What is the objective and how does each activity contribute to that objective?
2 What are the constraints that impose limitations on attaining that objective?

A common objective in transportation-type problems is to minimize transportation costs. In such problems each activity usually refers to transporting a product by a particular route. For each such activity we therefore need to obtain the cost of transporting a unit by that route. This unit cost appears in the objective function as the coefficient of the variable representing the amount shipped by that particular route.

The unit costs of transporting each unit in the mattresses problem are given

Table 15-1 The Unit Transportation Costs by Each Possible Route in the Mattress Problem

Transportation route	Decision variable representing the amount to be transported by this route	Cost of transporting each unit by this route
Origin 1 to destination 1	x_{11}	$3
Origin 1 to destination 2	x_{12}	7
Origin 1 to destination 3	x_{13}	5
Origin 2 to destination 1	x_{21}	5
Origin 2 to destination 2	x_{22}	4
Origin 2 to destination 3	x_{23}	6

in Table 15-1. With these unit costs we can formulate the cost-objective function as follows:

$$\text{Total transportation costs} = \$3x_{11} + \$7x_{12} + \$5x_{13} + \$5x_{21} + \$4x_{22} + \$6x_{23}$$

And what are the constraints upon minimizing total transportation costs? Usually, they are of two types as follows:

1 The condition that the capacity at every origin (for example, at every factory) be fully utilized. (This turns out not to be as restrictive as it appears.)

2 The requirement that the quantity demanded at every destination (for example, at every market region) be exactly fulfilled.

Taking the origin-capacity condition first, we must answer the usual question: What are the activities that utilize a particular origin capacity, and what is that capacity?

The activities that utilize, say, origin 1 capacity are those shipping activities where the product originates from origin 1 and goes to any of the possible destinations. Thus, in our mattress example, origin 1 capacity is utilized by the activity levels represented by x_{11}, x_{12}, and x_{13} (that is, by transporting units from origin 1 to destination 1, to destination 2, and to destination 3).

Each unit that we transport by each route uses up exactly 1 unit of the associated origin capacity, so that for every possible route (for every variable), the coefficient is 1. Thus, for a given shipping program (that is, so many units by each route) we could represent its total use of an origin capacity as follows:

$$x_{11} + x_{12} + x_{13} = \text{total use of origin 1 capacity}$$

For a program of transporting 3,000 units from origin 1 to destination 1, 4,000 units from origin 1 to destination 2, and 0 units from origin 1 to destination 3, we would have the following total use of origin 1 capacity.

$$x_{11} + x_{12} + x_{13} = \text{total use of origin 1 capacity}$$
$$3{,}000 + 4{,}000 + 0 = 7{,}000 \text{ (total use of origin 1 capacity)}$$

But the condition we must represent is the *full utilization* of the origin 1 capacity (and of every origin capacity). The capacity of origin 1 is 8,000. Thus, the sum of the units originating at origin 1 must sum to 8,000. We represent this condition by the following *equation:*

$$x_{11} + x_{12} + x_{13} = 8{,}000 \text{ (origin 1 capacity)}$$

All feasible programs must satisfy this and every other equation constraint. The program considered above is infeasible in terms of this constraint because the assumed program utilizes only 7,000 units of the capacity of origin 1, which obviously is less than the 8,000 capacity.

The capacity at the other origin (origin 2) is given in Table 15-2 (along with the quantities demanded at the destinations). For origin 2 we have the following equation constraint that must be satisfied.

$$x_{21} + x_{22} + x_{23} = 6{,}000 \text{ (origin 2 capacity)}$$

Part of the constraints in such transportation-type problems are comprised of origin-capacity constraints, and the rest are made up of destination-demand constraints. Usually, they, too, are all equation constraints. We will have a separate constraint equation for each origin capacity and a separate constraint equation for each destination quantity demanded.

Each destination demand can be fulfilled by shipments from one or more of the different origins. For example, in our mattress problem the destination 1 demand can be satisfied by transporting units from either origin 1 or origin 2 or from both origins. Since the destination 1 demand is 3,000 units (and it must be exactly fulfilled) we have the following equation constraint pertaining to the destination 1 demand that must be satisfied.

$$x_{11} + x_{21} = 3{,}000 \text{ (destination 1 quantity demanded)}$$

Table 15-2 The Capacity at Each Origin and the Quantity Demanded at Each Destination

Origin capacity	Destination quantity demanded
Origin 1: 8,000	Destination 1: 3,000
Origin 2: 6,000	Destination 2: 7,000
	Destination 3: 4,000

The entire set of origin-capacity and destination-demand constraints, along with the objective function, for our mattress problem appears in the following formulation:

Minimize:
Total costs
$$= \$3x_{11} + \$7x_{12} + \$5x_{13} + \$5x_{21} + \$4x_{22} + \$6x_{23}$$
Subject to:

$$
\begin{array}{llll}
x_{11} + x_{12} + x_{13} & & = 8{,}000 \text{ (origin 1 capacity)} \\
x_{21} + x_{22} + x_{23} & = 6{,}000 \text{ (origin 2 capacity)} \\
x_{11} \qquad\qquad + x_{21} & = 3{,}000 \text{ (destination 1 demand)} \\
x_{12} \qquad\qquad + x_{22} & = 7{,}000 \text{ (destination 2 demand)} \\
x_{13} \qquad\qquad + x_{23} & = 4{,}000 \text{ (destination 3 demand)}
\end{array}
$$

THE TRANSPORTATION METHOD OF SOLVING THE PROBLEM

As indicated earlier, we can solve this problem as formulated by the simplex method. However, when it is of this form (where all the coefficients of the constraints are 1 and each constraint adds one more unknown), we can solve it by the more efficient transportation method. Let us illustrate this method in the section that follows.

The transportation method focuses on the use of tables, too, but they appear somewhat different from those in the simplex method. First, the variables do not appear explicitly in the usual transportation table. That is why in Table 15-3 we have shown the variables in parentheses in the cells of the table. Usually, we leave the cell blank; however, it is well to think of each cell as being associated with a variable such as we have indicated in Table 15-3.

In each such table we will have *a row corresponding to each constraint equation representing an origin capacity*. In our mattress problem we have two origins, and so we have just the two rows. The first row in Table 15-3 corresponds to the equation constraint representing the origin 1 capacity.

$$x_{11} + x_{12} + x_{13} = 8{,}000 \text{ (origin 1 capacity)}$$

In the usual table we drop several elements: the variable designation (x_{11}, x_{12}, and so forth), the plus signs, and the equation signs. As a matter of fact, all that would usually appear in the first row of the first table for the mattress problem is the origin 1 capacity of 8,000 at the far-right side as shown in Table 15-4.

We will consider various programs in our solution procedure (the transportation method), but to be sure the programs are feasible we must add the solution

Table 15-3   The Decision Variables and Equation Constraints that Are Implicit in a Transportation Table

	Destination 1 (East)	Destination 2 (West)	Destination 3 (Central)	Origin capacity
Origin 1 (East)	(x_{11})	$+ (x_{12})$	$+ (x_{13})$	$= 8{,}000$
Origin 2 (West)	(x_{21})	$+ (x_{22})$	$+ (x_{23})$	$= 6{,}000$
Destination demand	3,000	7,000	4,000	

Table 15-4   The Mattress Problem Placed in the Usual Transportation Table

	Destination 1 (East)	Destination 2 (West)	Destination 3 (Central)	Origin capacity
Origin 1 (East)	$3	$7	$5	8,000
Origin 2 (West)	$5	$4	$6	6,000
Destination demand	3,000	7,000	4,000	

values in each cell in each such row to see that they sum to the origin capacity in the right-hand margin of the table. Thus, in our solution procedure we act as if the addition and equality signs are still there for every row.

The destination-demand equation constraints are represented in the table, too. *Each column corresponds to a destination-demand equation constraint.* For example, the first column in Table 15-3 corresponds to the equation constraint representing destination 1 quantity demanded.

$$x_{11} + x_{21} = 3,000 \text{ (destination 1 quantity demanded)}$$

Although we have not inserted them in Table 15-3, there are addition signs implicitly between the cells (or variables) in each column and an equation sign at the bottom of each column of the table.

Thus, in our solution procedure we will have to be sure that the solution values in each column sum exactly to the destination demand at the bottom of each column.

Now we are ready to begin a discussion of the solution procedure known as the transportation method. It strongly parallels the four-step procedure of the simplex method discussed in Chapter 10. First, we shall discuss the preparatory steps that are necessary before we go to the four-step procedure of applying an optimality test, selection of incoming and outgoing variables, and obtaining a new solution.

Preparatory Steps that Include Obtaining an Initial Solution

If we have a problem that appears to be of the transportation type, there are several things to do before beginning the four-step solution procedure. They are as follows:

1 Put the problem in standard linear-programming form (or some analogous form).
2 Create a table that has as many rows as there are origin-capacity constraints and as many columns as there are destination-demand constraints. Insert each origin-capacity amount in the appropriate right-hand margin of each row, and identify the origin at the left-hand margin. Insert each destination quantity demanded at the appropriate bottom margin of each column, and identify the destination at the top of each column.
3 In the upper-left corner of each cell insert the appropriate unit cost for transporting a unit from the relevant origin to the relevant destination.
4 Obtain an initial feasible solution by the "northwest-corner rule."

For the mattress problem the first step already has been completed as shown above. Completing the second and third steps gives us the table shown in Table 15-4.

Obtaining an Initial Solution   As in the simplex method we need an initial basic feasible solution to begin the solution procedure. The simplest way to obtain an initial solution is by the "northwest-corner" rule. This rule simply means that we create a feasible solution by starting in the upper-left (northwest) corner of our table such as we have in Table 15-4. The basic idea is to *allocate as much as we can to the upper-left cell and then proceed by merely satisfying all the row and column equation constraints that we discussed earlier.*

In this type of problem it turns out that once we have made *a single allocation to a route* (that is, once we have assigned a particular value to a single variable) the rest of the table can be completed by satisfying the row and column equation constraints. This completed table provides a basic feasible solution.

Let us begin with the northwest-corner allocation in our mattress problem and then complete the table.

How much can we allocate to the northwest-corner cell, that is, cell (1, 1)? (*Note:* In referring to the cells, let us list the row number first and then the column number.)

To see how much we can allocate to that cell, we must look at *both* the origin 1 capacity (which is 8,000) and the destination 1 demand (which is 3,000). To satisfy the equation constraint in column 1 we must allocate no more than 3,000 to that cell. If we allocate exactly 3,000 we have then satisfied the column 1 constraint: 3,000 + 0 = 3,000.

Now, we can try to satisfy the row 1 constraint. Thus, we go across row 1 to cell (1, 2). How much can we allocate to this cell with a view to satisfying the row 1 constraint? We already have allocated 3,000 to cell (1, 1), and we would like to allocate to cell (1, 2) the remaining 5,000 in order to satisfy the row 1 constraint.

We can allocate 5,000 units to cell (1, 2) because destination 2 demand is 7,000. Allocating 5,000 to cell (1, 2) thus satisfies the row 1 constraint. We can now try to satisfy the column 2 constraint.

We have already allocated 5,000 units to cell (1, 2), and so 2,000 units need to be allocated to cell (2, 2) in order to satisfy the column 2 constraint: 5,000 + 2,000 = 7,000 (destination 2 demand). Therefore, we allocate 2,000 to cell (2, 2).

Once we satisfy a column constraint, we shift our attention to satisfying a row constraint (also, when we satisfy a row constraint, we shift our focus to satisfying a column constraint).

We have just satisfied the column 2 constraint, and so we shift to the row 2 constraint. We have already allocated 2,000 to cell (2, 2). Therefore, we must allocate 4,000 to cell (2, 3) in order to satisfy the row 2 constraint: 2,000 + 4,000 = 6,000. We allocate 4,000 to cell (2, 3).

Since we satisfied the row 2 constraint, our attention shifts to satisfying the column 3 constraint. But it is already satisfied by the 4,000 allocated to cell (2, 3). Thus, we have reached the "southeast" corner and this means we have finished the table (satisfied all the equation constraints) and have obtained an initial basic feasible solution. In Table 15-5 we record the amounts we have allocated to each cell and follow the practice of enclosing within circles the solution values of the basic variables (those variables not set to 0 to obtain a basic solution).

For any solution we can easily obtain its total cost by multiplying the solution values by their unit costs and summing the products (each unit cost being located in the upper-left corner of the appropriate cell). For our initial basic feasible solution, we have a total cost of $76,000.

$$\text{Total cost} = \$3(3,000) + \$7(5,000) + \$4(2,000) + \$6(4,000)$$
$$= \$76,000$$

Table 15-5   An Initial Solution for the Mattress Problem

	Destination 1 (East)	Destination 2 (West)	Destination 3 (Central)	Origin capacity
Origin 1 (East)	$3 ⟨3,000⟩	$7 ⟨5,000⟩	$5	8,000
Origin 2 (West)	$5	$4 ⟨2,000⟩	$6 ⟨4,000⟩	6,000
Destination demand	3,000	7,000	4,000	

Total cost = $76,000

But is our initial feasible solution the lowest-cost (the optimal) feasible solution? This is where we begin the four-step procedure:

1 Apply the optimality test.
2 Select the incoming variable.
3 Select the outgoing variable.
4 Obtain a new basic feasible solution.

Step 1: Apply the Optimality Test

We must determine if the initial feasible solution is the lowest-cost feasible solution. The application of the optimality test in the simplex method was quite easy because all that we had to do was to check the top row to see if there were any elements that had the appropriate negative or positive sign. Each of the elements in the top row indicated the rate of change in total profit (or cost) if a particular variable (activity) was brought in that currently was not under consideration (not in the program). We need the same kind of indicators here, but we have to do a little work to get them.

In transportation-type problems the activities that are not in the program (that is, the variables temporarily set to 0) are each associated with a vacant cell in the transportation table. For example, in Table 15-5, cells (1, 3) and (2, 1) are vacant. They are not in the current program under consideration (we could say that the vacant cells are associated with nonbasic variables). And what we need to know is this: the rate of change in total cost if each of these activities individually was brought into the program.

The way we get this rate of change in total cost is very straightforward. We simply try allocating *a single unit* to the vacant cell and then see how much it changes total cost. This is the *indicator* that we seek for each vacant cell.

If when computing these indicators we obtain a negative value, total costs will be lowered at that rate if that activity is used. If the indicator is positive in sign, it means that total costs will rise at that rate if the associated activity is brought in.

In Table 15-6 we try allocating a single unit to the vacant cell (1, 3). We show a +1 in the lower part of the cell to represent this unit increase in the amount shipped by that route. Of course, currently, there is nothing allocated to cell (1, 3).

But if we allocate 1 unit to cell (1, 3) our equation constraints will not be satisfied unless we make the appropriate adjustments in the rows and columns affected. (However, we must make the adjustments only in the circled cells in the rows and columns affected.) Thus, if we increase cell (1, 3) by 1 unit, we will have to decrease another circled cell in that same row by 1 unit in order to keep our row 1 equation constraint satisfied. (However, the circled cell in the same row that we decrease by 1 unit must have another circled cell in the same column.) Thus we decrease cell (1, 2) by 1 unit, which has a circled cell in the same column and also keeps the row 1 constraint satisfied: 3,000 + 4,999 − 1 = 8,000.

But decreasing cell (1, 2) by 1 unit disturbs column 2. Therefore, if we decrease cell (1, 2) by 1 unit we will have to increase a circled cell in column 2 by 1 unit. Which circled cell in column 2 shall we then increase by 1 unit? One that also has another circled cell in its row. Inasmuch as we have a very small example, we have just the one circled cell in column 2, cell (2, 2), and it

Table 15-6   Obtaining the Rate of Change in Total Cost if the Route "Origin 1 to Destination 3" Is Used

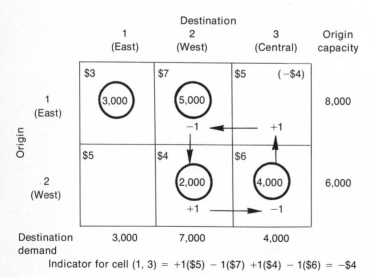

Indicator for cell (1, 3) = +1($5) − 1($7) +1($4) − 1($6) = −$4

also has another circled cell in its row, cell (2, 3). Thus, we increase by 1 unit cell (2, 2) in order to satisfy the column 2 constraint: 4,999 + 2,001 = 7,000.

However, the unit increase in cell (2, 2) disturbs row 2. We have to decrease cell (2, 3) by 1 unit in order to keep the row 2 constraint satisfied. Decreasing cell (2, 3) by 1 unit just offsets the original unit increase in cell (1, 3) from which we started.

In Table 15-6 we have connected with arrows the unit changes that would be necessary in the program if a unit were shipped by the route not in use and represented by cell (1, 3). Analogous loops will have to be traced out for each vacant cell in order to get an indication of the effect of its use upon total cost.

To get the *indicator* for cell (1, 3), we note the unit changes that would be necessary. Next, we want to know the cost effect of such a unit adjustment. This is obtained simply by multiplying each unit change (a unit increase or decrease) by its associated unit cost. In Table 15-6 we see that cell (1, 3) has a unit cost of $5. Therefore, a unit increase by that route would increase cost by $5 (the cost of a unit shipped by that route). But cell (1, 2) has a unit decrease, and its unit cost is $7. The net effect of all the unit adjustments associated with the original unit increase in cell (1, 3) is found to be −$4 as follows:

$$\text{Cost indicator for cell } (1, 3) = + 1(\$5) - 1(\$7) + 1(\$4) - 1(\$6) = -\$4$$

Thus, for each unit allocated to the now-unused route represented by cell (1, 3), total transportation costs will *decrease* by $4. We record the −$4 indicator within parentheses in the upper-right corner of cell (1, 3) for which the evaluation was made.

We need such an indicator for each vacant cell (that is, each nonbasic variable) in order to make the optimality test (to see if the current solution is optimal) and also to select the incoming and outgoing basic variables in order to arrive at an improved solution.

We have already seen from the −$4 indicator obtained for cell (1, 3) that the initial basic feasible solution is not optimal because costs can be reduced if that route is used. But it may be that using other currently unused routes may decrease costs at an even greater rate.

Our only other vacant cell in Table 15-6 is cell (2, 1). To get the cost indicator for this unused route, we try a unit increase for this route and repeat the adjustment procedure analogous to that which we did for cell (1, 3). Of course every adjustment loop is a bit different. We show the necessary unit adjustments for cell (2, 1) in Table 15-7. If we allocate 1 unit to the route represented by cell (2, 1), a unit decrease in that same row is necessary. Then that decrease necessitates an increase in cell (1, 2) and so forth. The net effect is to increase total transportation costs by $5.

$$\text{Cost indicator for cell } (2, 1) = + 1(\$5) - 1(\$4) + 1(\$7) - 1(\$3) = \$5$$

We record this cost indicator for cell (2, 1) within parentheses in the upper-right corner of that cell.

Table 15-7   Obtaining the Rate of Change in Total Cost if the Route "Origin 2 to Destination 1" Is Used

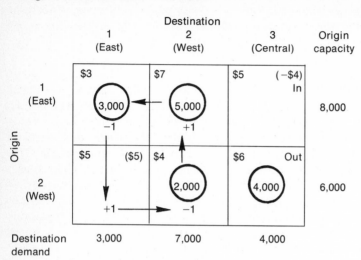

Indicator for cell (2, 1) = +1($5) − 1($4) +1($7) − 1($3) = $5

Now for the optimality test. With indicators in the upper-right corner of each vacant cell (the nonbasic variables), we examine them to see if any of the indicators are negative. If any are negative, we have not reached an optimal solution. In our mattress problem, we have a −$4 in cell (1, 3). Therefore, further reduction in total cost is possible. The next step is to select an incoming variable.

Step 2: Selecting an Incoming Variable

The selection of an incoming variable is made simply by identifying the *most negative* of the indicators in the vacant cells (the nonbasic variables). In our mattress example there is only one negative indicator, −$4 for cell (1, 3), and so it is also the most negative. Thus, cell (1, 3) represents the incoming variable. We note this by writing the word "in" within the cell.

Step 3: Selecting the Outgoing Variable

One of the routes currently under consideration (one of the basic variables in the current solution) will have to be dropped in the next basic solution. In short, we must select an outgoing variable from the current set of basic variables. The current basic variables are those with circled-cell values as shown in Table 15-7. One of these will have to be selected as the outgoing variable.

The key to the selection of the outgoing variable lies with the *incoming* variable. Here, the incoming variable is represented by cell (1, 3). For cell (1, 3) we *retrace* the unit-adjustment loop made to obtain the cost indicator for that cell (as shown back in Table 15-6). Looking at Table 15-6, we identify those basic variables (circled-cell values) that would have to be *decreased* by 1 unit if cell (1,

3) were increased by 1 unit. These cells are (1, 2) and (2, 3). Of these two cells we identify the one with the *lowest* solution value. It is cell (2, 3) with a value of 4,000. Cell (1, 2) is the other contender, but it has a higher value (5,000). Thus, the outgoing variable is associated with cell (2, 3), and in Table 15-7 we insert the word "out" within that cell.

Step 4: Obtaining a New Solution

The first step to take in obtaining a new solution is to identify the new set of basic variables. In our example, cell (1, 3), representing the incoming variable, is substituted for cell (2, 3), representing the outgoing variable.

Thus, we create a new table showing only the new set of basic variables with no values yet assigned. This is shown in Table 15-8. There is only one substitution of variables occurring in each table. Thus, each new table will have a single *new* basic variable (a single, new, circled cell) and a single, departed, basic variable (a single, old, circled cell).

It is with the new circled cell (associated with the new basic variable) that we begin to obtain the new solution. And here is a key point: The amount allocated to the new cell, here cell (1, 3), is *an amount equal to that which had been allocated to the old cell,* here cell (2, 3). Thus, since 4,000 units had been allocated to outgoing cell (2, 3) we allocate the same 4,000 units to incoming cell (1, 3). We insert this amount first in the new table as shown in Table 15-9.

Recall that once we have obtained a single value in the new solution we can then obtain the remaining solution values simply by seeing to it that each row and column equation constraint is satisfied by the values in the circled cells.

Table 15-8   The Basic Variables for the Second Solution of the Mattress Problem

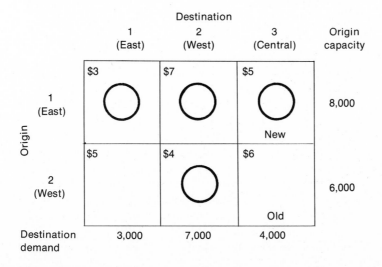

Table 15-9 The First Step in Obtaining the Second Solution—Allocating the Proper Amount to the New Cell

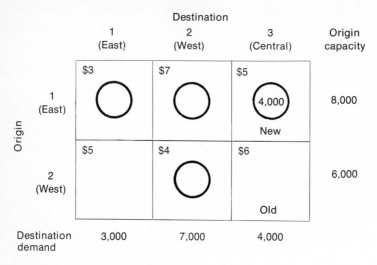

	Destination 1 (East)	Destination 2 (West)	Destination 3 (Central)	Origin capacity
Origin 1 (East)	$3 ◯	$7 ◯	$5 ◯ 4,000 New	8,000
Origin 2 (West)	$5	$4 ◯	$6 Old	6,000
Destination demand	3,000	7,000	4,000	

Table 15-10 The Second Solution of the Mattress Problem

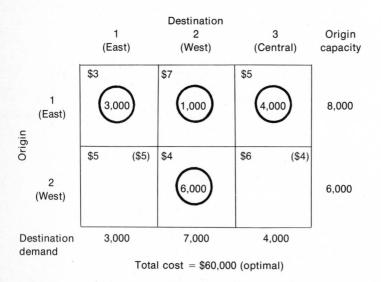

	Destination 1 (East)	Destination 2 (West)	Destination 3 (Central)	Origin capacity
Origin 1 (East)	$3 ◯ 3,000	$7 ◯ 1,000	$5 ◯ 4,000	8,000
Origin 2 (West)	$5 ($5)	$4 ◯ 6,000	$6 ($4)	6,000
Destination demand	3,000	7,000	4,000	

Total cost = $60,000 (optimal)

We complete the table in Table 15-10. Cell (1, 1) must have a value of 3,000 because it is the only circled cell in that column. Thus, we insert 3,000 within the circle in that cell. Cell (1, 2) must then have a value of 1,000 in order for the row 1 equation to be satisfied. Finally, the column 2 equation is satisfied only if cell (2, 2) has a value of 6,000. This 6,000 allocation to cell (2, 2) also satisfies the row 2 equation constraint. Thus, all equation constraints are satisfied, and we have a new basic feasible solution.

What is the total cost of the new solution? We can find out simply by multiplying each circled-cell value by the unit cost in the upper-left corner of the cell. This gives us a total transportation cost of $60,000 for the new program.

The new program decreased total costs by $16,000. Recall from Table 15-7 that the cost indicator was −$4 for the basic variable we brought in, cell (1, 3). The most we could allocate to the new cell (1, 3) was 4,000 units. Thus, since every unit allocated to the new cell would decrease total costs by $4, we actually could have anticipated that total costs would decrease by $16,000 if we allocated 4,000 units to the new cell.

The Optimality Test Again

After we obtain a new solution, we go back and apply the optimality test in order to know if we have reached an optimal solution. Our optimality test requires that we once again obtain cost indicators for each vacant cell and place the amount of the indicator in its position in the upper-right corner of that cell.

Working from the solution in Table 15-10, we have two vacant cells to evaluate, cells (2, 1) and (2, 3). The following gives us the cost indicator of $5 for cell (2, 1).

Cost indicator for cell (2, 1) = + 1($5) − 1($4) + 1($7) − 1($3) = $5

For cell (2, 3) we have the following:

Cost indicator for cell (2, 3) = + 1($6) − 1($4) + 1($7) − 1($5) = $4

Since none of the cost indicators is negative, we know that the last solution obtained is an optimal feasible solution. No other allocation will result in any lower total costs.

THE LOCATION OF NEW FACILITIES

Let us look at a simple illustration of the way in which the previous analysis of this chapter can help determine where to expand facilities or locate new ones.

Suppose that the quantity demanded at destination 3 (the Central region) is expected to increase from 4,000 to 5,000 units in the near future. More production facilities will be needed to produce the additional 1,000 units. Our main question is this: Should the expansion of facilities be undertaken at origin 1 (the East Coast) or at origin 2 (the West Coast)?

Of course in a real-world problem there are many factors to take into account, but our analysis in this chapter provides a way to determine (in terms of transportation costs to the buyers) whether the origin 1 capacity should be increased by 1,000 or if the capacity at origin 2 should be increased by 1,000 instead.

Table 15-11   Expanding the Production Facilities First on the East Coast and Then on the West Coast

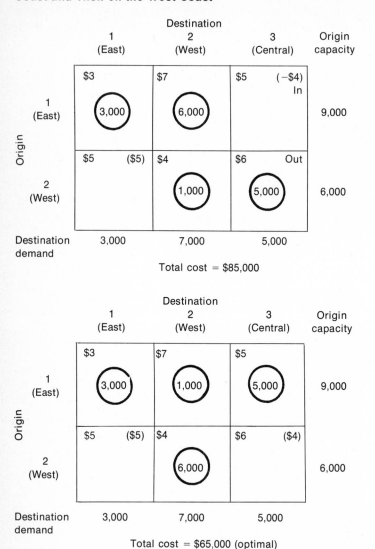

	Destination 1 (East)	Destination 2 (West)	Destination 3 (Central)	Origin capacity
1 (East)	$3 3,000	$7 6,000	$5 (−$4) In	9,000
2 (West)	$5 ($5)	$4 1,000	$6 Out 5,000	6,000
Destination demand	3,000	7,000	5,000	

Total cost = $85,000

	Destination 1 (East)	Destination 2 (West)	Destination 3 (Central)	Origin capacity
1 (East)	$3 3,000	$7 1,000	$5 5,000	9,000
2 (West)	$5 ($5)	$4 6,000	$6 ($4)	6,000
Destination demand	3,000	7,000	5,000	

Total cost = $65,000 (optimal)

In the left-hand section of Table 15-11 we have solved the problem if the origin 1 (East Coast) capacity is increased by 1,000 units. Minimum transportation costs are found to be $65,000.

In the right-hand section of Table 15-11 we solve the problem if the origin 2 (West Coast) capacity is increased by 1,000 units. Minimum transportation costs for this program are $62,000. Thus, in terms of transportation costs alone (and if

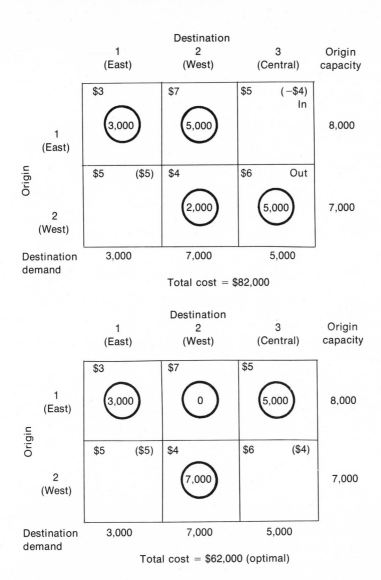

Total cost = $82,000

Total cost = $62,000 (optimal)

all assumptions hold) the best place to expand the production capacity is on the West Coast.

If we were to consider another (new) location of the additional production capacity (for example, in the Central region), a new origin 3 would have to be added with a new third row to our table. Unit costs of shipping items from the new origin 3 to each of the three destinations would have to be provided. Then the minimum transportation costs obtained from solving this new problem would be compared with the minimum transportation costs associated with the expansion of facilities at the existing production locations that we obtained in Table 15-11.

INSUFFICIENT DEMAND (OR EXCESS CAPACITY)

We have not stated it explicitly, but up to now we have been assuming that the sum of the quantities demanded at all the destinations equals the sum of the capacities at all the origins.

What happens then to our analysis if there is not sufficient demand to utilize the total capacity? That is, what happens if the total of the quantities demanded is *not* equal to the total capacity? How then do we obtain the program that satisfies the destination demands and also minimizes total transportation cost? Also, at what origin should we have the idle capacity? These are questions we shall try to answer in this section.

A Decrease in Demand at Destination 3

Suppose that in our mattress example the demand at destination 3 (the Central region) decreases from 4,000 units to 2,000 and there is no corresponding decrease at any of the origin capacities. How do we proceed?

The main point is that (in our analysis) we create a fictitious destination 4 to pick up any deficiency in demand so that the total quantity demanded (including the fictitious destination 4 demand) equals the total capacity.

Thus, we begin the problem at the top of Table 15-12. Destination 3 demand has decreased from 4,000 to 2,000, but we leave the capacities at the origins unchanged.

In the next table we create a fictitious destination 4 to pick up the insufficient demand. Here, the deficiency is 2,000, and so we assign a quantity demanded of 2,000 to the fictitious destination 4.

In the newly created cells for destination 4, we insert a unit cost of $0 since there will be no actual transportation cost incurred for any amounts allocated to these cells. It is simply a device to get our standard transportation method to work as it did in the previous sections. By creating the fictitious destination 4, we again have total quantity demanded equal to total capacity. We solve the new problem as usual. The minimum total cost to fulfill the quantities demanded at the destinations is seen to be $50,000. The optimal program is shown at the bottom of Table 15-12.

Where Should the Idle Capacity Be?   Our final table at the bottom of Table 15-12 shows where the idle capacity should be if transportation costs are to be minimized. Some interpretation is necessary, but the relevant information is in the fictitious destination 4 column.

Note that cell (1, 4) has a circled-cell value of 2,000. This means that in the optimal program 2,000 units will go from origin 1 to the fictitious destination 4.

Since this is a fictitious destination, it simply means that it does not go at all, and thus the idle capacity will be at the associated origin 1. The capacity of 8,000 at origin 1 will not be fully used.

Also, in solving this particular problem, we encountered something a little different from the previous problems. In getting the cost indicator for cell (1, 4) in the second table of Table 15-12, we had to make a unit-adjustment loop that involved a slightly more complicated loop. We had to "jump over" an adjacent circled cell in order to make the unit changes only in the cells with circled-cell values (the basic variables). The −$3 indicator was obtained as follows.

$$\text{Cost indicator for cell } (1, 4) = +1(\$0) - 1(\$7) + 1(\$4) - 1(\$0) = -\$3$$

EXCESS DEMAND (OR INSUFFICIENT CAPACITY)

The other possibility is that the total demand at the destinations may exceed the total capacity available at the origins. We represent such a .problem in Table 15-13 where the demand at destination 3 (the Central region) increases from 4,000 to 7,000 units, but it is not accompanied by a corresponding increase in the origin capacities.

This type of problem is handled in a fashion analogous to the preceding one. Only now we must create a fictitious origin 3 in our procedure and assign it a capacity of 3,000 units so that we can have total demand and total capacity equal.

Thus we add a new third row (for origin 3) to our table, as shown in Table 15-13, and insert the 3,000 capacity. Also, we insert unit costs of $0 in each of the cells associated with the fictitious origin 3 since these activities would involve no costs at all.

The final table in Table 15-13 shows the program that minimizes total transportation costs but fulfills the demand that can be satisfied with the limited "real" capacity. From the final table we see also that there are two solution values in the fictitious origin 3 row. There is a value of 1,000 in cell (3, 2) and a value of 2,000 in cell (3, 3). Since these two amounts are from the fictitious origin 3, they do not correspond to actual shipments. Thus, we see that it is the destination 2 demand that will be unfulfilled by 1,000 units and the destination 3 demand that will be unfulfilled by 2,000 units. This total unfulfilled demand (3,000) is the amount of the excess demand (and the amount of the fictitious origin 3 capacity).

An interesting consequence of the increase in destination 3 (Central region) demand is that it interferes with the fulfillment of destination 2 (Western region) demand even though there has been no change in the destination 2 demand. The increase in destination 3 demand by 3,000 units has the effect of causing destination 2's continuing demand of 7,000 units to be unfulfilled by 1,000 units. Also, only 1,000 of the 3,000-unit increase in demand at destination 3 (the Central region) will be fulfilled.

All this assumes that allocations are made on the basis of minimization of

Table 15-12   Insufficient Demand (or Excess Capacity) in the Mattress Problem

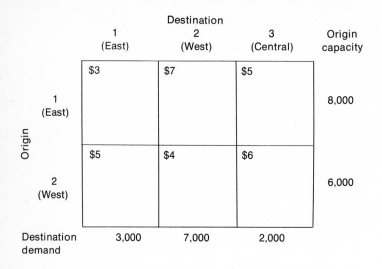

	Destination 1 (East)	2 (West)	3 (Central)	Origin capacity
1 (East)	$3	$7	$5	8,000
2 (West)	$5	$4	$6	6,000
Destination demand	3,000	7,000	2,000	

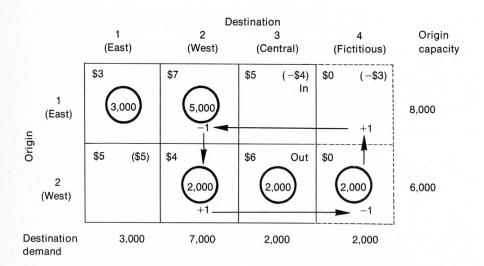

	Destination 1 (East)	2 (West)	3 (Central)	4 (Fictitious)	Origin capacity
1 (East)	$3 3,000	$7 5,000	$5 (−$4) In	$0 (−$3)	8,000
2 (West)	$5 ($5)	$4 2,000	$6 Out 2,000	$0 2,000	6,000
Destination demand	3,000	7,000	2,000	2,000	

total transportation costs. More complete models would incorporate production costs and other costs as well as the transportation costs. This can be done within the basic transportation model that we have developed.

(*Note:* In the second table appearing in Table 15-13, we have another unusual unit-adjustment loop in obtaining the cost indicator for cell (3, 1): + 1($0) − 1($0) + 1($6) − 1($4) + 1($7) − 1($3) = $6. The loop in obtaining the cost indicator for cell (2, 1) in the final table is unusual, too: +1($5) − 1($4) + 1($0) − 1($0) + 1($5) − 1($3) = $3.

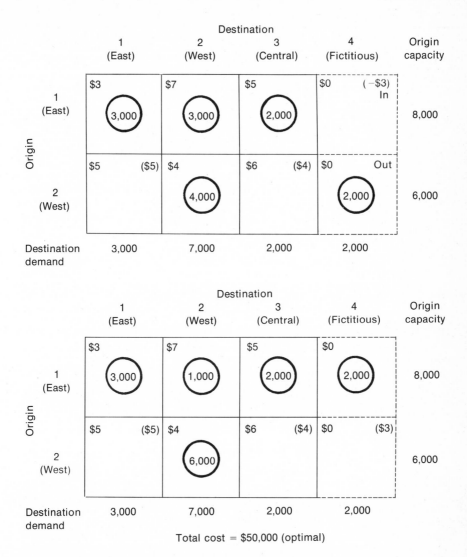

Total cost = $50,000 (optimal)

BREAKDOWN IN THE PROCEDURE: DEGENERACY

Occasionally, we will encounter a problem in which we cannot obtain a cost indicator for each vacant cell. This is due to our having too few circled-cell values (basic variables). This situation is referred to as *degeneracy* in the solution procedure.

There is really no serious problem, however. In such circumstances, we simply "create" a new circled-cell value (a new basic variable) in a vacant cell

Table 15-13   Excess Demand (or Insufficient Capacity) in the Mattress Problem

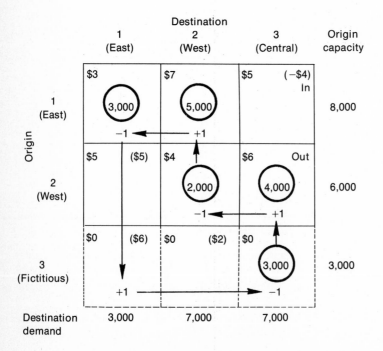

| | Destination | | | Origin |
	1 (East)	2 (West)	3 (Central)	capacity
Origin 1 (East)	$3	$7	$5	8,000
Origin 2 (West)	$5	$4	$6	6,000
Destination demand	3,000	7,000	7,000	

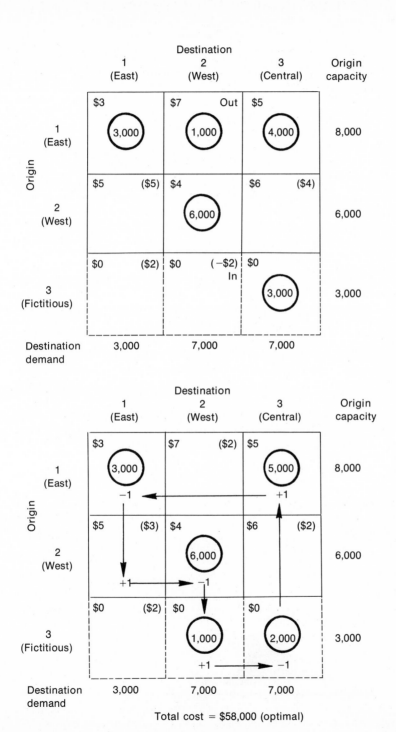

Total cost = $58,000 (optimal)

such that we can obtain a cost indicator for every remaining vacant cell, and then continue with our solution procedure as usual.

The value that we assign to the newly created circled cell is an extremely small amount. It is so small that we treat it as being equal to 0. However, we shall refer to this extremely small amount by the letter e.

To provide an example of degeneracy and how to deal with it, we have modified our mattress problem so that degeneracy is encountered. Suppose that destination 2 demand decreases from 7,000 to 5,000 and at the same time origin 2 capacity is decreased from 6,000 to 4,000.

The solution procedure is started at the top of Table 15-14, but we encounter difficulty in getting cost indicators for the vacant cells. But if we add a circled-cell value to cell (2, 1) we can continue with our computation of the cost indicators. Introducing the letter e to represent the extremely small amount allocated to the new basic cell (2, 1), we compute the necessary cost indicators. We proceed toward an optimal solution, treating e as being equal to 0 in any computations. In large problems we may have to insert more than one additional basic cell.

SUMMARY

1   For transportation-type problems there is a special solution procedure known as the *transportation method*.

2   The special terms in transportation-type problems are *origins* and *destinations*. The *activities* in these problems typically are the amounts to transport from each origin to each destination. What is usually sought is an optimal feasible program of such activities, that is, a pattern of shipment that minimizes total transportation costs.

3   In the usual linear-programming formulation the coefficients in the *objective function* represent the cost of transporting a unit from each origin to each destination. The constraints are all *equation constraints*. There is an equation constraint for each origin, specifying that each origin capacity be fully utilized. And there is an equation constraint for each destination, requiring that each destination demand be exactly fulfilled.

4   Beyond obtaining a minimum-cost pattern of transporting the products, the transportation method provides a means of studying where new production capacity should be located.

5   In the transportation method it is assumed that total demand at all destinations equal the total capacity at all origins. Where demand is insufficient, a *fictitious destination* is created whose demand is set equal to the demand deficiency. This then makes total demand and total capacity equal. Similarly, if total demand is in excess of total capacity, a *fictitious origin* is created whose capacity is set equal to the deficiency in the capacity.

PROBLEMS

15-1   A firm that makes paint products has manufacturing facilities on the East Coast and also in the Central region. The paint products are transported to various distributors and retailers throughout a large, national, market region. With a known demand from each distributor and retailer the least-cost program of shipments from each

Table 15-14 A Breakdown in the Solution Procedure (Degeneracy)

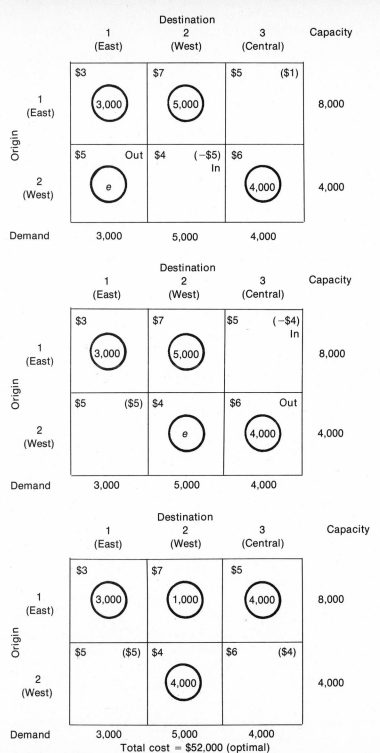

Destination

	1 (East)	2 (West)	3 (Central)	Capacity

Origin

1 (East): $3 | 3,000 | $7 | 5,000 | $5 ($1) | | 8,000

2 (West): $5 Out | e | $4 (−$5) In | | $6 | 4,000 | 4,000

Demand: 3,000 | 5,000 | 4,000

Destination

	1 (East)	2 (West)	3 (Central)	Capacity

Origin

1 (East): $3 | 3,000 | $7 | 5,000 | $5 (−$4) In | | 8,000

2 (West): $5 ($5) | | $4 | e | $6 Out | 4,000 | 4,000

Demand: 3,000 | 5,000 | 4,000

Destination

	1 (East)	2 (West)	3 (Central)	Capacity

Origin

1 (East): $3 | 3,000 | $7 | 1,000 | $5 | 4,000 | 8,000

2 (West): $5 ($5) | | $4 | 4,000 | $6 ($4) | | 4,000

Demand: 3,000 | 5,000 | 4,000

Total cost = $52,000 (optimal)

manufacturing facility to each distributor (or retailer) is desired. Let us form a simple version of the problem by grouping the distributors and retailers into three regions: the Eastern region, the Western region, and the Central region. The following additional data are available:

Origin capacities:
    Origin 1 (East Coast facility)   = 140
    Origin 2 (Central-region facility) = 200

Destination demands:
    Destination 1 (Eastern region) = 120
    Destination 2 (Western region) = 130
    Destination 3 (Central region) = 90

Unit transportation costs:
    Origin 1 to destination 1 = $ 3
    Origin 1 to destination 2 = $11
    Origin 1 to destination 3 = $ 5
    Origin 2 to destination 1 = $ 5
    Origin 2 to destination 2 = $ 7
    Origin 2 to destination 3 = $ 2

a   Formulate the problem in linear-programming form with an objective function, an equation constraint for each destination demand, and an equation constraint for each origin capacity.

b   Form a transportation table (as in Table 15-4) from the linear-programming formulation in *a*.

c   Solve the problem by the transportation method. What is the optimal solution and its total cost?

15-2 A manufacturer of steel products has production facilities at two locations; one facility is in the North Central region, the other in the Southern region. Buyers of the products are distributed over a large area, but let us group the buyers into four market regions: the Northeast region, the North Central region, the Southern region, and the Western region. The manufacturer desires to know the pattern of shipment from each production facility to each buyer that will minimize total transportation costs. The following demand and capacity data are available along with the unit transportation costs.

Origin capacities:
    Origin 1 (North Central facility) = 2,000
    Origin 2 (Southern facility)   = 1,000

Destination demands:
    Destination 1 (Northeast region)   = 600
    Destination 2 (North Central region) = 900
    Destination 3 (Southern region)   = 700
    Destination 4 (Western region)   = 800

Unit transportation costs:
    Origin 1 to destination 1 = $ 8
    Origin 1 to destination 2 = $ 3

Origin 1 to destination 3 = $ 6
Origin 1 to destination 4 = $12
Origin 2 to destination 1 = $10
Origin 2 to destination 2 = $ 6
Origin 2 to destination 3 = $ 4
Origin 2 to destination 4 = $11

a Formulate the problem in linear-programming form with an objective function and the necessary demand and capacity equation constraints.

b Form a transportation table (as in Table 15-4) from the linear-programming formulation in *a*.

c Solve the problem by the transportation method. Indicate the optimal solution and its total cost.

15-3 Let us make some parameter variations like those that often come up in the analysis of real-world problems. Suppose the paint manufacturer in Problem 15-1 finds that demand in the Western region is expected to rise in the next couple of years (demand in other regions remaining about the same). There is the desire to expand the production capacity of the firm to accommodate this increase in demand. But there is a problem regarding the location of the expansion. For example, should the facilities in the Eastern region be expanded or should the expansion take place in the Central region? Let us explore this and see what the effect is upon total transportation costs.

a Suppose the demand in the Western region increases by 75 units (from 130 to 205). Increase the capacity at origin 1 (East Coast facility) by 75 units (from 140 to 215). Solve for the optimal solution of this new problem and indicate the minimum total transportation costs.

b Go back to the original demand and capacity amounts in Problem 15-1. Let us determine the effect of expanding the facilities in the Central region. Again, increase the demand in the Western region from 130 to 205. But now increase the capacity at origin 2 (Central-region facility) by 75 units (from 200 to 275). Solve for the optimal solution of this new problem and indicate the minimum total transportation costs.

c Compare the minimum total transportation costs obtained in *a* and *b*. In terms of transportation costs alone, should the expansion of production facilities occur on the East Coast or in the Central region?

15-4 Let us go back to the original data for the paint manufacturer in Problem 15-1 and suppose that demand in the Eastern region will increase before additional facilities can be constructed at any producing location (assume all other demand amounts remain the same).

a If demand in the Eastern region increases by 75 units (and the production capacities remain unchanged), what is the optimal solution and its total cost? Use the transportation method to solve the problem.

b Interpret the solution obtained in *a*. Does the increase in demand of 75 units in the Eastern region go unfulfilled? Explain.

15-5 Let us examine again the original data for the paint manufacturer in Problem 15-1. Now suppose that demand in the Central region *decreases* by 35 units (from 90 to 55).

a Solve the new problem by the transportation method. Indicate the optimal solution and its total cost.

b   Interpret the solution obtained in *a*. In terms of transportation costs does the 35-unit decrease in demand in the Central region result in a 35-unit decrease in production at the facility in the Central region? Explain.

15-6   The *assignment problem* is a special type of transportation problem that can also be solved by the transportation method discussed in this chapter.

Some real-world problems arise where decisions must be made concerning the assignment of each of a number of different machines to one of a number of different locations, each of a number of persons to one of a number of different positions, and so on. When there are many *assignees* (many machines or persons) and many possible *assignments* (many locations or positions) the decision problem can be quite complex, especially since we usually want to take into account simultaneously the cost (or profit) associated with each possible assignment of each assignee.

In solving such assignment problems by the transportation method we simply treat each assignee (machine) as a separate "origin" and each assignment (location) as a separate "destination" and proceed as usual.

Of course the transportation method of solving such problems is more efficient than the simplex method, but if we have many assignment problems we should try to obtain a special assignment computer program (essentially a variant of the transportation method) that is even more efficient than the standard transportation method. (Incidentally, when we solve assignment problems by the transportation method we invariably encounter the "degeneracy" difficulty. It is easily overcome, however, by the procedure discussed in this chapter.)

Because only one machine can be assigned to each location, we will have an "origin capacity" of 1 for each assignee and a "destination demand" of 1 for each assignment. And, in the upper-left corner of each cell in our transportation table we place the rate of cost (or profit) of each assignee-assignment combination. (*Note:* If we use profits instead of costs our "optimality test" involves a test for any *positive* indicators and the selection of the incoming variable is determined by the largest positive indicator. However, the selection of the outgoing variable remains the same as in the cost-minimization procedure.)

a   Suppose our problem is that of assigning three machines to three different locations so that total cost is minimized. Using the transportation tables, obtain the least-cost assignment of machines to locations (including the minimum total cost) when the cost per hour for each assignment is as follows: [*Note:* In the degeneracy procedure place a new basic variable in cell (1,2) and also one in cell (1,3)]

	Location 1	Location 2	Location 3
Machine 1	$6	$4	$ 7
Machine 2	$5	$8	$10
Machine 3	$6	$9	$ 3

b   Does your solution make sense? Describe the optimal program in words.

c   Now suppose our problem is that of assigning three persons to three different positions so that total profit is maximized. Obtain the maximum-profit assignment of persons to positions (including the optimal total profit) when the profit, in hundreds of dollars per month, is as follows:

[*Note:* In the degeneracy procedure place a new basic variable in cell (1,2) and also one in cell (1,3).]

	Assignment 1	Assignment 2	Assignment 3
Assignee 1	$ 9	$11	$ 6
Assignee 2	$15	$ 8	$10
Assignee 3	$ 7	$14	$12

d In the optimal program of assignments in *c*, is each person assigned to the position where the monthly profit he generates is the greatest? Why or why not? What is gained through the use of formal assignment analysis?

Part Four

Other Approaches to Decision Problems

Chapter 16

Approaches to Inventory Decisions

So far in this book we have not examined any problems involving inventories. But the need for firms and other organizations to hold stocks of materials, supplies, and finished products is apparent in virtually every operation. Consumers, too, are faced with the need to keep some amounts of particular products on hand.

But how large should these stocks of products and materials be? For both firms and consumers this is the primary inventory decision problem.

BACKGROUND FOR INVENTORY ANALYSIS

At the outset, you might well ask: "What is it that in a deeper sense creates this need for inventories?" Before answering this question try to imagine an economic system that has no need to hold inventories at all.

Thus, in a very simplified way let us think of an economic system as a sort of huge machine (or assembly line) operating continuously, with consumers taking the products as they are turned out.

In this supersimplified view, resources would continuously flow into the machine and products would flow out, with really no need for inventories of finished products. Neither would there be a need for inventories of materials if they flowed into the machine at the rates they were needed.

But if any disruptions or chance variations were to occur in the continuous flow of materials and products, we can see that holding inventories at various points in the system could be quite vital.

The Presence of Uncertainty

Of course in real life there are disruptions and chance variations in these flows. First, there is the aspect of *uncertainty*.

With respect to consumers, the exact amount they will take on a given day (or even over a longer period of time) is not known with certainty. To accommodate them, stocks of products usually have to be held.

There is also some uncertainty with respect to the availability of materials (or other inputs to the firms). The times when the needed materials actually will be available for use normally cannot be known with exactness. Commonly, this is so because of delays on the part of suppliers or because of variability in the time it takes to transport items. Yet it is extremely important in some instances to have stocks of items available. For example, the lack of a single component part can stop an entire assembly line.

Production and Purchasing Tend
to Occur in Batches (or Blocks)

Another factor that creates a need for inventories is that both materials and finished products usually are purchased or produced in "batches" or "blocks" of some sort.

For example, in the case of purchasing, firms buy lumber by the carload and consumers buy gasoline by the tankful.

Also, firms generally make products in batches of some sort; that is, the production per day of a particular product is typically undertaken at a much higher daily rate than the daily consumption rate of that same product.

Thus, after a production run of some amount, there is a shift to the making of some other product. With modern technology this is very common because greater production efficiencies are realized in producing at a faster rate.

But such modern production processes do require inventories of the finished products to be held, as demand for the products may be distributed over a fairly long period of time.

Of course whatever the reason for inventories, the basic inventory problem is this: How much of an inventory should be held?

HOW MUCH SHOULD BE ORDERED?

Real-world inventory decisions are often quite complex. They involve events (such as the amount of sales or the use of an item) that may occur over extended periods of time, and they also involve uncertainty with respect to the occurrence of such events. Therefore, we must be aware of the complicated nature of many inventory decisions encountered in actual work, even though at times we focus on some very simplified versions of such problems.

We Know the Demand for the Product over the Period

The basic inventory decision on how much of an item to hold usually reduces itself to answering the following question: How much of an item should be ordered? We refer to this amount as the *order quantity*.

If we happen to know the number of units of a product that will be used or demanded during some period of time (and we ignore any costs of holding the product over the period), the order-quantity decision is quite simple. We merely order an amount that is equal to the total amount that will be demanded.

An Illustration For example, if over a 20-day period the demand for a perishable prescription-drug item varies but is either 60, 80, or 100 (and nothing else) and we know in advance which amount it will be, we have a simple decision problem under *certainty* as represented in Figure 16-1.

In this example we assume that we know (for certain) that total demand will be 80 units. Thus, a probability of 1.00 appears on the branches leading to that event, with 0s appearing on all other branches leading to other events.

Also shown is the profit for each act-event combination. The profit is derived from a known (and constant) unit revenue of $12 and a unit cost of $7. (The unit cost is also known and constant, but it does not include the costs of ordering, of holding the item in inventory, or any other inventory costs. Also, we are assuming that the item has no value at all if it is not sold during the period.)

From Figure 16-1 we see (to no surprise) that the optimal number to order is 80 units, given that we know that 80 units will be demanded during the period. But we formed the tree mainly to get a view of the effect that uncertainty in demand has upon the problem of deciding on the quantity to order. Let us take a look at that general problem next.

When the Demand over the Period is Uncertain

In earlier sections we saw how the appearance of uncertainty in a decision problem can transform a fairly simple problem into a complicated one.

An Illustration Suppose we take the problem in Figure 16-1 and introduce some uncertainty into the demand. Now the firm's probability assessments are .10 for a demand of 60 units, .30 for a demand of 80 units, and .60 for a demand of 100 units. We represent this new problem in Figure 16-2.

Computing an expected profit for each act gives us a basis for determining the optimal quantity to order (using the maximization-of-expected-profit criterion). This optimal quantity to order is 100 units, which has an expected profit of $380.

But as is common in decisions under uncertainty, the optimal act indicated

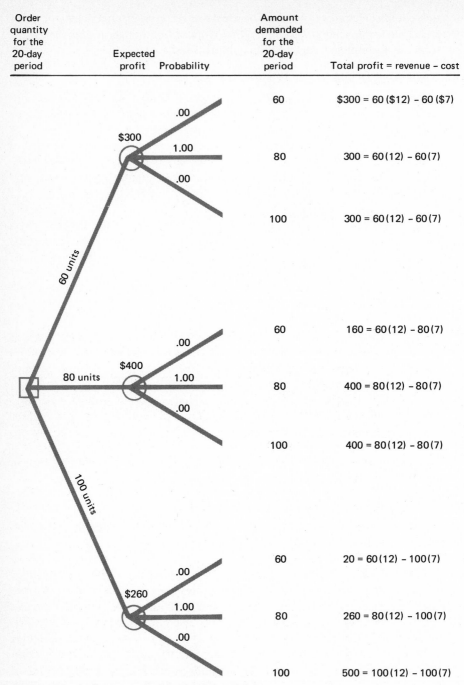

Order quantity for the 20-day period	Expected profit	Probability	Amount demanded for the 20-day period	Total profit = revenue – cost
		.00	60	$300 = 60 ($12) – 60 ($7)
	$300	1.00	80	300 = 60(12) – 60(7)
		.00	100	300 = 60(12) – 60(7)
60 units				
		.00	60	160 = 60(12) – 80(7)
80 units	$400	1.00	80	400 = 80(12) – 80(7)
		.00	100	400 = 80(12) – 80(7)
100 units				
		.00	60	20 = 60(12) – 100(7)
	$260	1.00	80	260 = 80(12) – 100(7)
		.00	100	500 = 100(12) – 100(7)

Figure 16-1 An inventory decision under certainty.

Order quantity for the 20-day period	Expected profit / Expected opportunity loss	Proba-biltiy	Amount demanded for the 20-day period	Profit	Opportunity loss
		.10	60	$300	$0
	$300 $150	.30	80	$300	$100
		.60	100	$300	$200
		.10	60	$160	$140
	$376 $74	.30	80	$400	$0
		.60	100	$400	$100
		.10	60	$20	$280
	$380 $70	.30	80	$260	$140
		.60	100	$500	$0

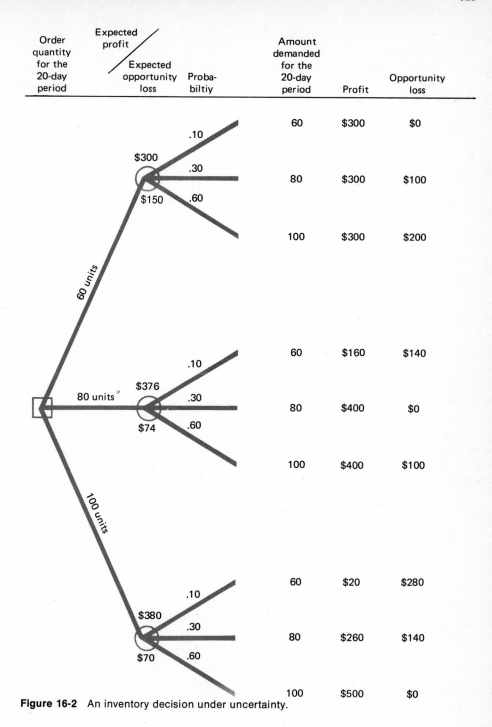

Figure 16-2 An inventory decision under uncertainty.

by our analysis (ordering 100 units) may, in retrospect, be a mistake. If the demand turns out to be 100, of course profits are $500. But if the demand is either 60 or 80, the ordering of 100 units is far from the best act.

The Expected Value of Additional Information

Recalling the concept of opportunity loss, we would say that the opportunity loss is $280 if the demand is 60 (and 100 are ordered). The opportunity loss is $140 if 100 are ordered and the demand turns out to be 80. Thus, the *expected* opportunity loss for the act (ordering 100 units) is $70. The expected "loss of profit" due to the uncertainty is $70 for the 20-day period.

Expected
opportunity
loss for the = .10 ($280) + .30 ($140) + .60 ($0) = $70
act "order
100 units"

From our discussion in Part Two of the book you will recall that the expected opportunity loss of the optimal act is equal to the expected value of perfect information. This, of course, is useful in assessing the value of obtaining additional information before making the order-quantity decision.

Thus, the concepts associated with decision making under uncertainty apply to inventory decisions as well as to other decisions under conditions of uncertainty. As expected, if we move toward more realistic inventory decisions, they become more complex. For example, the possible demand amounts often tend to be many; also, the alternative order quantities frequently become more numerous.

THE OPTIMAL ORDER QUANTITY OR "ECONOMIC ORDER QUANTITY"

When uncertainty in demand is considerable, we have seen above that it is important to try to assess the probabilities of various demand amounts and then incorporate the uncertainty into the order-quantity decision making.

In our example of decision making under uncertainty (in Figure 16-2) we made some assumptions that we should take notice of again. These simplifying assumptions enabled us to see quite clearly the impact of uncertainty upon the decision problem and how we can handle the uncertainty when we ignore other complicating aspects of the problem.

But we are now at a point where we should look at these other aspects of inventory decision problems. In doing this, we shall go back to assuming that we know the total demand for the period under consideration.

In other words, we shall ignore uncertainty again and focus on these other aspects of inventory problems in order to see how they affect the optimal order-quantity decision.

Of course in complex inventory decision problems in the real world, all the factors tend to exert some influence. But the relative degree of influence varies from situation to situation. Sometimes, it is one set of factors that is dominant, and at other times it is another set. As before, we see that the approach that is best to use in studying a given real-world problem depends very much upon which set of assumptions fits the reality best.

Taking into Account the Carrying Costs

Perhaps the main simplifying assumption we made in the example in Figure 16-2 was that of ignoring any costs of carrying (or holding) the items in inventory over the period.

Storage costs, deterioration costs, and interest foregone on the funds tied up in the inventory items are usually the main elements of carrying costs. Let us refer to these costs simply as *carrying costs*. In the section that follows we want to see how such costs affect the optimal order-quantity decision.

Remember that we are now assuming that we know the total demand for the period under consideration. In Figure 16-1 we assumed such certainty (specifically, that we knew in advance that the amount demanded would be 80 units for the 20-day period).

Our optimal order quantity in that example was to order 80 units. This meant that 80 units were ordered and received at the beginning of the period and were all sold (or used) by the end of the period. Thus, there were some units that would be carried in inventory essentially over the entire period, with other units being carried over just parts of the period because they were sold sometime during the period.

Since in Figure 16-1 we ignored any carrying costs of such items being held in inventory, our optimal order-quantity decision was simply to order 80 units at the beginning of the period. But when carrying costs are taken into account, that may not be the best order quantity.

The Average Inventory Level   As we try to take into account the carrying costs, we become concerned with the usually changing inventory level during the period. This is so because total carrying costs are associated with the number of units in stock over the period (such as an average of the amounts in stock each day). As a matter of fact, we could simply count the items in stock each day and take their average. This would give us an *average inventory level* over the 20-day period.

But a quicker and less costly way of getting an estimate of the average inventory level for the period is to take the average of the inventory levels at the beginning of the period and at the end of the period.

For example, if at the beginning of the period the inventory level is 80 units and at the end of the period it is 0 units, the average inventory level is 40 units: $(80 + 0) \div 2 = 40$. This method, however, implicitly assumes a constant daily rate of sales or daily rate of usage. But in some problems this may well not be the case.

We show in Figure 16-3*a* the declining inventory level from the beginning of the 20-day period to the end. The entire 80 units are in inventory at the beginning of the first day and, there is a decline to 0 units at the end of the twentieth day.

Thus, we are assuming a constant daily rate of sales (or usage) for the period. It is 4 units per day: $80 \div 20 = 4$. Also, the average inventory is 40 as given by the height of the graph at the midpoint in the period, that is, at the end of 10 days.

Up to now we have considered placing only one order during the entire 20-day period. But if it is possible to order the item in smaller amounts (and to do this more frequently during the 20-day period), we would suspect that our average inventory level could be reduced. This, in turn, could decrease the carrying costs, since total carrying costs are directly related to the average inventory level.

In Figure 16-3*b* we show the inventory levels associated with ordering 40 units at two different times. The first order of 40 units gives us an inventory of 40 at the beginning of the first day, and it decreases to 0 by the end of the tenth day. Then, a second order increases our inventory level back to 40 units at the

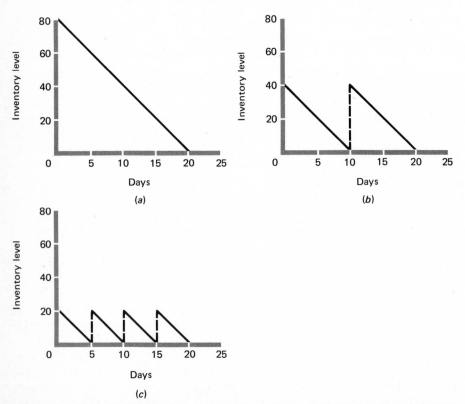

Figure 16-3 The inventory level over the 20-day period *(a)* when the order quantity is 80 units; *(b)* when the order quantity is 40 units, and *(c)* when the order quantity is 20 units.

beginning of the eleventh day. By the end of the twentieth day, the inventory level is 0 again.

What is the average inventory level in Figure 16-3*b* when 40 units are ordered every 10 days of the 20-day period? Of course we suspect that it would be lower because the actual inventory level can never be higher than 40 (when an order has just been received), and usually it is less than 40.

We see from the graph in Figure 16-3*b* that at the beginning of the first day 40 units are in stock, and by the end of the tenth day the inventory level falls to 0. Thus, over this 10-day period the average inventory level is 20 (the average of the inventory levels at the beginning and end of the 10-day period): (40 + 0) ÷ 2 = 20.

The same pattern is repeated for the next 10-day period. It has an average inventory level of 20, also. Thus, for the entire 20-day period the average inventory level is also 20 units. Therefore, *to compute the average inventory level for an entire period* (here, 20 days), we need only *take the order quantity* under consideration (now 40 units) *and divide it by 2*. We state it more formally as follows:

$$
\begin{array}{l}
\text{Average} \\
\text{inventory} \\
\text{level for} \\
\text{a given} \\
\text{order} \\
\text{quantity}
\end{array}
=
\dfrac{\text{order quantity}}{2}
$$

For an order quantity of 40 discussed above, we have the following:

$$
\begin{array}{l}
\text{Average} \\
\text{inventory} \\
\text{level for} \\
\text{an order} \\
\text{quantity} \\
\text{of 40 units}
\end{array}
=
\dfrac{40}{2}
= 20
$$

If the order quantity were to be reduced further, say to 20 (with an order placed every 5 days), we would have a still lower average inventory level. The inventory levels for this order quantity are shown graphically in Figure 16-3*c*. For an order quantity of 20 the average inventory level is 10: 20 ÷ 2 = 10. In Table 16-1 we summarize the average inventory levels for the three selected order quantities.

In Table 16-2 we obtain the total carrying costs for the 20-day period for each of the three order quantities. We assume the carrying cost per unit over the 20-day period to be $3.

Multiplying the average inventory level for the 20-day period by $3 gives us a measure of the total carrying costs for the 20-day period. Clearly, the total

Table 16-1   The Average Inventory Level for Each of Three Selected Order Quantities

Total demand for the 20-day period	Order quantity (the quantity ordered each time, given a total demand of 80 units for the 20-day period)	Number of orders in the 20-day period	Average inventory level (the order quantity divided by 2)
80	80	1	40
80	40	2	20
80	20	4	10

Table 16-2   The Total Carrying Costs over the 20-Day Period for Each of the Three Selected Order Quantities

Total demand for the 20-day period	Order quantity	Number of orders in the 20-day period	Average inventory level	Carrying cost per unit per day	Total carrying costs for the 20-day period
80	80	1	40	$3	40($3) = $120
80	40	2	20	$3	20($3) = $ 60
80	20	4	10	$3	10($3) = $ 30

carrying costs decrease as the order quantity is made smaller (and we order more frequently to satisfy the total demand of 80 units for the 20-day period).

Taking into Account the Ordering Costs

But there are other costs that we have not yet mentioned. Invariably, there are costs (especially wage and salary costs) associated with placing orders, making payments for orders, receiving the items from each order, and placing each order as it is received into inventory. We refer to these costs associated with ordering activities simply as *ordering costs*.

Ordering costs are assumed to be essentially the same total amount for each order (that is, they are assumed to be the same whether the order quantity is 20, 40, or 80). Thus, the ordering costs do not include the cost of the items, only the costs associated with obtaining the items and getting them into inventory. Therefore, these costs are directly related to the number of orders placed in a period. In our example above, when more orders were placed, we should have thought about incorporating ordering costs, too. We do this now in Table 16-3.

Table 16-3 The Total Inventory Costs over the 20-Day Period for Each of the Three Selected Order Quantities

Total demand for the 20-day period	Order quantity	Average inventory level	Carrying costs per unit per day	Total carrying costs for the 20-day period	Number of orders in the 20-day period	Ordering costs per order	Total ordering costs for the 20-day period	Total inventory costs (total carrying costs plus total ordering costs for the 20-day period)
80	80	40	$3	$120	1	$30	$ 30	$150
80	40	20	$3	$ 60	2	$30	$ 60	$120*
80	20	10	$3	$ 30	4	$30	$120	$150

*Minimum

We obtain the ordering costs for the period simply by multiplying the number of orders placed by the cost per order.

Each order-quantity decision involves deciding how many orders to place during the 20-day period to satisfy the total demand of 80 units. If the order quantity is 80 units, only one order is needed. However, if the order quantity is 40 units, two orders are needed to satisfy the demand of 80 units.

In Table 16-3 we assume the cost per order to be $30. Thus, an order quantity of 80 incurs a total ordering cost of $30 (1 order × $30 = $30), whereas an order quantity of 40 units results in a total ordering cost of $60 for the 20-day period: 2 orders × $30 = $60.

The Optimal Order Quantity or "Economic Order Quantity"

In studying Table 16-3 we see that as the order quantity is reduced (and orders are placed more frequently) the *total ordering costs* for the 20-day period *rise*. However, the *total carrying costs* for the 20-day period *decrease* as the order quantity is reduced (because the average inventory level is lowered). Thus, the optimal order quantity in a given situation depends very much upon the relationship between ordering costs and carrying costs.

In the extreme-right column of Table 16-3 the total carrying costs and the total ordering costs for each of the order quantities of 80, 40, and 20 are summed. Thus, from these three order quantities we can identify the one with the lowest total inventory-associated cost. We see that the best of these three order quantities is 40 in terms of minimizing the total inventory costs as we have described them.

A graph of the general relationship of the two types of inventory costs is shown in Figure 16-4. The graph corresponds to the data in Table 16-3, but smooth curves have been drawn through the points to indicate the general relationship.

Various order quantities are represented on the horizontal axis in Figure 16-4, and costs are represented on the vertical axis. Thus, we see graphically the point made earlier about ordering costs and carrying costs: total ordering costs for a given period decrease as the order quantity increases, and total carrying costs for the given period increase as the order quantity increases.

The sum of the two types of costs gives the *total inventory costs* for each order quantity. As shown in the upper section of Figure 16-4, total inventory costs typically will decline as the order quantity is increased from 0, but eventually they will rise as the order quantity reaches larger amounts (with carrying costs dominating due to the large average inventory levels).

Thus, there is an order quantity that is associated with the minimum point on the total-inventory-cost curve. Identification of the optimum order quantity is shown in Figure 16-4 by dropping a perpendicular line to the horizontal axis from the minimum point on the total-inventory-cost curve. In Table 16-3 we considered just three possible order quantities and happened to have included the optimal order quantity of 40. The graph in Figure 16-4 represents the general case of considering many more possible order quantities.

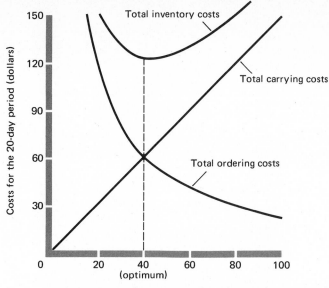

Figure 16-4 Total inventory cost and its components (carrying costs and ordering costs) in relation to the order quantity.

The graph in Figure 16-4 is also associated with the determination of the optimal order quantity by means of a formula, often called the *E.O.Q. formula* (for "economic order quantity").

Let us now illustrate the solution to our familiar problem by using the E.O.Q. formula. This formula is based on the following statement that we have already discussed:

$$\begin{matrix} \text{Total} & & \text{total} & & \text{total} \\ \text{inventory} & = & \text{carrying} & + & \text{ordering} \\ \text{costs} & & \text{costs} & & \text{costs} \end{matrix}$$

In more detail it becomes

	Total carrying costs			Total ordering costs	

$$\text{Total inventory costs} = \begin{pmatrix} \text{carrying} \\ \text{costs} \\ \text{per unit} \\ \text{over} \\ \text{the} \\ \text{20-day} \\ \text{period} \end{pmatrix} \begin{pmatrix} \text{Average} \\ \text{inventory} \\ \text{level} \end{pmatrix} + \begin{pmatrix} \text{ordering} \\ \text{costs} \\ \text{per} \\ \text{order} \end{pmatrix} \begin{pmatrix} \text{number} \\ \text{of orders} \\ \text{placed in} \\ \text{the} \\ \text{20-day} \\ \text{period} \end{pmatrix}$$

And more compactly,

	Total carrying costs	Total ordering costs

$$\text{Total inventory} = \quad c_c\,\frac{q}{2} \quad + \quad c_o\,\frac{d}{q}$$
$$\text{costs}$$

where q = order quantity (amount ordered each time)
  d = total demand for the 20-day period
  c_c = carrying cost per unit for the 20-day period
  c_o = ordering cost per order

Thus, for any order quantity selected we can substitute into the formula the appropriate values and obtain the associated total inventory costs. For an order quantity of 20 we have the following:

$$
\begin{aligned}
\text{Total inventory costs (for an order quantity of 20)} \;
&= c_c\,\frac{q}{2} + c_o\,\frac{d}{q} \\
&= \$3\left(\frac{20}{2}\right) + \$30\left(\frac{80}{20}\right) \\
&= \$30 + \$120 \\
&= \$150
\end{aligned}
$$

Although it can be shown more convincingly by more advanced mathematical methods, we can see graphically from Figure 16-4 an important relationship between the minimum point on the total inventory-cost curve and the graphs of total carrying cost and total ordering cost.

The relationship is this: The minimum point on the total inventory-cost curve will always be directly above the point of intersection of the total carrying-cost graph and the total ordering-cost graph.

Thus, if we drop a perpendicular line from the minimum point on the total inventory-cost curve to the horizontal axis, it will pass through the point of intersection of the graphs of total carrying cost and total ordering cost. The point on the horizontal axis associated with the perpendicular line identifies the optimal order quantity for the problem. For our particular problem the optimal order quantity is seen to be 40 units.

But we are working toward the use of the E.O.Q. formula to determine the optimal order quantity for all such problems, and the next step in this direction builds upon the relationships described in the previous paragraphs. It is this: If the total carrying-cost graph and the total ordering-cost graph intersect at the q-value (the order quantity) when total inventory costs are at a minimum, then we can say that *at the optimal order quantity the two types of costs must be equal.*

Thus, if we use the term $c_c\, q/2$ to represent total carrying costs and the term $c_o d/q$ to represent total ordering costs, we can set them equal to one another as follows:

$$c_c\, \frac{q}{2} = c_o\, \frac{d}{q}$$

or

$$\frac{c_c\, q}{2} = \frac{c_o\, d}{q}$$

By cross multiplying, we have

$$c_c\, q^2 = 2\, c_o\, d$$

$$q^2 = \frac{2\, c_o\, d}{c_c}$$

$$q = \sqrt{\frac{2\, c_o\, d}{c_c}}$$

Optimal
order
quantity
(or E.O.Q.)
$$q = \sqrt{\frac{2 c_o\, d}{c_c}}$$

For our particular problem discussed above, we substitute for c_o the $30 ordering cost per order, for c_c the $3 carrying cost per unit for the 20-day period, and for d the 80 units of demand over the 20-day period.

Optimal
order
quantity,
(or E.O.Q.)
$$q = \sqrt{\frac{2(\$30)(80)}{\$3}} = \sqrt{1{,}600}$$
$$= 40$$

The optimal order quantity of 40 is the very same optimal order quantity illustrated graphically in Figure 16-4 and in table form in Table 16-3. Once we have become familiar with the E.O.Q. formula, the direct use of it is the most effective and accurate way to identify the optimal order quantity.

But What if Demand Is Uncertain?

The simple E.O.Q. formula assumes that total demand for the period (and the other constants in the problem) do not change from their assumed values. But very often total demand for a period may not turn out to be the same as that assumed.

For example, in our problem above we assumed a total demand of 80 units for the 20-day period. But suppose that although 80 is our best estimate of demand we also believe that the actual demand may well be higher or lower than 80.

What can we do? We can make a simple *sensitivity test* to see how much the optimal order quantity will change if the total demand is some amount other than the 80 we assumed.

Upon doing this we find the optimal order quantity does not change greatly as the total demand is changed. For example, if we go to extremes and assume a total demand of 45 for the entire period (instead of 80), we find that the optimal order quantity falls only from 40 to 30. And when total demand is 125, the optimal order quantity rises only to 50.

Thus, the point to be made here is that if minor errors occur in the estimate of demand for the entire period, the optimal order quantity will change by only a small amount, and from a practical standpoint this helps make the E.O.Q. formula very useful.

WHEN TO PLACE THE ORDER: THE REORDER LEVEL OF INVENTORY

Perhaps we are all familiar with the problem of trying to decide *when* to reorder some item so that our stock of it is not depleted before the new order arrives.

It turns out not to be a difficult decision problem if we know just when we will run out of stock and exactly how long it takes to replenish the stock. What makes it difficult is when there is uncertainty in the demand for the item or uncertainty in the time it takes for replenishment of the stock. We shall explore uncertainty in demand in a later section, but right now let us examine further the "reorder decision" under conditions of certainty.

If in our prescription-drug product above we know for sure that we will run out of stock 10 days from now and that it takes 3 days to replenish the stock, we simply place an order 7 days from now so that the order is received in time to avoid being out of stock.

The Reorder Level of Inventory (or Reorder Point)

In much practical inventory decision making it becomes desirable to express such a decision procedure in terms of a *reorder inventory level* (or *reorder point*), that is, the inventory level at which time a new order is to be placed.

To obtain the reorder point in a problem, we need to know the length of the replenishment period (also referred to as the *lead time*). As we implied above, this refers to the time it takes to replenish the stock of an item. The date at which time an order is placed usually has to "lead" the date at which time the order will be needed.

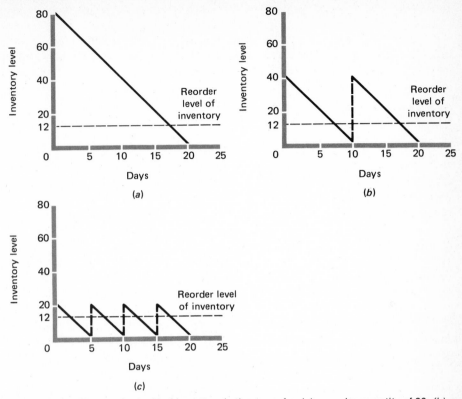

Figure 16-5 The reorder level of inventory is the same for *(a)* an order quantity of 80, *(b)* an order quantity of 40, or *(c)* an order quantity of 20.

Let us suppose that this replenishment period (or lead time) is 3 days, as assumed above. But another factor we need to know is the *rate* at which the item is sold or used. Suppose it is 4 units per day.[1]

Thus, with a replenishment period of 3 days we would want to place the order 3 days before the inventory level reaches 0. But what would the *inventory level* be 3 days before it reaches 0? It would be 12 units, because "backing up" in time from an inventory level of 0 would mean that each day 4 more units would be in inventory. Backing up 3 days would mean that 12 units would be in inventory. Thus, that is the inventory level when a new order should be placed. We say that the reorder point is at an inventory level of 12 units.

We also show in Figure 16-5 that the reorder point is the same for all the order quantities we considered. Thus, generally, we have the following expression:

---

[1]This rate of demand (or rate of use) is equal to the slope (absolute value) of the associated inventory-level graph in Figure 16-3*b:* rise $\div$ run $= (-40) \div 10 = -4$. The absolute value of -4 is 4.

$$\begin{matrix} \text{Reorder} \\ \text{level of} \\ \text{inventory} \end{matrix} = \begin{pmatrix} \text{rate of} \\ \text{sales} \\ \text{(or use)} \\ \text{of the} \\ \text{item} \end{pmatrix} \begin{pmatrix} \text{length of the} \\ \text{replenishment} \\ \text{period (or} \\ \text{lead time)} \end{pmatrix}$$

And (just as we indicated above) the reorder level for our prescription-drug example is found to be 12 units.

$$\begin{matrix} \text{Reorder} \\ \text{level of} \\ \text{inventory} \end{matrix} = (4)(3)$$

$$= 12$$

PROTECTION AGAINST BEING OUT OF STOCK: KEEPING A SAFETY STOCK OF SOME AMOUNT

In our E.O.Q. formula (and the associated analysis) we have been assuming that we know the rate of demand (or rate of use) for an item. But in real-world problems often we cannot be so sure of the rate of demand. Thus, the depletion of an inventory of an item cannot be foreseen accurately. Of course it is not uncommon for actual inventory levels to go to 0 before a new order arrives.

Being out of stock is undesirable to the firm both from a short- and long-run standpoint. First, sales are often lost because of a shift by the buyer to another supplier. Such lost sales usually result in immediate lost profits.

Additionally, there is often an extended loss of a customer due to being out of stock. Thus, from a long-run point of view the loss in sales and profit is commonly much greater than that associated with a single lost sale.

There are two main ways that the firm can deal with this problem. One way is to try to get the customer to take delayed delivery of the item; that is, delivery would occur when the stock is replenished. This arrangement is sometimes referred to as the *backordering* of an item. These backorders are usually the first to be filled when a new shipment of the item arrives.

In many situations, however, the backordering approach is of very limited usefulness because customers have immediate alternative sources where their demands can be fulfilled.

The second major way of dealing with the out-of-stock problem is to keep an extra amount of inventory on hand to help meet any demand in excess of that expected. This extra amount of inventory is called a *safety stock* of the item.

In Figure 16-6 we show a possible safety-stock amount of 4 units for our prescription-drug example (where an optimal order quantity of 40 was found). In this safety-stock approach we will actually have 4 units in inventory even when the inventory level in our analysis is 0. But of course the safety-stock items would be indistinguishable from the other items in the inventory.

The usual time when an item is out of stock is during the replenishment

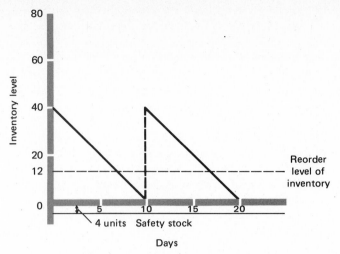

Figure 16-6   A safety stock amount of 4 units.

period (or lead time) of the item. It is then that the actual inventory level is low. Therefore, the actual demand amount that occurs during that period will determine whether or not the item becomes out of stock.

In our prescription-drug example we obtained a reorder point of 12. Thus, when the inventory level reaches 12 units, the replenishment period begins with 12 units still being available. (This reorder point is shown again in Figure 16-6.) In our original analysis we assumed that 12 units would be demanded over this replenishment period of 3 days: daily rate of demand × length of replenishment period = (4) (3) = 12.

Demand Amounts and Their Probabilities during the Replenishment Period

But now we must face up to uncertainty in demand. We are now saying that amounts other than 12 units may be demanded during the replenishment period. Suppose these demand amounts are 8, 12, 16, or 20 units.

These amounts may have been demanded during such replenishment periods in the past. Suppose the relative frequency of each demand amount can be obtained and is as follows:

Amount demanded during replenishment period	Relative frequency of this demand amount during replenishment
8	.15
12	.60
16	.20
20	.05

Then, let us use these relative frequencies as the probabilities of the various demand amounts in such future replenishment periods. We summarize these probabilities in Table 16-4.

Now if the actual demand turns out to be either 8 or 12 units during the replenishment period, we would *not* go out of stock. The units available are 12, and the demand is either 8 or 12. But if the demand amounts are either 16 or 20, we *will* go out of stock and will incur some adverse consequences as discussed earlier.

Keeping a safety stock of some amount will reduce such out-of-stock occurrences and the adverse consequences associated with them. We can see from our example above that if we keep a safety stock of 8 units, there could be no unfilled demand (under our assumed demand amounts) because even if the demand is 20 during the replenishment period (the highest possible demand), our usual stock of 12, supplemented by the safety stock of 8 units, will allow all 20 units of demand to be filled.

Safety-Stock Costs: Carrying Costs of the Safety Stock and Expected Costs of Being Out of Stock

Of course there are costs (particularly carrying costs) associated with keeping a safety stock. And the larger the safety-stock amount the higher are the total safety-stock carrying costs. However, carrying a large safety stock decreases the expected cost of being out of stock.

Of course what is desired is the identification of the safety-stock amount with the lowest total safety-stock costs. But first we must find the expected out-of-stock costs for each safety-stock amount that we might consider holding.

To obtain for each safety-stock amount the expected cost of being out of stock (for a single replenishment period), we construct the tree shown in Figure 16-7. We are considering the safety-stock amounts of 0 units (no safety stock at all), 4 units, or 8 units.

The possible demand amounts during the replenishment period with their

Table 16-4 Demand Amounts and Their Probabilities during the Replenishment Period

Demand amount during the replenishment period (the lead time)	Probability of this demand amount occurring
8	.15
12	.60
16	.20
20	.05

Act: Safety stock amount chosen (with the reorder inventory level of 12 units)	Expected cost of being out of stock	Probability	Amount demanded during replenishment period (lead time)	Unfulfilled demand (amount of stockout): 12 units available for the period	Cost of not satisfying the amount demanded, $20 per unit

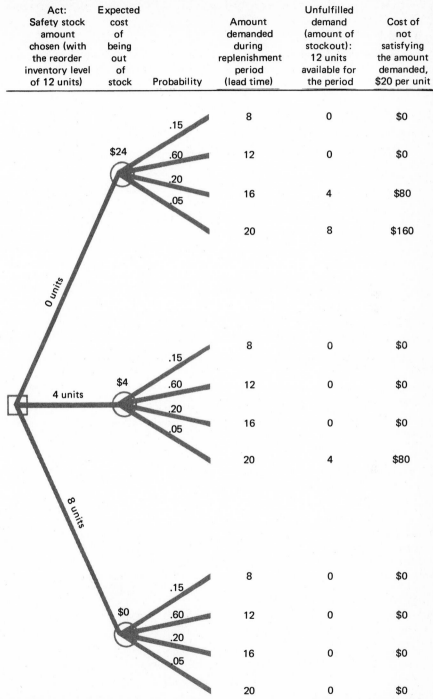

Figure 16-7 Obtaining the expected cost of being out of stock for the three safety stock amounts (0, 4, and 8 units).

Table 16-5 Total Safety-Stock Costs for the Selected Safety-Stock Amounts

Optimal order quantity	Number of orders during the 20-day period	Reorder inventory level	Safety-stock amount	Expected cost of being out of stock with this safety-stock level for each replenishment period	Expected cost of being out of stock (2 periods)	Total additional carrying cost of this safety-stock level for the 20-day period	Total safety-stock costs (expected cost of being out of stock plus the cost of carrying the safety stock)
40	2	12	0	$24	2($24) = $48	0($3) = $ 0	$48
40	2	12	4	$ 4	2($ 4) = $ 8	4($3) = $12	$20 (minimum)
40	2	12	8	$ 0	2($ 0) = $ 0	8($3) = $24	$24

probabilities of occurrence are also shown. For each act-event combination, we obtain the unfulfilled demand and the cost of its nonfulfillment. We assume that each unit of demand that is unfilled incurs a "cost" of $20 per unit (due to lost sales and profits, perhaps over an extended period of time).

Computing the expected cost for each act (each safety-stock amount) gives .us $24 for a safety stock of 0 units, $4 for 4 units, and $0 for 8 units. We record these expected costs for *one* replenishment period in Table 16-5. Since there are two such replenishment periods during the 20-day period in our problem (when the optimal order quantity is 40), we must multiply each of the expected costs by 2. This gives us $48 for a safety stock of 0 units, $8 for 4 units, and $0 for 8 units. We record these results in Table 16-5, too.

We see clearly in Table 16-5 that by increasing the safety-stock amount high enough we can eliminate any out-of-stock costs. But of course the higher safety-stock amounts incur higher safety-stock carrying costs.

Recalling that in our problem the carrying cost per unit for the entire 20-day period is $3, we simply multiply each safety-stock amount by $3. This gives us carrying costs of $0 for a safety-stock amount of 0 units, $12 for 4 units, and $24 for 8 units.

Finally, summing the carrying costs and the total expected cost of being out of stock for each safety-stock amount gives us $48 for 0 units, $20 for 4 units, and $24 for 8 units. Clearly, of the three safety-stock amounts considered, the minimum total safety-stock costs are associated with a safety-stock amount of 4 units.

SUMMARY

1 The basic inventory decision problem is that of choosing an *order quantity* (that is, an amount of an item to order).

2 If total demand for a period is known (and the minimization of carrying costs plus ordering costs is of primary concern) the optimal order quantity is most quickly obtained through the use of the *E.O.Q. formula* (the economic-order-quantity formula).

3 The *reorder level of inventory* is determined by the *rate of demand* (or rate of use) of an item and the *replenishment time (lead time)*. Multiplying the rate of demand by the replenishment time gives the reorder level of inventory (the point at which a new order is placed).

4 The *safety stock* of an item refers to an additional amount of inventory kept to reduce the chances of being out of stock on an item. The optimal safety-stock amount depends on the relationship between the carrying costs of various safety-stock levels and the expected cost of being out of stock (for various safety-stock levels). The optimal safety-stock amount is that which minimizes the sum of these two types of costs.

PROBLEMS

16-1 Suppose that in the problem shown in Figure 16-2 the probabilities of the total demand amounts are the following (instead of those appearing in the original problem:

Total demand amount	Probability of this demand amount
60	.10
80	.40
100	.50

a   If only one order is to be placed for the entire 20-day period, what is the optimal order quantity using the maximization-of-expected-profit criterion?

b   What is the expected cost of uncertainty in this inventory decision problem? Why is it not $0? Explain.

c   Do the new probabilities increase or decrease the probability of decision error under the optimal act (optimal order quantity)? Explain.

d   What is the most that should be paid for receiving any additional information about the demand before making the decision on the order quantity? Explain.

16-2   A bookstore for the coming year has to decide on the number of copies to order of a new book (a travel guide for motorists). First, the total demand for the coming year must be estimated. Suppose this assessment results in the following demand amounts and their associated probabilities:

Demand amount (copies)	Probability of this demand amount
100	.10
200	.20
300	.40
400	.30

The order quantities considered are four in number: 100, 200, 300, or 400. Selling price per copy is $10 (and constant). Acquisition cost per copy is $6 (and constant). Unsold units are assumed to have no value, and no carrying costs or ordering costs are to be taken into account.

a   Construct a tree of the order-quantity decision representing the act-event combinations with their appropriate profit consequences (unit profit is to be interpreted as selling price less acquisition cost).

b   Insert the appropriate probabilities on the branches leading to the demand amounts. Determine the expected profit for each act and identify the optimal order quantity under the maximization-of-expected-profit criterion.

c   What is the "expected cost of uncertainty" in this decision problem? Why is it not $0?

d   What is the expected value of perfect information in this problem? Explain the basis for its value.

e   If any unsold copies can be disposed of for $2 per copy, does the optimal order quantity change? Does the expected value of additional information change (for example, the expected value of perfect information)? How much does it change? Why?

16-3 a Suppose that in the prescription-drug problem discussed in this chapter (and illustrated in Table 16-3) the carrying costs per unit for the 20-day period are increased (from $3 to $12). Does this carrying-cost change tend to increase or decrease the optimal order quantity?

b After the change in carrying costs in *a* what is the optimal order quantity?

16-4 a Let us now go back to the original prescription-drug example (in Table 16-3) and consider only an increase in total ordering costs from $30 per order to $120 per order. Does this ordering-cost change tend to increase or decrease the optimal order quantity?

b Determine the optimal order quantity after the change in ordering costs in *a*.

16-5 a Now let us consider a simultaneous 200 percent increase in *both* carrying costs (per unit over the 20-day period) and total ordering costs (per order) in the original prescription-drug problem in Table 16-3. Do these changes tend to increase or decrease the optimal order quantity?

b After the changes in *a* what is the optimal order quantity? Does your answer make sense? Explain.

16-6 In the bookstore example in Problem 16-2, suppose total demand for the year is assumed to be 300 copies (that is, total demand is assumed to be known). Thus, given a total demand of 300 copies, let us consider different order quantities that will satisfy the total demand for the year but that will also minimize total inventory costs (carrying costs plus ordering costs). The following inventory costs are assumed to be applicable:

Carrying cost per copy for the year = $1
Ordering cost per order = $6

a Compute the carrying costs and ordering costs for order quantities of 50, 100, and 150. Place the results in a table (along the lines of Table 16-3 for the prescription-drug example).

b From the set of three order quantities selected for analysis in *a*, which has the minimum total inventory cost?

c Using the E.O.Q. formula, determine the optimal order quantity. Is it one of the three selected for analysis in *b*?

d What is gained through the use of the E.O.Q. formula?

16-7 Suppose in the bookstore example in Problem 16-6 the demand amount for the year (assumed to be known) is 400 copies, instead of 300, and the carrying costs per copy per year are one-third higher, too. Using the E.O.Q. formula, determine the optimal order quantity under these conditions. Does your solution make sense to you? Explain.

16-8 In the prescription-drug example illustrated in Table 16-3 suppose the replenishment time (lead time) is 5 days instead of 3 days. What then is the reorder level of inventory?

16-9 In the original prescription-drug example (shown in Table 16-3) what is the reorder inventory level (to the nearest whole number) if the total demand for the 20-day period is 125 instead of 80? Assume that the replenishment time and all other data are the same as in the original problem.

16-10 Let us continue with the bookstore example as it appeared in Problem 16-6. Recall that the total demand was 300 copies for the coming year (365 days).

a What is the rate of demand per day?

b   Compute the reorder level of inventory (to the nearest whole number) if the replenishment period (lead time) is 12 days.

16-11   Continuing with the bookstore problem as it appeared in Problem 16-6, let us determine the optimal safety-stock level if the demand probabilities are the following during the replenishment period: (Assume the cost of being out of stock is $4 per unit. Also, use any data in Problem 16-6 that is needed.)

Demand amount during replenishment period	Probability of this demand amount
5	.10
10	.40
15	.30
20	.20

a   Construct a tree along the lines of the one in Figure 16-7 to obtain the expected cost of the safety-stock levels of 0, 5, and 10.

b   Construct a table (similar to the one in Table 16-5) in order to determine the optimal safety-stock amount.

c   What is the optimal safety-stock amount?

Chapter 17

Markov Processes
and Decisions

In this chapter we return to the analysis of decision under uncertainty that was undertaken in Part Two. There we investigated procedures primarily related to one-time decisions where the outcomes of the acts were uncertain.

In those earlier sections, we really said nothing about repeating a decision, except perhaps to give some intuitive meaning to such elements as expected profit and expected cost. And in those discussions we made an important assumption. We assumed that the probabilities of the states (the basic events) *held constant* from one time to the next. The only changes that came about in the probabilities of the states occurred when additional information was received (such as a test outcome) which in turn permitted a revision of the (prior) probabilities of the states.

With respect to many real-world situations, however, there is a need to modify the probability assignments of the states for each run of a chance process *in light of the state that occurred in the just-previous run*. The general probability model that permits a representation of this situation is the *Markov-process model*. In this chapter we shall examine briefly its main properties and its major assumptions.

Also, we shall illustrate types of problems where the Markov-process model represents quite well the real situation to be studied. The main feature of this model is that it can represent those real-world chance processes where the probabilities of the states are affected by the state that occurred in the immediately preceding run of the chance process.

This development in our study also allows the time factor to be incorporated more explicitly into the analysis. The inclusion of the element of time permits an analysis of decision making over more than one time period, with the probability assignments to the states being affected by the occurrence of the state in the immediately preceding period. First, however, let us examine the Markov process apart from any decision.

MARKOV PROCESSES

A Markov process is a chance process in which there is a set of possible states (events), one of which occurs in a given period of time, whose probabilities of occurrence *depend only upon the state occurring in the immediately preceding period.* These probabilities are often referred to as *transition probabilities* because over many periods a *movement* from one state to another usually occurs. (However, the concepts can be applied to problems where time is not a factor. Then the use of the term "stages" is more appropriate than "periods.")

Also, these probabilities may be called *conditional probabilities* because the probability assignments to each of the states depend upon the immediately preceding state. A useful way to represent the possible states in a Markov-process model and their transition probabilities is by a *transition diagram,* such as that shown in Figure 17-1.

In this illustration there are three possible states with the given transition probabilities placed on the arrows that indicate the direction of possible movement from one state to another. Thus, given that state 1 has occurred in the preceding period, the probability of moving to state 2 in the next period is .90 and the probability of remaining in state 1 is .10. There is no arrow from state 1 to state 3. This indicates that this movement is impossible. Implicitly, there is a probability of .00 assigned to this transition.

Similarly, given that state 2 or state 3 has occurred in the immediately preceding period, the probabilities of the occurrence of states 1, 2, and 3 are seen represented in Figure 17-1. That the transition probabilities of a Markov-process model are *conditional* probabilities is made even clearer when we place the states and their probabilities in the tree shown in Figure 17-2. The probabilities of the states clearly depend upon the preceding state.

In the earlier discussions in Part Two we encountered differing conditional probabilities of the states, but those conditional probabilities were dependent on such factors as test outcomes (or sample outcomes) and were obtained by using Bayes' formula, which combines prior and additional test information (or sample information). Here in the Markov-process models the only basis for the probability assignments to the states is the knowledge of the immediately preceding state.

The transition probabilities remain fixed from period to period (at least in the common Markov-process models). This may, at first, suggest that the Markov-

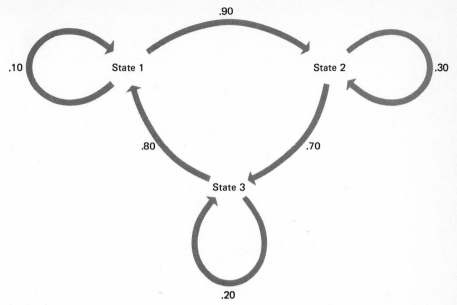

Figure 17-1   Transition diagram of a Markov process.

process model has very limited application. Of course it is limited, as all models are, and also in a particular way, but the potential usefulness still is quite great.

At first glance, one of the concepts that the Markov-process models seem not to represent very well is the generally accepted idea that all actual events are in a sense created from previous actual events (but not necessarily events in the immediately preceding period). In the Markov-process analysis, this long stream of influence from past events is definitely not denied; it merely represents this influence through those events of the immediately preceding period. (However, the definition of the immediately preceding period in an application can vary.) This feature of the Markov-process model does constitute an important limitation on its usefulness, but at the same time this very characteristic that limits its application enhances its practical value where it does correspond satisfactorily to a segment of reality. One reason for its great practical value is that the empirical data needed (transition relative frequencies to provide the transition probabilities) are usually much easier to obtain for a Markov-process model than for many other contending models.

Probability of the Process Being in a Particular State after a Specific Number of Periods

One of the questions that arises in connection with Markov-process models is this: After a specific number of future periods have elapsed, what is the probability that the process is in a particular state? Let us illustrate this. Suppose in the example shown in Figure 17-1 we want to know the probability that the process is

Current
state
of the
process

State
of the
process in
next
period (stage)

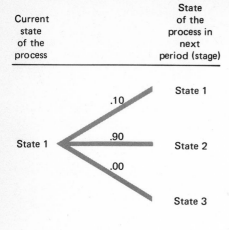

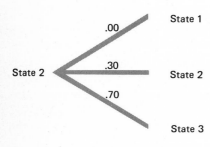

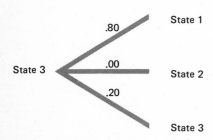

Figure 17-2 Conditional probabilities in
a Markov-process model.

in state 3 at the end of two periods. To obtain this probability we have to know first the current (or immediately preceding) state of the process.

Suppose that the process is in state 1. Then, in the first period the conditional probabilities of moving to states 1, 2, or 3 are .10, .90, and .00, respectively. In the second period it is possible still to be in state 1, and the conditional probabilities of states 1, 2, and 3 are the same as in the first period. However, in the first period it is possible to move to state 2, and thus the probabilities of states 1, 2, and 3 (given that particular state) are .00, .30, and .70, respectively.

Perhaps the tree diagram in Figure 17-3 represents this sort of thing best. Also, it facilitates the computation of the probability of being in a particular state at the end of a specific number of periods. The tree diagram in Figure 17-3 represents the case of two periods. If we multiply through the tree, we obtain the probabilities in the right-hand column of Figure 17-3.

These probabilities are called *joint probabilities* because they are the probabilities of the joint occurrence of particular states (events). For example, moving through the uppermost branches of Figure 17-3 represents the occurrence of state 1 in the first period and state 1 in the second period. This joint occurrence is the *product* of their separate probabilities as obtained by multiplying through the uppermost branches of the tree. It is found to be .01: (.10)(.10) = .01.

Ordinarily, it is possible (at the end of some specific number of periods) to be in a particular state with more than one history of state transitions, but from Figure 17-3 we can see that the other routes by which the process might be in state 1 at the end of two periods each has a joint probability of .00.

However, the process can be in state 2 at the end of two periods with two different histories: state 1 in the first period and state 2 in the second, or state 2 in the first period and state 2 in the second. Since these joint occurrences are mutually exclusive, we can add the probabilities .09 and .27, giving us the probability of .36 of the process being in state 2 at the end of two periods.

The most probable state of the process at the end of two periods is state 3. It is .63 and can be accomplished only by going to state 2 in the first period and to state 3 in the second period. Of course there is the high probability of .90 on the movement to state 2 in the first period and a relatively high probability of .70 of going to state 3 from state 2 in the second period.

For more periods and more states the basic procedure is the same. Only more computation is involved. Also, we note that the joint probabilities in Figure 17-3 sum to 1.00 because it is assumed that the process must be in one of the specified states at the end of two periods.

VARIATION IN RAW MATERIALS AS A MARKOV PROCESS

In Part Two of this book we examined a packaging-machine problem in which there was uncertainty with regard to the quality of materials to be used in a packaging process. There it was assumed that the quality of the materials could be either good or poor. Part of the problem at that time involved the choice of

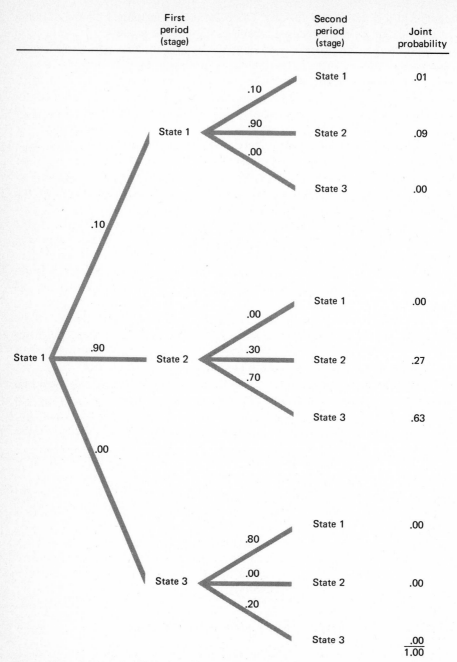

Figure 17-3   Joint probabilities in a Markov-process model.

using an old machine or a new machine in the packaging activity. For the moment, however, let us postpone any analysis involving decisions and focus only on the chance process involved in obtaining either good- or poor-quality materials.

In Part Two we assumed that the (prior) probabilities assigned to the states (events) "good-quality materials" and "poor-quality materials" were based on simple relative frequencies of the receipt of "good-quality materials" and "poor-quality materials" in past shipments. For example, when 20 out of 100 of the past shipments had been of poor quality, a probability of 20 percent was assigned to the state "poor-quality materials" in the future.

Now we shall begin to think about this same problem in terms of a Markov-process model. We shall obtain the probabilities of the states in a slightly different way. Provided we collected the data such that it reveals the chronological sequence of the shipments, we could, for example, obtain the relative frequency of the state "poor-quality materials" given that the just-previous shipment had been of poor quality.

Suppose that past shipments of poor quality were followed by shipments of poor quality 14 out of 20 times. This *conditional* relative frequency of 70 percent provides one of the *conditional* (transition) probability assignments to the "poor-quality-materials" states in the future, if we represent the process by the Markov model. Of course all the other transition probabilities of the states could be similarly derived. The transition diagram in Figure 17-4 provides us with an assumed set of such transition probabilities.

In this particular application of a Markov-process model something of interest, for example, may be the probability that the next three shipments all will be of good quality or the probability that at least two of the next three shipments will be of good quality (given that the last shipment was of good quality). From Figure 17-5, by multiplying through the uppermost branches of the tree, we can obtain the probability that the next three shipments will be of good quality. It is .512. The probability that at least two of the next three shipments will be of good quality is .736, obtained by adding the appropriate joint probabilities: $.512 + .128 + .048 + .048 = .736$. For more numerous shipments and states the procedures are the same.

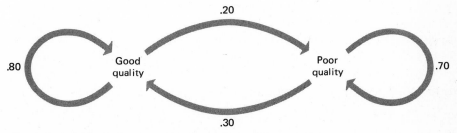

Figure 17-4 Transition diagram for the raw-materials example.

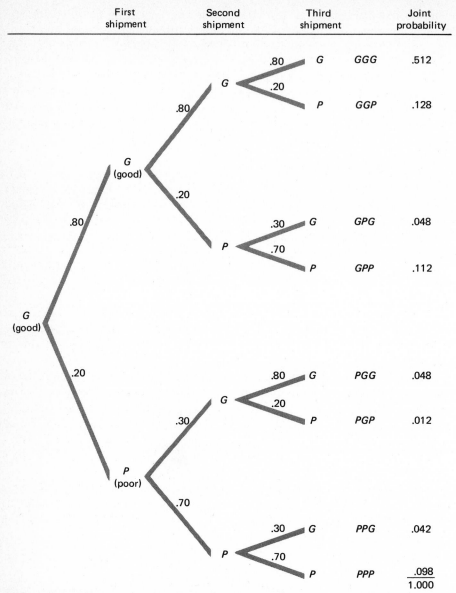

Figure 17-5 Joint probabilities in the raw-materials example.

MARKOV PROCESSES AND DECISIONS

Up to now in this chapter we have examined the main characteristics of a simple Markov-process model and some of its potential applications. The primary aim has been to construct a model that may aid in the *prediction* of particular events, such as the occurrence of good-quality or poor-quality materials in future shipments.

Recall that in the example just discussed we obtained only the probabilities of particular states (events) occurring at some time in the future. No effort was made to relate the Markov-process models to any problems of *choice* (or decision) within the firm. Upon reflection we must realize that uncertainty regarding the reality that is represented by a Markov-process model may well affect the possible revenue or profit outcomes of various acts (or policies) that can be taken by the firm. It is time to examine this point.

Alternative Acts and Expected Profits

As we studied decision problems in Part Two, we followed the procedure of listing the alternative courses of action (acts) and then listing the possible events (states) that could occur with each course of action. For each act-event combination we obtained a profit or some other consequence of interest.

With probabilities assigned to the basic events, we were able to compute an expected profit for each act. Then, using the maximization-of-expected-profit criterion, we selected one of the courses of action to implement in the real-world problem.

In this chapter we want to extend those procedures to problems where the probabilities assigned to the states are obtained by a Markov-process probability model. Thus, some aspects of the procedure discussed in this section are old and some are new.

In order to get a diagram that represents clearly the possible profits of the act "use old machine" and their associated probabilities, we insert in Figure 17-6 the amounts on the branches next to the probabilities associated with the occurrence of each of the events. Thus, we see that if the last shipment has been of good quality, the probability of the next shipment being of good quality is .80, with a profit of $100. The other possible state is that the shipment will be one of poor quality, with a probability of .20 and a profit of $60.

For the act "use new machine" the profits are different from what they were for the act "use old machine." For this act in Figure 17-7 we have placed the appropriate profit amounts on the arrows next to the probabilities. Given that the

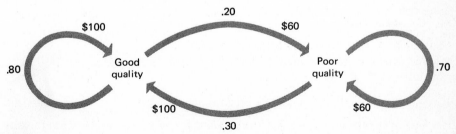

Figure 17-6 Transition probabilities and the conditional profits for the act "use old machine."

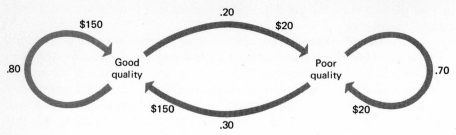

Figure 17-7 Transition probabilities and the conditional profits for the act "use new machine."

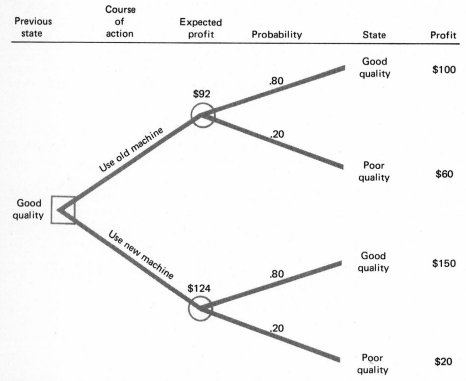

Figure 17-8 Determination of the optimal act looking ahead one period, given that the last shipment was of good quality.

last shipment was of poor quality, the profits for this act are $20 or $150, with probabilities of .70 and .30, respectively.

The Optimal Act for Two Periods: A Fixed-Policy Model

Our next step is to examine a procedure for selecting the best act looking ahead *two* periods. Procedures that we develop taking into account two periods in the future are also applicable for any number of periods. However, considerably more computation is involved when the number of periods is great.

In Figures 17-8 and 17-9 we illustrate the procedure for just one period. It is similar to that which we used in Part Two. However, we want to extend the procedure to include two future periods.

When we have more than one period in our analysis, a question immediately arises. Do we want a model in which a decision is to be made *after* each period? Or, do we want one where a decision is made at the beginning (taking into account all periods) but not permitting a choice at the end of each period. The latter model shall be referred to as a *fixed-policy* model, whereas the former is called an *adaptive-policy* model.

We represent the decision problem for one period in Figures 17-8 and 17-9. In Figure 17-8, the last shipment has been of good quality; thus, for the next period the probability of the next shipment being of good quality is .80 and of poor quality, .20.

Using the profits for each act-event combination as shown in Figures 17-6 and 17-7, we compute an expected profit of $92 for "use old machine" and an expected profit of $124 for "use new machine." Thus, given that the last shipment was of good quality, the optimal act (looking ahead one period) is "use new machine."

On the other hand, if the last shipment has been of poor quality, the tree in

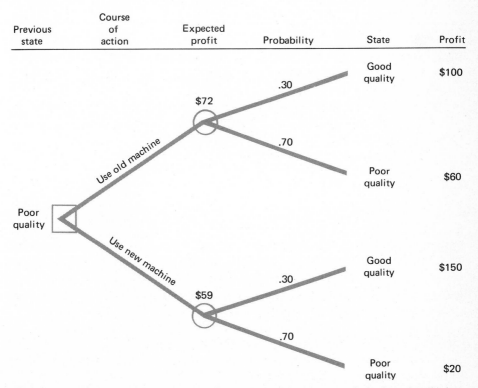

Figure 17-9 Determination of the optimal act looking ahead one period, given that the last shipment was of poor quality.

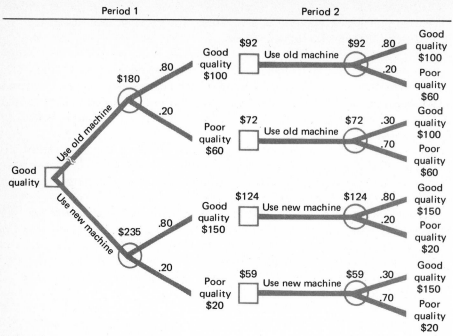

Figure 17-10   A fixed-policy model.

Figure 17-9 shows the appropriate analysis. In this case the act "use old machine" (with an expected profit of $72) is superior to the act "use new machine" (with an expected profit of $59).

In examining the procedures where two or more periods are involved, let us look at the fixed-policy model first. We shall use the familiar machine example to illustrate this.

Using a tree, the problem takes the form shown in Figure 17-10. Here, the preceding shipment has been of good quality, and we are looking ahead two periods. Under this model, the act chosen in period 1 is the one that will be maintained throughout both periods. Thus, in the upper half of the tree in Figure 17-10 we lay out the possible paths under one fixed policy: "use old machine." In the lower half of the tree the possible paths for the act (policy) "use new machine" are similarly set down.

As in earlier decision trees, we lay out from left to right in chronological sequence the possible acts and events with their associated probabilities and profits. Then, we start working *backward* through the tree, computing expected profits at chance points, and selecting an optimal act at the choice points.

Thus, in Figure 17-10, as we work backward through the tree, we compute the expected profits for period 2 of $92, $72, $124, and $59. Since this is a fixed-policy model, the expected profits each are moved back to a point just posterior to the state of the preceding period.

But as we move these expected profits backward we see that there is something else to consider: *the profits from period 1*. We see in the uppermost branches of Figure 17-10, period 1 profits of $100 for "use old machine" and "good-quality materials," and $60 for "use old machine" and "poor-quality materials."

Considering the first period alone, the expected profit is $92: .80 ($100) + .20 ($60) = $92. But we are considering more than period 1. *For period 2* we have an expected profit of $92 if the act-event combination in period 1 is "use old machine" and "good-quality materials." The probability is .80 that we will reach a point where this expected profit of $92 is effective.

The other (conditional) expected-profit possibility pertaining to period 2 is $72. It is the expected profit for period 2 if the period 1 state is "poor-quality materials." The probability of reaching this state (and thus of getting to the point where the expected profit of $72 is effective) is .20.

Therefore, *in period 1* we see a probability of .80 associated with the (conditional) expected profit of $92 (for period 2) and a probability of .20 associated with the (conditional) expected profit of $72 (for period 2). The expected profit of these (conditional) expected profits is $88: .80 ($92) + .20 ($72) = $88. This is the expected profit for period 2 even before the state of the shipment for period 1 is known.

To get an expected profit for "use old machine" for two periods under this fixed policy, we can simply add the two expected profits of $88 (for period 2) and $92 (for period 1). This gives us a "total" expected profit of $180 for holding to that policy (use old machine) for the two periods.

Similarly, for the act "use new machine" we repeat the analysis and computations. As shown in Figure 17-10, the total expected profit for this act (fixed for the two periods) is $235 and is optimal. Thus, if we are to stay with the same course of action for two periods, the act "use new machine" has the higher total expected profit.

The Optimal Sequence of Acts for Two Periods: An Adaptive-Policy Model

A development beyond the fixed-policy model is the adaptive-policy model. In this analysis a choice of acts is made available at the end of each period. As shown in Figure 17-11, at the end of period 1 it is possible to shift to another act for period 2.

In the machine example, the new machine may be used in period 1, but for period 2 a shift to "use old machine" is possible. Actually, such a shift would be desirable if for period 1 the quality of the shipment turned out to be poor. This can be seen in Figure 17-11.

Generally, as we work back through the tree in Figure 17-11 we compute the expected profits, select the acts with the maximum expected profits, move these expected profits backward, and incorporate them in the computations of the total expected profits as shown in the previous section.

We can see that for period 1 the optimal act is "use new machine." For period 2 the optimal act is "use new machine" if in period 1 the quality of the

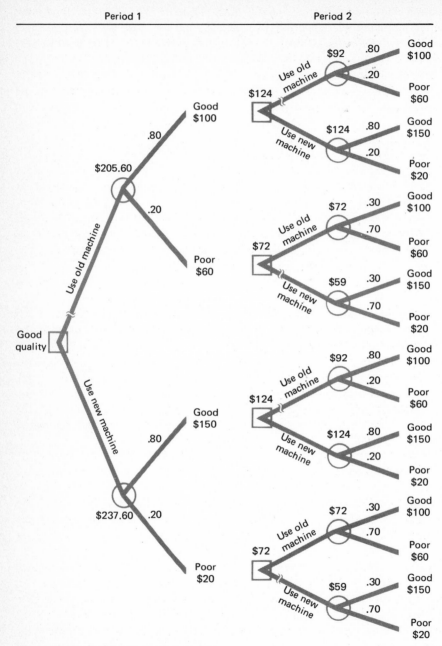

Figure 17-11 An adaptive-policy model.

shipment was of good quality. If the shipment was of poor quality, the optimal act for period 2 is "use old machine."

Thus, it is not surprising to find that under this adaptive-policy model the total expected profit of the optimal act (at the beginning) is higher than under the fixed-policy model ($237.60 compared with $235). The adaptive-policy model permits more flexibility in decision making so that we may respond to events as they unfold.

MARKOV PROCESSES AND DECISIONS: THE TRANSITION PROBABILITIES AFFECTED BY THE ACT CHOSEN

The purpose of this section is to illustrate another type of Markov-process model used in decision under uncertainty. We shall examine an optimization procedure (model) in which a Markov-process model is a component of a larger model. (The term "dynamic programming" sometimes is used to refer to such optimization procedures because they involve the element of time and changes occurring over time).

The key idea in the type of model discussed in this section is that the transition probabilities of the underlying Markov process *are affected by the act chosen.* (So far in this chapter we have assumed that the probabilities of the states are independent of the acts chosen.) Let us illustrate this model for two periods with an example of a firm that has to make a decision on whether to advertise a product or not.

Example: An Advertising Decision

The level of sales of a firm may be in one of two possible states. The level of sales may be in a satisfactory state or in an unsatisfactory state. Let us refer to the satisfactory state as state 1 and the unsatisfactory state as state 2.

Also, suppose that from past data we obtain the transition probabilities as shown in Figure 17-12. Now we have *two* transition diagrams because we have two sets of transition probabilities and profits.

Given that sales in the past period were satisfactory, under policy I (no advertising) the probability of satisfactory sales in the next period (the process staying in state 1) is .60, and the probability of unsatisfactory sales (going to state 2), .40. Given the same state of satisfactory sales in the past period, if policy II (advertising) is followed, the probability of satisfactory sales in the subsequent period is .70, whereas for unsatisfactory sales it is .30. The assumed transition probabilities for policy II indicate that the advertising policy increases the probability of the process remaining in state 1 (satisfactory sales) if it is currently in that state and also increases the probability of movement to state 1 (satisfactory sales) if the process currently is in state 2 (unsatisfactory sales).

To be noted, too, is that the profits for the act-event combinations are different for the two policies. For example, if policy I (no advertising) is the act taken and satisfactory sales occur, the profit is $20, whereas if policy II (advertis-

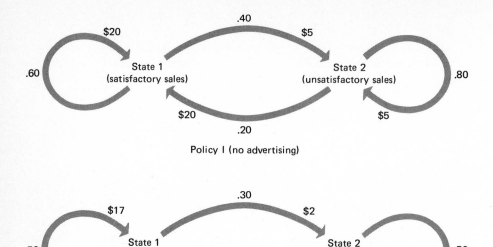

Figure 17-12 Transition probabilities and conditional profits for policy I (no advertising) and for policy II (advertising).

ing) is chosen and satisfactory sales occur, the profit is $17. The profits associated with policy II (advertising) are lower, reflecting the additional (advertising) costs involved. All the relevant profits and transition probabilities are shown in Figure 17-12.

As before when we studied such a problem, we lay out the sequence of acts and events (here, the sequence of states, acts, and states). This we do in Figure 17-13 for two periods. Then, we insert the appropriate transition probabilities and profits. Remember that these probabilities and profits are dependent upon the states and acts.

Now we are in a position to begin working back through the tree. At the right side of Figure 17-13 we compute for period 2 the expected profit at each chance point. Then, where choice points are encountered (as we move toward the left), we reverse our view and look forward (to the right) to examine the expected profit at each chance point. The optimal act in that period is indicated by the maximum expected profit. Then we move this optimal expected profit back (to the left) to the decision point. The optimal expected profits for period 2 then become elements in the computation of the total expected profit for period 1.

Working back through the tree to the left in Figure 17-13 we obtain a total expected profit of $26.20 for policy I (no advertising) in period 1 and $25.15 for

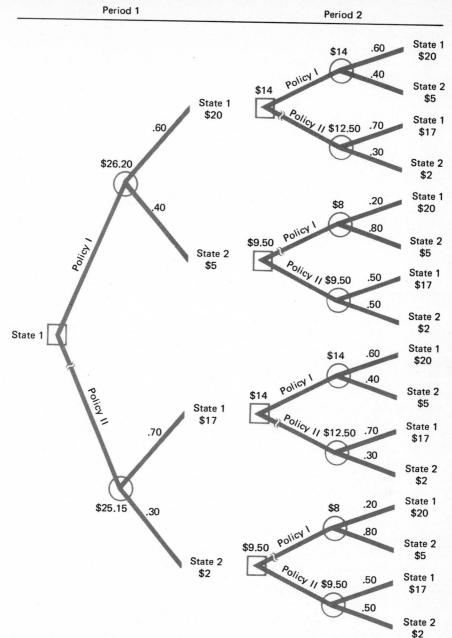

Figure 17-13 An adaptive-policy model where the transition probabilities and conditional profits are affected by the act taken.

policy II (advertising). We see that the optimal act in period 1 is policy I (no advertising) given the current state is state 1 (satisfactory sales).

In period 2, the optimal policy depends upon the state that occurs in period 1. From Figure 17-13 we see that the optimal act is policy II (advertising) if state 2 (unsatisfactory sales) occurs. Otherwise, policy I (no advertising) would be optimal.

In addition to providing the set of optimal policies to follow over time, the above example can illustrate again the value of being able to change policies at the end of each period. Under the adaptive procedures just discussed, the maximum total expected profit obtained was $26.20 (as shown in Figure 17-13). This is higher than the total expected profit of $25.60 for the best fixed policy (no advertising) for the two periods. The computation of the maximum expected profit of $25.60 under a fixed policy is not shown but would perhaps provide a useful exercise for the reader. All the procedures discussed here extend to problems with many acts and many states.

SUMMARY

1 A *Markov-process model* can be used to represent those situations in which the probabilities of the states (the basic events) in a chance process are affected by the state (event) that occurred in the immediately preceding period (or run of the chance process).

2 The probability of the process moving from one particular state to another is referred to as a *transition* probability. It is also a *conditional* probability because the probability of movement to a particular state depends upon the current (or immediately preceding) state.

3 A *transition diagram* shows the possible states in a model and the (transition) probabilities of movement from one state to another.

4 Markov-process models may be used for *prediction* purposes only, or they may be used for *decision-making* purposes by incorporating the courses of action that are open at particular points.

5 A *fixed-policy model* incorporates a procedure in which a choice of a course of action is made at the beginning of a specific number of periods and no change is permitted from period to period. An *adaptive-policy model* allows a change in the course of action after each period.

6 Both the fixed-policy models and the adaptive-policy models can be modified to permit the acts (the courses of action) to affect the transition probabilities as well as the profits of the act-event combinations.

PROBLEMS

17-1 Consider the transition diagram in Figure 17-4 in this chapter. But let us now replace those transition probabilities with the following probabilities:

		To:	
		State 1 (good-quality materials)	State 2 (poor-quality materials)
From:	State1 (good-quality materials)	.70	.30
	State 2 (poor-quality materials)	.20	.80

a   Form a transition diagram of the problem and insert the appropriate transition probabilities on the branches (arrows).

b   If the last shipment of materials was of poor quality (state 2), what is the probability that the *next two* shipments will be of poor quality?

c   What is the probability of the process being in state 2 (having received poor-quality materials) at the end of two periods (that is, after the receipt of two future shipments)?

17-2   A Markov process has the following transition probabilities.

		To:		
		State 1	State 2	State 3
From:	State 1	.40	.60	.00
	State 2	.20	.30	.50
	State 3	.70	.00	.30

a   Form a transition diagram for this Markov process, including the insertion of the transition probabilities on the branches (or arrows).

b   If the process begins in state 1, what is the probability of its being in state 1 at the end of two periods (stages)?

c   What is the probability of the process being in state 1 after three periods (assuming it begins in state 1)?

d   Is it most probable that the process will be in state 3 at the end of three periods if it starts in state 1? Explain.

17-3   Suppose the behavior of individual automobile buyers is viewed as a Markov process. Let us suppose there are only two brands of automobiles; one we shall refer to as brand A, the other as brand B.

     The states of this process are defined as follows:

State 1: Last purchase was of brand A.

State 2: Last purchase was of brand B.

In a Markov process a movement from one state to another state is assumed. In this application, the movement from state 1 to state 2 (for instance) refers to a consumer having bought brand A at the last purchase and buys brand B on the next purchase. The probability of this transition and others is given as follows:

		To:	
		State 1 (brand A)	State 2 (brand B)
From:	State 1 (brand A)	.60	.40
	State 2 (brand B)	.30	.70

a Form a transition diagram for the problem and insert the appropriate probabilities on the arrows.

b At the end of two additional (future) purchases what is the probability of the consumer being in state 2 (last purchase was of brand B) given that he or she started in state 2?

17-4 Let us pursue an extension of Problem 17-3. Now let us define each state of the process of automobile buying in terms of *the last two purchases*. For instance, state 2 now refers to having bought brand A on the next-to-last purchase and brand B on the very last purchase, and state 3 refers to having purchased brand B and then brand A during the last two purchases.

We define all the states as follows (and include the transition probabilities):

		To:			
		State 1 (A A)	State 2 (A B)	State 3 (B A)	State 4 (B B)
	State 1 (A A)	.65	.35	.00	.00
From:	State 2 (A B)	.00	.00	.50	.50
	State 3 (B A)	.55	.45	.00	.00
	State 4 (B B)	.00	.00	.30	.70

    a   Construct a transition diagram for this Markov process. Insert the transition probabilities on the branches (arrows).

    b   Looking at the transition diagram in *a,* make a guess as to whether a buyer (now in state 2) is more likely after *two* more purchases to be in state 1 (last two purchases are of brand A) or in state 4 (last two purchases are of brand B).

    c   Using a probability tree to make the computation, obtain the probability of the buyer in *a* being in state 1 (last two purchases are of brand A) after two more purchases.

    d   What is the probability of the buyer in *a* being in state 4 (last two purchases of brand B) at the end of two more purchases? Was your guess in *b* correct?

17-5 Let us examine a decision problem involving a Markov process. Suppose it is a slight variation of the decision problem in Figure 17-8 in this chapter.

       The problem is to decide whether to use the new machine or to use the old machine in packaging some items. Uncertainty exists with regard to the quality of the materials to be used.

       Suppose the new transition probabilities are those given in Problem 17-1. The profits of the act-event combinations are the same as in Figure 17-8.

    a   Given that the last shipment of materials was of good quality, which machine should be used if we wish to maximize expected profit?

    b   If the last shipment had been of poor quality, which machine should be used?

17-6 Let us continue with Problem 17-5, but now we want to maximize expected profit over *two* future periods using the fixed-policy approach.

    a   If the last shipment was of good quality, which is the best machine to use over the two periods?

    b   What is the optimal expected profit over two future periods following the policy obtained in *a?*

    c   If the last shipment was of poor quality, which is the best machine to use over the two periods?

    d   What is the optimal expected profit over two future periods if the policy obtained in *c* is used?

17-7 Continuing with Problems 17-5 and 17-6, let us investigate the use of an adaptive-policy approach.

    a   Given that the last shipment of materials was of good quality, which machine should be used in the first period and what is the optimal expected profit looking ahead two periods?

    b   Given that the last shipment was of poor quality, what is the optimal act in the first period and what is the optimal expected profit over two future periods?

17-8 Compare the optimal expected profit obtained in Problem 17-6*b* under a fixed policy with that obtained in Problem 17-7*a* using an adaptive policy. Is there a gain in expected profit using an adaptive policy? If so, how much? Explain the basis for any gain.

17-9 Analogous to what was done in Problem 17-8, compare the optimal expected profit that you obtained in Problem 17-6*d* with that obtained in Problem 17-7*b* using an adaptive policy. Indicate the amount of any gain in expected profit and its basis.

17-10 Suppose the transition probabilities associated with state 1 under Policy I in Figure 17-12 are changed to the following:

       $P(\text{state 1} \mid \text{state 1}) = .55$ (instead of .60)
       $P(\text{state 2} \mid \text{state 1}) = .45$ (instead of .40)

a With all other transition probabilities and profits remaining as given in Figure
   17-12, what is the optimal policy in the first period looking ahead for two
   periods (using an adaptive-policy approach)?
b What is the optimal expected profit over the two future periods?

Chapter 18

Project Analysis:
PERT and CPM

Occasionally, each of us uses the term "project" to refer to some of our undertakings. The undertakings we call projects usually are not trivial in terms of the cost involved (such as the amount of our time used and that of other resources), nor are they trivial in terms of the benefits expected when the undertaking is completed.

Usually, the *amount of time* it takes to complete a project is of primary (or initial) interest. But perhaps the most distinguishing characteristic of all is that a project has a beginning and also has an end. In this way it is in contrast to the continuous-process operations that are typical in petroleum refining and the chemical industries.

Although the term "project" is very broad, some of the clearest examples of projects are illustrated by the following: the building of an airplane, the construction of a house, or the making of an airport.

Many such projects are now planned and undertaken with the aid of formal *project analysis*. Such formal analysis technically is known as PERT (for Program Evaluation and Review Technique) or CPM (for Critical Path Method). (Also, formal project analysis constitutes a part of the broader field of "network analysis.")

Project analysis can be thought of as a formalization and extension of the project planning and analysis that traditionally has been done in a more or less informal way.

As we indicated above, primary attention in project analysis is given to the identification of the minimum amount of time necessary to complete the project. Usually, secondary consideration is given to the costs incurred in completing the project and the use of scarce and limited resources.

The two formal methods for the analysis of projects (PERT and CPM) are very similar, and in many respects they are indistinguishable. Although both methods were developed in the 1950s, they emerged more or less independently from one another.

To the present day, both methods are being further refined and developed. Also, applications are being extended to new types of problems. Some of the more recent applications (such as in budgeting activities and in new-product introduction) are quite different, outwardly at least, from the early applications.

PERT had its first applications on military projects (such as the building of the first nuclear-powered submarine). CPM has been associated from its beginning with applications in the building-construction industry. At the present time, however, applications of at least one of the two types of project analysis are found in virtually every industry.

DEFINITIONS: PROJECTS AND JOBS

There are some concepts in PERT and CPM that have special meanings. We have already referred briefly to the term "project." Now, however, we want to examine carefully the more technical meaning of this term and others in formal project analysis. (*Note:* We shall mainly follow the definitions as they appear in CPM. The CPM definitions and concepts are a bit simpler, but they are very close to the meanings of the terms in PERT.)

Projects and Jobs

First, in formal project analysis a *project* is defined as an undertaking with a beginning and with an end.

But, also, a project is described by the elements (the "steps" or "tasks") of which it is comprised. We call these elements *jobs*.

Thus, in any project there is a set of *jobs* that must be completed in order for the *project* to be completed.

For example, in the project of making an airport, the job of grading the earth for the runways and the job of pouring the concrete for the runways are two separate elements (jobs) in the project (making the airport). (*Note:* In many PERT discussions, jobs, as we have defined them, are referred to as "activities.")

HOW LONG DOES EACH JOB TAKE?

In project analysis we are usually interested in how soon an entire project can be finished. Since a project is made up of a number of jobs, we must find out how long each job takes to complete. Thus, we want to associate with each job the amount of time it takes for it to be completed.

Identification of Immediately Preceding Job

Also, it is important to determine which jobs must be completed *before* other jobs can begin. Moreover, it is important to know which jobs can be done *at the same time*. Therefore, we examine each job in the project to see how much time it will take and, also, what job or jobs (if any) must precede it.

Project Tables and Project Diagrams

The jobs that comprise a project, the time needed to complete each of the jobs, and which jobs must precede other jobs can be represented either in a *project table* or in a *project diagram*.

In Table 18-1 we see the jobs that are included in the project of building a house.

At the top of Table 18-1 we list the job that must be the first one completed. Then, succeeding jobs are listed.

Also, we record in the second column the time needed to complete each job. In the third column we identify the immediately preceding job (or jobs) that must be completed before that particular job can begin.

In Figure 18-1 we see the same project represented in a *project diagram*. Here, each job is represented by a separate box in which a description of the job appears, together with an estimate of the time needed to complete the job.

In forming the project diagram we place at the extreme-left side the job that must be completed first. Then, from left to right, the succeeding jobs are represented.

For example, the first job appearing at the left in Figure 18-1 is "lay the foundation." It can be followed by either of the two following jobs: "erect the walls" or "pour the basement floor."

Also, we say that the job "lay the foundation" is an *immediately preceding*

Table 18-1 Project Table for Building a House

Job	Time needed for completion	Immediately preceding job (the job or jobs that must be completed before this job can begin)
Lay the foundation	5 days	None
Erect the walls	3 days	Lay the foundation
Pour the basement floor	2 days	Lay the foundation
Erect the roof	1 day	Erect the walls
Install the heating system	3 days	Erect the roof and pour the basement floor
Plaster the interior walls	6 days	Install the heating system

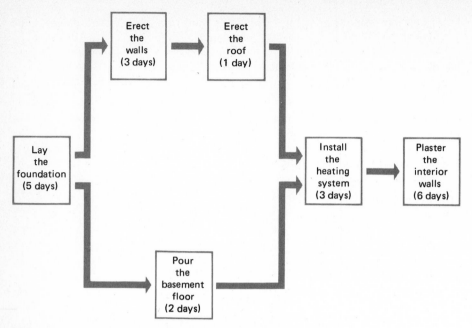

Figure 18-1   A project diagram for the project of building a house.

job to both "erect the walls" and "pour the basement floor." In the project diagram this is shown by the arrows from the immediately preceding job (lay the foundation) to the jobs "erect the walls" and "pour the basement floor."

The job "erect the roof" is immediately preceded by the job "erect the walls." The job "install the heating system" has *two* immediately preceding jobs: "erect the roof" *and* "pour the basement floor." Both of these immediately preceding jobs must be completed before the heating system can be installed.

From the project diagram in Figure 18-1 we can tell there are two immediately preceding jobs to "install the heating system" because there are two arrows leading into the box representing the job of installing the heating system. If a job had three immediately preceding jobs, we would have three arrows leading into the box.

"Plaster the interior walls" has only one immediately preceding job. It is the job "install the heating system."

Thus, the project diagram (with its boxes and arrows) represents the jobs in a project, the time it takes for each job to be completed, and the necessary sequence in which the jobs must be completed.

THE SOONEST A PROJECT CAN BE FINISHED: TARGET TIME

In both Table 18-1 and Figure 18-1 we have the jobs in the project represented, along with the amount of time needed for the completion of each.

Being interested in how soon the entire project can be completed, might we not then determine this either from Table 18-1 or Figure 18-1 by simply adding together the times it takes for the jobs? Doing this gives us a total of 20 days for the completion of the project.

Generally, however, this procedure does *not* give us the minimum time it takes to complete the project. Why not? It is because some jobs can be done simultaneously.

For example, in Figure 18-1 we can see that the job "pour the basement floor" can be done at the same time the jobs "erect the walls" and "erect the roof" are being done.

Consequently, the 2 days it takes to pour the basement floor should not be added to the time it takes to complete the other jobs because it can be done at the same time. Instead of 20 days, the minimum time it takes to complete the entire project is only 18 days.

In effect, the 2 days it takes for the job "pour the basement floor" (that can be done concurrently with others) is subtracted from the total of the days it takes to complete all the jobs.

A More Formal Procedure

For larger projects we need a formal procedure for accurately identifying the minimum time it takes to complete a project. In the more formal analysis we refer to this minimum time for the completion of the project as the *target time* for the project.

The procedure that gives us the minimum time in which a project can be completed (the target time) is illustrated in the project diagram in Figure 18-2.

Above each box (for each job) we write the phrase "can be started in ——— days." Below each box we insert the words "can be finished in ——— days."

As we work from left to right in the project diagram in Figure 18-2, we ultimately reach the last job in the project. When we determine the number of days in which the last job in the project can be finished, we have identified the number of days in which the entire project can be finished. This is what is called the *target time* of the project. Now let us illustrate this in terms of the project diagram in Figure 18-2.

We begin with the job "lay the foundation." Since there are no other jobs preceding this job, we can start it right away; that is, it can be started in 0 days. Thus, we insert a 0 in the blank above the box.

The job "lay the foundation" takes 5 days to complete. Therefore, this job can be finished in 5 days from the beginning of the project. The general procedure by which we get the number of days in which a job can be finished (the number below the box) is by adding the number of days *in* the box to the number of days in which the job can be started (the number *above* the box).

Thus, for the first job ("lay the foundation") we indicate 0 days above the box. Since 5 days for job completion appears in the box, we simply add the 5 days in the box to the 0 days above the box. This gives us 5 days (below the box) in which the job can be finished.

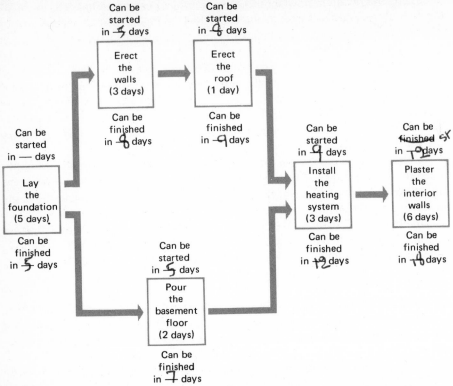

Figure 18-2 The first step in identifying the minimum time in which the project can be completed.

We go to the next job (or jobs) where the arrow (or arrows) leads us. It does not matter which one we consider first, but let us first take the job "erect the walls."

In how many days from the beginning of the project can this job be started? Five days. It can be started when the immediately preceding job "lay the foundation" is finished. That job can be finished in 5 days. Therefore, the job "erect the walls" can be started in 5 days. We record 5 days above the box representing this job.

In how many days can the job "erect the walls" be finished? Eight days. We simply add the number of days in the box (3 days) to the number of days above the box (5 days).

Turning to the job "pour the basement floor," we record above the box that it can begin in 5 days from the time the project starts. It takes 2 days to complete this job, and so the number of days in which it can be finished is 7.

The job "erect the roof" is immediately preceded by the job "erect the walls." Erection of the roof can begin when the walls are erected. We determined earlier that erecting the walls can be finished in 8 days. Thus, the job "erect the roof" can be started in 8 days from the beginning of the project. Since "erect the roof" takes 1 day to complete, we have 9 days in which it can be finished.

More than One Immediately Preceding Job   The job "install the heating system" is represented by a box in Figure 18-2 with two arrows pointed toward it. This means there are two immediately preceding jobs to "install the heating system." They are "erect the roof" and "pour the basement floor."

This means that *both* of the immediately preceding jobs must be finished before the job "install the heating system" can begin.

Since "erect the roof" can be finished in 9 days and the job "pour the basement floor" can be finished in 7 days, how soon can the job "install the heating system" begin?

Obviously, it will have to be 9 days because both jobs will have to be completed. Since "install the heating system" takes 3 days to complete, the job can be finished in no less than 12 days from the beginning of the project. In Figure 18-2 we record this below the box representing the job "install the heating system."

Thus, the general procedure for jobs that have more than one immediately preceding job is to take the *largest* of the finishing times (number of days) of the immediately preceding jobs and assign this time (number of days) to the earliest starting time for the job with more than one immediately preceding job.

The Last Job in the Project   The last job in our project of building a house is "plaster the interior walls." It has one immediately preceding job, "install the heating system." Thus, this last job can be started in 12 days from the beginning of the project. Since plastering the walls takes 6 days, the job can be finished in 18 days from the beginning of the project.

Inasmuch as this is the last job in the project, the 18 days to this job's completion represents also the earliest time in which the entire project can be finished. Therefore, we say the target time of the project is 18 days. The completed project diagram appears in Figure 18-3.

HOW MUCH FREEDOM DO WE HAVE IN SCHEDULING THE JOBS IN A PROJECT?

From a very practical standpoint it is useful to know the *latest* time that each job can be started and still not delay the earliest completion time of the project (the target time). In other words, it is desirable to know which jobs have *slack time* in them.

Also, if we can identify the jobs that *must* be completed on time to prevent the project completion time from being delayed, then perhaps special attention can be devoted to them in order to assure that the project is completed on time. Such jobs that must be completed on time are called *critical jobs*.

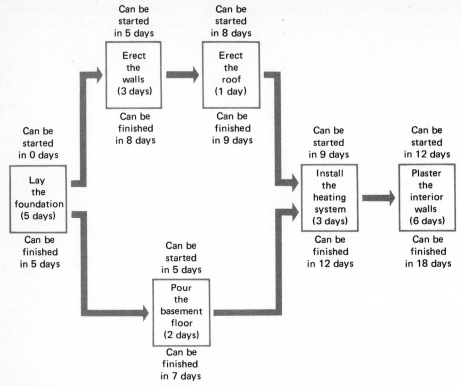

Figure 18-3 Identifying the 18-day target time (the earliest time the project can be finished).

Identifying Critical Jobs and Those with Slack Time

We want a general procedure that will indicate to us in large projects whether a particular job is a critical one (it must be completed on time) or if it is one that has slack time and can be delayed.

Again, we direct our attention to the project diagram of our project of building a house. Beginning with the diagram in Figure 18-3, we ultimately obtain the one that appears in Figure 18-4.

In Figure 18-4 we have made additional statements about each job. We have placed an additional statement above and an additional one below each box. The new statements are enclosed in parentheses.

Above each box we record the time each job *must be started* in order for the entire project to be completed on time. Below each box we have the time when each job *must be finished* in order for the project to be completed on time.

Critical jobs are those jobs where the number of days before a job *can* be finished is the same as the number of days in which it *must* be finished.

Alternatively, critical jobs can be defined as those jobs where the number of days before the job can be started is the same as the number of days by which it must be started.

From the project diagram in Figure 18-4 we can see that all the jobs in the project are critical jobs except the job "pour the basement floor." We note that it *can* be finished in 7 days and *must* be completed in 9 days.

Thus, there is *slack time* in the job "pour the basement floor." Its completion can be delayed 2 days without delaying the completion time of the project. But as we have noted before, it is the only job with any slack time in this project.

Obtaining the Times Each Job Must Be Started and Finished

How do we obtain the times that each job must be started and finished? We obtain these times by working *backward* (from right to left) through our project diagram.

We begin with the *last* job "plaster the interior walls" and note *when it can be finished*. It can be finished in 18 days. Then, we insert within parentheses

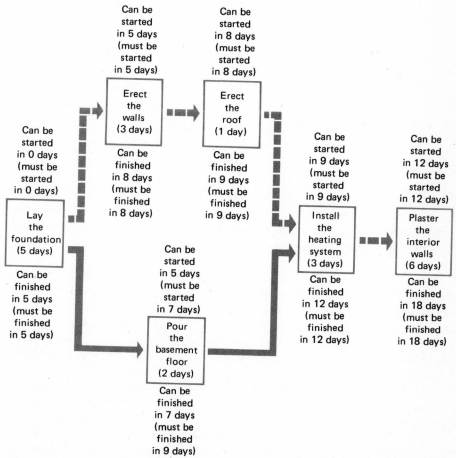

Figure 18-4 Identifying the jobs that have slack, the critical jobs, and the critical path.

below the box that this job *must* be finished in 18 days (to make the target time of 18 days).

Working in reverse fashion, we move *upward* through the box representing the job "plaster the interior walls" and *subtract* the number of days it takes to complete that job. After doing this, we record above the box that the job *must be started* 12 days from the beginning of the project: 18 days − 6 days = 12 days.

The next job in our reverse order is "install the heating system." Since the job "plaster the interior walls" must be started in 12 days, its immediately preceding job "install the heating system" must be finished in 12 days. We record this within parentheses below the box representing the job "install the heating system."

More than One Immediately Preceding Job   Moving upward through the box representing the job "install the heating system," we subtract 3 days of completion time from the 12 days in which it must be finished. Thus, we record above the box the 9 days by which this job must be started.

There are two immediately preceding jobs to the job "install the heating system." Therefore, we record under each of the boxes representing these immediately preceding jobs (erect the roof and pour the basement floor) that each of these jobs must be finished in 9 days from the beginning of the project.

The job "erect the roof" must then be started in 8 days, and the job "pour the basement floor" must be started in 7 days.

The job "erect the walls" immediately precedes the job "erect the roof," which must be started in 8 days. Therefore, "erect the walls" must be finished in 8 days. Also, since it takes 3 days for the job "erect the walls," it must be started in 5 days.

When One Job Immediately Precedes Two or More Other Jobs   Finally, the job "lay the foundation" is an immediately preceding job to two other jobs (erect the walls and pour the basement floor). The job "erect the walls" must be started in 5 days, and the job "pour the basement floor" must be started in 7 days.

Thus, when must the immediately preceding job "lay the foundation" be finished? Obviously, it must be finished in 5 days because it must be completed before the other two jobs can begin.

This last job illustrates the point that when one job immediately precedes two others (and each of these two jobs has a different time by which it must be started), the *smaller* of the two times is selected as the time the immediately preceding job must be finished. In our example it is 5 days.

Moving upward through the box representing the job "lay the foundation," we then record that this job must be started in 0 days if the target time of the project is not to be delayed.

As we reexamine the project diagram in Figure 18-4, we see once again that all the jobs are critical jobs except one. It is the job "pour the basement floor."

Identifying the Critical Path of the Project

If in a project diagram we connect the critical jobs from the beginning of the project to the end, we have a *critical path* of the entire project. Let us designate the critical paths in our project diagrams (as in Figure 18-4) by a special marking of the arrows connecting the boxes representing the jobs on the critical path.

Every job on the critical path must be completed on time in order for the entire project to be completed on time. Every project has at least one critical path. And every critical job lies on a critical path.

EXTENSIONS OF PROJECT ANALYSIS

In our brief introduction to project analysis we have focused mainly on its usual primary aim, which is to find out how soon a project can be completed. At times, however, we may wish to modify the analysis to take into account any uncertainty in the times it takes for jobs in the project to be completed.

Also, we may wish to study the cost effects of acquiring more resources so that the target time of a project can be shortened. More advanced discussions on project analysis may include such extensions and modifications.

SUMMARY

1   Many of our undertakings of consequence can be planned and implemented more effectively using formal project analysis (that is, PERT or CPM, which is a part of "network analysis").

2   In project analysis, the primary or initial aim is that of discovering the shortest time in which a project can be completed.

3   A *project* can be described in terms of the elements (the "steps" or "tasks") of which it is comprised. These elements are called *jobs*.

4   In any project there is a set of jobs that must be completed in order for the entire project to be completed.

5   In order to identify the shortest time in which a project can be completed, we must first determine how long it takes to complete each of the jobs in the project.

Second, we must determine which jobs must be completed before other jobs can begin.

Third, we need to know which jobs can be done at the same time.

6   A *project table* or a *project diagram* is useful in representing (a) the jobs in a project, (b) the time needed to complete each job, and (c) those jobs that must precede other jobs.

7   A project diagram is especially useful in determining the shortest time in which a project can be completed. This minimum time is called the *target time* of the project.

8   Working backward through the project diagram, we can determine how much freedom we have in scheduling and completing the jobs in a project.

Those jobs that must be completed on time to prevent the project completion time from being delayed are called *critical* jobs.

Those jobs whose completion can be delayed without delaying the project completion time are jobs with *slack time*.

9   A *critical path* of a project refers to a sequence of jobs through the entire project comprised entirely of critical jobs. Every such job must be completed on time, or the target time of the project will not be realized. Every project has at least one critical path.

PROBLEMS

18-1   Let us think of the making of a special-type door as a project. The time needed for each job and the immediately preceding jobs are given as follows:

Job	Time needed for completion	Immediately preceding job or jobs
A Draw plans	1 day	— None
B Obtain wood	3 days	A Draw plans
C Obtain glass	2 days	A Draw plans
D Obtain latch and lock	1 day	A Draw plans
E Cut wood sections	1 day	B Obtain wood
F Cut glass sections	1 day	C Obtain glass
G Form and sand wood sections	2 days	E Cut wood sections
H Assemble wood sections	1 day	G Form and sand wood sections
I Install glass	1 day	H Assemble wood sections and cut glass sections F
J Install latch and lock	1 day	I Install glass

a   Construct a project diagram for the project of making the special-type door in which you represent each job, the time needed for its completion, and the order in which the jobs must be completed.

b   From the project diagram in *a* obtain the earliest time each job can be started and the earliest time each job *can* be finished.

c   What is the minimum time in which the entire project can be finished (the target time)?

18-2   a   From the project diagram in 18-1*b* obtain the time that each job *must* be started and *must* be finished in order not to delay the completion time of the entire project?

b   What are the critical jobs in the door-making project?

c   Draw heavy, dark arrows on your project diagram in 18-1*b* to designate the critical path of the project.

d   Which jobs in the door-making project have slack time and how much?

18-3   Suppose we wish to represent as a project the budgeting activities involved in the introduction of a new product.

We have made the following list of jobs with the time needed for their completion and also the order in which they must be completed.

Job	Time needed for completion	Immediately preceding job or jobs
Develop new product	20 weeks	None
Obtain estimate of demand	6 weeks	Develop new product
Obtain competitors' product prices	2 weeks	Develop new product
Make production plans	3 weeks	Obtain estimate of demand
Decide on product price	1 week	Obtain estimate of demand and obtain competitors' product prices
Estimate production costs	2 weeks	Make production plans
Make up budget	3 weeks	Estimate production costs and decide on product price

a Make a project diagram for the budgeting-related activities in which the above information is represented.

b Indicate on your project diagram in *a* the earliest time each job *can* be started and the earliest time it *can* be finished.

c How soon can the budget be prepared?

18-4 a Now indicate on your project diagram in Problem 18-3*a* and *b* the time each job *must* be started and *must* be finished in order not to delay the budget-completion date.

b Draw heavy, dark arrows on your budget-preparation project diagram in Problem 18-3*a* and *b* to designate the critical path.

c Which jobs in the budget-preparation project have some slack time and how much?

18-5 Many of us are familiar with the periodic servicing of a car. To get more familiar with project analysis, suppose we think of this servicing as a project and relate its elements to the concepts of this chapter. (*Note:* There is sufficient labor to permit any jobs to be done simultaneously if it is technically possible.)

Job	Time needed for completion	Immediately preceding job or jobs
Place car on hoist	3 minutes	None
Drain oil	6 minutes	Place car on hoist
Lubricate chassis	14 minutes	Place car on hoist
Rotate the tires	10 minutes	Place car on hoist
Remove old oil filter	3 minutes	Drain oil
Install new oil filter	3 minutes	Remove old oil filter
Remove car from hoist	2 minutes	Install new oil filter and lubricate chassis and rotate tires
Add new oil	5 minutes	Remove car from hoist
Check battery	2 minutes	Remove car from hoist
Move car to parking lot	3 minutes	Add new oil and check battery

We list on page 379 jobs to be completed in this project of servicing a car. Also shown are the minutes each job takes, along with the immediately preceding job or jobs (if any).

a   Construct a project diagram for the servicing of a car in which all the above information is represented.

b   Record on the project diagram in *a* the earliest time each job can be started and the earliest time it can be finished.

c   What is the target time of the project? Discuss its meaning, especially in relation to the assumption of certainty in time each job takes.

18-6   a   In the car-servicing project diagram in Problem 18-5*a* and *b* record the time each job must be started and must be finished so that the completion time of the project will not be delayed.

b   Indicate with heavy, dark arrows on your project diagram in Problem 18-5*a* and *b* the critical path of the project.

c   What is the earliest time the project can be completed if one of the critical jobs takes 2 minutes longer than planned?

d   What is the earliest time the project can be completed if *each* critical job takes 2 minutes longer than planned?

e   What is the earliest time the project can be completed if each noncritical job takes 2 minutes longer than planned?

Chapter 19

Simulation: A Supplementary Method for Making Predictions and Decisions

In Chapter 1 we noted that much progress has been made in recent years in the use of quantitative models for prediction and decision making. We made the comment that better predictions and decisions often can occur with appropriate use of such models.

The chapters since then have illustrated different models that can be used to represent important elements in various types of complex real-world situations. Once the model is constructed, we have seen how the use of logical analysis (usually some type of mathematical analysis) allows us to obtain predictions (or optimal courses of action) with respect to the real situation in which we are interested.

This chapter, however, focuses upon an important *supplement* to the use of such mathematical analysis. It is called *simulation*.

However, before we examine this procedure in detail, let us look at some of its main features and see how it compares with other procedures we have used.

BACKGROUND ON SIMULATION

An important point to recognize at the outset is that if we wish to improve our ability to predict and make decisions with respect to some part of reality we can proceed in two main ways.

Experiment Directly with Reality

One way is *to experiment directly with the reality,* usually by manipulating some element (or elements) in the reality and then observing the results.

Construct a Model of the Reality

The other main way involves a couple of steps. First, *we construct a model of the reality* (such as the mathematical models illustrated in earlier chapters). Then, once the model is constructed, there are *two* general ways to proceed in using the model to make predictions or to obtain optimal courses of action.

Obtain a Solution by Analytical Procedures   One of the ways of using the model is *to apply one or some of the many procedures of mathematical analysis.* Most of this book so far has dealt with the use of such procedures to obtain a prediction or an optimal course of action.

Obtain an Approximate Solution by Simulation: Experiment with the Model   The other way of using the model is by *experimenting with the model,* that is, by manipulating elements in the model and then observing the results. This is to be contrasted sharply with experimentation *directly with the reality.*

Repeated experiments with elements in the model generate results which, when evaluated properly, provide a basis for prediction and decision in the real situation on which the model was based. This is the essence of the procedure called *simulation.*[1]

The Rise of Simulation

In some situations, experimenting directly with the reality can be the most useful way to proceed. Because it is virtually impossible to capture in a model all the significant elements and relationships in reality that affect events and outcomes of interest to us, there is simply no perfect substitute for manipulating the reality itself.

The Value and Limitations of Experimenting Directly with Reality   Trying out a new course of action in reality can yield results that are more valuable (or more conclusive) than trying out the same course of action within the confines of a model (which does not correspond exactly to the reality).

But direct, repeated, experimentation with reality can be very costly, and sometimes it is simply not possible. At best, only a few manipulations with

---

[1]In some studies, physical models are constructed instead of (or in addition to) mathematical models. Then experiments are made with the physical model. Such experimentation on a physical model also is called "simulation."

An illustration of this occurs in the designing of hulls of ships. A small-scale model of the full-size hull is constructed which is immersed in a tank of water. Experiments are then made on the physical model that yield useful results for improving the design of the hull. In business and economic simulation studies, virtually all the experimentation is done with mathematical models of the reality rather than with physical models.

reality usually can be undertaken. This means, for example, that very few alternative courses of action can be tried out. Thus, it may be quite unlikely that anything near the best course of action can be identified. This would tend to be especially true where the direct experience with the reality has been quite limited.

The Value and Limitations of Models Solved by Analytical Procedures Of course one of the big gains from using mathematical models is that one can consider the effect of taking many different alternative courses of action under many different conditions. And we can consider taking these alternative different courses of action *in advance* of actually taking a course of action in the reality.

Analytical operations on the mathematical models are very efficient in this respect when the model yields to such procedures. But sometimes the model cannot be solved in this way.

However, simulation can pick up right where analysis leaves off. Although simulation methods generally are not as efficient as the analytical methods (when both can be applied to the same model), they can provide a good estimate of the optimal courses of action (using the very models that do not yield to analytical procedures).

Mathematical knowledge, at times, seems to be so complete that there appears to be nothing in reality too complex to be represented and analyzed in terms of mathematical models.

The fact is, however, that our present reality abounds with practical problems that cannot be handled satisfactorily by current analytical procedures. Usually, we can construct equations, inequalities, and probability distributions to represent satisfactorily parts of the real-world problem, but quite often there is no mathematical analysis available to obtain a solution (or an optimal course of action) that takes into account all the interrelated components of the model.

It is right here that simulation methods come in to provide much-needed help. To be sure, if a model can be solved using mathematical analysis, it is highly preferable to do so because it is relatively quick and rather low in computational cost.

However, when mathematical analysis bogs down, we are happy to have simulation procedures that permit us to "grope" toward the best prediction or best course of action. It is relatively slow and somewhat high in computational cost, but it can provide useful predictions and decisions in complex situations that lie beyond the reach of current analytical methods.

The rise in the use of simulation methods has been greatly facilitated by developments in high-speed electronic computers. The heavy and high-speed computation required in many current simulation studies could not have been accomplished prior to the electronic computer.

The usefulness of some of the many developments in modern analytical procedures (particularly, decision analysis and linear programming) has been discussed and illustrated in the previous chapters of this book.

But despite the progress in these ways, there are (as we have noted) particular types of problems that continue to elude the procedures of current analytical methods. This is especially so when it is necessary to represent in the mathematical model uncertainty, time factors, and numerous nonlinear relationships.

In the remainder of this chapter we shall focus on simulation methods associated with the inclusion in the model of uncertainty and time. First, we shall examine an illustration involving only uncertainty. Then, we shall look at the use of simulation in an inventory decision model, where both uncertainty and time are incorporated into the model.

SIMULATION: UNCERTAINTY REPRESENTED IN THE MODEL

Let us look at the way in which uncertainty is handled in simulation methods by taking a simple model where a solution actually can be obtained by the analytical procedures of probability.

Of course in practical work, simulation methods tend to be used only in cases where the analytical methods do not provide a solution. But if we apply simulation methods to the very same model on which we have used the analytical procedures, we shall be able to see how the two methods compare with each other.

An Illustration: The Packaging-Machine Example

Perhaps you recall the decision problem under uncertainty that we discussed in Chapter 2. In that problem a choice had to be made on whether to use a new packaging machine or an old one before we knew the quality of the packaging materials to be used by the machine.

We repeat part of that problem in Figure 19-1. It shows the uncertainty and profit outcomes only for the act "use new machine."

Also, note in Figure 19-1 that the probability now is .50 of receiving materials of good quality (and thus incurring a profit of $240). The probability is .50 (also) of receiving a poor-quality shipment and incurring a profit of $80.

In previous chapters, for each such course of action considered, we computed an expected profit. Then, the act with the highest expected profit was selected as the optimal act. This procedure is an illustration of the analytical procedures (referred to above) that are used to identify an optimal course of action.

Thus, in Figure 19-1 we compute an expected profit for the act "use new machine." It is $160: .50 ($240) + .50 ($80) = $160.

In this section we want to illustrate how we can *approximate* this expected profit of $160 by the methods of simulation (this type of simulation is sometimes called "Monte Carlo" simulation).

To be sure, we already have obtained the expected profit of the act, but it turns out that in some types of large, complex problems we cannot do this. However, by simulation we can get an approximate expected profit.

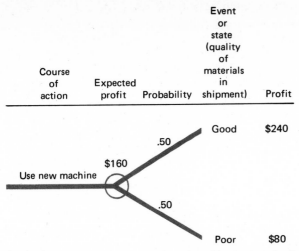

Course of action	Expected profit	Probability	Event or state (quality of materials in shipment)	Profit
		.50	Good	$240
Use new machine	$160			
		.50	Poor	$80

Figure 19-1   The uncertain events and profit outcomes for the act "use the new machine."

Recall that we referred to simulation as a procedure in which we manipulate the model or "try out" different alternative courses of action. In this example of simulation we repeatedly go down the single path "use new machine."

But to do this we need some random device that will in the long run send us down the path to "good-quality materials" 50 percent of the time and to "poor-quality materials" 50 percent of the time.

Simulating the Occurrence of Chance Events: Flipping a Coin   An ordinary (fair) coin is such a random device; and when the possible chance events are only two (with each event being equally probable), the outcome of a flip of the coin could be used to determine which event occurred (that is, in our experiment on the model).

But we have to decide in advance of this coin flipping just which event corresponds to the head on the coin and which to the tail.

Suppose that we agree in advance that if a head faces upward after the coin is tossed we will say that the event "good-quality materials" occurred; and, if a tail faces upward, the event "poor-quality materials" occurred. We summarize this association in Table 19-1.

On the first toss of the coin, suppose it comes to rest with the *head* facing upward. Then, we would say that the event "good-quality materials" occurred. And, when that event occurs, along with the act "use new machine," we incur a profit of $240.

We toss the coin again which represents another run of the chance process. Suppose this time the *tail* faces upward. Now, as indicated in Table 19-1, we say the event "poor-quality materials" has occurred. A profit outcome of $80 is associated with this event when it is combined with the act of using the new machine.

Table 19-1   The First Step in Simulating the Chance Occurrence of Receiving Good-Quality Materials or Poor-Quality Materials

Possible event (quality of materials)	Profit outcome (using the new machine)	Probability of this event and profit outcome	Assignment of heads and tails (in advance) to simulate the occurrence of this event and profit outcome
Good	$240	.50	If a head occurs, let us say this event occurred
Poor	80	.50	If a tail occurs, let us say this event occurred

Table 19-2   Simulating the Receipt of Five Shipments of the Materials

Outcome in tossing the coin	Simulated event (the quality of the materials)	Simulated profit outcome (using the new machine)
First toss is a head	Good	$240
Second toss is a tail	Poor	80
Third toss is a tail	Poor	80
Fourth toss is a tail	Poor	80
Fifth toss is a head	Good	240

In Table 19-2 we summarize the results of five tosses of the coin. This represents "going through" the tree (in Figure 19-1) five times with the event and profit outcomes being determined by chance in accordance with the .50–.50 probabilities.

We have simulated five events and their associated profit outcomes. Therefore, if we take an average of the simulated profit outcomes, we have an approximation to the long-term average profit of this act. This long-term average tends to be equal to the expected profit that we computed above.

From Table 19-2 we see that the average of the five simulated profit outcomes is $144. The expected profit (as shown in Figure 19-1) is $160.

Thus, we see something very typical of simulation studies. It is this: The average of the simulated profit outcomes (or other outcomes) will deviate by some amount from the expected profit (or expected outcome). Generally, the more simulations that are done, the smaller will be the deviation of the average simulated profit outcome from the expected profit outcome.

Of course, deviations of this type are to be expected from such experimentation or sampling. And the deviations tend to be larger when the simulations are few, as they are in our example. If we had done 25 or 30 simulations instead of the 5 (which we chose to do for ease of illustration), we would very likely obtain an average much closer to the expected profit, $160.

Simulating the Occurrence of Chance Events: Using Random Numbers
The use of coin tossing to simulate the occurrence of events and outcomes of a chance process essentially limits us to those chance processes with two events and two (profit) outcomes with equal probabilities.

What is needed is a more flexible random device or procedure that permits us to simulate chance processes with numerous events, each, perhaps, with a different probability of occurrence.

Such a procedure is obtained by using numbers that have been generated in a random fashion. Random numbers (or random digits) are usually generated by a physical process or through the use of a mathematical expression. These methods are analogous to the rather limited coin-flipping method discussed above or the drawing of names (or numbers) out of a hat.

There are computer subroutines available that generate sequences of random numbers. Also, published tables of random numbers are available. In Table 19-3 we reproduce part of a page of a widely used book that is mostly comprised of random digits.

Table 19-3   A Table of Random Digits*

6744	6861	5915	3509	9600	7692
2416	9160	9608	8607	2835	5955
1739	8380	8934	7863	6181	3916
3131	7385	8872	1696	5199	6562
5885	4583	3965	0518	3613	8231
1694	5596	5359	4404	2063	1201
7958	5147	5166	9694	4724	7691
7314	0993	3627	2353	2745	7082
5422	1391	6726	1791	6537	6456
8377	4092	2025	9241	8878	8499

In the construction of such a table, each digit had an equal chance of "being drawn" (of being generated by a random device). Since there are 10 digits (1, 2, 3, 4, 5, 6, 7, 8, 9, and 0), each digit had a probability of $\frac{1}{10}$ of being drawn.

Therefore, before looking at a table of random digits we would have to say that the probability of, say, the digit 7 appearing in the upper-left corner of the table (or in any other position in the table) is $\frac{1}{10}$. This is the same probability we would attach to any of the other digits appearing in any particular position in the table.

To simulate a chance process involving 10 events (each having a probability of occurrence of $\frac{1}{10}$), we can simply associate event 1 with the occurrence of the digit 1, event 2 with the occurrence of the digit 2, and so on. Of course we must always decide on the correspondence between the events and the digits *before* going to the table of random digits. Otherwise, we may not be allowing the simulated events to occur in accordance with the probabilities that were originally specified.

To illustrate the use of a table of random digits to simulate chance events, let us return to the packaging-machine example in Figure 19-1. True, we simulated this chance process by tossing a coin, but the equivalent procedure using the table of random digits may be worth noting.

The first step is to construct a table such as the one appearing in Table 19-4. For each possible event and profit outcome we list the associated probabilities of .50 and .50. Then, we assign the random digits 1, 2, 3, 4, and 5 to the event "good-quality materials."

To the event "poor-quality materials" we assign the digits 6, 7, 8, 9, and 0. If any of the digits 1, 2, 3, 4, or 5 occurs, we say that the event "good-quality materials" occurred. If 6, 7, 8, 9, or 0 occurs, we say the event "poor-quality materials" occurred.

But are we representing the correct probabilities (.50 and .50) of the events in this simulation? Yes, because each digit has a $\frac{1}{10}$ probability of occurring. Thus, the probability of the digit 1 or 2 or 3 or 4 or 5 occurring is simply the sum

Table 19-4 Assignment of Random Numbers to Simulate the Chance Occurrence of Receiving Good-Quality Materials or Poor-Quality Materials

Possible event (quality of materials)	Profit outcome (using the new machine)	Probability of this event and profit outcome	Random numbers assigned to simulate the occurrence of this event and profit outcome
Good	$240	.50	1, 2, 3, 4, and 5
Poor	80	.50	6, 7, 8. 9. and 0

**Table 19-5 Simulating the Receipt of
Ten Shipments of the Materials**

Random number drawn	Simulated event (quality of materials in shipment)	Simulated profit outcome (using new machine)
6	Poor	$ 80
2	Good	240
1	Good	240
3	Good	240
5	Good	240
1	Good	240
7	Poor	80
7	Poor	80
5	Good	240
8	Poor	80
		$1,760

Average of the simulated
profit outcomes
$$= \frac{\$1,760}{10} = \$176$$

of their individual probabilities (the occurrence of each digit being mutually exclusive). Thus, the .50 probability of the event "good-quality materials" is correctly represented by the .50 probability of "drawing" 1 or 2 or 3 or 4 or 5 in the table of random digits: $\frac{1}{10} + \frac{1}{10} + \frac{1}{10} + \frac{1}{10} + \frac{1}{10} = \frac{5}{10}$.

In Table 19-5 we show 10 simulations of the chance process represented in Figure 19-1. We decided in advance to start in the upper-left corner of the table of random digits (Table 19-3) and proceed down the first column of digits. Since we want to do 10 simulations, we took the first 10 digits in the first column and placed them in Table 19-5.

Then, since we assigned random digits to these events in Table 19-4, we use that assignment to determine which event occurred when each random digit occurred.

For example, the first digit is 6. This digit is in the set of digits that is associated with the event "poor-quality materials." Thus we say this event occurred in the first simulation. And with this event the profit outcome of $80 occurs.

The second digit is 2, which simulates the occurrence of the event "good-quality materials" with a profit outcome of $240. The remainder of Table 19-5 is completed in this same fashion.

The final step in the simulation of the chance process is that of obtaining an average of the simulated profit outcomes. From Table 19-5 we see that it turns

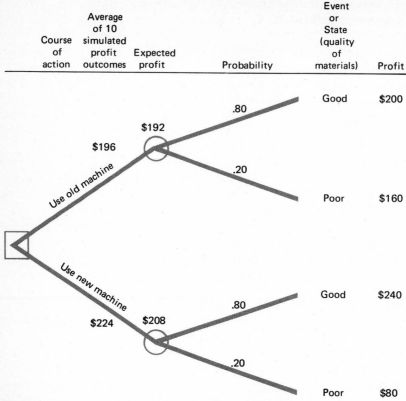

Course of action	Average of 10 simulated profit outcomes	Expected profit	Probability	Event or State (quality of materials)	Profit
			.80	Good	$200
		$192			
	$196				
Use old machine			.20	Poor	$160
			.80	Good	$240
Use new machine	$224	$208			
			.20	Poor	$80

Figure 19-2 A two-act decision problem under uncertainty.

Table 19-6   The New Assignment of Random Numbers Due to the New Probabilities

Possible event (quality of the materials)	Probability of this event	Random numbers assigned to simulate the occurrence of this event
Good	.80	1, 2, 3, 4, 5, 6, 7, and 8
Poor	.20	9 and 0

out to be $176. Thus, the average of our 10 simulated profit outcomes deviates, too, from the expected profit of $160.

Simulating Chance Events with Unequal Probabilities   But most chance events and outcomes do not occur with equal probabilities. Thus, we must use a little ingenuity in order to use the table of random digits where each digit has the same probability of .10. Let us illustrate this with an example related to the one in Figure 19-1.

The example in Figure 19-2 repeats the original packaging-machine problem in Chapter 2 with the very same acts, events, probabilities, and profit outcomes. We have unequal probabilities on the events now (.80 and .20), and there is the problem of choosing one of the two acts.

In this simple illustration we can compute the expected profit for each act ($192 and $208), and, by using the maximization-of-expected-profit criterion, we can select an optimal act ("use new machine" with an expected profit of $208).

But to gain some familiarity with the procedures of simulation, suppose for the very same problem we attempt to select the optimal course of action after 10 simulations using the table of random digits. (In real-world applications the simulations should be many more.)

First, we must make a table (such as the one in Table 19-6) in which we assign random digits to the events. Because we want to have the event "good-quality materials" occur 80 percent of the time in the simulations, we assign the digits 1 through 8 to the occurrence of this event, and the digits 9 and 0 to the occurrence of the other event, "poor-quality materials."

Let us simulate the occurrence of an event (and its profit outcome) in this chance process 10 times. Therefore, we must obtain 10 random digits from Table 19-3. They can come from any place in the table, but let us decide in advance to start at the top of the second column of digits from the upper-left corner and proceed downward. This gives us the random numbers appearing in the extreme left-hand column of Table 19-7.

From our random-number assignments in Table 19-6, we see that the occurrence of the first number, 7, represents the occurrence of the event "good-quality materials." If this event is combined with the act "use new machine," the profit outcome is $240. If it is combined with the act "use old machine," it is $200.

In Table 19-7 we record the events and profit outcomes associated with each random number drawn.

The final step again is to compute the average of the simulated profit outcomes. But now we have two acts, and so we have an average simulated profit outcome for each of the acts. For the act "use new machine" it is $224, and for "use old machine" it is $196.

We went back to Figure 19-2 and inserted the average of the 10 simulated profit outcomes for each act where it is easy to compare them with the associated expected profits.

The main point is that by the procedures of simulation we have illustrated an alternative (or supplementary) method of deciding on a particular course of action (or of making a prediction).

We see from Figure 19-2 that our simulation procedure identifies the act "use new machine" as being optimal—the same act identified as optimal by the computation of the expected profit for each act. The act "use new machine" has

Table 19-7   Using Simulation Methods to Select a Best Course of Action

Random number drawn	Simulated event (quality of materials)	Simulated profit outcome using new machine	Simulated profit outcome using old machine
7	Good	$ 240	$ 200
4	Good	240	200
7	Good	240	200
1	Good	240	200
8	Good	240	200
6	Good	240	200
9	Poor	80	160
3	Good	240	200
4	Good	240	200
3	Good	240	200
		$2,240	$1,960
Average of simulated profit outcomes	$2,240 = —— = 10	$224 for using new machine	$1,960 —— = 10 $196 for using old machine

an average simulated profit of $224 (compared with an expected profit of $208), and the act "use old machine" has an average simulated profit of $196 (compared with an expected profit of $192).

Although the packaging-machine problem just discussed lends itself to either method of choosing a course of action, the methods of simulation can be applied to complex problems that do not yield to analytical methods (such as those methods involving expected profits). It is time to turn our discussion toward such a problem.

SIMULATION: UNCERTAINTY AND TIME BOTH REPRESENTED IN THE MODEL

We have noted that in many real-world problems there is uncertainty that we wish to represent in a model. Additionally, it may be important that time is taken into account as well. Some important changes in reality may be associated with the passage of time.

In doing this we can obtain a model that corresponds more closely to the real situation with which we are concerned. But unfortunately, the more realistic model is often a more complex model and the increased complexity may make it difficult or even impossible to solve by analytical means.

It is in cases such as these that simulation methods can be very useful. Let us illustrate some of the main steps in this method with a not-too-complicated inventory-decision example.

An Inventory Example

Suppose a bookstore wishes to carry a standard desk-size dictionary in stock. Demand is uncertain, and the replenishment of stock cannot be immediate (it takes some time).

There is the usual inventory decision problem. What quantity should be ordered and at what time should the order be placed?

We saw in the earlier chapter on inventories that frequent orders of small amounts generally keep carrying costs low but incur high ordering costs due to the many orders placed. Large and infrequent orders reduce ordering costs, but they cause high average inventories and relatively high carrying costs.

In the earlier chapter on inventories we saw that the E.O.Q. (economic order quantity) model adequately incorporated such carrying costs and ordering costs as long as the demand was known. You may have noticed that we did not satisfactorily incorporate uncertainty and time into the discussion on the E.O.Q. model.

It is often difficult in large and more realistic inventory decision problems to represent uncertainty and time in a model so that analytical procedures will obtain an optimal order quantity and the time the order should be placed.

Of course our bookstore example is still a very simplified one, but let us use it to illustrate how simulation can provide us with an estimate of the best order quantity and reorder point.

The relevant data in this inventory decision model are as follows:

Demand amounts (per day): 1, 2, 3, or 4 units with probabilities of .10, .40, .30, and .20, respectively

Carrying costs (per unit per day): $.50

Ordering costs (per order): $6.00

Replenishment time (lead time): 2 days

Objective: To identify a combination of an order quantity and a reorder point (reorder inventory level) that minimizes total inventory costs (carrying costs plus ordering costs).

Trying Out Different Inventory Decision Rules by Simulation A common simulation procedure that attempts to obtain an estimate of the best inventory decision rule (the best order quantity and reorder point) in a particular situation is to simulate a large number of days (or weeks or whatever is relevant), first, using one decision rule, and then, repeating the simulation for the same number of days using another decision rule, and so on.

For example, in our bookstore problem we shall make separate simulation runs of 10 days using each of the following inventory decision rules:

a   Order 6 units when present inventory plus orders not yet received is less
than 8 units.
b   Order 9 units when present inventory plus orders not yet received is less
than 8 units.
c   Order 12 units when present inventory plus orders not yet received is less
than 8 units.

The simulation runs give us an average inventory cost per day for each of the
three inventory decision rules. Then, from the set of three decision rules that
have been tried out in the simulation runs, we can easily identify the one that
incurs the lowest inventory cost per day.

In this introductory discussion we shall keep matters as simple as possible to
illustrate the procedure clearly. First, we shall consider only the three selected
decision rules, each having the same reorder point of 8 units but with a different
order quantity. The procedure would be the same if we considered different
reorder points, too (which we would likely want to do in a practical application).

Also, we shall simulate only 10 days using each of the three decision rules.
This is definitely too short a simulation run to get results in which we can place
much confidence. The simulation run should be for several hundred days for
each of the decision rules to get reliable estimates of inventory costs.

Obviously, hand computations for such large runs would be too burden-
some. Therefore, we see why most simulations of practical problems require the
use of the computer.

Getting Ready for the Simulation Run   Let us, then, simulate 10 days using
each of the above decision rules and see which one of the three incurs the
lowest average inventory cost per day.

We have uncertainty in demand, and so one of the first steps we will want to
take is to assign random numbers to each of the demand amounts so that we can
simulate the demand occurrences each day in accordance with the given probabilities. In Table 19-8 we make an appropriate assignment of random numbers to
the demand amounts.

Let us "try out" for 10 days the first of the three decision rules. Under this
decision rule we shall place an order of 6 units whenever the present inventory
plus the units on order is less than 8.

We can represent our simulation run most simply by constructing a table
such as the one appearing in Table 19-9.

In the first column (from the left) we simply record the day numbers in our
simulation run. Since the run is for 10 days, our table will be comprised of 10
rows.

For each day we want to simulate a demand amount in accordance with the
given probabilities. In Table 19-8 we made the necessary random-number assignments. Therefore, once we decide where to obtain the random numbers we are
ready to begin.

Suppose we decide in advance to use the third column of digits in Table 19-3.

Table 19-8 The Assignment of Random Numbers to Simulate the Occurrence of the Daily Demand Amount in the Inventory Problem

Demand amount each day	Probability of this demand amount	Random numbers assigned to simulate the occurrence of this demand amount
1	.10	1
2	.40	2–5
3	.30	6–8
4	.20	9 and 0

We need 10 random numbers, and so the single column of digits is sufficient. These random numbers are: 4, 1, 3, 3, 8, 9, 5, 1, 2, and 7.

We simply associate a random number with each day in order to simulate the demand for that day. Thus, the second column in Table 19-9 is comprised of the random numbers in the order in which they appear in the table. Then, from the assignments of the random numbers that we made in Table 19-8, we obtain a simulated demand amount for each day.

For example, for day 1 the random number is 4. From Table 19-8 we see that this random number is associated with a demand amount of 2. The simulated demand amounts for the other 9 days are similarly obtained.

The next six columns of Table 19-9 are concerned with inventory levels and the amounts on order each day over the 10-day simulation run. The other remaining columns require two main steps: the first is the daily application of the assumed decision rule in order to determine whether or not an order should be placed that day; the second is the daily calculation of the inventory costs (carrying costs and ordering costs).

In starting our simulation run, suppose that at the beginning of day 1 the inventory is already at 5 units. Also, 6 units were ordered 2 days ago.

Thus, we insert 5 in the column headed "inventory beginning today." We insert 6 in the column "amount ordered 2 days ago." And we place a 0 in the column "amount order 1 day ago" since none was ordered then.

Our job now is to complete the rest of the table. The end result is the completed table shown in Table 19-10. But let us work through the first few days of the simulation run to see how the completed table was formed.

Simulation of Day 1 In day 1 the simulated demand amount is 2 units. Thus, if the inventory at the beginning of day 1 is 5 units, the inventory at the end of day 1 must be 3 units. We record this in the table.

Table 19-9 The Simulation Table Ready for a 10-Day Run of the Inventory Problem

Simulated daily demand			Inventory beginning today	Inventory at end of today	Amount on order		Amount available for inventory tomorrow	Previous orders plus end-of-today inventory	Amount to order today	Inventory costs		
Day	Random number drawn	Simulated demand amount			Amount ordered 1 day ago	Amount ordered 2 days ago				Carrying costs today	Ordering costs today	Inventory costs today
1	4	2	5		0	6						
2	1	1										
3	3	2										
4	3	2										
5	8	3										
6	9	4										
7	5	2										
8	1	1										
9	2	2										
10	7	3										

Table 19-10 The Results of the 10-Day Simulation Run of the Inventory Problem with an Order Quantity of 6 Units

Simulated Daily Demand					Amount on Order					Inventory Costs		
Day	Random number drawn	Simulated demand amount	Inventory beginning today	Inventory at end of today	Amount ordered 1 day ago	Amount ordered 2 days ago	Amount available for inventory tomorrow	Previous orders plus end-of-today inventory	Amount to order today	Carrying costs today	Ordering costs today	Inventory costs today
1	4	2	5	3	0	6	9	9	0	$ 4.50	$ 0.00	$ 4.50
2	1	1	9	8	0	0	8	8	0	4.00	0.00	4.00
3	3	2	8	6	0	0	6	6	6	3.00	6.00	9.00
4	3	2	6	4	6	0	4	10	0	2.00	0.00	2.00
5	8	3	4	1	0	6	7	7	6	3.50	6.00	9.50
6	9	4	7	3	6	0	3	9	0	1.50	0.00	1.50
7	5	2	3	1	0	6	7	7	6	3.50	6.00	9.50
8	1	1	7	6	6	0	6	12	0	3.00	0.00	3.00
9	2	2	6	4	0	6	10	10	0	5.00	0.00	5.00
10	7	3	10	7	0	0	7	7	6	3.50	6.00	9.50
										$33.50	$24.00	$57.50

Next, we must obtain the inventory amount that will be available tomorrow. This is simply the sum of the inventory at the end of today (day 1) plus the amount ordered 2 days ago (it will arrive in such time that it will be available on the third day from the time the order was placed). Thus, the amount of inventory available tomorrow (for day 2) is 9: 3 + 6 = 9.

For the next column, we need to obtain the present inventory (end of day 1) plus the amounts on order. For day 1, this is 9: 3 + 6 = 9. To this amount we apply our decision rule: Order 6 units if the present inventory plus the amounts on order is less than 8 units. For day 1 it is not less than 8 (it is 9), and so no order is placed in day 1 (therefore, we insert 0 in this column).

The last three columns pertain to inventory costs. Carrying costs for each day are obtained simply by multiplying the carrying cost per unit per day (here it is $.50) by the amount of inventory available for tomorrow (here in day 1 it is 9 units). Thus, for day 1 the carrying cost is $4.50: (9) ($.50) = $4.50. And, since no order is placed in day 1, the ordering costs are $0. Therefore, total inventory costs for day 1 are $4.50: $4.50 + $0 = $4.50.

Simulation of Day 2 For day 2 our first step is to insert the correct inventory amount at the beginning of that day. Actually, it was determined in day 1 and was called "inventory available for tomorrow." Thus, we observe that it was 9 in the day 1 row, and so we merely insert a 9 in the day 2 row in the column "inventory available at the beginning of today."

The second step we take for day 2 is to update by 1 day the amounts on order. Nothing was ordered in day 1, and so in day 2 the amount ordered 1 day ago will be 0. Back in the day 1 row, we also see that nothing was ordered 1 day ago (from day 1). Thus, for the day 2 row we note with a 0 that nothing was ordered 2 days ago (from day 2). In the day 1 row we also see the 6 units ordered 2 days ago (from day 1). Thus, for the day 2 row these 6 units no longer will be on order; they will have gone into the inventory available for tomorrow (for day 2).

Now, for day 2 we look at the simulated demand amount. It is 1 unit. Therefore, the inventory at the end of day 2 is 8. The amount available for inventory tomorrow also is 8 since there was nothing ordered 2 days ago.

The present inventory (at the end of day 2) plus the units on order also is 8. Applying the decision rule does not result in an order being placed in day 2, either. Finally, the carrying costs for day 2 are $4.00: 8 ($.50) = $4.00. Since there are no ordering costs, total inventory costs for the day are $4.00.

Simulation of Day 3 For day 3 we update again. The inventory at the beginning of day 3 is 8, the same as that indicated in day 2 for the next day. And nothing is on order.

The inventory at the end of day 3 is 6 because the simulated demand amount is 2. The inventory available for the next day also is 6. And present inventory (at end of today) plus the amount on order is 6. Thus, the application of the decision rule (order 6 when present inventory plus units on order is less than 8) requires an order of 6 units to be placed in day 3. Of course only orders of 6 units are possible under this decision rule.

For day 3 the carrying costs are $3.00: 6 ($.50) = $3.00. The ordering costs are $6.00. Thus, the total inventory costs for day 3 are $9.00.

Simulation of Day 4 The inventory at the beginning of day 4 is 6. The amount on order is 6 units (placed 1 day ago). With a simulated demand amount of 2, the inventory at the end of day 4 is 4 units. The inventory available for the next day also is 4.

The present inventory (at the end of the day) plus units of order is 10: 4 + 6 = 10. Therefore, the application of the decision rule results in no order being placed for day 4. The carrying costs are $2.00, and this comprises the entire inventory costs for day 4.

Simulation of Day 5 The inventory at the beginning of day 5 is 4. And the 6 units that were ordered 1 day ago in day 4 now become 6 units ordered 2 days ago. At the end of today (day 5) they will go into inventory.

Thus, the amount available for inventory for tomorrow is 7. This is because the simulated demand of 3 leaves only 1 unit in inventory at the end of day 5. That 1 unit, augmented by the 6 units coming into inventory, gives a total of 7 units available for tomorrow.

In day 5, the present inventory, plus the amount on order, is also 7. Thus, when the decision rule is applied in day 5, a new order of 6 units is indicated. Carrying costs are $3.50 for the day, and ordering costs are $6.00. Thus, total inventory costs for day 5 are $9.50.

The rest of the days in the simulation run are similarly treated as seen in Table 19-10.

What is of particular interest in Table 19-10 is the average inventory cost per day using this decision rule. We see that for 10 days the total inventory costs are $57.50. Thus, the average inventory cost per day in $5.75: $57.50 ÷ 10 days = $5.75.

If for each of the other two decision rules we repeat the same simulation run for 10 days (with the same random numbers to simulate the demand and the same beginning inventory of 5 units and amount on order of 6), we would obtain an average inventory cost per day that would allow us to compare the three decision rules.

Thus, if we were to begin with Table 19-9 and when we reordered we would order 9 units (instead of 6), we would be simulating the use of one of the other decision rules. If we were to order 12 units when we reordered, we would be simulating the third decision rule.

We actually made these two additional simulation runs, one for each of the other two decision rules. The inventory costs for all three decision rules are summarized in Table 19-11.

From this set of three decision rules (but only with simulation runs of 10

Table 19-11   The Inventory Costs Under Three Different Decision Rules Obtained from a Simulation Run of 10 Days Under Each Decision Rule

Reorder level	Order quantity	Carrying costs for 10 days	Ordering costs for 10 days	Total inventory costs for 10 days	Average inventory cost per day
8	6	$33.50	$24.00	$57.50	$5.75
8	9	38.00	18.00	56.00	5.60 (minimum)
8	12	45.50	12.00	57.50	5.75

days), we identify the decision rule with the order quantity of 9 as the one with the lowest inventory cost per day.

We emphasize again that for practical problems we must make simulation runs of several hundred days in such cases in order to get good estimates of the inventory costs per day for each decision rule. Therefore, the decision rule that minimizes inventory costs per day cannot be identified with reliability unless the simulation runs are *much larger* than those used in our example. Also, more decision rules than three should be simulated. Consideration could then be given to decision rules involving different reorder inventory levels (reorder points) as well as different order quantities.

SUMMARY

1   If we wish to learn more about some part of reality and to make good decisions in the reality, we can proceed in two main ways:

a   We can *experiment directly with the reality* by manipulating some elements in the reality such as "trying out" different courses of action in the reality or

b   We can *construct a model of the reality* (such as the mathematical models discussed in this book). Then, once the model is constructed we can use it to make decisions or predictions in connection with the reality. These decisions or predictions can be obtained by two main procedures:

i   *by the application of analytical operations* such as those discussed prior to this chapter.

ii   *by experimenting with the constructed model,* that is, by manipulating some elements in the model such as "trying out" different courses of action in the model. This procedure, usually called *simulation,* is in contrast to experimenting directly with the reality.

2   Although we can construct models of complex segments of reality that represent the reality well, it frequently turns out that analytical procedures are not capable of providing a solution, such as a prediction or optimal course of action. It is in such instances that the method of simulation is especially useful in obtaining estimates or approximations to the analytical-type solutions.

3   In previous chapters on choosing a course of action under uncertainty, we usually computed an expected profit for each act and then identified the act with the highest expected profit as the best act to take. This involved what is called an *analytical procedure* of probability.

4   In this chapter we have seen that we can select an act under uncertainty by *simulating* the taking of each act a large number of times and observing the event and the profit outcome each time. The act with the largest average of the simulated profit outcomes is the indicated best act under the simulation procedure. In models too complex to be solved by analytical procedures, simulation is usually the only workable alternative. However, it is costly and cumbersome, and so it tends to be used only when analytical procedures fail.

PROBLEMS

19-1   Look up in a dictionary the meaning given to the word "simulation." Compare that definition with the special meaning associated with the term in simulation studies of the type discussed in this chapter.

19-2   In Table 19-2 we summarized the results of tossing a fair coin five times in order to simulate the occurrence of five events and the associated profit outcomes of "use new machine."

    a   Make your own simulation study of the average profit (using the new machine) by tossing a coin 25 times. Record the results in a table such as that in Table 19-2.

    b   Compute the average of your 25 simulated profit outcomes. Is the average you attained closer to the $160 expected profit (shown in Figure 19-1) than the $144 average that we obtained tossing the coin five times? If it is not, try another 25 tosses (50 tosses all together).

19-3   In Problems 2-1 and 2-2 we examined a decision under uncertainty for a timber-products firm. A decision had to be made on whether to produce plywood or regular lumber before the quality of the logs was known.

    a   Going back to the original data in Problems 2-1 and 2-2, obtain the expected profit for each act.

    b   Assign random numbers to the events in accordance with the probabilities given in Problem 2-2.

    c   Using the fourth column of digits in Table 19-3, simulate 10 times the chance process of receiving a good batch of logs or a poor one. Construct a table showing your results (as in Table 19-7).

    d   What is the average simulated profit outcome for each act?

    e   On the basis of your simulation study, which is the best act to take?

    f   How does your answer in *e* compare with the best act obtained by using the maximization-of-expected-profit criterion?

19-4   A decision on whether or not to drill for oil in a particular region was examined in Problem 2-10.

    a   From the data in Problem 2-10, what is the expected profit if drilling is undertaken?

    b   Assign random numbers to the possible events in accordance with the probabilities given in Problem 2-10.

    c   Using the fifth column of digits in Table 19-3 simulate 10 times the chance process of drilling for oil. Construct a table (as in Figure 19-7) that shows your results.

d On the basis of your simulation study, should the drilling take place?

e How does the average of the simulated profit outcomes compare with the expected profit?

19-5 In Figure 3-9 we examined a copying-machine problem that involved making two copies of a document. We could get 0, 1, or 2 good copies with probabilities of .25, .50, and .25, respectively.

a Assign random numbers to the possible values of the random variable (the number of good copies). (*Note:* Now we need to assign two-digit numbers to each outcome because we have two-digit probabilities. Each two-digit random number had a probability of occurrence of .01. Since 0 good copies has a probability of .25, we need to assign the numbers 01 through 25 to 0 good copies. The random numbers 26 through 75 are assigned to 1 good copy, and the random numbers 76 through 00 to 2 good copies.)

b Using the ninth through the twelfth columns of digits in Table 19-3, simulate 20 times the chance process of making two copies of the document. Construct a table (as in Table 19-7) that shows your results.

c What is the average number of good copies on the basis of your study? How does it compare with the expected number of good copies (as computed in Figure 3-9)?

19-6 In our discussion of the bookstore's inventory decision in this chapter, we illustrated in Table 19-10 a 10-day simulation run using the decision rule "order 6 units when present inventory plus units on order is less than 8 units."

Taking Table 19-9 as your starting point, do a 10-day simulation run using the decision rule "order 9 units when present inventory plus units on order is less than 8 units." Obtain a table such as the one in Table 19-10. Check your simulated inventory costs using this decision rule with those shown for this decision rule in Table 19-11.

19-7 Do a 10-day simulation run of the bookstore inventory decision problem (discussed in this chapter) using the decision rule "order 12 units when present inventory plus units on order is less than 8 units."

Use Table 19-9 as a starting point and obtain a completed table as in Table 19-10. See if your simulated inventory costs agree with those shown for this decision rule in Table 19-11.

Chapter 20

Waiting-Line Problems

The problem of lines (or "queues") forming to await service of some sort is common to each of us. It is an obvious inconvenience and cost to those waiting in line, both in terms of time and of lost opportunities for engaging in other activities. But the waiting lines also can incur costs to those supplying the service, particularly if some customers do not wait for the service, thereby reducing the potential revenue and profit for the firm. Sometimes, too, within a firm, employees may wait for some service which results in a cost in terms of lost production due to their idleness.

SOME OF THE CAUSES OF WAITING-LINE PROBLEMS

If the supplier of the service can foresee perfectly the demand for the service (the arrivals of customers) and if there are no considerations of cost in obtaining the resources necessary to provide immediate service for various possible demand amounts, waiting lines essentially could be avoided.

Thus, to eliminate waiting lines, perfect knowledge of the demand (the arrivals) is necessary, along with the availability of resources and supplies to accommodate any number of customers on an immediate basis.

In real situations, however, the arrivals (the demand amounts) cannot be foreseen perfectly, and, also, there usually is a substantial cost in acquiring the facilities and resources that would be necessary to provide the service on an immediate basis. Thus, waiting-line problems involve a kind of "tug of war" between the resource costs that would be incurred in order to provide more immediate service and the costs of having customers wait for service.

Waiting-line problems are found in virtually every industry and public-service activity. A few of these are listed in Table 20-1. The list suggests a much wider applicability of waiting-line models than we might initially assume.

In the next section we shall examine some of the concepts and terms that are common in waiting-line models. In a later section we shall look at the main considerations in making decisions with regard to waiting lines and we shall illustrate the simulation approach to the study of waiting lines. In a final section we shall illustrate the somewhat limited analytical methods in waiting-line studies.

We should point out that our treatment of waiting-line models is introductory. The discussion is in quite general terms in order that we may gain some perspective and a framework for more detailed waiting-line studies.

CONCEPTS IN WAITING-LINE MODELS

There are a number of concepts and terms that are perhaps unique to waiting-line models. The main concepts and terms are "waiting lines," "arriving units," "servers," and "service times."

Waiting Lines Defined

A waiting line usually forms when persons (or units) arriving to receive some service cannot be accommodated immediately. Thus, we define a waiting line

Table 20-1 Some Real-World Waiting-Line Problems

Arriving units	Servers	Waiting line
Cars in need of gasoline	Attendants at service stations	Cars
Customers with groceries	Checkout clerks at grocery store	Customers
Airplanes ready to land	Airport runways	"Stack" of planes
Trucks to be unloaded	Dock crews	Trucks
Machines in need of repair	Repair specialists	Idle machines
Patients in need of medical care	Doctors	Patients
Buildings on fire	Firefighters	Burning buildings
Cases to be tried	Judges	Cases to be tried

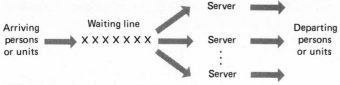

Figure 20-1 A typical waiting-line system.

simply as an accumulation of persons (or units) waiting to be provided with some service.

A diagram depicting a typical waiting-line system is shown in Figure 20-1. There is a flow of units into the system, a service is provided for each arriving unit, and then they depart from the system.

The Bathtub Analogy   Sometimes it is instructive to think of a waiting-line system as being roughly analogous to a bathtub with the faucet turned on and the drain partially open.

If the inflow of water is less than the outflow capacity, there is no accumulation of water in the tub. Neither is there an accumulation if the inflow of water and the outflow capacity are the same. Thus, it is essentially when the inflow of water is greater than the outflow capacity that water accumulates in the tub.

The analogy is closest to waiting-line problems when the inflow of water varies by chance, such as when random changes occur in the water pressure. Then, even though the outflow capacity and the *average* inflow of water may be the same, there would be periods of time when an accumulation of water would occur depending on the random changes in the water pressure (that is, for short periods of time the inflow would be greater than the outflow capacity).

Thus, the accumulation of water in a tub is analogous to the accumulation of units in a waiting line. And in waiting lines, as in bathtubs, the amount of the accumulation (the length of the waiting line) depends primarily on the rate of inflow to the system (arriving units) and the outflow capacity (the capacity for performing the particular service).

The Length of a Waiting Line   The length of a waiting line simply refers to the number of persons or units waiting for service. Sometimes it is defined to include the person or unit being served, and sometimes it is not.

An interesting point in connection with waiting lines is that there are applications in which the waiting line is not comprised of persons or units grouped at one particular point. Stalled cars on a cold morning awaiting service from a mechanic are in a waiting line of this type.

Waiting-Line Discipline   This concept refers to such items as the order in which units in the waiting line are served. In our discussions we shall assume the common "first-come-first-served" order of service.

In some models, however, *priorities* may be established (such as giving an airplane that is low on fuel first priority in landing). In still others, a *random selection* of those in the waiting line is the basis for selecting the next person or unit to receive service. This is common in telephone communications systems (one of the first areas in which waiting-line models were used) where the telephone calls are the "arriving units," the service is provided by the telephone circuits, and the waiting line is comprised of the incompleted calls. The next call that becomes completed usually is determined by chance and not by giving the person placing the first incompleted call the next opportunity for service.

Other aspects of waiting-line discipline are concerned with the number of separate waiting lines and whether or not those in the line ever leave. In some waiting-line models these aspects must be incorporated. In our discussions, we merely make note of these aspects and focus on the simpler models.

Arriving Units and the Servers

The persons or units arriving for a particular service are simply referred to as the *arriving units*. As shown in Table 20-1, they may be grocery-store customers wishing to check out, airplanes ready to land, filled trucks ready to be unloaded, or idle machines in need of repair.

The arriving units essentially constitute the demand for the service provided by the "servers." The *servers* are defined as the persons (or persons and equipment) that provide some particular service for the arriving units.

For the examples cited above, the servers are the grocery checkout clerks, runways of an airport, unloading crews at a dock, or repair workers who service the idle machines. Although the number of arriving units over a fairly long period of time is usually large, there may be only one server in the system. In our diagram in Figure 20-1, however, we depict the case of more than one server.

In the bathtub analogy we discussed the inflow of water and the outflow capacity. The accumulation of water in the tub clearly depends upon the relationship between the two.

In waiting-line models, the rate of arrivals (for example, so many arrivals per minute, hour, or day) represents the inflow to the system, and the outflow capacity depends upon the number of servers and the time it takes each of them to perform the service.

If there is just one server, the outflow capacity of the waiting-line system is simply the "service time" for one server. *Service time* is defined as the time it takes one server to provide the particular service to one customer. In our discussions we shall assume the service time to be constant, but in some cases it may vary and in an unpredictable way (such as the time it takes a doctor to see each patient). Thus, it may be necessary at times to incorporate into the model the probabilities of different service times.

An Illustrative Example: Unloading Trucks

Suppose an automobile manufacturer has the component parts that are needed in its assembly operations delivered by truck directly to its assembly facility from the various suppliers.

Loaded trucks arrive at the assembly facility throughout the day at the rate of 2 per hour. There is a dock crew of 2 persons, and the crew takes ½ hour to unload each truck. Thus, two trucks per hour can be unloaded by the dock crew of 2.

In this example the arriving units are the loaded trucks, and the servers are the two persons in the dock crew. But what about a waiting line? Will one form?

To determine whether or not a waiting line will form, we need some more information. Particularly, we need to know if the number of arrivals per hour varies from hour to hour. If it varies, perhaps we can know in advance just how it will vary. If there is uncertainty with regard to the number of arrivals, however, we need to know the probabilities of the various arrival possibilities.

The very simplest case would be where the trucks arrive at a constant (fixed) rate of 2 per hour (no more than 2 and no less than 2). The capacity of the servers (the dock crew of 2 persons) in unloading the trucks is 2 trucks per hour. Thus, we can see that in this special case 2 trucks would arrive each hour, within an hour both trucks would be unloaded, and no waiting line would form.

A slightly more complicated case would be one where the loaded trucks arrive at an *average* rate of 2 per hour but where the actual number of arrivals varies from, say, 0 to 5 trucks each hour. Now if the number of trucks arriving each hour could be known in advance, it would be possible to schedule the correct number of servers (the number of persons in the dock crew) so that whatever number of trucks arrive they could all be unloaded in an hour. The capacity of each server (each member of the dock crew) to unload trucks is assumed to be one truck per hour, and so if 5 trucks were known to be arriving in a particular hour, 5 servers could be scheduled for that hour.

A summary of this case, where a waiting line could be avoided even though there are variations in the number of arrivals, is shown in Table 20-2. Of course if

Table 20-2 When Variations in the Arrivals Can Be Known the Correct Number of Servers Can Be Scheduled to Avoid a Waiting Line

Number of trucks arriving per hour	The appropriate number of servers (number of persons in the dock crew) to avoid any waiting line (and idle-server time)
0	0
1	1
2	2
3	3
4	4
5	5

there is no attempt to schedule the servers in response to the known number of arrivals, a waiting line of trucks would likely occur at times.

The more typical case is where there is variation in the number of arriving units, but the variation cannot be predicted perfectly. Thus, there is uncertainty as to the actual number of arrivals each hour.

We indicated above that in cases involving uncertainty we need probabilities to associate with each of the possible number of arrivals. This requires the gathering of data on the relative frequency of different numbers of arrivals in those past periods closely analogous to the future period with which the study is concerned.

Suppose the relative frequency of arrivals permits us to obtain the probabilities as shown in Table 20-3. Then, computing the expected number of arrivals per hour, we find it to be 2 trucks: $.15(0) + .25(1) + .25(2) + .20(3) + .10(4) + .05(5) = 2$.

We now have the classic waiting-line model: the number of servers must be scheduled before the actual (future) arrivals are known. However, the expected number of arrivals is 2 trucks per hour. It might appear that a dock crew of 2 persons would be best because such a crew could unload 2 trucks per hour. But when there are chance variations in the number of arrivals, it turns out (as we shall see later) that it may not be best to schedule 2 servers.

In studying the best number of servers to schedule in the face of uncertainty, we need to compare the *cost of different service levels* (different numbers of servers) with the *expected cost of waiting*. Let us turn to that problem now.

DECISIONS WITH REGARD TO WAITING LINES

One of the main decisions to be made in connection with waiting-line systems pertains to the level of service to be chosen for the system. In many problems this reduces itself to the choice of the number of servers to be scheduled to serve the uncertain demand.

Although it is possible in some cases to consider measures designed to increase the efficiency of the servers (that is, reducing the service time per server), we shall focus on the *number of servers* as the principal factor affecting the level of service over which we have control.

But increasing the level of service by increasing the number of servers usually involves additional costs. We refer to the costs associated with different levels of service simply as *service-level costs*. If the level of service is changed by varying the number of servers, the total service-level cost tends to vary directly with the level of service.

For example, if each person in the dock crew in our trucking problem has an hourly wage cost of $7, the relevant total service-level cost for the three service levels involving 2, 3, and 4 servers is $14, $21, and $28 per hour, respectively, as shown in Table 20-4.

We also show in Table 20-4 (for each of the three selected service levels) the expected cost of waiting in line and the *total associated waiting-line costs* that

Table 20-3   Obtaining the Probabilities of the Arrival Possibilities from Two Weeks of Experience (80 Hours)

Number of trucks arriving per hour	Number of times (hours) that this number of trucks arrived in one hour	Relative frequency that this number of trucks arrived in one hour	Probability of this number of trucks arriving in one future hour
0	12	$12/80$ = .15	.15
1	20	$20/80$ = .25	.25
2	20	$20/80$ = .25	.25
3	16	$16/80$ = .20	.20
4	8	$8/80$ = .10	.10
5	4	$4/80$ = .05	.05
	80	1.00	1.00

Table 20-4   Identifying the Optimal Service Level

Service level (number of persons in the dock crew)	Cost of service level (dock-crew cost per hour)	Expected cost of waiting (expected cost per hour of driver delay)	Total associated waiting-line costs per hour
2	$14	$22.50	$36.50
3	21	4.50	25.50 (minimum)
4	28	1.00	29.00

were obtained from a 20-hour simulation study of the problem. We shall examine that study in the next section, but let us note here that the optimal service level depends essentially upon the relative magnitude of the service-level costs and the expected costs of waiting in line.

We noted above that total service-level costs typically *rise* as the level of service is increased (more servers are scheduled). The expected cost of waiting (due to expected cost of delay and lost productivity), however, *decreases* as the service level increases.

As shown in Table 20-4, our simulation study indicates that for the three selected service levels (where the number of servers alternatively was assumed to be 2, 3, and 4) the average cost of waiting is $22.50, $4.50, and $1.00 per hour.

As we shall see later, the basis for the cost of waiting in our simulation study was the loss of productive service from the idled truck drivers waiting for their trucks to be unloaded. It was assumed that a loss of $10 in productive service occurred for every hour a truck driver had to wait in line.

Thus, the total associated waiting-line costs (the sum of the service-level costs and the expected cost of waiting) in the right-hand column of Table 20-4 show that the minimum total cost is obtained at the service level corresponding to the use of 3 servers (3 persons in the dock crew).

In Figure 20-2 we see graphically the general relationships between these costs and the level of service. The minimum point on the total associated waiting-line cost curve identifies the optimal level of service on the horizontal axis.

A SIMULATION STUDY OF A WAITING-LINE PROBLEM

We have already revealed in Table 20-4 the main results of our simulation study of the trucking problem discussed earlier. Actually, it is not necessary to include in our simulation study the costs of the different service levels associated with changing the number of servers. These service-level costs are simply $14, $21, and $28 per hour for 2, 3, and 4 servers, respectively (each server's wage cost being $7 per hour).

But to get a measure of the expected cost of waiting we need a simulation study (or an analytical study in those cases where it is possible).

For our trucking example we have simulated 20 hours of operations. Again, we should emphasize that 20 hours is generally too short a period to enable simulation studies to provide a reliable estimate of the expected costs. But the basic procedure is the same if 200 hours are simulated instead of 20.

The basic data for the waiting-line model were given earlier. There is

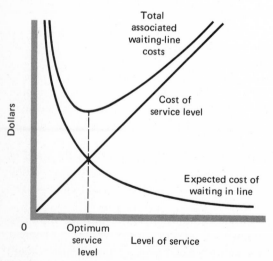

Figure 20-2   The general relationship between the waiting-line costs and the level of service.

Table 20-5   The Assignment of Random Numbers to the Arrival Possibilities

Number of trucks arriving per hour	Probability of this number of trucks per hour	Random numbers assigned to simulate the occurrence of this number of trucks per hour
0	.15	01–15
1	.25	16–40
2	.25	41–65
3	.20	66–85
4	.10	86–95
5	.05	96–00

uncertainty in the number of arrivals per hour, and this is represented by the probabilities associated with each of the arrival possibilities in Table 20-3. (The arrival possibilities are 0, 1, 2, 3, 4, or 5 with probabilities of .15, .25, .25, .20, .10, and .05, respectively.)

To simulate the number of trucks that arrive each hour, we must assign random numbers to each arrival possibility in accordance with the appropriate probabilities. This assignment is made in Table 20-5.

The service time for each server is 1 hour per truck. This means that it takes 1 server 1 hour to unload a truck. Two servers can unload two trucks per hour, 3 servers can unload 3 trucks per hour, and 4 servers can unload 4 trucks per hour.

Our primary aim in the simulation study is to estimate, under a given server schedule (such as 3 servers), the number of trucks each hour whose unloading is delayed an hour. This tally gives us a waiting line each hour (of course, it can be zero).

The number of trucks in the waiting line each hour in our simulation run gives us a basis for estimating the costs of waiting. If we multiply the number of trucks delayed an hour by the cost of driver idleness ($10 per hour), we obtain a cost of waiting for that hour. If we take an average of these hourly waiting costs for the 20 hours simulated, we have an estimate of the expected cost of waiting under that particular level of service.

Our first simulation run assumes there are 3 servers, that is, that there are 3 members of the dock crew. (To obtain the results in Table 20-4 it was necessary to repeat the simulation run assuming 2 servers were scheduled and then 4 servers.)

Our first task is to form a simulation table as shown in Table 20-6. The first column shows the simulation by hour number. The next two columns are concerned with simulating the number of truck arrivals each hour in accordance with the probability distribution of the arrivals in Table 20-5.

In advance, we decided to begin with the two-digit random numbers beginning at the top of columns 13 and 14 in Table 19-3. The first random number is 35.

OTHER APPROACHES TO DECISION PROBLEMS

Table 20-6   A Simulation Table for the Truck-unloading Problem

Hour	Random number (beginning at the top of columns 13 and 14 in Table 19-3)	Simulated number of trucks arriving this hour	Number of trucks ready to be unloaded this hour	Capacity of the dock crew (number of trucks that can be unloaded this hour)	Number of trucks actually unloaded this hour	Waiting-line length: number of trucks where the unloading is delayed until the next hour	Cost of waiting ($10 per hour of delay)
0						2	
1	35	1					
2	86	4					
3	78	3					
4	16	1					
5	05	0					
6	44	2					
7	96	5					
8	23	1					
9	17	1					
10	92	4					
11	09	0					
12	07	0					
13	63	2					
14	96	5					
15	18	1					
16	04	0					
17	94	4					
18	53	2					
19	91	4					
20	41	2					

Thus, for hour 1 the simulated number of trucks arriving is 1 truck. The random number 35 falls in the interval of random numbers (16–40) that were assigned to represent the occurrence of 1 truck arriving. (*Note:* For simplicity we shall assume that all trucks arriving in a given hour arrive shortly after the beginning of that hour.)

The second random number is 86, and so for hour 2 the simulated number of arrivals is 4 trucks. The random number 86 falls in the interval of random numbers 86–95 that was associated with the occurrence of 4 trucks arriving.

The next three columns in Table 20-6 are concerned with the number of trucks ready to be unloaded each hour, the number of trucks the dock crew *can* unload each hour (their capacity), and the number of trucks actually unloaded this hour (in the simulation).

Although the capacity of the 3 servers is the ability to unload 3 trucks per hour, only 2 trucks actually can be unloaded if only 2 trucks have arrived and are ready to be unloaded.

The next-to-the-last column in Table 20-6 keeps a record of the number of trucks whose unloading is delayed until the next hour. This gives us a measure of the trucks waiting in line each hour. We begin the simulation run (under the 3-server schedule) with a waiting line of 2 trucks from the previous hour. We refer to the previous hour as hour 0.

The very last column in Table 20-6 records the cost of waiting due to driver idleness. It is assumed that each hour of idleness results in a $10 loss of productive service for each driver so idled.

What we desire from our simulation run is a complete table, as shown in Table 20-7. This table is the same as that in Table 20-6 except that we have filled in the blank columns.

Thus, let us begin the simulation with 3 servers (that is, 3 persons in the dock crew) who have a capacity to unload 3 trucks each hour.

In hour 1, one truck arrives. Therefore, the number of trucks ready to be unloaded this hour is 3. With 3 persons in the dock crew, 3 trucks can be unloaded. Thus, there are no trucks whose unloading is delayed until the next hour. A cost of $0 is then inserted in the extreme right-hand column to indicate there is no cost of waiting in hour 1.

In hour 2 there are 4 arrivals. The number of trucks ready to be unloaded this hour is also 4 (0 trucks delayed from the previous hour plus 4 arrivals this hour). However, only 3 of the 4 trucks can be unloaded this hour, and so 1 truck is delayed. The delay of 1 truck for 1 hour idles 1 driver for an hour. The $10 per hour cost of idleness gives us a $10 waiting cost in the last column for hour 2.

In hour 3 there are 3 trucks arriving. The number of trucks ready to be unloaded this hour is 4 (1 truck delayed from the previous hour plus 3 arrivals this hour). Only 3 trucks can be unloaded this hour, and so the unloading of 1 truck is delayed. Again, the waiting cost is $10.

In hour 4 only 1 truck arrives. The number of trucks ready to be unloaded is 2. Thus, the actual number of trucks unloaded in this hour is 2. Three trucks could have been unloaded, but only 2 had arrived and were ready to be unloaded. Of course in this hour no trucks are delayed and no waiting costs are incurred.

In hour 5 no trucks at all arrive. With no trucks delayed from the previous hour and no new arrivals this hour, there are obviously no trucks to unload, and no trucks actually are unloaded. Of course the number of trucks delayed is zero, too. Thus, waiting costs for this hour are $0.

The rest of the 20 hours in the run are simulated in the same way.

When the table is completed, the last column in Table 20-7 provides us with the cost of waiting each hour for drivers of trucks whose unloading is delayed an hour. If we take a simple average of the waiting costs each hour, we find it to be $4.50 per hour. On the average, we say that the cost of waiting is $4.50 per hour when the number of persons in the dock crew is 3.

This $4.50 *average* cost of waiting (from our simulation using 3 servers) then

Table 20-7   The Simulation Results in the Truck-unloading Problem

Hour	Random number (beginning at the top of columns 13 and 14 in Table 19-3)	Simulated number of trucks arriving this hour	Number of trucks ready to be unloaded this hour	Capacity of the dock crew (number of trucks that can be unloaded this hour)	Number of trucks actually unloaded this hour	Waiting-line length: number of trucks where the unloading is delayed until the next hour	Cost of waiting ($10 per hour of delay)
0						2	
1	35	1	3	3	3	0	$ 0
2	86	4	4	3	3	1	10
3	78	3	4	3	3	1	10
4	16	1	2	3	2	0	0
5	05	0	0	3	0	0	0
6	44	2	2	3	2	0	0
7	96	5	5	3	3	2	20
8	23	1	3	3	3	0	0
9	17	1	1	3	1	0	0
10	92	4	4	3	3	1	10
11	09	0	1	3	1	0	0
12	07	0	0	3	0	0	0
13	63	2	2	3	2	0	0
14	96	5	5	3	3	2	20
15	18	1	3	3	3	0	0
16	04	0	0	3	0	0	0
17	94	4	4	3	3	1	10
18	53	2	3	3	3	0	0
19	91	4	4	3	3	1	10
20	41	2	3	3	3	0	0
				60	44		$90

$$\frac{\$90}{20} = \$4.50$$

may be used as an estimate of the expected cost of waiting in the real situation (using 3 servers). The simulation study is a way of getting an estimate of the vital expected cost of waiting shown in Table 20-4 for our trucking problem (and generally in Figure 20-2).

We repeated the 20-hour simulation run using only 2 servers and also using 4 servers. The average costs of waiting clearly decrease as the level of service is increased. A summary of the results appears in Table 20-4 where we also take into account the costs of the different service levels. As noted previously the results of our simulation study indicate that the optimal number of servers to schedule is 3. The total associated waiting-line costs are minimized at that level of service.

Additional Considerations

It is of interest to note that the best level of service indicated by our simulation study of the trucking problem is not the service level in which the servers' time is used most fully.

In many waiting-line studies, interest is at times centered on the "utilization rate" of the servers' capacity. The utilization rate simply refers to the proportion of the time the servers will be fully occupied in performing the service.

Our 20-hour simulation run using 3 servers in the trucking problem shows (in the sixth column of Table 20-7) the number of trucks unloaded each hour. The capacity of the 3 servers is, of course, 3 trucks per hour.

Looking down the sixth column shows there are many hours when the dock crew is not fully occupied. An average utilization rate can be obtained simply by summing the number of trucks actually unloaded (in column six) and then dividing the total of 44 by the capacity of the 3 servers for 20 hours (which is 60). This gives us a utilization rate of 73 percent: $^{44}\!/_{60} = .73$.

For the simulation run using 2 servers, the utilization rate was found to be 100 percent, and for 4 servers it was 55 percent. Thus, the optimal number of servers (3) clearly is not associated with the highest utilization rate of the scheduled servers. This, of course, is due to the fact that there are expected costs of waiting that more than offset the costs of providing a level of service in excess of that actually utilized.

AN ANALYTICAL APPROACH WHERE PROBABILITIES OF ARRIVALS CORRESPOND TO A PARTICULAR THEORETICAL PROBABILITY DISTRIBUTION

Perhaps most real-world waiting-line problems are best studied using the simulation methods previously discussed and illustrated. But such methods tend to be rather expensive and time-consuming. Therefore, whenever a waiting-line problem can be studied by analytical methods that are available, we want to use these methods in such cases.

It turns out that if the probabilities of arrivals correspond closely to a particular theoretical probability distribution (the "Poisson" probability distribution) essentially the same results we obtained above by the simulation procedures can be obtained by shorter and quicker analytical procedures. But as in the use of any theoretical distribution (that is, any model), we must be concerned about the adequacy of its fit to our particular real-world situation.

The Poisson probability distribution will not be discussed fully here. However, we might note that it refers to a family of probability distributions that are useful in the study of waiting-line problems. In Table 20-8 we show the probabilities of arrivals based on the Poisson distribution when the expected number of

Table 20-8   The Probability of Various Arrivals per Unit of Time That Are Assumed in a Poisson Probability Distribution Where the Expected Number of Arrivals Is 4

Number of Arrivals per Unit of Time	Probability
0	.018
1	.072
2	.144
3	.192
4	.192
5	.154
6	.102
7	.058
8 or more	.064
	1.000

arrivals is 4 per unit of time. If the expected number of arrivals is something other than 4, another set of probabilities is involved.

If the theoretical probabilities (as in Table 20-8) approximate the chances of occurrence of the uncertain events in our particular situation, then we can use some general expressions (formulas) to obtain results in which we may be interested. Such results, for example, may be the *expected waiting time* and the *expected cost of waiting* under a particular service level. In the background, of course, is the common problem of identifying the *optimal service level* (that is, the number of servers that will minimize the total associated waiting-line costs).

A Simple Example

Let us use a very simple example to illustrate an analytical procedure when uncertainty exists in the rate of arrivals. This uncertainty, we are assuming, is adequately represented by a Poisson probability distribution.

Suppose that a large manufacturing facility has a tool-service center that provides service and repairs to numerous tool users in the facility. They come to the center for service and repairs where there are three persons (servers) providing service. The users arrive at an average rate of 4 per hour. Of course during some hours the arrivals are more numerous than 4 and for other hours they are less than 4. It takes one-half hour to provide the service to each tool user, so the 3 servers have a capacity of providing service to 6 tool-users per hour.

In analytical approaches to waiting-line problems it turns out that the *expected utilization rate* is an important factor. As we noted earlier, it can be thought of as the proportion of the time the servers will be busy. More formally, we define it as follows:

$$\text{Expected utilization rate} = \frac{\text{expected arrivals per unit of time}}{\text{service capacity per unit of time}}$$

Its simplest interpretation is in the special case where the arrivals per hour are constant (not varying) and the service capacity is also constant. Suppose that exactly 4 arrivals occur every hour (at the beginning of each hour) and the service capacity is 6 per hour. This gives us an expected utilization rate of 4/6 (or .67).

Intuitively, we can see that all 4 arrivals can be served within the hour in which they arrive and no waiting line (beyond the hour) will form. And, of course, the servers will be busy only two-thirds of every hour.

We see also that when both the arrival rate and the service capacity are constant no waiting line will form as long as the service capacity is equal to or greater than the rate of arrivals. However, if the rate of arrivals is greater than the service capacity, a waiting line will grow indefinitely.

Now let us return to our example where there is uncertainty in the rate of arrivals. When the arrivals vary by chance (and the expected arrivals per hour are 4) there are some hours when the number of arrivals will be greater than the service capacity of 6 and some hours when they will be less. Thus, in those hours when the arrivals are greater than the service capacity, a waiting line tends to form.

The Expected Waiting Time It turns out that when the arrival probabilities correspond to a Poisson probability distribution (and the service capacity is constant, as well as being greater than the expected number of arrivals) the expected waiting time is given by the following expression:

$$\text{Expected waiting time} = \frac{\text{expected utilization rate}}{\text{service capacity}}$$

Thus, if the expected rate of arrivals is 4 and the service capacity is 6, we have an expected waiting time of 1/9 hour.

$$\text{Expected waiting time} = \frac{4/6}{6}$$
$$= 1/9 \text{ hour}$$

Therefore, when the arrival probabilities are of the appropriate form we see that we can obtain the expected waiting time quite directly.

Additionally, we can obtain the expected waiting time under other service levels (that is, with a different number of servers). For example, we may wish to estimate the waiting time when the number of servers in the tool-service center is 4 instead of 3.

This would change the service capacity from 6 to 8. We would expect this greater service capacity to decrease the expected waiting time. And it does. We find that the expected waiting time falls to 1/16 hour.

$$\text{Expected waiting time} = \frac{4/8}{8}$$
$$= 1/16 \text{ hour}$$

We do the same analysis for five servers, too, and then summarize our results in the first four columns of Table 20-9.

The Total Associated Waiting-Line Costs for Different Service Levels In the remaining columns of Table 20-9 we have compiled the costs of these three selected service levels and the expected cost of waiting based on the expected waiting times under the various service levels. In this problem we assume that each server has a wage cost of $6 per hour and each hour of waiting time for a tool-user incurs a cost of $144 (primarily due to lost production).

In the last column of Table 20-9 we sum the expected cost of waiting and the service-level cost for each service level. This permits us to identify the service level that minimizes the total associated waiting-line costs. We find the optimal service level to be that service level where four persons (servers) are in the tool-service center. Thus, if we are satisfied that our model represents the real situation adequately, we would recommend that an additional server be added to tool-service center (there now being three servers).

SUMMARY

1 The basic causes of waiting lines are (a) uncertainty in demand (that is, uncertainty regarding the number of persons or units that will arrive for service in some period) and (b) the fact that the provision of immediate service for any demand amount usually involves substantial resource costs. In some cases there is also uncertainty in the time it takes each server to provide the particular service (that is, there is uncertainty in the *service time*).

2 A *waiting line* is defined simply as an accumulation of persons or units waiting to be provided with some service. The *length* of the waiting line refers to the *number* of persons or units waiting for service. They need not be grouped at a particular point and thus may not necessarily form a physical "line."

Table 20-9 The Total Waiting-Line Costs for Three Different Service Levels Obtained by Analytical Methods

Service level (number of servers)	Service capacity per hour (number of tool-users that can be served)	Expected number of arrivals per hour (tool-users)	Expected waiting time by tool users (in hours)	Expected waiting costs ($144 per hour)	Service-level costs ($6 per hour per server)	Total associated waiting-line costs
3	6	4	$\frac{4/6}{6} = 1/9$	$16.00	$18	$34.00
4	8	4	$\frac{4/8}{8} = 1/16$	9.00	24	33.00 (minimum)
5	10	4	$\frac{4/10}{10} = 1/25$	5.76	30	35.76

3 *Waiting-line discipline* primarily refers to the order in which units in a waiting line are served. The most common bases for determining the order of service are: (a) "first come first served," (b) priorities, and (c) random selection.

4 The persons or units arriving for a particular service are called *arriving units*. The persons (or persons and equipment) that provide the service are called *servers*. The servers may be one or many. The arriving units in most applications are numerous.

5 If the number of arriving units per unit of time is *known* in advance (even though the number varies), the correct number of servers often can be scheduled to avoid a waiting line and also underutilization of the servers.

6 If the number of arriving units per unit of time is *uncertain,* it is essentially impossible to schedule the number of servers such that waiting lines do not ever form and underutilization of the servers does not occur.

7 The best number of servers to schedule under conditions of uncertainty in the number of arriving units depends upon the relationship of the cost of more servers and the expected cost of waiting in line. In short, additional servers *increase resource costs* but also *reduce the costs of waiting* in line. Thus, the best number of servers is that which minimizes the sum of the two types of costs (which we call *total associated waiting-line costs*).

8 Simulation studies of waiting-line problems usually seek an estimate of the length of waiting lines that would occur using different numbers of servers (different service levels). Often an additional aim is to obtain an estimate of the expected costs of waiting under different service levels. Thus, an estimate of the best number of servers can be obtained.

9 Analytical studies of waiting lines can be undertaken to determine the best number of servers, too. However, it is essentially limited to those situations where the uncertainty in the arrivals and service times can be satisfactorily represented by particular theoretical probability distributions.

PROBLEMS

20-1 Starting with Table 20-6, simulate the truck-unloading operation for 20 hours using 2 servers (2 persons in the dock crew) instead of 3.
   a What is the average cost per hour of waiting when 2 servers are used?
   b What is the service-level cost when 2 servers are used?
   c What are the total associated waiting-line costs using 2 servers?
   d Compare your answers in *a, b* and *c* with those given in Table 20-4 for 2 servers.

20-2 Starting with the table in Table 20-6, simulate the truck-unloading operation for 20 hours using 4 servers (4 persons in the dock crew).
   a Obtain the average cost per hour of waiting when 4 servers are used.
   b Compute the service-level cost when 4 servers are used.
   c What are the total associated waiting-line costs using four servers?
   d Compare your answers in *a, b,* and *c* with those given in Table 20-4 for 4 servers.

20-3 From your simulation results in Problem 20-1:
   a What is the utilization rate of the servers when 2 servers are used?
   b What is your estimate of the expected length of the waiting line of trucks?

20-4 From your simulation results in Problem 20-2:
  a Obtain the utilization rate of the servers when 4 servers are used.
  b Obtain an estimate of the expected length of the waiting line.

20-5 This problem involves three simulation runs with regard to a modified version of the truck-unloading problem discussed in this chapter. Now, we have probabilities of .05, .20, .30, .30, .10, and .05 associated with the arrival possibilities per hour of 0, 1, 2, 3, 4, and 5, respectively.
  a As was done in Table 20-5 in the original problem, assign two-digit random numbers to simulate the occurrence of the arrival possibilities in accordance with the probability distribution given above.
  b Starting with the table in Table 20-6 (except for the third column which will be new in light of your assignment of random numbers above), simulate the truck-unloading operations for 20 hours using 2 servers (2 persons in the dock crew).
  c Repeat what you did in *b* using 3 servers.
  d Repeat what you did in *b* using 4 servers.
  e From your three simulation runs, complete a table (as in Table 20-4) that shows for each service level the service-level cost, the expected cost of waiting, and the total associated waiting-line costs.
  f From the three different service levels, which does your simulation study indicate to be the best? Compare it with the results in Table 20-4 for the original problem and explain any differences in costs or the optimal service level.

20-6 This problem is a modified version of the original truck-unloading problem discussed in this chapter. The original probability distribution of arrivals is to be used. This problem involves three simulation runs, each using a different number of servers. The only modification of the original problem is this: New unloading equipment has been acquired that makes it possible for each person in the dock crew to unload 1½ trucks per hour instead of 1 truck per hour.
  a Starting with the table in Table 20-6, simulate the truck-unloading operations for 20 hours using 2 servers (2 persons in the dock crew).
  b Repeat what you did in *a* using 3 servers.
  c Repeat what you did in *a* using 4 servers.
  d From your three simulation runs, complete a table (as in Table 20-4) that shows for each service level the service-level cost, the expected cost of waiting, and the total associated waiting-line costs.
  e From the set of three different service levels, which does your simulation study indicate to be the best? Compare it with the results in Table 20-4 for the original problem, and explain any differences in costs or the optimal service level.

20-7 A manufacturer of automotive parts uses a large number of separate machines in its production operations. The machines occasionally break down and require repair, but this cannot be known in advance.

  From 200 days of experience it has been found that the number of machines needing repair per day are 0, 1, 2, 3, or 4 with (absolute) frequencies of 10, 50, 70, 50, and 20, respectively. A repair worker takes ½ day to repair each machine. His daily wage cost is $90. Lost profit per day from a machine being idled is $200.
  a Obtain a probability to associate with each "arrival" possibility (the number of machines needing repair).

b Assign random numbers to each "arrival" possibility in *a* in accordance with the appropriate probability.

c With 2 repair workers, simulate 20 days of operation using the columns of digits 17 through 20 in Table 19-3. Construct and complete a table along the lines of Table 20-7.

d Obtain the average cost per day of waiting (the average cost of machine idleness beyond the service time) when 2 repair workers are used (2 servers).

e Obtain the service-level costs with 2 servers.

f Obtain the total associated waiting-line costs when 2 servers are scheduled.

20-8 Using 3 repair workers (instead of 2), simulate 20 days of operation of the system described in Problem 20-7. (Use the same random numbers that you used in Problem 20-7).

a Obtain the average cost per day of waiting (average cost of machine idleness) when 3 repair workers are used.

b Compute the service-level cost for 3 servers.

c What is the total associated waiting-line cost for 3 servers?

20-9 Simulate 20 days of operation of the system described in Problem 20-7 when 4 repair technicians are used. (Use the same random numbers that you used in Problem 20-7.)

a What is the average cost per day of waiting when 4 repair technicians are used?

b Obtain the service-level cost for 4 servers.

c What are the total associated waiting-line costs for 4 servers?

d If you have done Problems 20-7 and 20-8, construct a table as in Table 20-4 showing the relevant costs for each level of service investigated.

e From the set of three service levels investigated, which one minimizes the total associated waiting-line costs?

20-10 Repeat your 20-day simulation study of the automotive-parts manufacturer's machine operations in Problem 20-7 with additional uncertainty in the time it takes a repair technician to repair a machine (the service time). Usually, each machine can be repaired in $\frac{1}{2}$ day, but 10 percent of the machines in need of repair require a full day of the repair technician's time. Let us investigate the costs associated with using 4 repair workers with uncertainty in the service time as well as in the rate of "arrivals."

a Assign random numbers to the two service-time possibilities.

b Construct and complete a simulation table along the lines of the one in Table 20-7. Beginning with the twenty-first column of random digits in Table 19-3, simulate the service-time occurrence for each machine in need of repair.

c What is the average cost of waiting using 4 servers?

d Compute the service-level costs using 4 servers.

e What are the total associated waiting-line costs using 4 servers?

f Compare your answers in *c, d,* and *e* with those obtained in Problem 20-9. Explain any differences.

20-11 Using 3 repair workers, simulate 20 days of operation of the system described in Problem 20-10.

a Obtain the average cost per day of waiting.

b Obtain the service-level costs for 3 servers.

c What are the total associated waiting-line costs for 3 servers?

20-12 Using 5 repair workers, simulate·20 days of operation of the system described in Problem 20-10.

    a Obtain the average cost per day of waiting using 5 repair workers.

    b Compute the service-level costs for 5 servers.

    c What are the associated waiting-line costs for 5 servers?

20-13 If you have done Problems 20-10, 20-11, and 20-12,

    a Construct a table as in Table 20-4 to show the costs associated with the waiting-line system.

    b From the set of three service levels, which is the best in terms of minimizing the total associated waiting-line costs? Explain any differences in the costs or the optimal service level compared with that obtained in Problems 20-7, 20-8, and 20-9.

20-14 Let us look again at the example represented in Table 20-9. Now, however, let us suppose the servers in the tool-service center require three-fourths of an hour to provide the service.

    a Obtain by the analytical method the expected waiting times when there are 3, 4, and 5 servers (that is, three different service levels).

    b Obtain for each of the three service levels in *a* the expected cost of waiting and the service-level cost.

    c Obtain for each of the service levels in *a* and *b* the total associated waiting-line costs. Also, form a table (as in Table 20-9) and identify the optimal service level from the three selected service levels.

20-15 Refer again to the original example in Table 20-9 where the best number of servers to schedule is determined by using an analytical method. Now, however, let us assume uncertainty in the service capacity as well as in the rate of arrivals.

    The most common theoretical probability distribution used to represent service-capacity uncertainty is the "exponential" distribution (with a "down-sloping" probability graph). When it is used along with the Poisson-distributed arrivals, the expected waiting time is given by *the ratio of the expected utilization rate to the amount by which the expected service capacity exceeds the expected rate of arrivals*.

    a Using the relevant data in Table 20-9 and an expected service capacity of 6, obtain the expected waiting time.

    b From your results in *a* and the relevant data in Table 20-9 obtain the expected waiting costs with the expected service capacity of 6.

    c Assuming that an expected service capacity of 6 is associated with a service level of 3 servers, obtain the total associated waiting-line costs for this service level.

    d Discuss the meaning of your answer in *c* and compare it with that obtained in Table 20-9 for a constant service capacity of 6. What is the effect of the uncertainty in the service capacity?

20-16 Let us continue with Problem 20-15, using any relevant data from Table 20-9. We shall now consider the different service levels of 3, 4, 5, and 6 servers with expected service capacities of 6, 8, 10, and 12, respectively.

    a Obtain a table (as in Table 20-9) showing the total associated waiting-line costs for each of the four service levels.

    b Which is the optimal service level?

    c Discuss your answer in *b* and compare it with that obtained in Table 20-9 where there was no uncertainty in the service capacity.

Chapter 21

Interdependent Decision Making and the Game-Model Approach

It is rather appropriate for the final chapter of this book to focus on a common real-world problem that is extremely complex and difficult to represent in a model, particularly in a quantitative model.

The problem is one we call *interdependent decision making*. The main characteristic of this type of decision problem is that decisions are to be made by two or more *decision makers* and the consequence to each decision maker significantly depends upon the course of action taken by the others.

Thus, *additional* uncertainty appears in many decision problems from this source. There still may be uncertainty with regard to, say, the presence of oil in a particular region or the state of a market for a product at a particular time. But additional uncertainty can come from not knowing the course of action a rival firm will choose. The rival's price, production, and advertising decisions can well affect the profit and sales of a firm, and very often this cannot be known in advance.

AN ILLUSTRATIVE EXAMPLE OF INTERDEPENDENT DECISION MAKING

The general interdependent decision problem can be illustrated by a simplified example. Suppose two firms have independently developed new television sets that are quite similar. Each firm is ready to introduce its product in a large national market, and each is attempting to decide whether its regular advertising program for such new products should be undertaken or if a "heavy" advertising program is preferable.

Where there are only two firms making this product, it is obvious that the profit to each firm will be affected by the advertising program undertaken by the other firm. And this can be a source of uncertainty for each of the firms.

But there still may be uncertainty for each firm with respect to the entire market for the new product. Let us suppose that the market for the new product can be classified as either good or poor, with probabilities of .60 and .40, respectively.

We can, of course, look at the decision problem from either firm A's standpoint or from firm B's. In Figure 21-1 we construct a decision tree from firm A's view, assuming for simplicity that firm A *knows* that firm B will engage only in a regular advertising program. Under this assumption (which removes the uncertainty about firm B's actions) the optimal course of action for firm A is to engage in a regular advertising program.

Still looking at the decision from firm A's standpoint, in Figure 21-2 we assume that it is known that firm B will engage in a heavy advertising program. Under this assumption the optimal course of action for firm A is to undertake a heavy advertising program, also.

Uncertainty from both the market and the rival firm's advertising action is represented in Figure 21-3. Now it is assumed by firm A that there is a .70 chance that firm B will engage in a heavy advertising program. Under this assumption we see in Figure 21-3 that the expected profit from firm A is maximized under a *regular* advertising program.

AN EXTREME APPROACH: THE DECISION MAKERS IGNORE EACH OTHER

The procedure illustrated in Figure 21-3 works very nicely if firm B makes its decision essentially ignoring firm A's possible advertising decisions. But this perhaps is not fully true in most real-world problems of this type. More commonly, rival firms take into account, to some extent at least, the possible actions of each other.

Thus, from a practical standpoint firm A's .70 probability assignment to firm B's advertising heavily is very easily upset if firm B starts thinking about the way firm A is thinking. As a matter of fact, if firm B knows that firm A is assigning a probability of .70 to its (firm B's) advertising heavily (and if it also knows the other data in Figure 21-3 for firm A), firm B could see what firm A's optimal act is under these assumptions and then could make its own decision, validly assuming that firm A is going to engage in a regular advertising program. Therefore, firm B could advertise heavily and make large gains at firm A's expense.

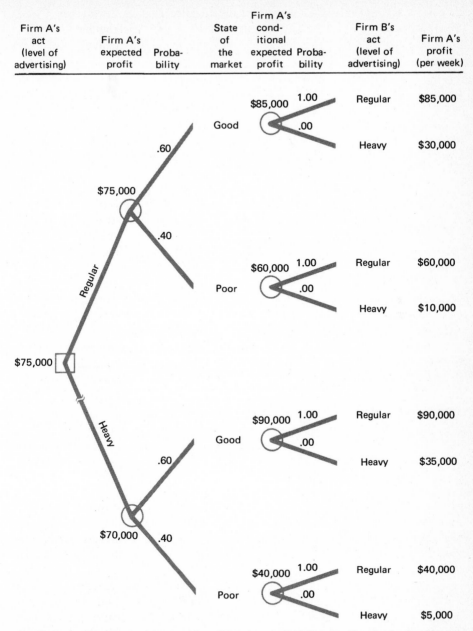

Firm A's act (level of advertising)	Firm A's expected profit	Probability	State of the market	Firm A's conditional expected profit	Probability	Firm B's act (level of advertising)	Firm A's profit (per week)
			Good	$85,000	1.00	Regular	$85,000
					.00	Heavy	$30,000
Regular	$75,000	.60					
		.40	Poor	$60,000	1.00	Regular	$60,000
					.00	Heavy	$10,000
	$75,000						
			Good	$90,000	1.00	Regular	$90,000
					.00	Heavy	$35,000
Heavy		.60					
	$70,000	.40	Poor	$40,000	1.00	Regular	$40,000
					.00	Heavy	$5,000

Figure 21-1 Firm A's decision problem if it is known that firm B will not advertise the new product heavily.

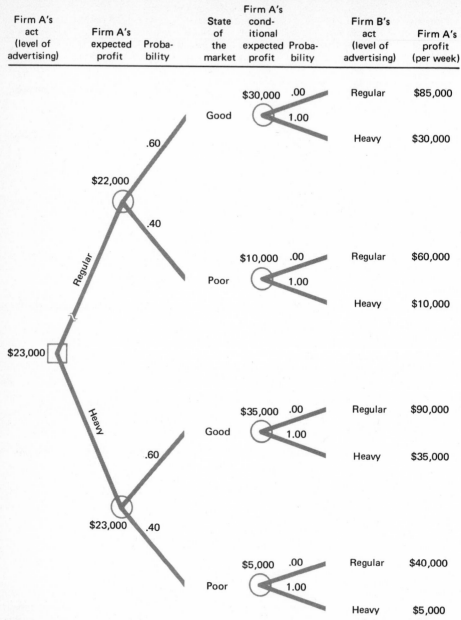

Firm A's act (level of advertising)	Firm A's expected profit	Proba- bility	State of the market	Firm A's cond- itional expected profit	Proba- bility	Firm B's act (level of advertising)	Firm A's profit (per week)
				$30,000	.00	Regular	$85,000
			Good		1.00	Heavy	$30,000
		.60					
	$22,000						
		.40					
				$10,000	.00	Regular	$60,000
			Poor		1.00	Heavy	$10,000
$23,000							
				$35,000	.00	Regular	$90,000
			Good		1.00	Heavy	$35,000
		.60					
	$23,000	.40					
				$5,000	.00	Regular	$40,000
			Poor		1.00	Heavy	$5,000

Figure 21-2 Firm A's decision problem if it is known that firm B will advertise the new product heavily.

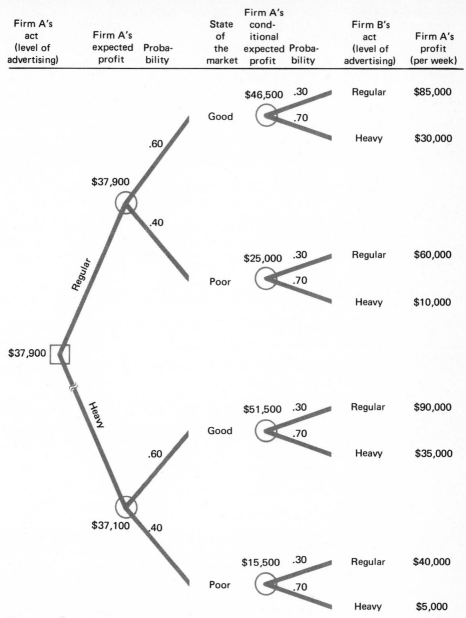

Figure 21-3 Firm A's decision problem if it assesses the probability to be .70 that firm B will choose to advertise the new product heavily.

THE OTHER EXTREME APPROACH: THE DECISION MAKERS
TAKE INTO ACCOUNT THE OTHER'S POSSIBLE ACTIONS

The age-old dilemma of interdependent decision making is no doubt the basic reason for the origin and continuing interest in "game" models (or the theory of "games"). Although this type of decision problem is old, it was not until the 1940s that game models of the type we discuss in this section appeared. Many decision problems, such as the advertising example discussed above, are analogous in some respects to the decision making by the players in many types of games. This, of course, is the reason for the use of the term "game" models and "game" theory.

But it is perhaps unfortunate that the term "game" has been used to refer to models of interdependent decision making because it does not convey the great importance of understanding and improving decision making of this type.

True, in thinking about such real-world problems, it is useful to exploit their similarity to parlor games. But also there is a big class of complex and important real-world problems that need to be better understood and confronted. Identifying these problems closely with relatively trivial games can undermine a general awareness of the actual significance of the problems.

The Game-Model Approach

In this section we go to the other extreme and assume that each decision maker takes fully into account the possible actions of the other decision maker. This is the basic premise of the game-model approach.

In the game-model approach it is often thought best to start with a table, such as the one appearing in Table 21-1 for the two firms in the advertising-decision problem.

In this example, each firm has only two courses of action that it will

Table 21-1   Profit Outcomes to Firm A from the Various Combinations of Actions by Firm A and Firm B (Assuming a Good Market for the Product)

| | | Firm B's courses of action: | |
		Regular advertising	Heavy advertising
Firm A's courses of action:	Regular advertising	$85,000 to firm A	$30,000 to firm A
	Heavy advertising	$90,000 to firm A	$35,000 to firm A

consider, and this is assumed to be known by each firm. (In other problems the courses of action might be numerous.) The profit outcome to firm A of each combination of choices is given in the body of the table. (Also, we are assuming here that there is no other uncertainty, such as uncertainty regarding the state of the market. We are, in fact, simply assuming that it is a good market. However, uncertainty regarding such factors as the state of the market can be incorporated later.)

The classical game models represent attempts to begin an understanding and improvement in interdependent decision making in complex situations. They should be thought of as first steps, and, as we might expect in such initial attempts, some rather severe simplifying assumptions are made.

Of course in making such simplifying assumptions, the model does not fit closely to as many real-world decision situations as we would like. But it is a start in studying decision making in complex situations, some of which have profound significance for all of us.

In summary, the main assumptions of the game-model approach are essentially as follows:

1   Each decision maker restricts his or her choice of acts to those specified and also knows the alternative courses of action to be considered by the other decision maker.

2   The decision makers know the consequences to each decision maker from each possible combination of actions. (This assumption and the first one mean that each decision maker knows what is in a table such as the one in Table 21-1.)

3   The gain to one decision maker is directly at the expense of the other decision maker. (This is an assumption of the most common-type game models, known as "zero-sum" models, meaning that the algebraic sum of the outcomes to the decision makers is zero.)

A Rational and Stable Decision for Both Firms: An Informal Analysis

Starting with the problem as it is represented in Table 21-1, let us examine the problem from firm A's standpoint.

If firm A knows what firm B's choice will be, there is essentially no difficulty in making a decision. For if firm B chooses a regular advertising program, it is best for firm A to advertise heavily and obtain the high $90,000 profit.

And if firm A knows that firm B will advertise heavily, it is best for firm A to advertise heavily, also. This combination would bring $35,000 in profit to firm A. Thus, as we summarize in the upper section of Table 21-2 the best choices for firm A in the face of either of firm B's actions, we see that it is best to advertise heavily.

In the lower section of Table 21-2 we look at the problem from firm B's point of view. Because it is assumed that the profit to firm A is directly at firm B's expense, we can represent firm B's profit maximization by having firm B select its best act by identifying the minimum profit outcome to firm A.

Table 21-2   Looking at Each Firm's Best Choice in the Face of All the Possible Acts by the Other Firm

If firm B's act is	Firm A's best act is	The profit to firm A is
Regular advertising	Heavy advertising	$90,000
Heavy advertising	Heavy advertising	$35,000

If firm A's act is	Firm B's best act is	The profit to firm A is
Regular advertising	Heavy advertising	$30,000
Heavy advertising	Heavy advertising	$35,000

If firm A undertakes a regular advertising program, it is best for firm B to advertise heavily and get firm A's profit down to $30,000. And if firm A advertises heavily, it is also best for firm B to advertise heavily.

Therefore, what we have just done is to determine that the best act for firm A is to advertise heavily in the face of any of firm B's actions. Also, for firm B it is best to advertise heavily, regardless of firm A's advertising program. Thus, the best choice for each firm is to advertise heavily. The profit outcome from this combination of actions is $35,000 (to firm A).

We also call this joint decision an "equilibrium solution" because it is a stable one. By this we mean that in the face of the (best) course of action taken by either decision maker there is no change in action that would lead to a preferable outcome to either decision maker.

For example, for firm A, in the face of heavy advertising by firm B, there would be no gain for firm A to go to a regular advertising program. And for firm B, in the face of a heavy advertising program by firm A, there would be no gain in taking a regular advertising program instead. This stability can be seen by studying Table 21-1.

A More Formal Solution Procedure

A more formal solution procedure that identifies the best course of action by each decision maker is that shown in Table 21-3.

Essentially, we repeat what was done informally above. For each row in the table we select the minimum profit outcome and record it at the right-hand margin of that row. We are selecting for firm A the "worst" outcome that can occur from each of its possible courses of action. It is $30,000 for a regular advertising program and $35,000 for a heavy advertising program.

Then, from the row minimums we identify the highest profit (we also use the contraction "maximin value" to refer to this "maximum value of the set of minimum values").

Similarly, we obtain for each column the maximum profit outcome. To firm B this is the worst that can happen from a given course of action—to have firm A's profits be the largest. (Remember firm A's profits are at firm B's expense.)

If firm B undertakes a regular advertising program, the maximum profit to firm A is $90,000, and if it advertises heavily, the maximum is $35,000. Thus, to firm B the "best of the worst profit outcomes" is the lowest one. It is $35,000.

More formally, the minimum of the column maximums is $35,000. Thus, the contraction "minimax" is used to refer to this value, and the entire solution is sometimes referred to as the "minimax solution." Also, it is termed an "equilibrium" solution because the maximum of the row minimums ($35,000) is equal to the minimum of the column maximums.

Perhaps a fuller understanding of the above solution to the decision problem is gained if we look at the results of the solution in terms of the decision trees in Figure 21-4.

In Figure 21-4a we look at the decision from firm A's point of view. Since it was assumed in the above solution that firm A could see that firm B's best act was to advertise heavily, a probability of 1.00 is implied for this occurrence. Thus, we place this probability on the branches leading to this occurrence. The result is that for firm A the optimal act is to advertise heavily, with an expected profit of $35,000.

It is interesting to see the analogous decision tree for firm B. To firm B the probability is 1.00 that firm A will advertise heavily. Thus, the best act for firm B is to advertise heavily, also. The act with the minimum expected profit for firm A ($35,000) is to advertise heavily.

Table 21-3   Identifying the Maximum of the Row Minimums for Firm A and the Minimum of the Column Maximums for Firm B

| | | Firm B's courses of action: | | Row minimums |
		Regular advertising	Heavy advertising	
Firm A's courses of action:	Regular advertising	$85,000 to firm A	$30,000 to firm A	$30,000
	Heavy advertising	$90,000 to firm A	$35,000 to firm A	$35,000 (maximum of row minimums)
	Column maximums	$90,000	$35,000 (minimum of column maximums)	

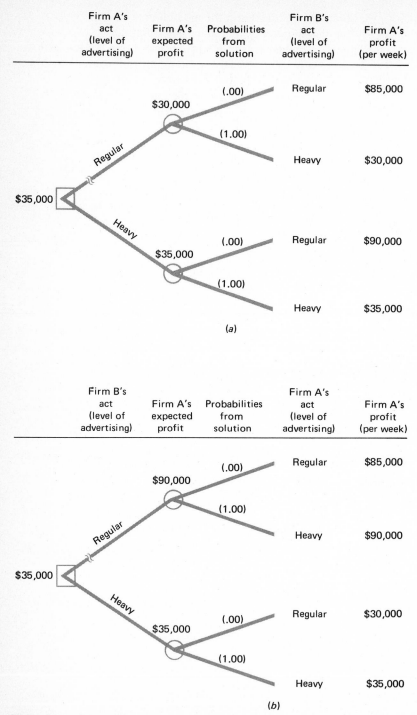

Figure 21-4 The decision trees for *(a)* firm A and *(b)* firm B that are implied in the game-model solution of the advertising example (assuming the market for the product to be good).

A GAME-MODEL APPROACH TO UNION-MANAGEMENT WAGE NEGOTIATIONS

Of course real-world union-management negotiations are very complex matters, and perhaps we are pushing things a bit far to use such an example to illustrate another aspect of the game-model approach to interdependent decision making. But even though some gross oversimplifications are made, many persons maintain that valuable insights are gained by thinking of the problem in this way.

Anyway, here goes. Suppose that the management of the firm has just two courses of action that it is considering in upcoming wage negotiations. One course of action is to take a "moderate line" in the negotiations, and the other is to take a "hard line."

Analogously, the leadership of the union is considering the very same two alternative courses of action. (In contexts such as this one the term "strategy" is often used interchangeably with "a course of action.")

Thus, the two courses of action for each "party," and the resulting outcomes in terms of a basic hourly wage increase, are shown in Table 21-4.

As before, such as in the earlier advertising example, each party knows the courses of action the other is considering, and each knows the outcome from each combination of actions. In other words, it is assumed that both management and the union know what is in Table 21-4 and that they are motivated by no other considerations.

In obtaining a solution to this decision problem, we start by recording in the right-hand margin for each row the worst that could happen as far as the firm is concerned. Thus, we identify the maximum wage increase associated with each course of action. It is $1.20 if a moderate line is taken and $1.00 if a hard line is followed. The best of these worst outcomes is $1.00 (the minimax value).

Table 21-4   Hourly Wage-Increase Outcomes of Various Combinations of Actions by the Firm and the Union

| | | The union's courses of action: | | Row maximums |
		Take a moderate line	Take a hard line	
The firm's courses of action:	Take a moderate line	$1.20	$ .80	$1.20
	Take a hard line	$ .60	$1.00	$1.00 (minimum of the row maximums)
	Column minimums	$ .60	$ .80 (maximum of the column minimums)	

From the union's standpoint the worst that can happen is the outcome with the lowest wage increase. Thus, for each column we identify the lowest wage increase. It is $.60 for a moderate-line strategy and $.80 for a hard-line strategy. The maximum of the column minimums is $.80 (the maximin value).

Thus, our work so far identifies that the best act for the firm and for the union to take is a hard line. But this is not a stable combination of decisions because the minimax and the maximin values are not equal.

What does this mean? It means that for each party it is preferable in light of the other party's act to take an act different from the one initially identified from either the minimax or the maximin values. In the face of a hard-line strategy on the part of the union, it would be worthwhile for the firm to take instead a moderate line (rather than a hard line) with a wage-increase outcome of $.80 instead of $1.00.

But if the firm takes a moderate-line strategy instead, the union, in turn, would find it worthwhile to take a moderate-line strategy. Then, the firm would be encouraged to go back to a hard-line strategy and, in turn, the union would do so as well. We would be back where we started only to begin the circle again.

What is the way out of this dilemma? One of the more profound contributions of game theory has been this: If there is not an equilibrium solution in terms of "pure" strategies (such as there was in the advertising example), there is one in terms of a *probability mixture* of the pure strategies. *Pure strategies* are defined as those courses of action that are considered by each party in the problem.

By a *probability mixture* of the pure strategies (called a "mixed strategy"), we mean a selection of the pure strategies on the basis of a set of probabilities, the particular probabilities being determined by an extension of the minimax solution procedure used in the earlier advertising example.

The Best Mixture of Strategies for Each Party

When we have a problem in which the minimax and maximin values are not equal, we do not have a stable solution. However, we can obtain an equilibrium solution by determining the appropriate probability mixture of strategies for each party.

In rough terms, this means that the selection of a strategy by each decision maker is best determined by a chance process with a probability being assigned to each possible course of action, the probabilities assigned being those obtained in a special minimax solution procedure.

What is the nature of this special solution procedure? The best place to begin is with Table 21-5. The body of the table is the same as that in Table 21-4. But we have inserted the letter p in the right-hand margin of the row pertaining to the firm's taking a moderate-line strategy.

The letter p in this row refers to the probability to be associated with the firm taking a moderate-line strategy. The problem is essentially one of solving for a best value for p. Once we obtain the best p-value for the firm, we have found

Table 21-5   The First Step in Solving a Problem Requiring a Probability Mixture of the Strategies: Associating p with a Particular Act

		The union's courses of action:		The probability for the firm to associate with taking this act
		Take a moderate line	Take a hard line	
The firm's courses of action:	Take a moderate line	$1.20	$ .80	p
	Take a hard line	$ .60	$1.00	1.00 − p
	The probability for the union to associate with taking this act	p	1.00 − p	

the best probability for the firm to assign to the taking of that act. Since there is just one other act (take a hard line), its associated probability is the rest of the probability and is obtained by subtracting the obtained p-value from 1.00: $1.00 − p$.

Thus, looking at the problem from the firm's viewpoint, we let p represent the probability to be associated with the firm's moderate-line strategy. From the firm's view we look at the possible outcomes (wage increases), first in the face of a moderate-line strategy by the union, and then, against a hard-line union strategy. It turns out that the expected wage increase in the first situation is given by the following:

> In the face of a moderate-line strategy
> by the union, the expected wage
> increase to the firm is $= \$1.20\ p + \$.60\ (1.00 − p)$

And, when confronted with a hard-line union strategy, the expected wage increase to the firm changes to the following:

> In the face of a hard-line strategy by
> the union, the expected wage increase to
> the firm is $= \$.80\ p + \$1.00\ (1.00 − p)$

For the decisions to be stable (that is, at the equilibrium solution) the two foregoing expected wage increases would be equal. Thus, we set the two above equations equal to each other and solve for p as follows:

$$\$1.20p + \$.60\ (1.00 - p) = \$.80p + \$1.00\ (1.00 - p)$$
$$\$1.20p + \$.60 - \$.60p = \$.80p + \$1.00 - \$1.00p$$
$$\$.60p + \$.60 = -\$.20p + \$1.00$$
$$\$.80p = \$.40$$
$$p = .50\ \text{(the probability to be associated with the firm's moderate-line strategy)}$$
$$1.00 - p = .50\ \text{(the probability to be associated with the firm's hard-line strategy)}$$

Thus, the minimax solution for the firm is to make a selection of a strategy whereby the moderate-line strategy has a probability of .50. This, of course, means that a probability of .50 is also associated with the hard-line strategy.

Practically speaking, the firm would then employ a chance device, such as the table of random numbers, to make its choice of strategy. For example, it could assign the numbers 01 through 50 to taking a moderate-line strategy and 51 through 00 to taking a hard-line strategy.

Then, planning to go to a table of random numbers, such as in Table 19-3, it could be decided in advance to pick the two-digit number in the upper-right corner of our random-number table. It is 92, and so the firm chooses a hard-line strategy. Of course the union would not know that a hard-line strategy was selected by the firm, but it is assumed that the probability mixture assigned to the firm's two strategies could be determined by the union.

Next, we repeat the above steps for the union. In viewing the problem from the union's standpoint, we associate the letter p with its taking the moderate-line strategy, too. Thus, in Table 21-5 we record a p at the bottom margin of the column associated with the union taking a moderate-line strategy.

The union looks first at its decision in the face of a moderate-line strategy by the firm and then in the face of a hard-line strategy. The expected wage increase in the first case is given by the following:

In the face of a moderate-line strategy
by the firm, the expected wage
increase to the union is $= \$1.20\ p + \$.80\ (1.00 - p)$

And, given a hard-line strategy by the firm, the union's expected wage increase is as follows:

In the face of a hard-line strategy by the
firm, the expected wage increase to the
union is $= \$.60\ p + \$1.00\ (1.00 - p)$

To solve for the best p-value for the union (that is, the best probability to associate with its taking a moderate-line strategy), we set the two equations equal to each other.

$$\$1.20p + \$.80 (1.00 - p) = \$.60p + \$1.00 (1.00 - p)$$
$$\$1.20p + \$.80 - \$.80p = \$.60p + \$1.00 - \$1.00p$$
$$\$.40p + \$.80 = -\$.40p + \$1.00$$
$$\$.80p = \$.20$$
$$p = .25 \text{ (the probability to be associated with the union's moderate-line strategy)}$$
$$1 - p = .75 \text{ (the probability to be associated with the union's hard-line strategy)}$$

Thus, the maximin solution for the union is to select a strategy whereby the moderate-line strategy has a probability of .25 and the hard-line strategy a probability of .75.

The union, too, would use some random device such as a table of random numbers to make its strategy selection. Suppose it assigned the numbers 01 through 25 to its taking the moderate-line strategy and 26 through 00 to its taking the hard-line strategy. Then, suppose the union chose to take the two-digit number in the lower-right corner of Table 19-3. Since that number is 99, the union would choose a hard-line strategy, too. The wage increase would be $1.00 as shown in Table 21-5.

The stability of this solution is seen in the decision trees for the firm and the union in Figure 21-5. In Figure 21-5a we represent the firm's situation. The probabilities associated with the firm's acts (and those of the union, too) come from the solution above. The expected wage increase for the firm is thus $.90.

In Figure 21-5b we see that the union has the very same expected wage increase of $.90. Thus, we see a result that is analogous to that in the earlier advertising problem where the minimax value and the maximin value were equal at the equilibrium solution involving only pure strategies.

For larger problems, we should note that it turns out to be best to formulate the problem in linear-programming form and solve it by the simplex method. We shall not take this step in this book.

APPROACHES TO DECISION SITUATIONS
BETWEEN THE EXTREMES

Perhaps most real-world situations involving interdependent decision making lie between the two extremes we have discussed. Decision makers usually do not ignore fully the possible effects that other decision makers have on the outcomes. Nor do they typically have nearly as much knowledge of the situation that is assumed in the usual game-model approach.

What, then, can we say about the many situations that lie between these extremes? One useful way to proceed may be to start with the approach that appears to fit best the real situation of interest. Sometimes this would lead us to the game-model approach, and at other times it could be the one-sided approach discussed earlier in this chapter (and also in Part Two of this book).

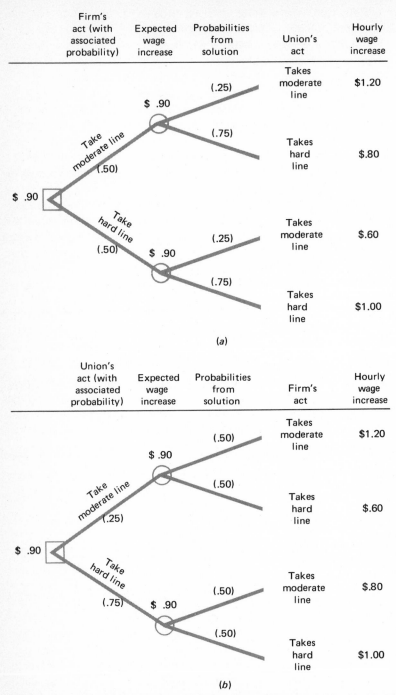

Figure 21-5 The decision trees for (a) the firm and (b) the union that are implied in the game-model solution of the wage-bargaining example.

If the situation seems close to the game-model approach, the concepts and procedures of that approach may provide a useful way to think about the problem. But we should be quite honest about the game-model approach. It does not provide anything like clear-cut guidance to the decision makers when any of the model's assumptions are not fulfilled.

Since the fit of game models to our situations of interest is often poor, we find that the more promising approach may be the less ambitious one. We might start with the more one-sided approach to the interdependent decision problem that we discussed earlier.

Assigning probabilities to another decision maker's acts may often be the best way to start, realizing that we may change them as soon as there is evidence that he is taking into account our decision when he is making his decision.

This one-sided approach may work better than we think because many actual situations are so complex (with many alternative courses of action and possible consequences) that a decision maker may simply not be able to take enough of the situation into account for it to be thought of in terms of the game-model approach.

Perhaps as more effort is devoted to these in-between types of interdependent decision problems we shall have more approaches and models so that more guidance can be provided.

SUMMARY

1 *Interdependent decision making* refers to decision making by two (or more) parties where the consequences to each party significantly depend upon the course of action taken by the other party.

2 There are two extreme approaches in studying real-world decision making of the interdependent type. One approach (the *one-sided approach*) assumes that the other decision maker ignores your thinking when he makes his decision. The other extreme approach (the *game-model approach*) assumes that each decision maker takes fully into account the possible actions of the other decision maker.

3 The one-sided approach in interdependent decision analysis only involves the assignment of probabilities to the occurrence of particular actions on the part of another decision maker. But these probabilities are subject to change as evidence appears that the other decision maker is taking our thinking into account.

4 If a problem fits the game-model approach, a stable (equilibrium) solution can be obtained. However, if a problem does not fit the game-model closely, little guidance is provided for the decision makers.

PROBLEMS

21-1 Suppose the two television set manufacturers discussed in this chapter have the following data instead of that in the text. Profits in the table are those of firm A.

State of the market is good:

| | | Firm B's acts: | |
		Regular advertising	Heavy advertising
Firm A's acts:	Regular advertising	$25,000	−$10,000
	Heavy advertising	$40,000	−$ 5,000

State of the market is poor:

| | | Firm B's acts: | |
		Regular advertising	Heavy advertising
Firm A's acts:	Regular advertising	$15,000	−$15,000
	Heavy advertising	$30,000	−$20,000

    If the probability is .70 that the state of the market is good (and .30 that it is poor), what is the best act for firm A if its is known that firm B is going to engage in a regular advertising program?

21-2 Continuing with Problem 21-1, suppose instead it is known that firm B is going to engage in a heavy advertising program. What is the best act for firm A and its expected profit?

21-3 Suppose in Problem 21-1 the action of firm B is uncertain but that a probability of .60 is assigned by firm A to firm B's undertaking a heavy advertising program. What is firm A's best act and its expected profit?

21-4 Suppose in Problem 21-1 that the state of the market is good but uncertainty exists for both firms with respect to the act that will be taken by the other firm.

    Treat the problem by the game-model approach and solve for the equilibrium solution. Explain why it is an equilibrium solution.

21-5 Suppose that the state of the market in Problem 21-1 is poor but uncertainty remains for the firms with respect to the other firm's advertising decision.

    Think of the problem in terms of the game-model approach and solve for the equilibrium solution. Explain why it is an equilibrium solution.

21-6 Suppose the wage-increase outcomes for the union-management wage-negotiation problem in Table 21-4 are such that the $.60 outcome and the $.80 outcome are interchanged. What is the best mixed strategy for the firm? Give some meaning to your solution.

21-7 In the union-management problem in Problem 21-6, what is the best mixed strategy for the union?

21-8 Construct a tree for the firm in Problem 21-6 along the lines of the one in Figure 21-5a. Insert the probabilities obtained in Problems 21-6 and 21-7.

21-9 Construct a tree for the union in Problem 21-7 as in Figure 21-5b. Insert the probabilities obtained in Problems 21-6 and 21-7. Discuss the meaning of the expected wage increase and its relationship to that obtained in Problem 21-8 for the firm. What is it that indicates that the mixed-strategy solution for each party is an equilibrium solution?

Suggestions for Further Reading

PART ONE BACKGROUND AND INTRODUCTION

Ackoff, Russell L. "Operations Research," *International Encyclopedia of the Social Sciences,* The Free Press, New York, 1968, vol. 11, pp. 290–294.

Bross, I. D. J., *Design for Decision,* The Macmillan Company, New York, 1953.

Encyclopaedia Britannica, "Operations Research," 1974, vol. 13, pp. 594–602.

Koopmans, Tjalling C., *Three Essays on The State of Economic Science,* McGraw-Hill Book Company, New York, 1957, Part II.

Lindley, D. V., *Making Decisions,* Interscience Publishers, a division of John Wiley & Sons, Inc., New York, 1971.

Raiffa, Howard, *Decision Analysis,* Addison-Wesley Publishing Company, Reading, Massachusetts, 1968.

Thompson, Gerald E., *Statistics for Decisions,* Little, Brown and Company, Boston, 1972.

Thrall, Robert, C. H. Coombs, and R. L. Davis (editors), *Decision Processes,* John Wiley & Sons, Inc., New York, 1954.

PART TWO DECISION ANALYSIS

Bierman, Harold, Jr., Charles P. Bonini, and Warren H. Hausman, *Quantitative Analysis for Business Decisions,* 4th ed., Richard D. Irwin, Inc., Homewood, Illinois, 1973.

de Finetti, Bruno, "Probability: Interpretations," *International Encyclopedia of the Social Sciences,* The Free Press, New York, 1968, vol. 12, pp. 496–504.

Edwards, Ward, "Decision Making: Psychological Aspects," *International Encyclopedia of the Social Sciences,* The Free Press, New York, 1968, vol. 4, pp. 34–41.

Fishburn, P. C., *Utility Theory for Decision Making,* John Wiley & Sons, Inc., New York, 1970.

Goldberg, Samuel, *Probability: An Introduction,* Prentice-Hall, Inc., Englewood Cliffs, New Jersey, 1960.

Hadley, G., *Introduction to Probability and Statistical Decision Theory,* Holden-Day, Inc., Publisher, San Francisco, 1967.

Hogarth, Robin M., "Cognitive Processes and the Assessment of Subjective Probability Distributions," (with comments by Robert Winkler and Ward Edwards), *Journal of the American Statistical Association,* June 1975, pp. 271–294.

Horowitz, Ira, *An Introduction to Quantitative Business Analysis,* 2d ed., McGraw-Hill Book Company, 1972.

Magee, J. F., "Decision Trees for Decision Making," *Harvard Business Review,* July–August 1964.

———, "How to Use Decision Trees in Capital Investment," *Harvard Business Review,* September–October 1964.

Mosteller, F., R. E. K. Rourke, and G. B. Thomas, Jr., *Probability with Statistical Applications,* 2d ed., Addison-Wesley Publishing Company, Reading, Massachusetts, 1970.

Newman, Joseph W., *Management Applications of Decision Theory,* Harper & Row, Publishers, Incorporated, New York, 1971.

Raiffa, Howard, "Bayesian Decision Theory," in *Recent Developments in Information and Decision Processes,* edited by Robert E. Machol and Paul Gray, The Macmillan Company, New York, 1962.

Savage, L. J., "Bayesian Statistics," in *Recent Developments in Information and Decision Processes,* edited by Robert E. Machol and Paul Gray, The Macmillan Company, New York, 1962.

Schlaifer, Robert, *Analysis of Decisions under Uncertainty,* McGraw-Hill Book Company, New York, 1969.

———, *Introduction to Statistics for Business Decisions,* McGraw-Hill Book Company, New York, 1961.

Thompson, Gerald E., *Statistics for Decisions,* Little, Brown and Company, Boston, 1972.

Winkler, Robert, *Introduction to Bayesian Inference and Decision,* Holt, Rinehart and Winston, Inc., New York, 1972.

PART THREE LINEAR-PROGRAMMING ANALYSIS

Anderson, David R., Dennis J. Sweeney, and Thomas A. Williams, *Linear Programming for Decision Making,* West Publishing Company, St. Paul, Minnesota, 1974.

Baumol, William J., *Economic Theory and Operations Analysis,* 3d ed., Prentice-Hall, Inc., Englewood Cliffs, New Jersey, 1972.

Bierman, Harold, Jr., Charles P. Bonini, and Warren H. Hausman, *Quantitative Analysis for Business Decisions,* 4th ed., Richard D. Irwin, Inc., Homewood, Illinois, 1973.

Dantzig, George B., *Linear Programming and Extensions,* Princeton University Press, Princeton, New Jersey, 1963 (advanced).

Dorfman, Robert, Paul A. Samuelson, and Robert Solow, *Linear Programming and Economic Analysis,* McGraw-Hill Book Company, New York, 1958.

Hillier, Frederick S., and Gerald J. Lieberman, *Introduction to Operations Research,* 2d ed., Holden-Day, Inc., San Francisco, 1974.

Spivey, W. Allen, and Robert Thrall, *Linear Optimization,* Holt, Rinehart and Winston, Inc., New York, 1970 (advanced).

Thompson, Gerald E., *Linear Programming,* The Macmillan Company, New York, 1971.

Wagner, Harvey M., *Principles of Operations Research,* Prentice-Hall, Inc., Englewood Cliffs, New Jersey, 1969.

van de Panne, C., *Linear Programming and Related Techniques,* North-Holland Publishing Company, Amsterdam, 1971.

Vandermeulen, Daniel, *Linear Economic Theory,* Prentice-Hall, Inc., Englewood Cliffs, New Jersey, 1971.

PART FOUR OTHER APPROACHES TO DECISION PROBLEMS

Bierman, Harold, Jr., Charles P. Bonini, and Warren H. Hausman, *Quantitative Analysis for Business Decisions,* 4th Ed., Richard D. Irwin, Inc., Homewood, Illinois, 1973.

Churchman, C. W., R. L. Ackoff, and E. L. Arnoff, *Introduction to Operations Research,* John Wiley & Sons, Inc., New York, 1957.

Gaver, D. P., and G. L. Thompson, *Programming and Probability Models in Operations Research,* Brooks/Cole Publishing Company, Monterey, California, 1973.

Hillier, Frederick S., and Gerald J. Lieberman, *Introduction to Operations Research,* 2d ed., Holden-Day, Inc., San Francisco, 1974.

Horowitz, Ira, *An Introduction to Quantitative Business Analysis,* 2d ed., McGraw-Hill Book Company, New York, 1972.

Howard, Ronald A., *Dynamic Programming and Markov Processes,* M.I.T. Press, Cambridge, Massachusetts, 1960.

Kemeny, J. G., A. Schleifer, Jr., J. C. Snell, and G. L. Thompson, *Finite Mathematics with Business Applications,* 2d ed., Prentice-Hall, Inc., Englewood Cliffs, New Jersey, 1972.

Levin, Richard I., and Charles A. Kirkpatrick, *Quantitative Approaches to Management,* 3d ed., McGraw-Hill Book Company, New York, 1975.

Luce, R. Duncan, and Howard Raiffa, *Games and Decisions,* John Wiley & Sons, Inc., New York, 1957.

Magee, J. F., *Production Planning and Inventory Controls,* McGraw-Hill Book Company, New York, 1958.

Miller, D. W., and M. K. Starr, *Executive Decisions and Operations Research,* 2d ed., Prentice-Hall, Inc., Englewood Cliffs, New Jersey, 1969.

Miller, R. W., "How to Plan and Control with PERT," *Harvard Business Review,* March–April 1972.

Morse, P. M., *Queues, Inventories, and Maintenance,* John Wiley & Sons, Inc., New York, 1958.

Plane, Donald R., and Gary A. Kochenberger, *Operations Research for Managerial Decisions,* Richard D. Irwin, Inc., Homewood, Illinois, 1972.

Richmond, Samuel, *Operations Research for Management Decisions,* The Ronald Press Company, New York, 1968.

Shubik, Martin, *Game Theory and Related Approaches to Social Behavior,* John Wiley & Sons, Inc., New York, 1964.

von Neumann, John and Oskar Morgenstern, *Theory of Games and Economic Behavior,* Princeton University Press, Princeton, New Jersey, 1944 (advanced).

Wiest, J. D. and F. Levy, *A Management Guide to PERT/CPM,* Prentice-Hall, Inc., Englewood Cliffs, New Jersey, 1969.

Index

Index

Abstraction in constructing a model, 5
Act-event combination:
  consequence of, 18–19
  defined, 17
Activity:
  defined, 144
  its meaning in a transportation problem,
    287
  level of, 149
  and a production process, 244–245
Adaptive-policy model, 357–359
Additional information:
  expected cost using, 116–117
  expected profit using, 78–92, 97–113
  expected revenue using, 94–95
  expected value of, 79–92, 110–113, 324–
    325
    in inventory problems, 324–325
  value of, 77, 84, 89–90
Additivity assumption in linear
  programming, 159

Arriving units, 404, 406
Artificial variable, 212–215
Assignment problem, 314–315
Average (mean), 19, 52
Average inventory level, 325–330

Basic feasible solutions, 195–196
Basic solutions, 196
Basic variables, 196
Bayes, Thomas R., 56
Bayes' formula, 68
Bayesian posterior probability, 56–70
Bayesian procedure, 56–70

Carrying costs, 325
Certainty assumption in linear
  programming, 160
Chance process, 16
Conditional probability, 54–70

Constant, 7
Constraints:
  equation, 210–218
  "greater-than" inequality, 210, 218–221
  "less-than" inequality, 150–151
  mixture of equations and inequalities,
    221–224
Cost of uncertainty, 120
CPM (PERT), 367–368
Criteria for decision making:
  maximization: of expected profit, 16, 20
    of expected revenue, 23, 94–95
    of expected utility, 125–135
  minimization: of expected cost, 24–25,
    42–44, 116–117
    of expected opportunity loss, 120–124
  pessimist (maximin and minimax), 21
Critical jobs, 373–375
Critical path, 375

Decision tree, 15–18, 78–92, 100–104,
    119–130
  under prior information, 78–79
  and using additional information, 78–
    92, 100–104
Degeneracy, 307–310
Destinations, 287
"Diet type" linear-programming problem,
    227–228
Divisibility assumption in linear
    programming, 159–160
Dual linear programming problem, 235–238

Economic (optimal) order quantity, 324,
    330–336
Event:
  chance, 16
  compound, 31–35
    probability of, 36–38
  simple, 30–31
    probability of, 35
Excess demand (insufficient capacity),
    305–306
Exhaustive events, set of, 26
Expected cost, 24–25, 42–44, 116–117
  of uncertainty, 120
  using additional information, 116–117

Expected cost:
  using perfect information, 116–117
  of waiting, 408–409
Expected deviation, 44–46
Expected net gain from sampling, 112–113
Expected opportunity loss, 120–124
  as a measure: of cost of uncertainty, 120
    of expected value of perfect
      information, 121–124
Expected profit, 16, 20
  for each act, 19
  relation to average profit, 19
  using additional information, 78–92, 97–
    113
  using perfect information, 79–87, 101–
    103
Expected revenue, 23, 94–95
  using additional information, 94–95
  using perfect information, 94–95
Expected squared deviation (variance),
    46–50
Expected utility, 125–135
Expected value, 40–41, 50
  of additional information, 79–92, 110–
    113, 324–325
  of perfect information, 79–87, 101–103,
    121–124
Expected waiting time, 417–418
Exponential probability distribution, 422

Feasibility, 153–154
Feasible programs, 153–154
Feasible region, 153–154
Fictitious destination, 304–305
Fictitious origin, 305–306
Fixed-policy model, 354–357

Imperfect predictor, 66, 84–91, 101–113
  expected profit using, 84–91, 101–113
  expected value of, 89–90, 101–113
Imputed total profit, 238–239
Incoming variable, 200–201, 298
Infeasibility, 153
Initial probability tree, 60, 70, 85, 88, 105–
    106
  for imperfect predictor, 85
  for perfect predictor, 88

Insufficient demand (excess capacity), 304–305
Integer programming, 271, 279–281
Interdependent decision making, 423–439
  game-model approach to, 428–437
    equilibrium solution in mixed strategies, 433–437
  one-sided approach to, 423–427

Joint and marginal probability table, 61–63, 85, 89, 108
Joint probability, 61–62

Lead (replenishment) time, 314–336
Linear programming:
  assumptions of, 157–160
  "diet-type" problem, 227–228
  with equation constraints, 210–218, 288–291
  with "greater-than" inequality constraints, 210, 218–221
  with "less than" inequality constraints, 150–151
  maximization problems in, 143–156
  minimization problems in, 215–221, 288–291
Linear-programming formulation of a problem, 161, 288–291
Linearity (proportionality) assumption in linear programming, 157–159
  in the constraints, 158–159
  in the objective function, 157–158
Location of new facilities, 301–306

Marginal contribution to profit, 178–186, 230–235
Marginal contribution to revenue, 253–260
Marginal probability, 62–70
Markov processes (chains):
  adaptive-policy model, 357–359
  and decision making, 352–362
  defined, 345–347
  fixed-policy model, 354–357
  transition diagram of, 346–347
  transition probabilities of, 346–347
Median, 52

Mode, 52
Models:
  certainty (deterministic), 8–9
  defined, 4–6
  predictions from, 7–8
  quantitative, 4–8
  and reality, 4–9
  uncertainty (probabilistic), 14
    decision making under, 14–15
  verbal, 4–6
"Moving back through the tree," 82–84
Multiple objectives, 271–273
Multiplication rule, 36–37
Mutually exclusive events, set of, 26

Network analysis, 367
Nonbasic variables, 196
Noncritical jobs, 373–375

Objective function, 149–156
  plotting an, 154–156
Operations research, 3
Opportunity loss, 118–124
  under certainty, 119–120
  defined, 119
  expected, 121–124
    minimum (of best act), 121–124
  as measure of the cost of uncertainty, 120
  under uncertainty, 120–124
Optimal basic feasible solution, 196
Optimal feasible program, 156
Optimal order quantity (economic order quantity), 324, 330–336
Optimal sample size, 110–112
Optimal service level, 410–411, 416–418
Optimality test, 200–201, 295–298
Order quantity, 321
Ordering costs, 330
Origins, 287
Outgoing variable, 201–202, 298–299

Parameter, 177–178
Parameter variation, 177–186, 253–264
  with more than one production process, 253–264

Parametric-programming analysis, 168, 177–186, 253–264
  with more than one production process, 253–264
Perfect information (perfect prediction), 66, 79–87, 101–103, 121–124
  expected profit using, 79–87, 101–103
  expected value of, 79–87, 101–103, 121–124
  in inventory problems, 324–325
Perfect predictor (perfect information), 66, 79–87, 101–103, 121–124
  expected cost using, 116–117
  expected profit using, 79–87, 101–103
  expected revenue using, 94–95
  expected value of, 79–87, 101–103, 121–124
  in inventory problems, 324–325
PERT (CPM), 367–368
Piecewise linear programming, 273–278
Piecewise linear relations, 158–159
Pivot element, 201–203
Poisson probability distribution, 415–416
Posterior information, 54–56
Posterior probability, 55–70
Primal linear programming problem, 233
Prior information, 54–56, 78
Prior probability, 54–70
Probability:
  Bayesian posterior, 56–70
  conditional, 54–70
  defined, 16
  graph, 40–43
  joint, 61–62
  marginal, 62–70
  posterior, 55–70
  prior, 54–70
  relative frequency interpretation, 26–30
  subjective (personalistic interpretation), 26–30
  transition, 346–347
  tree, 15–16, 40–43, 107
    initial, 60, 70, 85, 88, 105–106
    reverse, 62–63, 70, 108–109
  unconditional, 56, 59
Process:
  as an activity, 244–245
  level of, 245–246
  ray, 247–249
Project analysis, 367–368

Project diagram, 369–370
Project table, 369–370
Proportionality assumption in linear programming, 157–159
  in constraints, 158–159
  in objective function, 157–158

Random-digit table, 387
Random sample, 97
Random variable, 39–50
  defined, 39, 50
  expected deviation of, 44–46
  expected squared deviation (variance) of, 46–50
  expected value of, 40–41
  range of, 44
  standard deviation of, 49–50
Range:
  of possible outcomes of chance process, 44
  of random variable, 44
Range analysis, 232–235, 256–260
  graphic, 232–235
  using the simplex tables, 256–260
Reorder level of inventory, 334–336
Replenishment (lead) time, 334–336
Reverse probability tree, 62–63, 70, 108–109
Risk-averse decision maker, 133–135
Risk-neutral decision maker, 133–135
Risk-seeking decision maker, 133–135

Safety stock, 336–341
Sample information:
  expected profit using, 97–113
    for different sample sizes, 112–113
  expected value of, 97–113
    for different sample sizes, 112–113
Sensitivity analysis:
  in inventory problems, 333–334
  in linear programming, 168–177
Servers, 404, 406
Service capacity, 416–418
Service-level costs, 408–409
Service time, 404, 406
Simplex method:
  with equation constraints, 213–215
    computational steps, 213–215
    preparatory steps, 213–215

Simplex method:
   with "greater-than" inequality
      constraints, 218–221
      computational steps, 218–221
      preparatory steps, 218–221
   with "less-than" inequality constraints,
      196–205
      computational steps, 200–205
      preparatory steps, 196–197
Simplex tables, 197–208, 258–259
Simulation:
   compared to analytical procedures, 383
   defined, 381–382
   of an inventory problem, 393–400
   of a waiting-line problem, 410–415
Slack time, 373–375
Slack variable, 193–194
Standard deviation, 49–50
State (event), 60
Subjective judgment:
   of chance, 29
   of value (preference), 29
Surplus variable, 219–220
Systems analysis, 3

Target time, 370–371
Total inventory costs, 330–333, 399–400
Total profit, as a constraint, 271–273
Transition diagram, 346–347
Transition probabilities, 346–347
Transportation method, 286–310
   computational steps, 294–301
   preparatory steps, 293–294
Tree:
   decision, 15–18, 78–92, 119–130
      main, 78–92
   probability, 15–16, 40–43
      initial, 60, 70, 105–109
      reverse, 62–63, 70, 108–109

Uncertainty:
   cost of, 120
   decision under, 14–15
   in inventory problems, 320, 323
Unconditional probability, 56, 69
Utility:
   expected, 125–135
   graphs, 131–135
      concave, 131–135
      convex, 133–135
      straight line, 131–135
   modern theory of, 124–135
   values, 125–135
      how to obtain for a decision maker,
         127–132
Utilization rate, 415–417

Variable:
   artificial, 212–215
   basic, 196
   defined, 7
   nonbasic, 196
   random, 39–50
   slack, 193–194
   surplus, 219–220
Variance (expected squared deviation),
   46–50
Venn, John, 30
Venn diagram, 30–38
   with probabilities of simple and
      compound events, 34–38
   representing compound events, 32–35
   representing simple events, 30–32

Waiting-line discipline, 406
Waiting line problems (queues), 403–418
   using an analytical approach, 415–418
   using a simulation approach, 406–415